I0814167

READING *the* GOSPELS *as* CHRISTIAN SCRIPTURE

• READING •
CHRISTIAN
SCRIPTURE

VOLUMES AVAILABLE

Reading the New Testament as Christian Scripture
Constantine R. Campbell and Jonathan T. Pennington

Reading the Prophets as Christian Scripture
Eric J. Tully

Reading the Gospels as Christian Scripture
Joshua W. Jipp

READING *the* GOSPELS *as* CHRISTIAN SCRIPTURE

A LITERARY, CANONICAL, AND THEOLOGICAL INTRODUCTION

JOSHUA W. JIPP

Baker Academic
a division of Baker Publishing Group
Grand Rapids, Michigan

Published by Baker Academic
a division of Baker Publishing Group
Grand Rapids, Michigan
BakerAcademic.com

Printed in the United States of America

Library of Congress Cataloging-in-Publication Data
Names: Jipp, Joshua W., author.
Title: Reading the Gospels as Christian scripture : a literary, canonical, and theological introduction / Joshua W. Jipp.
Description: Grand Rapids, Michigan : Baker Academic, a division of Baker Publishing Group, [2024] | Includes bibliographical references and index.
Identifiers: LCCN 2023026222 | ISBN 9781540963345 (cloth) | ISBN 9781493444342 (ebook) | ISBN 9781493444359 (pdf)
Subjects: LCSH: Bible. Gospels—Criticism, interpretation, etc. | Bible. Gospels—Canonical criticism. | Bible. Gospels—Introductions.
Classification: LCC BS2555.52 .J57 2024 | DDC 226/.06—dc23/eng/20230825
LC record available at https://lccn.loc.gov/2023026222

Unless otherwise indicated, Scripture quotations are the author's own.

Italics in Scripture quotations have been added for emphasis.

Baker Publishing Group publications use paper produced from sustainable forestry practices and postconsumer waste whenever possible.

25 26 27 28 29 30 31 8 7 6 5 4 3 2

Contents

Preface

Christianity is centered on the person of Jesus. The claim is so obvious as to appear unnecessary, and yet as Christians we must consistently search to know, understand, and love this person Jesus if we would continue to faithfully bear the name "Christian." While all of the Scriptures are essential as the Word of God and testify in their own way to God's saving and revealing activity, the Gospels hold a unique role in the Christian canon, as they provide us with four accounts of Jesus of Nazareth, the climax of God's saving history and purposes. We will see that the Gospels are assumed as the bedrock stories for the rest of the New Testament writings and that they see themselves as the climax of the story of Israel found in the Old Testament. Within the Gospels, we find the origins and reasons for the church's practices of praying the Lord's Prayer (Matt. 6:9–13; Luke 11:2–4), for celebrating the Lord's Supper (Luke 22:14–30), and baptizing (Matt. 3:13–17). We find the foundations for the double love command: love God and love neighbor (Matt. 22:24–30). We see here the story of Jesus, whose life and character are the model for all disciples who not only confess that he is their saving Lord and Messiah but also commit to walking in his footsteps (1 Cor. 8:11–13; 11:1; 1 Pet. 2:21–25). But the Gospels do not only present Jesus as an important first-century figure from whom we can learn; they declare that this Jesus is alive as the one who has been raised from the dead. They declare that the resurrected and ascended Jesus is still present in the world and with his people by means of the Holy Spirit, the Paraclete, as John says. And so, Christians can read the Gospels looking to learn about the past, what God has done in the person of Jesus, and read the Gospels expectantly, knowing that this Jesus is alive and powerfully at work in the world and the church. Our very lives, our values, our character are put to the question when we seek Jesus and encounter him through the written word of the Gospels. My hope is that this book will act as a guide for your own personal engagement with these fascinating and life-giving texts.

The book is divided into three parts. The first part of the book centers on historical questions: What kinds of texts are the Gospels? Why are they called "Gospels"? Where did they come from? Why do we read four Gospels? I hope that spending time on these historical questions will enable you to appreciate the joys and challenges involved in reading four lives of Jesus.

The second part of the book asks, How do we read the Gospels? I focus on three large topics or areas of inquiry that I believe are important for a good reading of the Gospels: history, narrative, and theology/discipleship. In order to read the Gospels well, we must take into account the following: (1) these texts are two thousand years old and therefore require some awareness of ancient historical matters; (2) the Gospels are literary narratives, and so we do well to think about how to read stories well—how to account for setting, characterization, plot, and intertextuality; and (3) the Gospels are calling their audience to encounter the living Jesus and to follow him; they are, in other words, deeply interested in convincing you to be a certain kind of person and to live a particular way of life.

And the third part of the book involves a fairly in-depth examination of each of the four Gospels under the three headings of history, narrative, and discipleship. I do not try to be comprehensive in terms of touching on every pericope, but I do try to set forth the major distinctives and themes of each Gospel.

Acknowledgments

Over the years, when people have heard about my vocation as a New Testament professor, they have frequently asked: "What is your favorite course to teach?" I love all the courses I teach, but the one that rises to the top for me is our course on the canonical Gospels. I can think of nothing more important or more meaningful than spending time with a community of learners—disciples of Jesus—prayerfully reflecting on Jesus's teachings, his character and way of life, and the saving events of his incarnation, kingdom proclamation and activity, crucifixion, resurrection, and ascension. One of my goals, both in my life and in my teaching, has been to try to reflect on how every aspect of my life and existence is (or should be) influenced by Jesus's way of life and saving deeds. Readers will find my own attempts to reflect on some of these topics in the chapters on discipleship. I am grateful for the opportunity to write this book, and I hope it reflects the joy and meaning I have found in reading and teaching the Gospels.

The first group of people to whom I am indebted and to whom I want to express thanks are the teachers and scholars who have shaped my reading of the Gospel writings. I was encouraged by my publisher, and understandably so, to try to keep the scholarly references to a minimum. I tried, but I don't think I succeeded as well as was probably expected. This is due to the fact that I have been so deeply formed and shaped in my understanding of the Gospel writings by so many teachers and scholars. My debt to them is evident on each page. I cannot even begin to give comprehensive individual thanks to everyone, but I would not have been able to teach my course at TEDS or write this book apart from the likes of Helen Bond, David Pao, Richard Bauckham, Dorothy Jean Weaver, Joel Green, Jonathan Pennington, Marianne Meye Thompson, Morna Hooker, Luke Timothy Johnson, Mark Goodacre, Loveday Alexander, Craig Koester, Mark Allan Powell, and Michael Bird—among so many others.

This leads me to the second group of people that I am indebted to and to whom I want to express my thanks—the students in the various iterations of my Gospels course at TEDS. From our in-class discussions, the papers they have written, and our time together outside of class, they have taught me, encouraged me, and excited me about what following Jesus's way of life might look like in our current time and place. What would it look like for us to imagine Jesus's way of life as the basis for Christian leadership, for responses to societal challenges of mass incarceration and immigration, for our doctrine of the atonement, for how and why to pray, for how to be a Christian who struggles with doubt, and for how to love our enemies in practical ways? I have been formed by the types of questions they have asked and the responses they've fleshed out in their reading of the Christian Gospels. I would like to thank my students for the way they have shaped me and this book.

I also want to say thank you to my incredible graduate assistants, who offered so much assistance and encouragement as I wrote this book. In addition to the menial tasks involved in securing permissions and creating the index, they offered help in terms of creative help for the layout of the content, artwork, and much more. They have brought an incredible amount of joy, stimulation, and fun to my time at TEDS. Thank you Tyler Carrera, Lanie Walkup, and Cooper Bryan.

Abbreviations

Old Testament

Gen.	Genesis	Eccles.	Ecclesiastes
Exod.	Exodus	Song	Song of Songs
Lev.	Leviticus	Isa.	Isaiah
Num.	Numbers	Jer.	Jeremiah
Deut.	Deuteronomy	Lam.	Lamentations
Josh.	Joshua	Ezek.	Ezekiel
Judg.	Judges	Dan.	Daniel
Ruth	Ruth	Hosea	Hosea
1 Sam.	1 Samuel	Joel	Joel
2 Sam.	2 Samuel	Amos	Amos
1 Kings	1 Kings	Obad.	Obadiah
2 Kings	2 Kings	Jon.	Jonah
1 Chron.	1 Chronicles	Mic.	Micah
2 Chron.	2 Chronicles	Nah.	Nahum
Ezra	Ezra	Hab.	Habakkuk
Neh.	Nehemiah	Zeph.	Zephaniah
Esther	Esther	Hag.	Haggai
Job	Job	Zech.	Zechariah
Ps(s).	Psalm(s)	Mal.	Malachi
Prov.	Proverbs		

New Testament

Matt.	Matthew	1 Cor.	1 Corinthians
Mark	Mark	2 Cor.	2 Corinthians
Luke	Luke	Gal.	Galatians
John	John	Eph.	Ephesians
Acts	Acts	Phil.	Philippians
Rom.	Romans	Col.	Colossians

1 Thess.	1 Thessalonians	1 Pet.	1 Peter
2 Thess.	2 Thessalonians	2 Pet.	2 Peter
1 Tim.	1 Timothy	1 John	1 John
2 Tim.	2 Timothy	2 John	2 John
Titus	Titus	3 John	3 John
Philem.	Philemon	Jude	Jude
Heb.	Hebrews	Rev.	Revelation
James	James		

Deuterocanonical Works

Bar.	Baruch	2 Macc.	2 Maccabees
1 Macc.	1 Maccabees	Sir.	Sirach

Bible Versions

CSB	Christian Standard Bible	NLT	New Living Translation
NASB	New American Standard Bible (1995)	NRSV	New Revised Standard Version
NIV	New International Version (2011)	NRSVue	New Revised Standard Version, updated edition

General

ca.	circa
cf.	*confer*, compare
e.g.	*exempli gratia*, for example
i.e.	*id est*, that is
//	parallel(s)

PART 1

From Jesus of Nazareth to the Fourfold Gospel

History, Literature, Theology

Who is Jesus? For millennia Christians have turned to the Gospels of Matthew, Mark, Luke, and John in order to answer this question and to encounter the wisdom of Christ and his teaching. Devoted readers of the Gospels will inevitably spend time studying and pondering the rich content of these texts as they pursue wisdom and spiritual growth and seek to worship Christ. And, in the third and major part of this book, we'll explore the rich theological and literary texture of the Gospels with an eye toward how they lead us—and have led others—into wisdom, discipleship, prophetic witness, and worship of Christ. But at some point, almost every reader will likely pause to ask some questions about the nature, origins, and purpose of these texts. Why four Gospels instead of one? Why *these* Gospels and not others—such as the Gospel of Thomas? Why are these Gospels so similar to one another and yet, in some ways, obviously different? Are the Gospels historically accurate? My mother, for example, has asked me more than a few times questions like the following:

If other Gospels were written about Jesus, why aren't they also in our Bible?

Why did the pastor skip over the story of the woman caught in adultery (John 7:53–8:11) in her sermon series on the Gospel of John?

Why is there only one demon-possessed person in Luke's Gospel but two in Matthew's?

Do we really know that the Gospels are historically accurate?

More questions could be added, and maybe you'd like to add your own, but the essential concerns here are these: What kinds of books are the Gospels? Where did they come from? And how do we read them?

What Are the Gospels?

Why Are the Gospels Called "Gospels"?

It is anything but trivial, it is worth reminding ourselves, that the first four books are not just named for their authors (Matthew, Mark, Luke, and John) but rather are "*The Gospel* according to Matthew" (and Mark, Luke, and John). The connection with these apostles (or associates) is indeed important, but our first order of business is to understand why these texts are called "Gospels." Most educated persons in the first century were familiar with a variety of different literary genres—for example, histories, dramatic tragedies, epistles, philosophical treatises and dialogues, and biographies. But none of them would have been familiar with "Gospel" as a genre classification for a literary text. And yet after the first couple hundred years of the Common Era, we find a proliferation of texts titled "Gospels"—not only the four canonical Gospels but so-called Apocryphal Gospels such as the Gospel of Thomas, the Gospel of the Hebrews, and the Gospel of Mary. Why, then, call these narrative accounts of Jesus "Gospels"?

The Gospel in Isaiah

First, it is crucial we recognize that the language of "gospel" stems primarily from the Old Testament. While it's true that the language of "good news" (in the plural) is frequently used to speak of important Roman imperial events such as the birthday of Caesar or the visit of an imperial dignity, the primary context for gospel language is the canonical book of Isaiah. In Isaiah "good news" is the proclamation that God has been faithful to the promises he made to his people and has acted to establish himself as the king of Israel. In Isaiah 40:1–11, the prophet announces the good news that God has come to be with his people: "Get you up to a high mountain, O Zion, herald of good news; lift up your voice with strength, O Jerusalem, herald of good news, lift it up, do not fear; say to the cities of Judah, 'Here is your God!'" (40:9 NRSVue). Throughout this prophetic oracle there is a strong emphasis on verbal proclamation—that is, the declaration of what God is doing. God's manifestation of his kingship over Israel is indeed good news as it results in salvation, liberation, peace, restoration of the land, an outpouring of God's Spirit, and justice and freedom for the oppressed (Isa. 40:1–11; 52:7–12; 61:1–4).[1] Isaiah's "gospel" oracles, which occur interspersed throughout Isaiah 40–66, presume the situation of Israel's exile and judgment due to the sins of the people (see 40:1–2). Thus, Isaiah's "gospel" oracles anticipate Israel—and all those who attach themselves to the God of Israel—experiencing comfort, peace, and cosmic restoration. One helpful summary of these gospel oracles puts it this way: "A new chapter in God's plan is about to unfold: God's glorious, kingly presence of ages past will manifest itself again, in a universal fashion, and he will save his flock as a mighty, tender king."[2] 1.1

The Proclaimed Gospel and Messiah Jesus

Second, already within earliest Christianity the language of "gospel" or "good news" (noun, *euangelion*; verb, *euangelizō*), language that clearly predates the composition of the Gospels, is used frequently to describe the story of Jesus the Messiah and the good news of his salvation of humanity. The apostle Paul, for example, consistently uses language such as "gospel of God" and "gospel of Christ" to summarize his preaching (Rom. 1:1, 9; 15:16; 1 Cor. 9:12; 2 Cor. 4:4; 9:13; Gal. 1:7; Phil. 1:27; 1 Thess. 2:2, 8, 9; 3:2; 2 Thess. 1:8; 1 Tim. 1:1). Paul's references to the gospel consistently demonstrate that the term refers to his proclamation—that is, the oral announcement that God has done something of great significance for the world in the person of Jesus of Nazareth.

On a few occasions, Paul gives short, creed-like summaries of the content of the gospel. If we look at

SIDEBAR 1.1

The Gospel of Isaiah

- "O Zion, messenger of good news, shout from the mountaintops! Shout it louder, O Jerusalem. Shout, and do not be afraid. Tell the towns of Judah, 'Your God is coming!' Yes, the Sovereign LORD is coming in power. He will rule with a powerful arm. See, he brings his reward with him as he comes. He will feed his flock like a shepherd. He will carry the lambs in his arms, holding them close to his heart. He will gently lead the mother sheep with their young" (Isa. 40:9–11 NLT).
- "How beautiful on the mountains are the feet of the messenger who brings good news, the good news of peace and salvation, the news that the God of Israel reigns! . . . The LORD has demonstrated his holy power before the eyes of all the nations. All the ends of the earth will see the victory of our God" (Isa. 52:7, 10 NLT).
- "The Spirit of the sovereign LORD is upon me, for the LORD has anointed me to bring good news to the poor. He has sent me to comfort the brokenhearted and to proclaim that captives will be released and prisoners will be freed. He has sent me to tell those who mourn that the time of the LORD's favor has come, and with it, the day of God's anger against their enemies. To all who mourn in Israel, he will give a crown of beauty for ashes, a joyous blessing instead of mourning, festive praise instead of despair" (Isa. 61:1–3a NLT).

Romans 1:1–5, 1 Corinthians 15:1–5, and 2 Timothy 2:8–13, along with the assistance of Philippians 2:6–11 and Galatians 4:4–7, we can see that the gospel centers on the particular identity and narrative of Jesus as God's Messiah.[3] 1.2

Paul consistently narrates the gospel and the identity of Jesus Christ within the matrix of Israel's Scriptures.[4] God's promises to David for a messianic descendant who would reign over God's people stand behind Romans 1:1–5 (2 Sam. 7:12–14; Ps. 2:6–8); Paul explicitly claims that Jesus's death *and* resurrection took place "according to the Scriptures" (1 Cor. 15:3b, 4); the prophet Isaiah provides the language for Paul to declare in Philippians 2:10–11 that the enthroned Christ is worthy of receiving worship (see Isa. 45:23). God's gospel, then, centers on the good news of God's faithfulness to his scriptural promises to send the Davidic, messianic Son of God—the one who became incarnate, was crucified, resurrected, and enthroned to God's right hand.

SIDEBAR 1.2

The Gospel in Paul

1. **Messianic identity:** Jesus of Nazareth is both God's Son and the Davidic Messiah (Rom. 1:3–4; Gal. 4:4–6; 2 Tim. 2:8).
2. **Incarnation:** The preexistent Son, the one who is in the form of God, was made incarnate and took on real human flesh (Rom. 1:3, Gal. 4:4–6, Phil. 2:6–7).
3. **Suffering and death:** Messiah Jesus lives a life of obedience and service that culminates in his death on the cross for the sins of humanity (1 Cor. 15:3; Phil. 2:8).
4. **Resurrection and enthronement:** God raises Jesus from the dead and installs him with power as the singular heavenly king and Lord. God's resurrection and enthronement of the Messiah takes place by means of the Spirit such that the risen Messiah is now able to dispense the Spirit to his people (Rom. 1:4; Phil. 2:9–11; 1 Cor. 15:4–5).
5. **Universal mission and call for response:** God's gospel is good news for all people—both Jews and gentiles—and, therefore, Paul's mission is to bring about "the obedience of faith among the gentiles" (Rom. 1:5). The proclamation that Jesus is exalted at God's right hand will result in universal confession of Jesus's lordship (Phil. 2:10–11). Therefore, Paul's proclamation of the gospel constantly calls forth a response of faith, confession, repentance, and a transformed life (Rom. 1:16–17).

These five points are not a formula that occurs in every text, but they do highlight some of the main features that Paul emphasizes when he speaks of the gospel. We might summarize the occurrences of the gospel in this way: "Throughout the New Testament Epistles the 'gospel' refers to *the oral proclamation about Jesus the Christ* (meaning the anointed Davidic King)—who he was; what he accomplished through his life, death, and resurrection; the promise of his future return to establish God's reign; and the concomitant call to repent and have faith."[a] We should also keep in mind here that the written Gospels show an important transition from "gospel" being used to describe oral proclamation to it being used also for written books about Jesus.

The Gospel and Salvation

But there is a third obvious aspect of this gospel that we must note: the announcement of God's gospel is good news because it is the means whereby God brings salvation for all people. The Isaianic oracles said as much. Paul unpacks the significance of the gospel (Rom. 1:1–4) when he states, "I am not ashamed of the gospel. For it is the power of God *for salvation* to everyone who believes, first to the Jew and also the Greek" (Rom. 1:16). The gospel reveals that Christ's death and burial provide atonement for sins (1 Cor. 15:3–4). The gospel ensures that those who belong to Christ will live, reign, and share eternal glory with Jesus (2 Tim. 2:10–13). 1.3

Messiah Jesus Proclaims and Embodies the Gospel

A fourth aspect of the gospel should now be noted: the importance of the term "gospel" to the Synoptic Gospels' (Matthew, Mark, Luke) presentation of Jesus's ministry. While Paul and the other New Testament Epistles predate the Fourfold Gospel, we can see that the canonical Gospels also speak of Jesus proclaiming "the gospel" and often use the term to summarize Jesus's teaching and ministry. There are very good reasons, in fact, for thinking that Paul's emphasis on the gospel derives from Jesus of Nazareth's distinct and memorable use of the term. The Gospel of Mark, most likely the earliest of the four Gospels, begins with what looks to be a title for his work: "The beginning of the gospel of Jesus Christ" (Mark 1:1). Thus, Mark's prologue, the introduction to his action-packed story about Jesus, both begins (1:1) and concludes with a reference to the gospel: "After John had been handed over, Jesus came into Galilee proclaiming *the gospel of God*, saying, 'The time is filled up and the kingdom of God has drawn near; repent and believe *in the gospel*'" (1:14–15). Within Mark's prologue, we see the familiar elements of the fulfillment of the prophetic oracles of Isaiah (1:2–3), the call for faith and repentance (1:4–5, 15), the presence of the powerful Holy Spirit (1:8, 12), and the obedient, Spirit-empowered, messianic Son of God, who proclaims the gospel of God's kingdom (1:9–13). In the Gospel of Matthew, the narrator strategically locates two important descriptions of Jesus proclaiming "the gospel of the kingdom" (Matt. 4:23; 9:35). This *inclusio* (a bookend or bracket) functions to bracket Matthew 5–9 as one unit and so thereby associates the gospel with Jesus's teachings (chaps. 5–7) and his acts of mercy and compassion seen in healings, exorcisms, and table fellowship (chaps. 8–9). Like Mark's prologue, which is framed by the repetition of "gospel," so also Matthew's bracketing of Jesus's teaching and acts with references to the gospel of the kingdom works to establish the identity and activity of Jesus of Nazareth as the revelation of the gospel. It is also helpful to note that Matthew reports Jesus later drawing on the prophetic oracles of Isaiah, specifically Isaiah 61, to summarize his own ministry: "The blind see and the lame walk, those with skin disease are cleansed and the deaf can hear, the dead are raised and the poor have the gospel proclaimed to them" (Matt. 11:5). For both Mark and Matthew, we again see that the emphasis on the gospel and the kingdom of God "means that *God is coming* with power and in

SIDEBAR 1.3

The Gospel of King Jesus

In his book *The King Jesus Gospel*, Scot McKnight argues that the gospel is not to be singularly identified with forgiveness of sins or justification by faith. Rather, there are four crucial aspects of the New Testament gospel. First, the gospel is framed by the story of Israel. Jesus is Israel's Messiah, who brings the story of God's people to their climax. Second, the gospel is focused on Jesus's lordship. "Jesus is seen as suffering, saving, ruling, and judging because he is the Messiah and the Lord and the Davidic Savior. He is now exalted at the right hand of God."[b] Third, the gospel involves inviting people to embrace the truth about King Jesus. Fourth, the gospel brings salvation and redemption.

fulfilment of the promises to set things right, to defeat evil and establish righteousness so that people live in keeping with his will and character."[5]

In Luke's Gospel, the author uses the verb form of "proclaim the gospel" to describe Gabriel's message to Zechariah (Luke 1:19), the angelic message to the shepherds (2:10), and John the Baptist's exhortations and calls for repentance to the people (3:18). Luke's infancy narrative makes it abundantly clear that Jesus of Nazareth is God's anointed Son, born in the line of David, who has come to save and rescue his people. But it is in Jesus's first major sermon, in the synagogue of his hometown, Nazareth, where the Lukan Jesus's proclamation of the gospel is held up front and center (4:16–30). Here Jesus takes up the words of Isaiah 61 (and a line from Isa. 58): "The Spirit of the Lord is upon me; he has anointed me to proclaim good news to the poor; he has sent me to preach release for the captive and sight for the blind, to bring release for the oppressed, and to proclaim the year of the Lord's favor" (Luke 4:18–19). Later we will see that this episode is programmatic for Luke's Gospel, as it articulates many of the major themes of Jesus's ministry. But for now, it is enough to note that these first public words of Jesus in the Gospel of Luke portray Jesus as God's messianic agent who, in fulfillment of the Old Testament promises, will reveal and enact God's salvation for his people. Luke can, then, use the verb "proclaim the gospel" throughout his narrative to summarize Jesus as the agent of this saving good news (e.g., 4:43; 7:22; 8:1; 9:6). In Luke, the language of "proclaim the gospel" stands as a summary for the entirety of Jesus's Spirit-empowered ministry as Jesus provides liberation, freedom, and mercy to his people.

We have seen that there is great significance in the specific language of "Gospels" to describe the first four books of the New Testament canon. Calling these books "Gospels" alerts us to the following:

1. The prefiguration of the gospel in Israel's Scriptures, specifically the prophet Isaiah, and the depiction of Jesus as inaugurating God's promise to restore, heal, save, and shepherd his people.
2. The invocation by the New Testament Epistles of the language of "gospel" to describe their oral proclamation that Jesus is God's anointed Messiah sent to save his people. Already before the Gospels were written, the language of "gospel" was used to speak of Jesus as the Son of God, who became incarnate, faithfully suffered unto death on a cross, and was raised from the dead and exalted to God's right hand.

3. The identification of Messiah Jesus—his incarnation, life, death, and resurrection—with the salvation of humanity. Jesus's life is "good news" precisely because it is humanity's singular hope.
4. The depiction of Jesus, in the Gospels, as one remembered for proclaiming the gospel and often in connection with the inauguration of the kingdom of God.

For many of us, it's all too easy to reduce the gospel to something that, while nevertheless true, is incomplete in its ability to capture the full identification of the life and story of Jesus. The gospel is not, for example, justification by faith or even salvation; the gospel is "the narration of the saving Story of Jesus—his life, his death, his resurrection, his exaltation, and his coming again—as the completion of the Story of Israel."[6] The gospel, then, is not an idea, a philosophy, a plan for a better life; the gospel is, rather, the story of what God has done in space and time to reclaim the cosmos and humanity *in the person of Jesus of Nazareth*. As we read through the canonical Gospels, we will do well to remember that the gospel *just is* the good news of Messiah Jesus and his complete story as the ground of our salvation.

Who Titled These Books "Gospels"?

If the title "Gospel" is so important to these four books, then it's worth exploring whether the authors titled them as such or whether these titles were added later. Book titles often function to provide readers with a quick and pithy description of what they'll find should they choose to read the book. Sometimes a title is a clear and obvious description of a book's content; other times a title functions to provoke or elicit curiosity. It may seem trivial at first, but the titles of the works we are studying tell us some extremely important information about what kinds of texts these are and how to read them.

Each one of our writings has the inscription or title "The Gospel according to X." Within the actual body of the text, the author does not make any obvious claims about his authorial identity such as one finds in, for example, epistolary writings where Paul, Peter, James, and others explicitly speak of their personal identity. Even Luke's Gospel, which does refer to Theophilus as its addressee in the prologue (Luke 1:1–4), lacks any reference to the name of the author. This lack of explicit references to the author, along with the possibility that the titles were added at a later date, after the actual composition, has suggested to some that the Gospels are technically anonymous. Some have suggested that the names Matthew, Mark, Luke, and John were added later when there was competition among other Christians (i.e., so-called heretics) for the legitimate take on Jesus. On this view, the titles "The Gospel according to X" were added later, perhaps in the early second century, when the four Gospels began to circulate together or when heightened expectation for Christ's imminent return had waned. The Gospel of John's lack of references to "gospel" (in either the noun or the verb form) might indicate the unlikelihood of the author himself titling the work "the Gospel of John." Some have even argued that the anonymity of these texts reflects a sense of humility in their concern to give complete attention to their subject matter: Jesus of Nazareth.

Figure 1.1. Manuscript 𝔓75, leaf 2a.8r, which includes *"Euangelion Kata Loukan . . . Euangelion Kata Iōanēn"* (The Gospel according to Luke . . . The Gospel according to John)

While there's much we don't know for certain here, it is by no means impossible that the titles are original from the time of their circulation at least.[7] The evangelists may have had their own descriptions or titles for their works—for example, "the book of the genealogy of Jesus Christ" for Matthew's Gospel (Matt. 1:1), or "the beginning of the gospel of Jesus Christ" for Mark (Mark 1:1), or "an orderly account" for Luke (Luke 1:1–4).[8] John simply refers to his work as a *biblion*, a "book" (John 20:30). If the Gospel of Mark is the earliest of the Gospels, and we'll soon see that there are good reasons for thinking this, then the first words of Mark's Gospel—"The beginning of the gospel of Jesus Christ" (Mark 1:1)—may have influenced the superscriptions of the other Gospels when they were published and then circulated. Even if Mark did not specifically title his work a "Gospel," the opening lines make the classification of his writing (and the other three canonical Gospels) as a Gospel understandable. At least by the middle of the second century CE, the four texts were being referred to as Gospels (e.g., 2 Clement, Didache, Justin Martyr).

Thus, the possibility that the title "The Gospel according to X" is *original to the time of the circulation of each Gospel* is suggested by the following considerations. First, while the order of the four Gospels does vary in the earliest manuscripts, there are no later descriptions that give double or multiple titles to the same Gospel. And there is an abundance of second-century literature that explicitly names (again, entirely consistently) the authors/titles.[9] We would expect that if the Gospels had circulated anonymously for any period of time, we would have at least some evidence of the same Gospel being classified with two or more titles. But, instead, the later witness from the second and third centuries is entirely uniform with respect to the consistency of the titles, and this suggests that the Gospels originally circulated with their titles.[10] Second, it was remarkably rare in the ancient world that books circulated anonymously. And the early Christians would have needed some kind of name or way for identifying their written texts about Jesus. Third, with respect to Luke's Gospel, it is highly unlikely that a text dedicated to a named individual (Theophilus) would have circulated apart from the title bearing Luke's name. Fourth, if the Gospels began as anonymous literature, the question remains as to why they would later be assigned to the particular individuals Matthew, Mark, Luke, and John. The apostles Matthew and John are somewhat understandable here, but would there not be more obvious, perhaps more authoritative apostolic witnesses from which to choose? Fifth, assuming that Matthew and Luke both used the Gospel of Mark as a source for their own Gospels, it would be surprising that they would do so apart from knowledge of the authorial origins of Mark's Gospel. Again, each of the four Gospels is consistently designated as "The Gospel according to X," and the simplest explanation is that this is due to the likelihood that the Gospels had their traditional names associated with them at the time of their publication and circulation.

What Kind of Book Is a Gospel?

Whether we do so consciously or not, all of us intuitively recognize that there are different rules and expectations for our reading of texts that correspond to the classification of the text we're reading. Literary classification, or genre, helps me to determine how to interpret what I read. I do not read the *Chicago Tribune* in the same way I read an Agatha Christie mystery novel; I do not even read twenty-first-century scholarship on the Gospel of John in the same way that I read the Gospel of John. We tend to intuitively develop the requisite skills for interpreting contemporary texts simply through our embeddedness in our own sociocultural context; but this can be trickier for reading and understanding texts that are historically and/or culturally outside of our context. Determining what kind of texts the Gospels are, then, can help us develop wise sensibilities for how to read them well.

We have already explored the fact, as well as its significance, that the primary designation for canonical Gospels is "Gospel." Whether or not the four authors were responsible for the titles of these works, we have seen that the early and unanimous designation of these texts as Gospels activated a certain set of expectations for readers concerning the narrative about Jesus they would find in these books. Indeed, these four texts contain many differences in emphasis from one another—especially when we compare the Synoptic Gospels with that of John. But clearly the designation of each one as a Gospel, as well as their collection together into the canonical Fourfold Gospel, indicates that their narratives about Jesus were seen as similar enough to be grouped together.

In addition, other early Christian testimony sometimes refers to the stories and sayings about Jesus, whether in their oral or written form, as sayings or words of Jesus (e.g., Polycarp, *To the Philippians* 7:1–2; 1 Clement 13:1–4). In the early second century, Papias wrote five volumes titled *Expositions of the Sayings of the Lord* (Papias, *Fragments* 3.1). Justin Martyr loves to speak of the Gospels as "Memoirs of the Apostles" (e.g., *First Apology* 66.3; 67.3; *Dialogue with Trypho* 100.4; 101.3).[11] In the next chapter we'll see that references to Gospel traditions as sayings, testimony, and memoirs of Jesus provide important information for the oral tradition of our Gospel texts; but, for now, we can briefly note that these designations provide little help in terms of classifying the literary genre of our four Gospels. While a variety of proposals have been made for the best literary classification for the Gospels, two proposals rise to the top in terms of their influence: (1) the Gospels are without literary precedent and represent a unique and creative kind of Christian writing; (2) the Gospels are closest in form to ancient biographies (*bioi*).

Form Criticism and the Quest for the Literary Genre of the Written Gospels

In the early twentieth century, prominent biblical scholars known as form critics, mostly working in Germany, developed a method and certain set of arguments that convinced many that the Gospels were utterly unique (sui generis) and could not be fitted into a genre classification. The primary goal of form criticism actually centered on establishing the preexisting oral forms of the Gospel tradition based on their use within the early Christian communities. So one finds the sayings and stories of Jesus categorized according to various forms. 1.4

These forms are categorized together due to the identification of stereotyped patterning of

SIDEBAR 1.4

Different Gospel Forms

- Controversy dialogues (e.g., Mark 2:1–12; 3:1–6)
- Miracle stories (e.g., Mark 1:40–45; 4:35–41)
- Sayings and parables (e.g., Matt. 5–7; Mark 4; Luke 12)
- Tales and legends (e.g., Mark 5:1–20; Luke 7:11–17)
- The passion narrative (e.g., Mark 14–15)[c]

the Jesus tradition. It is supposed that these individual written Gospel units (each referred to as a "pericope") had an earlier life-setting (*Sitz im Leben*) and served specific purposes within the early Christian communities. Stories and memories of Jesus, in other words, were retold, adapted, and creatively expanded in order to meet the particular needs of the Christian communities. So, a miracle story may provide an apologetic defense for the supernatural power of Jesus; an authoritative pronouncement story may provide instruction regarding how followers of Jesus should live; Jesus's teachings and wise sayings provide catechetical instructions for disciples. Thus, while a particular pericope often has some relationship (though not always) to the historical Jesus, many form critics suppose that the Gospel traditions provide direct evidence for the beliefs of the earliest Christian churches (rather than Jesus himself).

One can see here that form critics are generally not very interested in anything like the literary or theological unity and creativity of the final written Gospel text. The Gospel texts are instead viewed as the depository of the collected oral traditions about Jesus. As a result, one will repeatedly find form critics describing the written Gospels with the language of "sui generis" (i.e., "entirely unique" or "original creation"); and this results in something of a moratorium on quests for comparative work between the written Gospels and other texts with respect to genre.

Many of the methods of form criticism have been abandoned and convincingly critiqued. But two important insights have enduring significance. First, the raw materials for our four evangelists were indeed the prior oral traditions regarding the sayings and stories of Jesus. That is to say, before the Gospels were written texts, the earliest Christians passed on their memories of Jesus orally. To give just one example, when we look at the unit of Mark 1:16–3:6, the text divides neatly into individual pericopes that can be separated quite easily from one another as stand-alone healing stories (e.g., 1:29–31; 1:32–34), controversy dialogues (e.g., 2:1–2), and pronouncement stories (e.g., 2:15–17; 2:23–28). There are no clear geographical or temporal markers within the unit, and each pericope could be placed elsewhere by Mark without any noticeable surprise on the part of the reader. Thus, it's very likely that Mark has collected individual (and previously oral) units of memories of Jesus and arranged them together by his own creative hand.[12] Mark imposes a framework on these distinct units in a way that is analogous to supplying the string for a handful of pearls. We'll see, in fact, that this view actually accords quite nicely with our most important patristic testimony regarding the origins of the Gospels.

Second, while one need not suppose that the Gospel traditions were creatively shaped and molded at will by the early church, there's no reason to deny the strong likelihood that specific memories of Jesus were preserved and remembered precisely because of their relevance and usefulness for the earliest Christians. John's Gospel concludes by emphasizing precisely this point. More stories and information could have been provided, but John has intentionally selected his stories and sayings from Jesus in order to convince his readers that the Messiah is Jesus of Nazareth (John 20:30–31). Third, while the idea of a truly "unique" or "creatively original" genre hardly makes sense, there are indeed surprising aspects of the Gospel narratives that do not neatly conform to Greco-Roman biographies.

The Four Gospels as Ancient Biographies/Lives of Jesus

Despite their being explicitly and consistently referred to as Gospels (not *bioi*) and containing some unusual features for an ancient biography, there is a strong consensus that each of the four Gospels most closely resembles the genre of ancient Greco-Roman biography. We have numerous ancient Greco-Roman biographies that focus on telling the story of a well-known, sometimes notorious or infamous, individual. David Aune provides a crisp description of ancient biography: "A biography relates the significance of a famous person's career (i.e., his character and achievements), optionally framed by a narrative of origins and youth, on the one hand, and death and lasting significance on the other."[13] Note that literary genres are descriptive; they are not inflexible formulas that authors must follow.[14] While we should be careful that we do not pigeonhole the Gospels into a static and rigid genre, we should also expect that any text will share some characteristics, some type of family resemblance, with other writings. Genre should be thought of as dynamic, rather than static and conventional, thereby allowing the author to engage in surprising and creative adaptation of its forms. Despite a large number of divergences within ancient biography, two characteristics of the genre are obvious: "first, a concern to commemorate a great life, and second, a moralistic desire to learn from it."[15]

Biographies overlapped with or, perhaps better, were considered a subset of ancient historiography, but the focus of a biography was obviously dominated by the particular life and character of the individual rather than by wars, politics, and so forth. Biographies are distinguished from ancient works of history, in part, due to their (often) overt and explicit attempts to elicit praise or blame for their character; they are also, generally, of medium length and chronologically ordered in terms of basic life events, though with flexibility to include the hero's teachings and actions as the author saw fit.[16] Thus, many of them are explicitly encomiastic as they memorialize

SIDEBAR 1.5

Examples of Ancient Biographies

Emperors: Suetonius, *Lives of the Caesars*
Philosophers: Xenophon, *Memorabilia*; Lucian, *Nigrinus* and *Demonax*; Philostratus, *Life of Apollonius*
Kings: Isocrates, *Evagoras*
Military leaders, statesmen, and lawgivers: Plutarch, *Parallel Lives*
Religious figures: Philo, *Life of Moses*

a figure from the ancient past for their wisdom, achievements, benefit to society, character, and so forth. 1.5

As is the case with all literary classifications, there is room for flexibility and creative adaptation when writing a biography. Biographies share obvious affinities with history and epideictic rhetoric (i.e., praise/blame of an individual), and this combination often results in a distinct type of work. 1.6

Returning to the four Gospels, we can see that each of them shares numerous features with ancient biographies.[17] With respect to titles, prefaces, and other opening features, we have seen that Matthew starts with "the book of the genealogy of Jesus Christ, Son of David, son of Abraham" (Matt. 1:1); Mark's Gospel starts with "the beginning of the gospel of Jesus Christ" (Mark 1:1); Luke has a lengthy and somewhat technical preface (Luke 1:1–4); and John also begins with a lengthy prologue for his biography about Jesus (John 1:1–18) and concludes with an explicit expression of his authorial purpose (20:30–31). Whereas Mark's Gospel moves straight into Jesus's adult years and public ministry, both Matthew's and Luke's Gospels include stories about Jesus's birth (Matt. 1:18–25; Luke 1:5–2:40) and genealogies that connect Jesus to the people of Israel and their great heroes (Matt. 1:2–18; Luke 3:23–38), and Luke even includes a story from Jesus's childhood (Luke 2:41–52). On the assumption that Mark's Gospel is the earliest, these additions further confirm that Matthew and Luke understood both their works and Mark to be that of a biography. Each Gospel obviously focuses with near exclusivity on the subject of Jesus. Only on the rarest of occasions does the narrator take the reader into a new geographical setting apart from Jesus's presence (see, e.g., Mark 6:14–29). The bulk of each Gospel centers on Jesus's teachings and his great deeds with an obvious emphasis on his character and manner of life. The authors draw on stories, sayings, short vignettes, and lengthier discourses in order to create their narrative about Jesus. Each Gospel is chronologically consistent and sensible, while primarily structured topically and without strong interest in precise chronological and geographical details. All four Gospels also demonstrate a strong interest in Jesus's death and his virtue and fortitude during his sufferings. These features of the four Gospels have rightly convinced most scholars that the appropriate literary classification for Matthew, Mark, Luke, and John is that of ancient biography. While John's Gospel has obvious differences with the Synoptic

Gospels, it should be emphasized that it too shares all of these same genre features of ancient biography.

Why would an author choose to write a biography? A variety of authorial purposes have been advanced, but here I mention three of the most prevalent and important as it pertains to our understanding of the Gospels. First, the most frequently articulated purpose is that of sharing ethics or morals for the audience to imitate by holding up a great figure from the past (e.g., Lucian, *Demonax*; Plutarch, *Parallel Lives*). When one writes a life of a philosopher or a religious teacher, the text functions as a literary memorial for the person's character and teachings.[18] Second, some biographies appear to attempt to legitimate a controversial figure. That is, they may seek to overturn a false depiction of the hero and rehabilitate their character (e.g., Xenophon, *Memorabilia*; Porphyry, *Life of Pythagoras*). Different interpretations of the life and teaching of the heroes are possible, and a biography can function to show its readers "the right way" to interpret the figure. Third, some are written, it would seem, primarily to inform

SIDEBAR 1.6

Literary Characteristics of Ancient Biographies

While there are all kinds of differences between ancient Greco-Roman biographies, they nevertheless share most of the following literary characteristics.[d]

1. Title: "The Life of . . ."
2. Preface or prologue: Opening words (often) set forth the purpose or the plan of the work.
3. Birth and lineage: Biographies often include considerations of the hero's birth and unusual omens, ancestry and ethnicity, growth and development as a child including his education.
4. Subject: In ancient biographies the individual character dominates the subject matter. One sees this especially clearly in that the subject of the verbs disproportionately have that character as the subject.
5. Geographical setting: The geographical location typically is dictated by the subject matter of the biography. The author rarely takes the reader to a geographical location without the primary figure.
6. Characterization: Ancient biographies were fascinated with the virtues, vices, and general characteristics of their subject. Unlike contemporary novels and biographies, ancient biography is much less interested in the particular individuality or psychological motivations of their subject matter; rather, the focus is often on virtue and character. This is such an important feature of ancient biographies that it is worth quoting some of Plutarch's opening words in his *Life of Alexander*:

> For it is not Histories that I am writing, but Lives; and in the most illustrious deeds there is not always a manifestation of virtue or vice, nay, a slight thing like a phrase or a jest often makes a greater revelation of character than battles where thousands fall, or the greatest armaments, or sieges of cities. . . . So I must be permitted to devote myself rather to the signs of the soul in men, and by means of these to portray the life of each, leaving to others the description of their great contests. (1.2–3)[e]

The text is illuminating because it indicates that Plutarch seems to see historiography as focused on wars, battles, sieges, and great events, whereas biography is looking for "signs of the soul in men." Plutarch will write, then, in a way that shows us the particular character—whether virtuous or otherwise—so that his readers can emulate or avoid what they see. While Plutarch is the most explicit, the majority of ancient biographies, in fact, focus on ethical characteristics of their subject and invite the audience to imitate or avoid what they see.

7. Sayings, stories, and exploits of the character: The body of the biography is, unsurprisingly, dominated by the central actions, exploits, and teachings or sayings of the main character.
8. Manner of death: Many of the biographies manifest an intense interest in the final hours and death of their hero. Did the figure die a noble death, demonstrating courage and consistency in the face of opposition, or die shamefully, manifesting fear and lack of courage?

and entertain one's audience (e.g., Suetonius, *Lives of the Caesars*; Tacitus, *Agricola*).

How does identifying the Gospels as examples of ancient biography aid us in our reading of these texts? Let me suggest four implications. First, it is worth stating the obvious: the "gospels are nothing less than Christology in narrative form."[19] For each of the Gospel authors, divine "revelation belongs supremely to a life."[20] Biography is an appropriate genre for the evangelists, given their conviction that salvation and revelation are found in a single person. Everything we read in the Gospels has as its function the illumination of the identity and actions of Jesus of Nazareth. Unlike some of the claims of the form critics, the decision of the evangelists to write their Gospels in the form of ancient biography indicates a significant passionate interest in preserving the past history of their founding figure.

Second, if the Gospels are ancient biographies, we should expect only basic chronological accuracy in the ordering of the stories. In other words, the text should flow well in terms of appropriately narrating the order of the major events in the life of Jesus; but we should not expect the Gospels to be overly concerned with giving detailed chronological precision. Ancient biographies allowed for authors to exert flexibility in terms of how they arranged the body of the text, and thus each Gospel author could exert personal creativity in the arrangement of the sayings and stories of Jesus. It is well known that having four canonical narratives about Jesus means that there are sometimes quite considerable differences in the placement of the stories and sayings of Jesus. And this presents the challenge of whether the Gospels can (and need to) be harmonized. Nowhere are these differences, especially as it pertains to chronology, more apparent than in those between John's Gospel and the Synoptic Gospels. And yet there is no reason why John's Gospel, if it is indeed understood as ancient biography, cannot depart from Mark's outline and arrangement of material.[21] Understanding the Gospels as ancient biographies does not solve all of these challenges, but it does help us avoid bringing unrealistic expectations regarding (our definition of) historical accuracy to the Gospels.

Third, we have seen that one of the major functions of ancient biography was moralistic in that it holds up a figure as one worthy of emulation and/or admiration. If the Gospels, then, are Christology in narrative form, we can also say that they are calls for discipleship for would-be followers of Jesus. "If the goal of the evangelists is (at least in part) to present Jesus as a model of God-ward virtue, then we should receive them as such, keeping this goal as an important part of what it means to interpret the Gospels and read them well."[22] This feature of ancient biography fits neatly with the Gospels' consistent exhortation to follow Jesus. Jesus invites disciples,

"Come after me" (Mark 1:17), to take up their cross and follow him (Mark 8:34), to take his yoke and learn from him (Matt. 11:29), to follow his example of sacrificial love (John 13:12–15), and to imitate his own hospitality practices (Luke 22:24–27). By virtue of their study and listening to the teaching and actions of Jesus, readers of the Gospels can learn both who Jesus was and how to follow him.[23] A good reading of each of the four Gospels will clarify how they function to call their readers to follow the character and virtue of Jesus.

Before we conclude our look at the Gospels as ancient biographies, we should note some of the surprising features of these texts, as they help us see how revolutionary and creative our four Gospels are.[24] Most simply, the exalted claims made for Jesus in the four Gospels are unique. Jesus alone is the center point of history, the fulfillment of God's plans and purposes for the cosmos and humanity, the one who brings Israel's Scriptures to their fulfillment (e.g., Matt. 1:2–17; Mark 1:2–3; Luke 4:18–19). He is the singular one worthy of humanity's worship because he is both God and human (Matt. 28:18–20; Luke 24:50–53). He alone is the one who is able to save and rescue humanity from their sins (Matt. 1:21; Mark 2:1–12; Luke 4:18–19; John 5:23–30). And he is still alive as the risen and enthroned king in heaven; as such, the living Jesus is still active and can be prayed to (John 14:12–14). Jesus promises his followers that he will be present among them even after his death (e.g., Matt. 18:20; 28:20; John 14–17). These features make for an unusual biography in that the subject matter is not simply a wise philosopher or a courageous and strategic military hero; rather, he is the living Jesus, who alone reveals God and can save humanity.

Summary

We have explored the question "What are the Gospels?" by examining the meaning of the term "Gospel," the origin of the titles "Gospel according to X" for the work of the four evangelists, and ancient biography as the best literary (genre) classification for the four Gospels.

We can summarize the main points with an emphasis on their implications for how we read the Gospels as we move forward.

1. The designation "Gospel" to refer to our (canonical) written stories of Jesus activates Isaiah's prophetic oracles that centered on the proclamation that God was coming to be with his people, to restore their cities and land, to pour forth his Spirit, and to save and rescue

his people (Isa. 40:1–11; 52:7–12; 61:1–4). The references to these portions of Isaiah within all four Gospels, often on the lips of Jesus, confirms that the gospel is nothing less than the fulfillment of God's redemptive activity as foretold by Isaiah (e.g., Matt. 3:3; Mark 1:2–3; Luke 4:18–19; John 1:23). When we read our four Gospels, we can expect, therefore, that we will find each author, in his own and unique way, showing us how Jesus brings Israel's Scriptures, specifically the prophetic promises of Isaiah, to their surprising fulfillment.

2. Paul and other early Christians used gospel language to describe the oral proclamation that God had acted powerfully to reclaim the world and humanity in the person of Jesus of Nazareth. The gospel centers on Jesus's identity as the God-incarnate, Davidic, messianic king and the full story of his birth, life, death, resurrection, and heavenly enthronement. This corresponds to the written Gospels' depiction of Jesus himself as one who proclaimed the gospel (Matt. 4:23; 9:35; Mark 1:14–15; Luke 4:18–19). When we read the written Gospels, then, we will see that each of them identifies their story about Jesus *with* the gospel. In other words, the gospel is just the full and complete story of what God has done in Jesus the Messiah.
3. This gospel is good news because it is humanity's singular hope for salvation. Our written Gospels present the full and complete life of Jesus, including its climax in his crucifixion and resurrection, as the saving good news. Our reading of the Gospels will be attentive, as such, to how every aspect of Jesus's life both reveals God and is critically necessary for humanity's salvation.
4. While our four Gospels are technically anonymous in that they do not name the identity of their author, there are very good reasons for seeing their titles as "Gospel according to X" as stemming from the very beginning of their circulation.
5. The popular view propagated by form critics that the Gospels were sui generis in terms of literary classification does not now command wide scholarly assent. Form critics rightly emphasized that the Gospels had an *oral* prehistory and that the stories/sayings of Jesus served specific functions within the early Christian communities before their textualization. While there are distinctive and surprising aspects of the written Gospels, most now affirm that the Gospels share strong enough family resemblances so as to be labeled as ancient biographies.
6. Understanding the Gospels as examples of ancient biographies will result in our affirming the significance of past history to early

Christianity. We will also expect to find chronological coherence in their telling of the story of Jesus, but we will understand that the genre allows for a high level of flexibility in terms of how each Gospel author orders and arranges his material. In addition, we will not be surprised to find the Gospels holding up Jesus as an example to be emulated, as is often the case with ancient biographies, and as one to be greatly admired—or, more appropriately, as one to be worshiped.

Where Did the Gospels Come From?

We have seen why the first four writings of the New Testament are titled "Gospels"; we have explored the origins of the titles' association with the named individuals Matthew, Mark, Luke, and John; and I have argued that the Gospels, despite their distinctive and surprising elements, are best classified as examples of ancient biography. But we have not yet examined the question of how the written Gospels came to be. Where did the four evangelists get their material? Do the sayings and stories of Jesus stem from eyewitnesses of his ministry? How carefully was the prewritten Gospel tradition preserved? In this chapter we examine what we can know about how the stories and sayings of Jesus were preserved and transmitted as well as how we came to have four different and yet similar canonical Gospels.

Jesus the Teacher

Before we ask *how* the Gospel tradition was preserved and transmitted, we should remind ourselves of a quite obvious fact: Jesus of Nazareth was a teacher. Jesus was a gifted teacher and was able to communicate his message in a powerful manner through a variety of oral techniques. Luke's Gospel preserves the story of Jesus as a young boy teaching, debating, and astonishing all those listening to him in Jerusalem; the story clearly prefigures one of Luke's literary agendas: to portray Jesus as the superior teacher of God's people (Luke 2:41–52). Each of the four

Figure 2.1. Rembrandt van Rijn, *Christ Preaching* (The Hundred Guilder Print)

Gospels depicts others frequently referring to Jesus as teacher (e.g., Matt. 8:19; 9:11; Mark 9:17; 10:17; Luke 12:13; John 3:2). The Gospels preserve memories of Jesus as one who surprised the crowds, those in the synagogue, and the scribes with his unique and authoritative teaching abilities. At the conclusion of Jesus's famous Sermon on the Mount, Matthew shares that the "crowds were amazed at his teaching, for he taught them as one who had authority and not like their scribes" (Matt. 7:28–29). Mark peppers his narrative with statements and questions from the audience that heighten the tension as to Jesus's true identity: "What is this? A new teaching with authority!" (Mark 1:27; cf. 1:22; 6:3). Luke's Gospel shows how Jesus's teaching in the synagogue leads to surprise,

SIDEBAR 2.1

Jesus Taught by Means of Forms

Here are some of the forms that Jesus employed to convey his teachings:

- Lengthy discourses/sermons, such as the Sermon on the Mount (Matt. 5–7) and the Farewell Discourse (John 14–17).
- Memorable parables, such as those of the good Samaritan (Luke 10:25–37) and the sheep and the goats (Matt. 25:31–46).
- Exposition and interpretation of the significance of Israel's Scriptures (and images, festivals, and institutions found therein) (e.g., Matt. 11:2–16; Luke 4:16–21; John 7–8).
- Aphorisms, riddles, and pithy one-liners, such as "Do not think I have come to bring peace to the earth; I have not come to bring peace but instead a sword" (Matt. 10:34); "Be wise as serpents and innocent as doves" (Matt. 10:16); "Give to Caesar what belongs to Caesar; give to God what belongs to God" (Mark 12:17); "If David calls him Lord, how then can he be his son?" (Mark 12:37a); "He who does not take up his cross, deny himself, and follow me is not worthy to be my disciple" (Mark 8:34).
- Instructions and rules, such as missionary discourses (Matt. 10:1–42) and teachings on wealth (Luke 16:1–31).
- Invective and polemic against his opponents and detractors (Matt. 23; Luke 11:37–54).

shock, and even anger from those listening to Jesus's exposition (Luke 4:16–30; cf. Mark 6:1–6). John's Gospel portrays some fellow Jews as perplexed as to Jesus's gifted teaching abilities considering his lack of scribal education (John 7:15).[1] Even a cursory read of the Gospels shows us that Jesus was a powerful communicator who drew on a variety of oral forms and techniques. 2.1

The list of literary forms in the sidebar "Jesus Taught by Means of Forms" is by no means exhaustive, but it does illustrate the four Gospels' depiction of Jesus as an effective and powerful teacher. People respond to Jesus with amazement and astonishment, but quite often they are also puzzled and confused by his riddles, irony, and ambiguous speech (e.g., Matt. 19:24–26; Mark 4:10–12; John 3:1–8).[2] Furthermore, the Gospels obviously portray Jesus as a "rabbi" (e.g., Mark 9:5; 14:45; John 1:38, 49; 3:2) who is followed by a select group of "disciples" who listen to his teaching (Luke 6:12–16). The language of "disciple" in the Gospels basically means "student." And one of the primary tasks of Jesus's students was to learn, memorize, and pass along the teachings of their master (e.g., Luke 10:16; John 13:18–20).[3]

The Oral Transmission of the Gospel Tradition

We have noted the rather obvious point that Jesus of Nazareth was remembered as a great teacher—but he was one who did not leave behind any written texts. So, it is not at all surprising that Jesus's followers, especially his disciples/students, would orally preserve, proclaim, and transmit the stories and sayings about their Savior. In the previous chapter we noted that this is one of form criticism's enduring insights with which very few now would disagree: our written Gospels had a prior oral history and transmission. The oral transmission of the Gospel tradition refers to the process of passing on the sayings and stories of Jesus by word of mouth (rather than through written medium) within the time frame of a generation or two.[4] Why would Jesus's followers do this? They believed that God's revelation and salvation had taken place through a historical person; thus, detailed knowledge of who this person was, what he said, and what he did was essential to the faith of the earliest Christians. Jesus's teachings could, furthermore, be appealed to for their practical value in settling controversies (e.g., food laws in Mark 7:1–23) and the practical life of disciples (e.g., Matt. 6:9–13; Luke 11:5–13).[5] The evidence for the oral transmission of the Gospel tradition is at least threefold, as follows below.

New Testament Epistles Demonstrate Oral Transmission of the Gospel Tradition

Although dating the Gospels is tricky, we can be quite confident that the Gospels were written after the letters that Paul wrote. Readers of Paul often wonder why there isn't more explicit engagement with Jesus's teachings in the Pauline Epistles; however, many of Paul's most important statements about the significance of Jesus's death and resurrection presume that Paul had access to a narrative account of Jesus's sufferings, death, and resurrection (Rom. 4:25; 1 Cor. 11:23–26; 15:3–5; Phil. 2:6–11; Col. 2:13–15; 1 Thess. 4:14). As one scholar notes, "Without the narration of the Jesus tradition, the kerygma [proclamation] of Jesus's redemptive death would have been incomprehensible to the church from the beginning."[6] A similar point holds for Paul's depiction of Christ's character as one who embodied humility, service, and hospitality (Rom. 15:1–3; 1 Cor. 9:19–23; 10:24–11:1; 2 Cor. 10:1; Phil. 2:6–8); Paul's emphasis on Christ's character is more than simply a vague awareness of his virtue and almost certainly stems from his knowledge of concrete stories and sayings of Jesus.[7] And while Paul's Letters are not loaded with direct references to Jesus's teachings, we should not underestimate the obvious fact that Paul does indeed *know* and *transmit* teachings of Jesus and, on occasion, refers to them as "words of the Lord" (Rom. 12:14–21; 14:14; 1 Cor. 4:11–13; 7:10–11; 9:14; 11:23–25; 1 Thess. 4:15–17; 5:1–7).[8] Perhaps the most well-known examples here are Paul's appeal to Jesus's teaching on divorce and remarriage (1 Cor. 7:10–11; cf. Mark 10:1–12) and Paul's transmission of Jesus's words at the Last Supper (1 Cor. 11:23–26; cf. Luke 22:15–20). Furthermore, there are a handful of themes and phrases in Paul's Letters that seem to show unmistakable indebtedness to the prewritten Gospel tradition. For example, on fourteen occasions Paul's Letters refer to Jesus's central proclamation: the kingdom of God (Rom. 14:17; 1 Cor. 4:20; 6:9–10; 15:24, 50; Gal. 5:21; Eph. 5:5; Col. 1:13; 4:11; 1 Thess. 2:12; 2 Thess. 1:5; 2 Tim. 4:1, 18). Paul's summation of the Torah through Leviticus 19:18 ("You shall love your neighbor as yourself") seems to be an obvious allusion to Jesus's teachings on the first and second greatest commandments (Rom. 13:8–10; Gal. 5:13–14; cf. Matt. 22:35–40; Mark 12:28–31). His reference to "the law of Christ" may even allude to Jesus's teachings (1 Cor. 9:21–22; Gal. 6:2). Paul's statement to the church in Rome expressing his persuasion "in the Lord Jesus that nothing is common in itself" (Rom. 14:14) has obviously reminded many of Jesus's teaching on the food laws in Mark 7:1–23.

The early Christian letters of 1 Peter and James also demonstrate awareness of the prewritten Gospel tradition.[9] Often the epistles demonstrate obvious overlap with and allusion to sayings of Jesus, but the exact wording or form of the sayings diverges enough so as to provide evidence that the sayings and stories of Jesus were being passed on even before the Gospels were written. For example, the sayings of Jesus in James appear to be closest to the form found in Matthew's Gospel, and yet there are sufficient divergences to indicate that "James was drawing from a common pool of oral traditions rather than from a fixed literary source akin to Matthew."[10] 2.2

Paul's Letters, the Epistle of James, and 1 Peter all provide evidence that the earliest Christians preserved and orally transmitted the sayings and stories of Jesus *before* the writing of thc four canonical Gospels.

The Gospels Provide Evidence for the Oral Transmission of the Sayings and Stories of Jesus

When we compare the four Gospels with one another, we find that each author composes his gospel through stitching together *many of the same*

SIDEBAR 2.2

Gospel Traditions in the Epistle of James and the First Epistle of Peter

Epistles	Sayings of Jesus
James 1:5: "If any of you lacks wisdom, let him ask from the God who gives generously and without reviling, and it will be given to him."	Matthew 7:7: "Ask and it will be given to you. Seek and you will find. Knock and it will be opened to you."
James 4:2c: "You do not have because you do not ask."	Matthew 7:7a: "Ask, and it will be given to you."
James 2:5: "Has not God chosen the poor in the world to be rich in faith and heirs of the kingdom that he has promised to those who love him?"	Luke 6:20: "Blessed are you who are poor, for yours is the kingdom of God."
James 4:9: "Be miserable and mourn and weep. Let your laughter be turned to mourning and your joy to gloom."	Luke 6:21: "Blessed are you who hunger now, because you will be satisfied. Blessed are you who weep now, because you will laugh."
James 4:10: "Humble yourselves before the Lord, and he will exalt you."	Luke 14:11: "For all who exalt themselves will be humbled, and those who humble themselves will be exalted."
James 5:12: "Do not swear an oath, either by heaven or by earth or by any other oath."	Matthew 5:34–37: "Don't take an oath at all, neither by heaven, which is the throne of God, nor by earth. . . . Let your yes be yes and your no be no."

Epistles	Sayings of Jesus
1 Peter 1:13: "Gird up the loins of your mind by being entirely self-controlled, and set your hope completely on the grace to come to you at the revelation of Jesus Christ."	Luke 12:35: "Get dressed for service and keep your lamps burning."
1 Peter 2:7: "The stone that the builders rejected has become the chief cornerstone."	Mark 12:10: "Have you not read this scripture: 'The stone that the builders rejected has become the cornerstone'?"
1 Peter 2:19–20: "For this finds God's favor, if because of conscience toward God someone endures hardships in suffering unjustly. For what credit is it if you sin and are mistreated and endure it? But if you do good and suffer and so endure, this finds favor with God."	Luke 6:32: "If you love those who love you, what credit is that to you? Even sinners love those who love them" (NIV).
1 Peter 2:21: "For to this you were called, since Christ also suffered for you, leaving an example for you to follow in his steps."	John 13:15: "For I have given you an example: you should do just as I have done for you."

short units of material but often in strikingly different order.[11] This suggests that the evangelists are working with the same, or at least remarkably similar, source materials: the oral (and perhaps some written) Gospel traditions. The oral traditions about Jesus tended to be passed on in short individual anecdotes (*chreia*) rather than in complete narratives. Furthermore, there are very good reasons to also accept the *basic* form-critical suggestion that the oral Gospel tradition was employed in diverse settings and for specific purposes. In other words, early Christian communities likely drew on Jesus's sayings regarding the rituals of prayer, financial generosity, and practicing the Lord's Supper as they themselves sought wisdom and guidance for their own common life and identity. As different communities recycled and passed on Jesus's teachings and with different aims, it should not surprise us to find some level of flexibility and fixity in the transmission—getting the essential gist of who Jesus was and what he said, rather than his exact wording, precise geographical location, chronology, and so forth, which are just not quite the point. The narrator will often tell us that Jesus is in Galilee, a village, Jerusalem, or on a mountain; in other words, he provides enough information for the setting to be entirely realistic but with very scant detail and with almost no interest in any appealing to aesthetic sensory impulses. The Gospel authors, rather, relate their stories in such a way as to be relentlessly focused on the activity of Jesus. All of these features demonstrate strong similarities to the features of ancient oral narratives.[12]

Comparison of Gospel pericopes also shows how the same saying and story could be used for different purposes. For example, the Gospels of both Matthew and Luke contain the parable of the lost sheep. In Luke's Gospel, Jesus's parable is directed to the Pharisees and scribes who are grumbling over Jesus's table fellowship with outcasts and sinners (Luke 15:1–7); but in Matthew's Gospel, Jesus shares this same parable with his disciples to teach them the necessity of forgiveness and care for those already in the Christian community (Matt. 18:10–14). Jesus's teaching in the parable, then, is (largely) fixed, whereas the evangelist's use of Jesus's teaching is more flexible in terms of narrative arrangement.

In the preceding chapter I briefly noted the example of Mark 1:16–3:6. In this section of Mark's Gospel are five pericopes that lack chronological and geographical detail. Scholars like to say that they look like "pearls on a string" or "individual squares of a chocolate candy bar" in that they can be broken off the string/bar into their own self-contained entities. Furthermore, Mark (or perhaps at the level of the oral retelling Mark knew about) appears to have structured these five stories together as controversy stories that explain both Jesus's unparalleled authority and the hostility and opposition he is provoking. One scholar states the relationship between the oral traditions and the written Gospels this way: "The written gospel shape comes into being by imposing order and sequence on an essentially fluid, episodic cycle of traditional units which have a life of their own, both before and after they are taken up into the literary tradition."[13] 2.3

Some of the differences here certainly can be attributed to different literary and theological emphases on the part of Matthew and Mark, the fact that Jesus was an itinerant teacher who almost certainly repeated his teachings in different forms, or perhaps that Matthew and Luke derived their material from a shared written or oral source and rewrote it into its current form.[14] But it's also very likely that Jesus's teaching on love of enemy was remembered from the beginning and then continually passed on in oral form to address how the earliest Christians should live. The fact that one finds echoes of Jesus's teaching on love of enemy in Paul's writings (Rom. 12:14, 20a; 1 Cor. 4:12b) as well as other early Christian sources (1 Pet. 3:9;

SIDEBAR 2.3

Gospel Traditions

Matthew 5:43–48	Luke 6:27–28, 32–36	Romans 12:14	1 Peter 3:9; 2:20
"You have heard it said: 'You shall love your neighbor and hate your enemy.' But I say to you: Love your enemies and pray for those persecuting you so that you may be sons of your heavenly Father, for he makes the sun to rise on the evil and the good and he gives rain to the righteous and the wicked.	"But I say to those who listen: Love your enemies, do good to those who hate you. Bless those cursing you, pray for those reviling you."	"Bless those persecuting you; bless and do not curse."	"Do not pay back evil for evil or reviling for reviling, but instead give a blessing."
For if you love only those who love you, what reward will you have? Do not even the tax collectors do the same thing? And if you greet only your siblings, what more are you doing than others? Do not even the pagans do the same thing? For you shall be perfect as your heavenly Father is perfect."	"And if you love those who love you, what credit is that for you? For even the sinners love those who love them. And if you lend to those from whom you hope to get a return, what credit is that to you? Even sinners lend to sinners so that they may receive back the same. But love your enemies and do good and lend without expecting anything. For your reward will be great, and you will be called children of the Most High. For he is kind to the unkind and the evil. Be merciful just as your father is merciful."		"But if you do good and suffer for it and you endure, this is a credit before God."

Didache 1:3) adds further likelihood that the divergent wording of Jesus's words in Matthew and Luke derive, in part, from their oral transmission in the earliest Christian churches.

The Early Church Fathers Provide Evidence for the Oral Transmission of the Gospel Tradition

In the next section we'll explore some of this in more detail, but here it's relevant to note that we have early Christian testimony that indicates that the Gospel traditions circulated orally both before and after the work of the four evangelists.[15] The existence of marked sayings of Jesus that are *not* found in our written Gospels suggests that the Gospel tradition was preserved, at least in part, through oral transmission and remembrance. Scholars sometimes refer to this as *agraphon* ("not written" or "unrecorded"). For example, Clement of Rome says that he wants his congregation to "remember the words of the Lord Jesus, which he spoke as he taught with gentleness and patience" (1 Clement 13:1). Clement then appeals to the words of Jesus:

> Show mercy, that you may receive mercy; forgive, that you may be forgiven. As you do, so shall it be done to you. As you give, so shall it be given to you. As you judge, so shall you be judged. As you show kindness, so shall kindness be shown to you. With the measure you use, it will be measured to you. (1 Clement 13:2)

While one can find similar sayings in our written Gospels, there is nothing that exactly parallels what Clement explicitly refers to as "the words of the Lord Jesus" (see also 1 Clement 46:7–8). Even within the Acts of the Apostles we see Paul, in his speech to the Ephesian elders, appealing to an otherwise unknown saying of Jesus: "Remember the words of our Lord Jesus, for he himself said: 'It is more blessed to give than to receive'" (Acts 20:35b). Justin Martyr (likewise Clement of Alexandria, *Salvation of the Rich* 40.2) says, "Jesus Christ warned us, 'In whatsoever things I shall apprehend you, in them also shall I judge you'" (*Dialogue with Trypho* 47.5).

Papias the bishop of Hierapolis, writing at the very beginning of the second century CE, undertook the task of writing a five-volume work (sadly lost!) titled *Expositions of the Logia [Sayings/Accounts] of the Lord Jesus*. We'll return to Papias momentarily, but for now, let me simply note that his prologue establishes his method as centering on collecting information from designated tradents of the oral Gospel tradition. Papias declares, "I did not think that information from books would profit me as much as information from a living and surviving voice" (Eusebius, *Ecclesiastical*

History 3.39.4). Michael Bird notes, "The living voice of the Jesus tradition was a living memory."[16] In Justin Martyr's writings, he often cites Gospel traditions, stories, and sayings that are well known to us through the writings of the four evangelists, and refers to them as "The Memoirs of the Apostles" (e.g., *Dialogue with Trypho* 100.4; 101.3; 102.5; 103.6–8). Both Papias and Justin (among others) establish that what we have in our four Gospels derives from memory—that is, the remembered and orally transmitted sayings and stories of Jesus.

How Was the Gospel Tradition Remembered and Transmitted?

We've seen that Jesus was remembered as a great teacher and that his earliest followers and admirers orally transmitted sayings and stories about him from the very beginning. The four Gospels, then, are the written remains of memories of Jesus. What we have not yet examined, however, are the questions of *who* and *how*. Who preserved the memories of Jesus? How did they preserve and transmit these memories? These are incredibly complicated questions, and thoughtful responses to them invariably will show divergent viewpoints, given the complexity involved in handling our ancient sources and contemporary studies of memory. Here I provide what I take to be two of the most important features of any hypothesis for explaining how the Jesus tradition was offered: eyewitness testimony and the role of memory.

Eyewitness Testimony and the Transmission of the Jesus Tradition

Whereas form critics operated under the conviction that the memories of Jesus were anonymously transmitted and creatively reshaped in the early Christian churches, there are actually good reasons for seeing much of the Gospel oral tradition as the carefully preserved remains of eyewitnesses. Richard Bauckham's important (and controversial) book *Jesus and the Eyewitnesses* makes the most passionate and creative arguments for viewing all four Gospels as preserving the eyewitness testimony of the apostles.[17] Establishing this point does not mean that everything in the Gospels stems from eyewitness testimony, nor does it establish the Gospel accounts as "objective uninterpreted facts" (as if such a thing were possible).[18] It would be too simplistic to view the Gospels as having unmediated access to interviewing and questioning eyewitnesses; and, in the next section we'll soon see that the Jesus tradition was remembered, transmitted, and "carefully shaped to perform formative and normative functions for church communities."[19] Yet there are good reasons for seeing the basic elements of the

Gospel tradition as stemming from eyewitness accounts. Let's look at a few of what I consider to be Bauckham's strongest arguments.

The Gospel of Luke is our only written Gospel that includes a preface that purports to give a brief description of his method and purpose.

> Since many have undertaken to compile a narrative about the events that have been fulfilled among us, just as they were handed on to us *by those who from the beginning were eyewitnesses and servants of the word*, I, too, decided, as one having a grasp of everything from the start, to write a well-ordered account for you, most excellent Theophilus, so that you may have a firm grasp of the words in which you have been instructed. (Luke 1:1–4 NRSVue)

Luke refers here to the practice of what ancient historians call *autopsia*.[20] *Autopsia* refers to the process whereby a historian gathers information either by means of personal presence and experience or through contact with those who experienced said event. Stated another way, *autopsia* refers to "a visual means to gather information concerning a certain object, a means of inquiry, and thus also a way of relating to that object."[21] The ancient historians Herodotus, Thucydides, Polybius, Josephus, and others all refer to their written historical records as predicated on the collection of eyewitness testimony. Further, the language of "handed on to us" (*paradidōmi*) is the technical language used to describe transmitted shared tradition (e.g., 1 Cor. 11:23–26; 15:3–5). It would seem to indicate that it was the "servants of the word"—that is, the apostolic eyewitnesses—who passed on the Jesus tradition on which Luke's Gospel depends. Luke's description of basing his written Gospel on those who "from the beginning were eyewitnesses" is an obvious claim to have collected his information from those who participated in and saw the events firsthand. Luke's language of "from the beginning" and "servants of the word" helps to explain why one of the qualifications for the apostolic replacement of Judas Iscariot was that he must have "accompanied us during all the time that the Lord Jesus went in and out among us, beginning from the baptism of John until the day that he was taken up from us—one of these must become a witness with us to his resurrection" (Acts 1:21–22 NRSVue). In other words, one of the tasks of the twelve apostles was to be "servants of the word" (Luke 1:2)—that is, those entrusted with passing on the sayings and stories of Jesus. Luke's preface, then, indicates his intention to engage in the two major steps of history writing: (1) collect eyewitness testimony and (2) write one's work into a coherent, aesthetically pleasing narrative.[22] Bauckham summarizes, "Luke can tell the story 'from the beginning' because he is familiar with the traditions of those who were eyewitnesses 'from the beginning.'"[23]

SIDEBAR 2.4

Who Is the Beloved Disciple?

There is no consensus as to the identity of the Beloved Disciple in the Gospel of John. Some have suggested the following as possibilities:

- John the son of Zebedee
- An unnamed Judean disciple (1:35–39)
- Lazarus (11:1–44)
- Mary Magdalene (20:11–18)
- Thomas (20:24–28)
- A symbolic figure, a literary device used by the author to identify an ideal reader. As one Johannine scholar notes, "The point John's Gospel makes is that any reader who wishes to follow Jesus can become a beloved disciple by following his lead. From the pages of the story the beloved disciple beckons the reader: 'Follow Jesus as I have followed him, and you too can become a *disciple whom Jesus loves*.'"[a]

A similar dynamic is at work in the Gospel of John, where the author frequently uses the language of testimony to appeal to his role as an eyewitness to the events he records.[24] The Gospel of John's final words are, "This is the disciple who testifies about these things and has written them; and we know that his testimony is true. But there are many other things that Jesus did, which if every one of them were written down, I suppose that the world could not contain the books that would be written" (John 21:24–25). It seems hard to deny that this "Beloved Disciple" is claiming here to have some relationship to the written account of John's Gospel. Most simply, this would be as the actual author of the Gospel, though it is also *possible* that the relationship is less direct and that he claims only to be the source. Either way, the basic claim is that John's Gospel is based on the eyewitness testimony of the Beloved Disciple. This figure, while undoubtedly idealized and part of John's larger theological theme of testimony, is portrayed as "a real person who validates the historical message of the gospel."[25] This helps explain the frequent depictions of the Beloved Disciple as a special companion of Jesus who is uniquely capable of providing his own eyewitness account of Jesus's teaching in the upper room, the crucifixion, and the empty tomb (e.g., John 13:21–38; 19:26–27, 35; 20:1–10; 21:24). 2.4

While scholars have often viewed John's Gospel as supposedly more "theological" and "spiritual" than the Synoptic Gospels and thereby as not "real history," we should note here that John contains numerous historical, chronological, and geographical details that are irrelevant to the story *unless* they actually are attempts to preserve historical information.[26] 2.5

We should also note that some of the earliest Christian evidence for the oral transmission of the Gospel tradition describes it as stemming from eyewitnesses.[27] In his prologue to his *Expositions of the Logia of the Lord*, Papias describes his method in this way:

> I shall not hesitate to set down for you, along with my interpretations, everything I carefully learned then from the elders and carefully remembered, guaranteeing their truth. For unlike most people I did not enjoy those who had a great deal to say, but those who teach the truth. Nor did I enjoy those who recall someone else's commandments, but those who remember the

> commandments given by the Lord to the faith and proceeding from the truth itself. And if by chance someone who had been a follower of the elders should come my way, I inquired about the words of the elders—what Andrew or Peter said, or Philip, or Thomas or James, or John or Matthew or any other of the Lord's disciples, and whatever Aristion and the elder John, the Lord's disciples, were saying. For I did not think that information from books would profit me as much as information from a living abiding voice. (Papias, *Fragments* 3–4)[28]

SIDEBAR 2.5

Examples of Chronological and Geographical Notes in John's Gospel

- Chronology: Passover (2:13; 6:4; 11:55); Feast of Tabernacles (7:2); Feast of Dedication (10:22)
- Location: Cana (2:1); Jacob's well in Samaria (4:1–15); the pool of Bethesda near the Sheep Gate in Jerusalem (5:1–2); Bethany (11:1); Solomon's colonnade in Jerusalem (10:23)

Papias indicates that, even after the canonical Gospels had been written, he preferred the oral transmission of the Jesus tradition. His means of obtaining access to the Jesus tradition consists in his inquiring about "the words of the elders." Papias seems to describe two groups of people here: the Lord's disciples and elders *and* those who followed the elders. It is this later group that Papias describes as providing access, by means of their association with the Lord's disciples, to the Jesus tradition. Papias seems to describe the transmission, then, as running as follows: Jesus → disciples/elders → a group who followed the elders → Papias. What Papias is doing here should remind us of the practice of *autopsia*; that is, Papias is engaging in the good historiographic method of obtaining knowledge and information about Jesus from those who could provide eyewitness testimony to Jesus's teachings and activities. Michael Bird describes this well: "Papias does not regard the Jesus traditions as disengaged from the eyewitnesses who originated them, but he assumes that the authenticity of the tradition was based precisely on the surviving and remaining witnesses who gave their testimony to followers in the first place."[29]

Similar testimony for the oral transmission of the Jesus tradition by eyewitnesses can be found in Irenaeus, the bishop of Lyons writing toward the end of the second century CE. Irenaeus describes the clarity and vividness of his own memories of his early formation and learning from Polycarp of Smyrna. Specifically, Irenaeus recounts how Polycarp would tell of

> his intercourse with John and with the others who had seen the Lord; how he repeated their words from memory; and how the things that he had heard them say about the Lord, His miracles and His teaching, things that he had heard direct from the eye-witnesses of the Word of Life, were proclaimed by Polycarp in complete harmony with Scripture. To these things I listened eagerly at that time, by the mercy of God shown to me, not committing them to

writing but learning them by heart. (Irenaeus, *Letter to Florinus*, in Eusebius, *Ecclesiastical History* 5.20.6–7)[30]

Again, Irenaeus describes the oral transmission of the Gospel tradition as taking place as follows: Jesus → John and other eyewitnesses → Polycarp → Irenaeus.[31] Both Papias and Irenaeus have apologetic agendas: to validate the truthfulness and veracity of *their particular account* of the Gospel tradition. Nevertheless, students of the Gospels need to take seriously their basic claim that the Gospel tradition was largely transmitted from Jesus the teacher to his students and disciples who followed him. When Luke, Papias, and Irenaeus refer to their practice of finding their information from eyewitnesses, they are following standard historiographical practices.

Finally, the New Testament and early Christian writings provide evidence that Jesus's disciples, and other eyewitnesses, played an important role in transmitting the Gospel tradition. We have already seen the Gospels' remembrances as a powerful teacher and the Twelve (among other disciples) as marked for the role of listening and learning from Jesus's words and example (Luke 10:16; John 13:20).[32] Jesus's teaching makes it clear that for the Twelve, teaching and transmitting "what they have seen and heard is integral to their leadership roles, and this requires them to *recollect* whatever will promote the upbuilding of the community."[33] Early Christianity was marked by the early rise of numerous teachers (e.g., Acts 13:1; 1 Cor. 12:28–29; Eph. 4:11; Didache 13:2). James Dunn asks, "Why teachers? Why else than to serve as the congregation's repository of oral tradition?"[34] And we have had occasion to see not only that Paul himself passes on sayings and stories of Jesus but also that on one occasion he uses the formal language of the passing on of community tradition to describe the Lord's Supper (1 Cor. 11:23–26). The Gospels themselves name numerous individuals, in addition to the twelve apostles, who could function as a source for eyewitness testimony—for example, the women following Jesus (Luke 8:1–3), Jesus's brother James (Acts 12:17; 15:13–21), and Jesus's mother, Mary (Acts 1:14).[35] And, on occasion, one finds references to these early Christians offering testimony or actively remembering Jesus's teachings and actions (e.g., Mark 14:9; Luke 22:19; John 4:39; 12:17; 15:26–27; Acts 1:22; 10:37–39).[36]

Memories of Jesus and the Writing of the Gospels

There is a problematic tendency, surprisingly seen among both form critics and conservative scholars, to pit eyewitness testimony and community tradition against each other. This is a false dichotomy. We have seen that eyewitness testimony must be accounted for as one significant factor in the oral transmission of the Gospel tradition. But it is obvious that at some point before the writing of the Gospels, even if (as is very likely) the eyewitnesses continued to exert some control, the Gospel tradition becomes shared social memory, in that the community now transmits and performs the sayings and stories of Jesus for their own needs. Michael Bird states it this way: "Who Jesus is can be determined only by his effect on his followers. Because an impact happened, a tradition was created, a tradition that bore the marks of Jesus' influence and the disciples' memory."[37]

Some scholars use the language of "collective memory" here to describe "the *content* of beliefs about the past that members of a social group largely hold in common."[38] But we should not thereby mistakenly discount the reality that eyewitness testimonies about Jesus continued to exist only because of individuals and communities who remembered, retold, and passed on their memories of Jesus from the very beginning.[39] The setting for the transmission of the oral tradition about Jesus was found in "the preaching, apologetics, polemics, worship and discipline of the early church."[40] Concerns to do justice to the connection to eyewitness testimony should not, then, lead to devaluing the simultaneously important insight that the Jesus tradition was preserved and remembered because it was found to be meaningful to those Christians who shaped and transmitted the sayings and stories of Jesus. We do indeed have access to the past, to the historical event and saying, but *only* through the recollection and remembrance of individuals and communities who interpreted and transmitted their memories of Jesus.[41] The process of *autopsia*—the gathering of stories and memories from eyewitnesses—is the means, then, whereby the past and present join together. The eyewitnesses, and those who continued to hear and transmit the memories of Jesus, were not passive observers but, rather, participants in the events they describe.

Memory should not be understood along the notions of a simplistic view of the mind as a storehouse for retrieval; rather, the notion of collective memory refers to *how* "a group makes use of the past to construct its own identity through ritual, monuments, oral traditions, texts, accepted way of behaving and so forth."[42] We have access to the past, then, only through the structures, frameworks, and social necessities of the present. In other words, human memory is embedded within society; therefore, society provides the structures, scripts, and frames for how individuals and groups remember. Memory is the bridge, then, between the past and the present; memory enables the past to become truly and meaningfully alive to address the needs, challenges, and edification of the present rememberers.

To give one example, the early Christians did not simply transmit the *bare historical fact* of Jesus's death; rather, they remembered the past event of Jesus's death and its significance *through* interpreting it through the lens of Israel's Scriptures. This is sometimes referred to as "keying." Keying involves understanding a recent event or episode through the framework of an older sacred event.[43] For the Gospels, Jesus is frequently remembered through the mnemonic aids of the Scriptures. We can see this in numerous places but perhaps nowhere as obviously as in the accounts of Jesus's passion. Jesus's so-called triumphal entry in Mark 11:1–11 is laced with evocations of biblical scenes and prophecies of a coming warrior-like king who rides to the temple on a horse/donkey (e.g., 2 Sam. 16:2; 1 Kings 1:32–40; 2 Kings 9:13; Zech. 9:9–15; 1 Macc. 13:51).[44] Similarly, we see that the sufferings of the righteous Davidic king in the Psalter are appropriated by the Gospels as mnemonic aids for *remembering and interpreting* Jesus's death (e.g., Ps. 41:9 in Mark 14:18b; Ps. 42:6, 11; 43:5 in Mark 14:35; Ps. 69:21 and 22:18 in Mark 15:23–24; Ps. 22:1 in Mark 15:34).[45] Sacred biblical texts and episodes thereby enable the tradents of the Gospel tradition to remember and interpret the past events of Jesus's life and teachings. Again, historical fact *and* interpretation are present within the early Christians' remembrances of Jesus.

The Gospel of John perhaps provides the best illustration of the relationship between past and present as well as the role of the community in remembering the past.[46] In John's Gospel, Jesus speaks to the disciples of a time when he will send forth the Spirit who, he declares, "will testify about me; and you also will testify since you have been with me from the beginning" (John 15:26–27). The Spirit testifies about Jesus after the resurrection, and this enables the disciples also to testify to Jesus. Again, Jesus refers to the Spirit, after the resurrection, as one who "will teach you all things and will remind you of everything which I spoke to you" (14:26b). After Jesus has been raised from the dead and has sent the Spirit, John portrays the disciples as *remembering* what Jesus had said in key events during his ministry. This collective act of remembering what Jesus said during his temple cleansing (2:17, 22) and triumphal entry (12:16) is portrayed not along the lines of simply recalling information; rather, the remembering enables the disciples to understand the truth and significance of what Jesus said and did. Again, notice the relationship between past and present, between historical datum and interpretation. Collective memory here, once again, describes how the followers of Jesus—beginning with the eyewitnesses—were able to remember, perform, and articulate the past sayings and events of Jesus with scripts and frameworks that were meaningful to John's audience.

If collective memory is an inextricable component of the transmission of the Gospel tradition, we might ask, Is the memory historically accurate? This is a difficult question and, to some extent, one that is not entirely answerable. In fact, memory approaches to the Gospels are not set up to even answer this question; rather, they focus on how and why groups remember and transmit memories in new settings.[47] However, we can say the following: Some Gospel scholars have used memory to argue that, while it is impossible to affirm the historicity of specific sayings and details in the Gospel tradition, there are specific themes, motifs, types of sayings, and images that must put us in touch with reliable historical information about Jesus of Nazareth. In other words, the larger patterns of the Gospel tradition show that Jesus was consistently remembered as an exorcist, a powerful teacher, calling forth twelve apostles, crucified as a messianic claimant by Rome, and so on and so forth. These remembrances of Jesus are so frequent and well attested that it is virtually certain that they are in touch with genuine historically accurate memories about Jesus.[48]

Countering the excessive presentism found in form criticism, students of social and collective memory argue that the present usually corresponds to actual past historical events.[49] The present (story) and past (history) are related. Furthermore, those who draw on *contemporary* human memory studies to suggest the historical inaccuracy of the Gospels are making false comparisons. The four evangelists did not ask eyewitnesses or others to simply recall and retrieve memories of events that had taken place thirty to forty years before; as we have seen, the eyewitnesses and the earliest Christian communities transmitted sayings and stories of Jesus from the very beginning. As the Gospel tradition became social memory, the eyewitnesses and the Twelve likely still exerted some level of authority with respect to the tradition. The powerful impression that Jesus made on his followers was taken into the transmission of their sayings and stories from the beginning. In fact, it is difficult for most of us to appreciate how important and prevalent a role memorization, at times quite lengthy memorization, played in ancient society and its educational system.[50] This explains, in part, why some of Jesus's sayings—found in Gospel texts, Paul's Letters, and other early Christian writings—are remarkably similar. This is probably not because these sayings are literarily dependent on the same text but simply because the oral Gospel tradition was fairly stable and, much of it at least, committed to memory. If we approach the Gospels as sources that we can use for uninterpreted brute facts in order to reconstruct the real historical Jesus, then of course we are off on a false quest.[51] Most now recognize that there can be no bifurcation between historical fact and interpretation; *all history writing necessarily engages in interpretation*. The Gospels are testimony, and this testimony, as we have seen, is both historical and theological and is the bridge between past and present.[52] There is simply no way to avoid either of these poles.

Summary

In this chapter we have begun our exploration of what we can know about where our four Gospels come from and how they relate to the historical Jesus of Nazareth. We examined the Gospels' obvious depiction of Jesus as a great teacher who made a lasting impression on his followers and others who heard him. His teaching and major life events were not written down immediately; rather, we have seen that the Gospels themselves, early Christian writings such as Paul's Letters, and the early Christian testimony of Papias (among others) show that the Gospel tradition was transmitted orally. Finally, we saw that any explanation for how the oral Gospel tradition was transmitted needs to account for *both* the role of eyewitness testimony *and* its continued oral performance as social memory in the Christian communities.

We can briefly summarize the main points with an emphasis on their implications for how we read the Gospels as we move forward.

1. The most obvious and noncontroversial remembrance of Jesus from all four Gospels is that he was a powerful teacher who was able to communicate his message through diverse and memorable oral techniques such as parables, aphorisms, discourses/sermons, and scriptural interpretation. As we read the Gospels, we should take note of Jesus's ability to grab his audience's attention (and ours!) through the way he communicates. The Gospel authors will also use this as a means to highlight Jesus's astonishing authority.
2. Jesus's role as a great teacher, along with his calling of disciples (i.e., students), calls attention to an important fact about the transmission of the Gospel tradition. Jesus's disciples were to commit themselves to learning, studying, and presumably memorizing both his life and his teachings. Since they were representatives and emissaries of their teacher, we should reckon with one of their roles consisting in transmitting Jesus's teachings.
3. Before our four Gospels were written, sayings and stories of Jesus were transmitted orally by Jesus's followers and worshipers. Texts such as the Pauline Epistles, 1 Peter, James, the Didache, and other

early Christian writings demonstrate that early Christians were drawing on Jesus's teachings to address practical matters from the very beginning.

4. The Gospels themselves bear some of the hallmarks and features of oral tradition. They are often made up of many short units that show evidence of having been used by early Christians to share the same story about Jesus (stable/fixed) but capable of diverse performances to meet different needs (flexible). The oral transmission of the sayings and stories of Jesus is further supported by early church teachers/fathers such as Papias, Justin, and Irenaeus.
5. Despite the fact that the Gospels were written decades later, there are good reasons for viewing them as closely connected to eyewitness testimony. This accords with the explicit testimony of the Gospels of both Luke and John, who provide evidence for the ancient practice of *autopsia*—collecting information from those who participated in or observed the events (Luke 1:1–4; John 21:24–25). We have also seen that Papias, among others, claims that he prefers "the living voice" over the written word and that the information for his writings goes back to the eyewitnesses of Jesus.
6. But in addition to eyewitness testimony, the Gospels also stem from community tradition. The Jesus tradition becomes part of the community's social memory as they remember the past to address their present situation. In other words, the Gospel tradition is something that is remembered, transmitted, and performed in order to meet the specific needs of and to edify the Christian communities. Memory approaches, then, can help us see the inextricable relationship that exists between past and present, between history and interpretation in the Gospel tradition.

CHAPTER THREE

What Are the Relationships between the Four Canonical Gospels?

It is a fact of remarkable significance and surprise that Christians have four sacred stories about Jesus instead of just one! Even a first-time reading of the four Gospels will reveal to the reader both some obvious similarities and convergences as well as some striking differences. The first-time reader will likely recognize that the subject of John's Gospel is the same historical individual represented by the Synoptic Gospels but may also notice that John's is quite a different retelling than that of the first three Gospels. There is joy and angst that comes from having four Gospels.[1] There is indeed great joy when one learns to appreciate the theological and literary artistry of each of the four Gospels and when one recognizes that there's something of an ecumenical willingness to embrace Gospels with four different perspectives. But, of course, there can be some angst as one may experience some concerns precisely about their difference—difference in terms of chronology, arrangement of stories, seeming discrepancies in retellings of the story. And how does one explain the relationship between the three Synoptic Gospels and John's Gospel?

In this chapter we explore three questions. First, given the preference for the "living voice" and the oral transmission of the Gospel tradition, why were Gospels written in the first place? Second, we'll look at what is known as the "Synoptic problem" and ask, What is the relationship between Matthew, Mark, and Luke? Third, we'll look at the relationship between John's Gospel and the Synoptic Gospels, asking whether John is an independent account of Jesus's life and teachings or if he is, in some way, dependent on one of the Synoptics for his story.

Reasons for Writing a Gospel

In the preceding chapter I spent a long time establishing the point that the Gospel tradition was initially transmitted orally among followers and worshipers of Jesus. We also saw that the oral stories and sayings of Jesus were viewed as stemming from the testimony of eyewitnesses. A simple question arises: Why put the Gospel tradition into *written* textual form at all? Why did four different authors make the conscious decision to write a Gospel?

Writing a Gospel is quite clearly an attempt to provide a textually stable performance and interpretation of the oral tradition about Jesus.[2] Quite likely part of the motivation for writing a Gospel stemmed from the fact that the eyewitnesses had begun to die. Offering precise dates for the composition of our Gospels is difficult, but it's likely that they were written some thirty to even fifty years after the life and death of Jesus. When Papias describes his practice of gathering eyewitness testimony from those who had previously learned from the Lord's disciples, one of the implications seems to be that many—probably most—of the disciples had died. Thus, writing a Gospel obviously would preserve the eyewitness testimony *and* the collective/social memory of early Christian communities.

Luke's prologue (Luke 1:1–4) explicitly claims that his Gospel is written with knowledge of other written accounts: "I, *too*, decided, as one having a grasp of everything from the start, to write a well-ordered account for you, most excellent Theophilus" (1:3 NRSVue). At the very least it would seem that Luke is claiming to have access to particular Gospel traditions or eyewitness testimony that is not in the other written accounts; likewise, writing his written account enables him to preserve community memories and the interpretations/performances thereof in a more stable format. Thus, one quite obvious and broad reason for writing a Gospel would be the simple need for authoritative and accurate accounts of the memories of Jesus. The inextricable relationship between the historical Jesus and the faith of the church necessitates a stable and historically accurate account of the origins of their faith.

Once a Gospel is written, it also creates the opportunity to transmit the written text to other churches. This holds true for all of the written Gospels, but one can see this clearly in the Fourth Gospel where John explicitly notes his reason for writing: "These things have been written so that you may believe that Jesus is the Christ and that by believing you may have life in his name" (John 20:30–31). Whether the primary goal here is *evangelism* or *community edification*, John's purpose statement alerts us to how writing a Gospel served practical goals and purposes for the early Christians. For example, some have very plausibly argued that Matthew's Gospel was written, at least in part, for *catechetical reasons*—to draw on Jesus's teachings in order to teach converts about the meaning of their Christian faith. One of the purposes of Luke's Gospel may have been to help *navigate the relationship with Judaism and the synagogue*. Was God faithful to his promises? Why did the majority of Israel's leaders reject Jesus as the promised Messiah? How do we read the Scriptures of Israel in relation to Jesus and the church? Questions like these, and the relationship between so-called church and synagogue, set forth challenges to the earliest followers of Jesus; a written Gospel could provide a clear explanation for how to respond to these difficulties. A variety of reasons can be discerned for the writing of each of the Gospels. Primarily they were written at a time when the eyewitnesses were starting to die and there was a need for the collective memories of Jesus to find a stable form such that the saving significance of Jesus could be interpreted and transmitted to future generations.

The Synoptic Problem

Even a first-time reader of the Synoptic Gospels will be struck immediately by significant similarities between these Gospels, which are thrown into even greater relief when one compares them with John's Gospel. This is, in fact, why the first three Gospels are called "Synoptic": they can be "looked at" (Greek: *opsis*, "view, sight") "together" (Greek: *syn*, "with, together"). These similarities occur with respect to sharing so many of the same stories and the frequency with which the stories/sayings have the exact same wording (often for long stretches of the text). Furthermore, considering all of the different possibilities for how an author might arrange the Gospel tradition material, the fact that the Synoptic Gospels show so much similarity in terms of order suggests some type of literary relationship between the Gospels.[3] Likewise, the Synoptic Gospels often pass on the same parenthetical asides to their audience; so, for example, when Matthew and Mark (though not Luke) interrupt Jesus's eschatological teaching on the Mount of Olives with an aside to the reader, "let the reader understand" (Matt. 24:15; Mark 13:14), it seems very likely that there is a literary relationship between Matthew and Mark.

As a result, it's natural to ask, What is the relationship between Matthew, Mark, and Luke? Why are the Gospels so similar? Additionally, did one (or more) of the Gospel authors use another Gospel for source material? Can we determine which one was written first? Are the similarities to be accounted for through a drawing on of shared oral tradition, or did they actually have a written Gospel for source material? The attempt to answer these questions,

questions that center on explaining the relationship between the first three canonical Gospels, is often referred to as the "Synoptic problem" and is a great example of what scholars do when they practice "source criticism."[4]

Similarities and Differences between the Synoptic Gospels

One of the best ways to observe the similarities and differences between the Synoptic Gospels is through a Gospels synopsis.[5] A synopsis sets forth the parallel passages from the Synoptics next to one another to facilitate quick comparison and contrast. Let's look at a few examples (provided in the sidebars) and make some observations about the data before we look at solutions to the Synoptic problem. As we look for similarities and differences, this will also allow us the opportunity to account for the so-called raw materials or sources with which the Gospel authors work. 3.1

First, when there is an *obvious* parallel passage in each of the Synoptic Gospels, as in the example in sidebar 3.1, scholars use the term "triple tradition" to describe the parallels. While there are some slight divergences in Jesus's wording, each Gospel overlaps quite obviously with the others, even using the same wording for lengthy stretches. Even where there are slight differences in wording and phrasing, each Gospel text shows basic agreement with the others. Almost three-fourths of Mark's Gospel is triple tradition, whereas it makes up only one-fourth of Matthew's and Luke's Gospels.

SIDEBAR 3.1

Jesus's Call for Discipleship

Mark 8:34–9:1	Matthew 16:24–28	Luke 9:23–27
[34] Then he called the crowd to him along with his disciples and said: "Whoever wants to be my disciple must deny themselves and take up their cross and follow me. [35] For whoever wants to save their life will lose it, but whoever loses their life for me and for the gospel will save it. [36] What good is it for someone to gain the whole world, yet forfeit their soul? [37] Or what can anyone give in exchange for their soul? [38] If anyone is ashamed of me and my words in this adulterous and sinful generation, the Son of Man will be ashamed of them when he comes in his Father's glory with the holy angels."	[24] Then Jesus said to his disciples, "Whoever wants to be my disciple must deny themselves and take up their cross and follow me. [25] For whoever wants to save their life will lose it, but whoever loses their life for me will find it. [26] What good will it be for someone to gain the whole world, yet forfeit their soul? Or what can anyone give in exchange for their soul? [27] For the Son of Man is going to come in his Father's glory with his angels, and then he will reward each person according to what they have done.	[23] Then he said to them all: "Whoever wants to be my disciple must deny themselves and take up their cross daily and follow me. [24] For whoever wants to save their life will lose it, but whoever loses their life for me will save it. [25] What good is it for someone to gain the whole world, and yet lose or forfeit their very self? [26] Whoever is ashamed of me and my words, the Son of Man will be ashamed of them when he comes in his glory and in the glory of the Father and of the holy angels.
[9:1] And he said to them, "Truly I tell you, some who are standing here will not taste death before they see that the kingdom of God has come with power." (NIV)	[28] "Truly I tell you, some who are standing here will not taste death before they see the Son of Man coming in his kingdom." (NIV)	[27] "Truly I tell you, some who are standing here will not taste death before they see the kingdom of God." (NIV)

We can also immediately note that each Gospel differs with respect to the narrative frame.

> Matthew: "Then Jesus said to his disciples . . ."
> Mark: "Then he called the crowd to him along with his disciples and said . . ."
> Luke: "Then he said to them all . . ."

The differences in the narrative framing of each episode are something that the careful reader of the Gospels will find repeatedly, and this accords with our earlier observation regarding the stability of the oral Gospel tradition. Jesus's words are carefully transmitted, but there is flexibility for the Gospel writer in terms of how he works his sources / oral tradition into his Gospel. 3.2

In regard to the example in sidebar 3.2, we can make three observations. First, quite obviously there is no Markan parallel for the content of John's preaching. The overlap is between only Matthew and Luke. We refer to this as the "double tradition." There are about forty episodes that belong to the double tradition. Another good example of the double tradition is the temptation of Jesus, where Matthew and Luke both show clear signs of overlap with no Markan parallel (Matt. 4:1–11; Luke 4:1–13; cf. Mark 1:12–13). It's worth noting here that when scholars ask, "What accounts for the similarities between the double tradition?" there are two main responses. One option is to account for the similarities by positing literary dependence from one Gospel to another. Those who take this route usually will claim that Luke had access to Matthew's Gospel. Another option is to account for the similarities through positing a shared source. In other words, Matthew and Luke are independent of each other but they work from a shared written source. This hypothetical source is often referred

SIDEBAR 3.2

John's Preaching of Repentance

Matthew 3:7–10	Luke 3:7–9
7 But when he saw many of the Pharisees and Sadducees coming to where he was baptizing, he said to them: "You brood of vipers! Who warned you to flee from the coming wrath? 8 Produce fruit in keeping with repentance. 9 And do not think you can say to yourselves, 'We have Abraham as our father.' I tell you that out of these stones God can raise up children for Abraham. 10 The ax is already at the root of the trees, and every tree that does not produce good fruit will be cut down and thrown into the fire." (NIV)	7 John said to the crowds coming out to be baptized by him, "You brood of vipers! Who warned you to flee from the coming wrath? 8 Produce fruit in keeping with repentance. And do not begin to say to yourselves, 'We have Abraham as our father.' For I tell you that out of these stones God can raise up children for Abraham. 9 The ax is already at the root of the trees, and every tree that does not produce good fruit will be cut down and thrown into the fire." (NIV)

to as "Q" (from the German word *Quelle*, meaning "source"). A second observation is that, once again, we see a remarkable consistency in the use of the exact same words by Matthew and Luke to describe John's preaching. The fact that many of the parallels show such detailed similarity in the wording has led most scholars to argue for the necessity of a literary solution to the Synoptic problem; that is, the similarities have to be accounted for, at least in part, through some type of literary dependence. Typically, this literary dependence is presumed to involve access to *the written text*, but, as more scholars are now suggesting, it might also include familiarity with a stable oral tradition that one recalls through memory. Third, again we see divergence only in the narrative framing. Matthew has John the Baptist direct his words to the Pharisees and Sadducees (Matt. 3:7a), whereas Luke has the Baptist preach to the crowds going out to see him (Luke 3:7a).

Let's look at a third text now, one that's a bit trickier, in sidebar 3.3. 3.3

What can we say about this text? Certainly, all three Gospels appear to be recounting the same story (rather than two or three different healings). And there are some intriguing similarities in terms of wording, most notably Jesus's words about having to put up with a generation that is faithless and perverse (Matt. 17:17; Mark 9:19; Luke 9:41). But what's more striking is that the *same story* is communicated with remarkably very little verbal agreement. This alerts us to the possibility that the Gospel authors were not simply engaging in literary editing but also had access to different oral retellings of the Jesus tradition. In other words, we likely have here and elsewhere "examples of oral retelling of that shared tradition, retellings which evince the flexibility and elaboration of oral performances."[6] The evangelists, then, likely drew on memories of oral performances as one of their sources for their Gospels.[7]

A fourth type of material is stories and sayings that appear in only one Gospel. For example, Jesus's parable of the sheep and the goats in Matthew (Matt. 25:31–46) is classified as special Matthean material (referred to as "M"); Jesus's parables of the good Samaritan (Luke 10:25–37) and the rich man and Lazarus (Luke 16:19–31) are examples of special Lukan material ("L").

Once again, the Synoptic problem is devoted to trying to untangle the relationships between the three Gospels and to provide a convincing hypothesis as to why they share so many similarities despite some obvious divergences. Before one can make any headway, however, this question must be addressed: Does one Gospel provide the initial foundation story or building blocks for the others? In other words, can we determine the first original Gospel from which, perhaps, the others drew much of their material?

SIDEBAR 3.3

Jesus Heals a Boy Possessed by a Spirit

Matthew 17:14–18

14 When they came to the crowd, a man approached Jesus and knelt before him. 15 "Lord, have mercy on my son," he said. "He has seizures and is suffering greatly. He often falls into the fire or into the water. 16 I brought him to your disciples, but they could not heal him."

17 "You unbelieving and perverse generation," Jesus replied, "how long shall I stay with you? How long shall I put up with you? Bring the boy here to me." 18 Jesus rebuked the demon, and it came out of the boy, and he was healed at that moment. (NIV)

Mark 9:14–27

14 When they came to the other disciples, they saw a large crowd around them and the teachers of the law arguing with them. 15 As soon as all the people saw Jesus, they were overwhelmed with wonder and ran to greet him.

16 "What are you arguing with them about?" he asked.

17 A man in the crowd answered, "Teacher, I brought you my son, who is possessed by a spirit that has robbed him of speech. 18 Whenever it seizes him, it throws him to the ground. He foams at the mouth, gnashes his teeth and becomes rigid. I asked your disciples to drive out the spirit, but they could not."

19 "You unbelieving generation," Jesus replied, "how long shall I stay with you? How long shall I put up with you? Bring the boy to me."

20 So they brought him. When the spirit saw Jesus, it immediately threw the boy into a convulsion. He fell to the ground and rolled around, foaming at the mouth.

21 Jesus asked the boy's father, "How long has he been like this?"

"From childhood," he answered. 22 "It has often thrown him into fire or water to kill him. But if you can do anything, take pity on us and help us."

23 "'If you can'?" said Jesus. "Everything is possible for one who believes."

24 Immediately the boy's father exclaimed, "I do believe; help me overcome my unbelief!"

25 When Jesus saw that a crowd was running to the scene, he rebuked the impure spirit. "You deaf and mute spirit," he said, "I command you, come out of him and never enter him again."

26 The spirit shrieked, convulsed him violently and came out. The boy looked so much like a corpse that many said, "He's dead." 27 But Jesus took him by the hand and lifted him to his feet, and he stood up. (NIV)

Luke 9:37–43

37 The next day, when they came down from the mountain, a large crowd met him. 38 A man in the crowd called out, "Teacher, I beg you to look at my son, for he is my only child. 39 A spirit seizes him and he suddenly screams; it throws him into convulsions so that he foams at the mouth. It scarcely ever leaves him and is destroying him. 40 I begged your disciples to drive it out, but they could not."

41 "You unbelieving and perverse generation," Jesus replied, "how long shall I stay with you and put up with you? Bring your son here."

42 Even while the boy was coming, the demon threw him to the ground in a convulsion. But Jesus rebuked the impure spirit, healed the boy and gave him back to his father. 43 And they were all amazed at the greatness of God. (NIV)

Markan Priority

Whereas most scholars now view Mark's Gospel as chronologically prior to and as providing the most important source for both Matthew and Luke, for most of church history it was actually Matthew's Gospel that was assumed to have been written first. The arguments for Matthean priority are not particularly strong, and they seem to largely reflect the popularity of Matthew's Gospel in the early church and its (related) consistent placement at the head of the Fourfold Gospel. In the mid-second century Clement of Alexandria had suggested that the Gospels that include Jesus's genealogies are the earliest Gospels (Eusebius, *Ecclesiastical History* 6.14). And Augustine's influential *Harmony of the Gospels* argued that Mark was the abbreviator and abridger of the Gospel of Matthew (Luke was dependent on both Matthew and Mark). It seems likely that the canonical arrangement of the Gospels influenced Augustine's understanding of literary dependence.

Figure 3.1. An example of a canon table, which functions as an index of Gospel passages. The method was invented by Eusebius to show which passages were used by more than one evangelist. Written at Lande'vennec in Brittany, ca. 865–99.

However, very few scholars still hold to Matthean priority, as the weight has now emphatically shifted to viewing Mark's Gospel as the first and prior Gospel. Markan priority is, then, considered to be a central piece of the solution to the Synoptic problem. The weight of evidence for Markan priority is indeed strong.[8] First, while Augustine viewed Mark as abbreviating and abridging Matthew and Luke, it has proved too difficult to imagine that Mark would eliminate so much important material from his Gospel. Why would Mark fail to pass on the Lord's Prayer, Jesus's teaching in the Sermon on the Mount/Plain, the eschatological parables of the final judgment in Matthew, the Lukan parables of the prodigal son and of the good Samaritan? And given that Mark is actually much more verbose in his storytelling than Matthew or Luke, viewing his work as an abbreviator doesn't seem to make much sense. Using a Gospels synopsis to compare Mark and Matthew in parallel passages, we see that Matthew is actually the one who abbreviates. 3.4

SIDEBAR 3.4

Matthew the Abbreviator

Matthew 14:3–12

[3] Now Herod had arrested John and bound him and put him in
prison because of Herodias, his brother Philip's wife, [4] for John
had been saying to him: "It is not lawful for you to have her."
[5] Herod wanted to kill John, but he was afraid of the people,
because they considered John a prophet.

[6] On Herod's birthday the daughter of Herodias danced for
the guests and pleased Herod so much [7] that he promised with
an oath to give her whatever she asked. [8] Prompted by her
mother, she said, "Give me here on a platter the head of John
the Baptist." [9] The king was distressed, but because of his oaths
and his dinner guests, he ordered that her request be granted
[10] and had John beheaded in the prison. [11] His head was brought
in on a platter and given to the girl, who carried it to her mother.
[12] John's disciples came and took his body and buried it. Then
they went and told Jesus. (NIV)

Mark 6:17–29

[17] For Herod himself had given orders to have John arrested,
and he had him bound and put in prison. He did this because
of Herodias, his brother Philip's wife, whom he had married.
[18] For John had been saying to Herod, "It is not lawful for you
to have your brother's wife." [19] So Herodias nursed a grudge
against John and wanted to kill him. But she was not able to,
[20] because Herod feared John and protected him, knowing him
to be a righteous and holy man. When Herod heard John, he
was greatly puzzled; yet he liked to listen to him.

[21] Finally the opportune time came. On his birthday Herod
gave a banquet for his high officials and military commanders
and the leading men of Galilee. [22] When the daughter of Herodias came in and danced, she pleased Herod and his dinner
guests.

The king said to the girl, "Ask me for anything you want, and
I'll give it to you." [23] And he promised her with an oath, "Whatever you ask I will give you, up to half my kingdom."

[24] She went out and said to her mother, "What shall I ask for?"

"The head of John the Baptist," she answered.

[25] At once the girl hurried in to the king with the request:
"I want you to give me right now the head of John the Baptist
on a platter."

[26] The king was greatly distressed, but because of his oaths
and his dinner guests, he did not want to refuse her. [27] So he
immediately sent an executioner with orders to bring John's
head. The man went, beheaded John in the prison, [28] and
brought back his head on a platter. He presented it to the girl,
and she gave it to her mother. [29] On hearing of this, John's disciples came and took his body and laid it in a tomb. (NIV)

Conversely, it's easier to imagine both Matthew and Luke having access to and respecting the Gospel of Mark but also wanting to expand Mark with more source material. Hence, not only can we understand Matthew and Luke wanting to include additional teachings, parables, and activities of Jesus, but we can also explain why they would find it necessary for their biography of Jesus to include some stories of his birth and childhood (Matt. 1–2; Luke 1–2) as well as stories of his resurrection appearances and commission of his disciples (Matt. 28:1–20; Luke 24:1–53). Explaining Mark's omission of these stories proves more difficult than supposing Matthew and Luke are the ones who have incorporated them *and most of Mark's Gospel* into their own Gospels.

This would also explain why so much of Mark's Gospel appears in both Matthew (about 85 percent of Mark) and Luke (about 65 percent of Mark).[9] On this view—and this is a second argument for Markan priority—Mark's Gospel provided Gospel tradition that both Matthew and Luke respected and thereby incorporated (much of it at least) into their own Gospels. Mark's Gospel here looks as though it is "the middle term" for Matthew and Luke since it looks as though each of them is following the order of events in Mark's Gospel. How can one determine this? When Matthew departs from Mark's ordering of events, Luke continues to follow Mark's ordering; when Luke departs from Mark's ordering of events, Matthew continues to follow Mark's ordering. Relatedly, Matthew and Luke typically agree when they have Markan source material to follow; when Mark ends, and thereby no longer provides source material to be followed, Matthew and Luke disagree as they go their own unique way.

Third, there are places where Matthew and Luke seem to either improve Mark's language or omit some of his difficult statements (see sidebar 3.5). Mark's notoriously wordy redundancies are often deleted and abbreviated. Potentially theologically offensive statements are smoothed out. Mark's references to Jesus's anger are deleted. Negative slurs made against Jesus from Mark are toned down in Matthew and Luke. 3.5 3.6

Finally, many would argue that Matthew and Luke show evidence of a more explicit and higher Christology than what is found in Mark, and that this likely points to Markan priority as well. One can see this in, for example, Luke's christological use of the title "Lord" and Matthew's use of the titles "Christ/Messiah," "Son of Man," and "Son of David." To give a specific example, Matthew's description of Peter's confession "You

SIDEBAR 3.5

Matthew's and Luke's Editing of Mark

Mark 6:5	Matthew 13:58	
He could not do any miracles there, except lay his hands on a few sick people and heal them. (NIV)	And he did not do many miracles there because of their lack of faith. (NIV)	
Mark 3:5		**Luke 6:10**
He looked around at them in anger and, deeply distressed at their stubborn hearts, said to the man, "Stretch out your hand." He stretched it out, and his hand was completely restored. (NIV)		He looked around at them all, and then said to the man, "Stretch out your hand." He did so, and his hand was completely restored. (NIV)
Mark 1:32	**Matthew 8:16**	**Luke 4:40**
That evening after sunset the people brought to Jesus all the sick and demon-possessed. (NIV)	When evening came, many who were demon-possessed were brought to him, and he drove out the spirits with a word and healed all the sick. (NIV)	At sunset, the people brought to Jesus all who had various kinds of sickness, and laying his hands on each one, he healed them. (NIV)

SIDEBAR 3.6

Graham Stanton on Markan Priority

"If an early Christian writer knew both Matthew and Luke, it is difficult to see why he would ever want to write what eventually became Mark's gospel. Who would want to produce a much-truncated version of Matthew and Luke? Why was Mark unwilling to include either Matthew's Sermon on the Mount in chapters 5–7 or the shorter version in Luke 6:17–49? . . . On the basis of Marcan priority we can readily understand why Matthew and Luke should want to modify and expand Mark, and the methods and distinctive theological emphases of Matthew and Luke can be discerned with some confidence."[a]

are the Christ, the Son of the living God" (Matt. 16:16) is more expansive than Mark's "You are the Christ" (Mark 8:29b).[10] When compared with Mark, both Matthew and Luke seem to have heightened the Christology they found in Mark.

While answers to our questions about the Synoptic problem will never come with certainty and thereby remain at the level of hypotheses about what is most likely, the consensus that Mark was the original Gospel that served as a foundational source for Matthew and Luke shows no signs of being overturned.

Three Possible Solutions to the Synoptic Problem

A variety of solutions to the Synoptic problem have been proposed, but three in particular deserve closer attention. Providing a full explanation for each hypothesis and argument for their likelihood is outside the scope of what I'm able to do here; I have, however, listed the hypotheses in what I find to be least to most likely.

THE GRIESBACH HYPOTHESIS // TWO-GOSPELS HYPOTHESIS (MATTHEW FIRST)

I noted briefly that the popularity of Matthew's Gospel in the early church was often associated with the assumption that it was also the first Gospel. In the eighteenth century, New Testament scholar J. J. Griesbach (and more recently, William Farmer) argued for Matthean priority. Unlike Augustine's solution, however, this view sees Luke as the second written Gospel and dependent on Matthew for a source. Mark is dependent on both Matthew and Luke and abbreviates both Gospels; thus, instead of being first, Mark's Gospel is the last. The virtues of this proposal are its simplicity, as there is no need to posit any lost sources (such as Q). It also accords with the majority early church tradition, which posits Matthew as the first Gospel. In the next hypothesis we'll examine the so-called minor agreements between Matthew and Luke in the triple tradition; these minor agreements refer to similarity and overlap in wording between Matthew and Luke and against Mark. The Griesbach hypothesis can easily explain the existence of these minor agreements since it sees Luke as dependent on Matthew. The main critique of the Griesbach hypothesis is that very few are convinced of Matthean priority. It has simply not been possible to capture scholarly imagination for *why* Mark would compose his Gospel the way he did if he had access to both Matthew and Luke.[11] As Mark Strauss notes, "In too many cases, Matthew seems to be clarifying, revising, refining, and smoothing over a rougher and less refined Markan original."[12]

THE TWO-SOURCE HYPOTHESIS

Another possible explanation for the Synoptic relationships posits two early sources that were *independently* used by both Matthew and Luke. The first source is Mark's Gospel; as such, Markan priority is fundamental to this theory because it maintains that Mark's telling of the Jesus story was traditional and important enough for both Matthew and Luke to follow its language and arrangement of events quite closely (as we have seen). The second source, however, is a lost sayings source (Q), which Matthew and Luke used independently. Note here that this explains the so-called double tradition; common material that is present in Matthew and Luke but not Mark is explained as the result of their using the same source for their Gospel. In addition to Mark and Q, it is also sometimes posited that Matthew and Luke had access to their own special materials that uniquely show up in their Gospels. I briefly introduced this already as M and L.[13]

It's important to remember that advocates of the two-source hypothesis think that there are good reasons for denying Luke's use of Matthew's Gospel as one of its sources. Again, both Matthew and Luke write independently of each other. Whereas Luke (and Matthew) usually follows Mark's ordering of his material quite closely, Luke does not seem to follow Matthew's order at all; this would seem a major oddity if Luke was familiar with Matthew.[14] Likewise, if Luke knew Matthew's Sermon on the Mount (Matt. 5–7), why would he break it up into small units and scatter it throughout his Gospel (e.g., Luke 6:17–49; 11:1–13)? There are also instances where it would seem as though Matthew's special material would fit Luke's theology and agenda quite well, but surprisingly he doesn't draw on the material. For example, given Luke's emphasis on Jesus as the Davidic Messiah (Luke 1–2), why does he not keep Matthew's titular references to Jesus as "the Son of David" (Matt. 9:27; 12:23; 15:22; 21:9, 15)?[15]

Despite some detractors, it's probably fair to say that the two-source hypothesis has commanded scholarly assent from approximately 1850 to 2000. That is no small achievement! The theory has helped to solidify Markan priority among most scholars; however, its largest weakness is its positing of the hypothetical (now lost) sayings source known as Q. Almost all of the material in Q is sayings of Jesus (approximately 230 sayings); the positing of this source finds some analogies in the existence of other sayings Gospels/

sources (e.g., Gospel of Thomas).[16] On the one hand, the notion that there were oral or written sayings sources that preceded the writing of our Gospels is entirely plausible and has textual support. Although some scholars have moved from positing the possibility of this hypothetical sayings source to building large and imaginative claims about Christian origins regarding a "Q community" or a "Q theology," one can accept the more modest claim that a shared sayings source helps make sense of the double tradition.

On the other hand, there are some significant problems with the Q hypothesis. One of the biggest problems here is the so-called minor agreements between Matthew and Luke. These are places where Matthew and Luke *agree* in wording with each other but go *against* Mark's wording. On the two-source hypothesis, Mark and Luke write *independently* of each other (i.e., neither is using the other's Gospel as a source), so these minor agreements are difficult to explain on the two-source hypothesis. If neither Matthew nor Luke had access to each other, what would account for these perplexing agreements? Another problem is that often Matthew and Luke reproduce so-called Q material in a different arrangement (order) and with significant differences in wording. Finally, there are places where Mark overlaps with Q, but of course on this theory Mark does not use Q as a source, and so this oddity is also challenging to account for.[17]

THE FARRER/GOODACRE HYPOTHESIS (NO Q, MARKAN PRIORITY, LUKE USED MATTHEW)

The final solution to the Synoptic problem is one that was proposed by Michael Goulder and Austin Farrer and finds its most ardent contemporary advocate in Mark Goodacre. Like the two-source hypothesis, it affirms Markan priority. Its major innovation is dispensing with Q by arguing for Luke's dependence on Matthew. Thus, Luke uses both Mark and Matthew as sources for his Gospel. If one can demonstrate the likelihood of Luke's use of Matthew (rather than simply shared oral traditions), then, so the argument goes, one no longer needs to posit the hypothetical Q. This view reminds us there is absolutely no evidence for the existence of Q. An important plank in their argument is the existence of the minor agreements between Matthew and Luke (and against Mark). And indeed, there are "numerous minor agreements of Matthew and Luke against Mark in the triple tradition," so much so that they are often seen as "the Achilles' heel of the two-source hypothesis."[18]

Mark Goodacre's work is prescient of the growing attention to oral traditions and performances, and he makes a convincing argument that some of Luke's divergences are better explained through his knowledge of oral sources and performances. After establishing the possibility, on the basis of the minor agreements, that Luke knew and used Matthew, one is freed to allow Luke to be Luke. In fact, proponents of this view frequently note the strange bias among scholars for Matthew's way of reproducing Jesus's teachings; why should it be so surprising that Luke would rearrange and adapt his source material in order to create a new Gospel account? Thus, Luke seems to have an aversion to reproducing Jesus's long blocks of teaching in Matthew. Luke, therefore, may have rewritten the Sermon on the Mount in a more pithy and choppy manner, as is characteristic of his writing, and he intentionally interspersed the material throughout his Gospel. On this view, Luke "adapts" Matthew's material as he chooses and rewords the material as he deems appropriate.[19] This corresponds neatly to how, on this view, Luke rewrites Matthew's lengthy sermon on the parables (Matt. 10), which is interspersed throughout Luke's Gospel in *seven different locations*.[20]

Memory and Oral Tradition

The perceptive reader may be asking, "Given the emphasis on the oral transmission of the Gospel tradition, what role does this play in the above solutions to the Synoptic problem?" Much of the history of research on the Synoptic problem is anachronistic in its sometimes nearly exclusive assumptions that the evangelists are literary editors working with written sources before them. Perhaps this anachronism can be forgiven, given that we are not the inhabitants of an oral culture that is able to reproduce lengthy portions of material from memory. Hence, the impressive relationships between the Synoptic Gospels understandably strike most observants as something that could be possible only through a (nearly exclusive) literary model of working with written texts.

We have already noted, however, that more and more scholars are reckoning with the fact that the sayings and stories of Jesus were something that the evangelists, and those from whom they derived their material, would have had familiarity with through worship and oral performances in their communities. Likewise, there is more of a willingness to embrace the possibility that the evangelists may have had large portions of their source material committed to memory (not unlike what is often assumed to be the case for the apostle Paul and his citations of the Old Testament). In short, there is a strong likelihood that each of the evangelists would be able "to reproduce and manipulate their source material in memory in the course of composing their own Gospels."[21]

We have noted already examples where the Synoptic evangelists preserve different oral retellings and performances of the same story (Matt.

17:14–18; Mark 9:14–27; Luke 9:37–43). Likewise, it's highly questionable as to whether texts like Jesus's beatitudes in Matthew (5:3–12) and Luke (6:20–26) are best explained through literary dependence or through their drawing on the same source; much better, it would seem, is the view that these sayings were told and retold in the early Christian communities and thereby bear the hallmarks of fixity and flexibility that characterize oral tradition.[22] The obviousness of this is perhaps best exemplified through the similarities and differences in Matthew's and Luke's versions of the Lord's Prayer (Matt. 6:9–13; Luke 11:2–4). The overlap and differences here are best explained "via the flexibility of many tellings and liturgical performances of the Lord's Prayer in many places in the first century."[23] The implications of the past twenty years (or so) of research on the dynamics of memory and oral tradition are beginning to make their way into our understanding of the Synoptic problem; while there will likely be new developments and new paradigms or hypotheses that are established, it seems almost certain that these paradigms will involve both careful attention to written sources and the reality of oral traditions and performances.

The Gospel of John and the Synoptic Gospels

But what about John's Gospel? How, if at all, is it related to the Synoptic Gospels? This is not simply a modern question but rather one that was asked from the earliest periods of church history. Clement of Alexandria noted the differences when he referred to the Synoptics as "corporeal" (or "bodily") and John's Gospel as "spiritual" (Eusebius, *Ecclesiastical History* 6.14.7). Eusebius of Caesarea also noted the differences between John and the Synoptics and argued that John's Gospel was composed *after* John read the Synoptics since they lacked "what had been done in the earliest times and at the beginning of the preaching by Christ" (Eusebius, *Ecclesiastical History* 3.24.7). Augustine wrote his famous *On the Harmony of the Gospels* to show the consistency and truthfulness of the Gospel accounts, but he clearly recognizes that John presents serious challenges, as his attempt to harmonize the chronology of Jesus's temple incident results in his strange claim that Jesus cleansed the temple twice, at the beginning of his ministry and at the end.

Similarities and Differences between John and the Synoptics

I imagine that most first-time readers of the Gospels will quickly recognize two facts about John's Gospel and its relationship to the first three canonical Gospels. First, John's Jesus is recognizable as the same historical figure described by the Synoptics. Just a few of the obvious similarities include Jesus's healing of the sick or those with bodily ailments (John 4:46–54; 5:1–9; 9:1–41), Jesus's miracle of the multiplication of bread (6:1–15), references to Jesus as Messiah and Son of Man (1:19–51), Jesus's walking on water (6:16–21), and conflict with the leaders of Israel sparked by his controversial teachings (5:19–47; 8:21–59). He also undergoes the same fate as he journeys to the Jerusalem temple (12:12–19), gathers his disciples for teaching on his final days (chaps. 13–17), suffers and is crucified by the Roman authorities (chaps. 18–19), and is raised by God from the dead (chaps. 20–21). Just as the Synoptics write up their story in the literary framework of a biography, so John's Gospel is best classified as an ancient biography. We could explore more of these in detail, but they are obvious enough to make the point clear: the character of John's Gospel is *the same* character described in the Synoptic Gospels.

Figure 3.2. First-century Israel

But, second, the first-time reader is also likely to note some glaring differences between the Synoptics and the Gospel of John. John's Jesus, for example, engages in no exorcisms, teaches in lengthy discourses that do not overlap with his sermons in the Synoptic material, repeatedly performs "signs," talks little about wealth and possessions, and speaks with a heightened sense of irony. John provides no genealogy or birth story for Jesus but rather describes him as the divine *logos* (the "Word") who was with God (and, in fact, is God) at the beginning of creation (John 1:1–3). In our later chapters on John, we will also see that there are major differences in terms of geography and chronology between the Synoptics and John's Gospel.

Who Wrote the Gospel of John?

Developing a hypothesis for the literary relationship between John and the Synoptics requires at least some discussion of the authorship of John's Gospel. The Fourth Gospel does claim to stem from an authenticator of eyewitness testimony (the Beloved Disciple), and we have also seen that, while the Gospels are technically anonymous, their titles ("the Gospel according to X") are very early, as there is no evidence for any of them ever being confused or called by another name. While the evidence is by no means indisputable, the best explanation for the authorship of the Fourth Gospel is the traditional view that it is John the son of Zebedee from Jesus's inner circle among the twelve apostles.[24] As Craig Keener crisply states it, "The only possibly surviving figure in the Synoptics accorded as prominent a role as the Beloved Disciple has in the Fourth Gospel (John 13:23), yet unnamed in this Gospel (cf. John 21:2), is the apostle John."[25] The Fourth Gospel associates its Gospel traditions with the Beloved Disciple, who notes that his testimony is true (John 13:23; 18:15–16; 19:26–27, 35; 20:1–8; 21:7, 20, 24). Some view his testimony as necessarily coming from outside of the Twelve, given how much it differs from the Synoptics; while this is possible, it seems more likely that only one from the Twelve would be able to produce a Gospel that could compete with the Markan traditions (associated with the disciple Peter), especially given the prominence of the Beloved Disciple as one who appears reclining on Jesus's breast (John 13:23).[26]

While the external evidence might be apologetically motivated, the fact that early Christians (including Gnostics) posited John the son of Zebedee as the author should also be seriously considered. The witness of the church fathers to the disciple John as the author writing from Ephesus is weighty (e.g., Theophilus of Antioch, Irenaeus, Polycrates, Papias).[27] Both so-called orthodox or mainstream authors and Valentinian (Gnostic) authors ascribe the Fourth Gospel to the apostle John (e.g., Heracleon, Ptolemy). Church tradition asserts that both Polycarp and Papias (early second century) were students of John the disciple (Eusebius, *Ecclesiastical History* 5.20.5–6; Irenaeus, *Against Heresies* 5.33.4). Nevertheless, as is the case with our other Gospels, the author of the Fourth Gospel is remarkably disinterested in allowing us access to his authorial identity or personal experiences. Edwyn Hoskyns states this well: "There was a workshop in which the Fourth Gospel was fashioned, a workshop filled with particular ideas and particular experiences and containing, it seems, other Christian literature. . . . But the author has done his best, apparently with intention, to cover up his tracks. For his theme is not his own workshop but the workshop of God, and to this we have no direct access! . . . He has, in fact, so burnt himself out of his book that we cannot be certain that we have anywhere located him as a clear, intelligible figure in history. At the end of our inquiry he remains no more than a voice bearing witness to the glory of God."[28]

A Relationship between John and the Synoptics?

The question of whether, and if so *how*, John is related to the Synoptic Gospels continues to perplex those who puzzle over it. If John the son of Zebedee authored the Fourth Gospel, why does his account look so different from Mark's Gospel? Are the similarities between John and the Synoptics, especially in those places where they transmit the *same* stories (e.g., compare John 6:1–21 with Mark 6:35–52), to be accounted for by supposing that John knew or had access to a written Gospel, or perhaps through positing shared oral tradition, or is John's Gospel entirely independent of the Synoptic Gospel tradition?

Many have argued for the independence of John's Gospel from the Synoptics while also maintaining, however, that John draws on some of the same oral (prewritten) traditions. This allows one simultaneously to maintain the uniqueness of John's Gospel as its own independent and creative take on Jesus and also account for some of the obvious similarities. On this view, John's recounting of stories such as Jesus walking on water (6:16–21) and his triumphal entry into Jerusalem (12:16–21) is accounted for through access to shared material rather than by positing any type of literary dependence.[29] Those who argue for this view often claim that the similarities are too general and vague and lacking in close verbal parallels to provide any solid basis for positing a relationship of literary dependence.[30]

Others have argued that John's Gospel demonstrates clear awareness of Mark's Gospel and was written in order to provide a supplement for those who already knew that Gospel. On this view, John's Gospel "has its own integrity, with powerful narrative logic and development of its own. But at the same time it is so written that, for readers/hearers who are also familiar with Mark, it rarely repeats and largely complements Mark's narrative, and in such a way that chronological dovetailing of the two narratives can easily be accomplished."[31] We will look at this theory in more detail in our chapters on John's Gospel.

There is no clear consensus right now with respect to the origins of John's Gospel and its relationship to the Synoptics; there are a variety of plausible hypotheses that are difficult to fully prove or disprove. There are, however, a few claims that strike me as eminently likely. John's Gospel has its own unity and integrity; understanding John's Gospel does not require knowledge of Mark or the Synoptic oral tradition for it to make good sense. John clearly has his own reasons for writing (e.g., 20:30–31) as well as access to unique Jesus traditions that are not present in the Synoptic accounts. If Mark's Gospel stems from many of the eyewitness accounts of Peter, we may view John's Gospel as giving us access to "similar but different" traditions about what Jesus said and did. Whether there is a literary relationship between John and the Synoptics is incredibly difficult to know with any certainty; nevertheless, it does seem very likely that John assumed some familiarity with the story of Jesus as narrated by the Synoptic Gospels. We can easily imagine John writing his own Gospel with its own literary integrity and distinctive eyewitness traditions even as he assumes and incorporates Synoptic tradition into his Gospel.

Summary

Perhaps some readers feel as though there are a dizzying array of speculative hypotheses and are wondering something like the following: "Apart from becoming a professionally trained source critic who works on the Gospels, how am I to know what's likely and what's not? More importantly, why should I care?" Let me offer three reasons why we should care and appreciate the questions (and answers) posed by source criticism. First, while we as Christians read the Fourfold Gospel as the Word of God, our attention to these questions helps remind us that the Gospels did not simply fall from the sky written by the hand of God. A serious reckoning with the similarities, differences, and potential relationships between the Gospels helps us appreciate what kinds of texts these are and protects us from having unrealistic and mistaken expectations of them. Second, using a Gospel synopsis to engage in close comparative work of parallel passages ("reading horizontally") helps us pay closer attention to what is really there in the text. There may be no better way to learn the particular details of individual Gospels than the use of a Gospels synopsis to compare parallel texts. This can help the reader discern some of the distinctive literary and theological emphases of the author or lead to a better appreciation for how a particular evangelist "writes" and shares the sayings and stories of Jesus. Third, there are important exegetical consequences that come with questions posed by source criticism. For example, if Mark's Gospel was one of the primary sources for the other Synoptics, our readings of Matthew and Luke can profit through seeing some of the ways they modify Mark.

In this chapter, we have seen the following:

1. There are numerous reasons an author would choose to write up the oral traditions about Jesus into a Gospel book. When the eyewitness of the Jesus tradition started to die, there was a desire to preserve

Criticisms and Anxieties over Multiple Gospels

Throughout the centuries of church history, Christians have believed that the Scriptures are the Word of God and are therefore truthful in all that they affirm. When one reads through any single *one* of the four Gospels, one finds a story that is internally consistent, ordered, and realistic in the presentation of its plot, history, and geography. But when we start reading *four* Gospel writings together and begin to notice differences between them in terms of the arrangement and ordering of the material, significant differences in their characterization of Jesus, and apparent inconsistencies between parallel passages, this can present some difficult challenges for how we might continue to affirm the full truthfulness of the Gospel texts. 4.1

SIDEBAR 4.1

Differences in Gospel Material

Temple Cleansing

Mark	John
Mark 11:15–17 places the cleansing of the temple at the end of Jesus's ministry.	John 2:13–22 places the cleansing of the temple at the beginning of Jesus's ministry.

Jesus's Emotions in His Death

Mark	Luke
In Mark's Gospel we see Jesus going to his death distraught and filled with troubling emotions as he cries out, "My God, my God, why have you forsaken me?" (Mark 15:34).	Luke's portrait of Jesus is of one who is almost Stoic-like, comforts others on his way to the cross, and cries out, "Father, into your hands I commit my spirit" (Luke 23:46).

Genealogies

Matthew	Luke
Matthew 1:6–7 has David's son Solomon as part of Jesus's family line.	Luke 3:31 has David's son Nathan as part of Jesus's family line.

The Gerasene Demoniac(s)

Matthew 8:28 NASB	Mark 5:1–2 NASB	Luke 8:26–27 NASB
When He came to the other side into the country of the Gadarenes, two men who were demon-possessed met Him as they were coming out of the tombs. They were so extremely violent that no one could pass by that way.	They came to the other side of the sea, into the country of the Gerasenes. When He got out of the boat, immediately a man from the tombs with an unclean spirit met Him.	Then they sailed to the country of the Gerasenes, which is opposite Galilee. And when He came out onto the land, He was met by a man from the city who was possessed with demons; and who had not put on any clothing for a long time, and was not living in a house, but in the tombs.

The Centurion's Confession

Mark 15:38–39	Luke 23:46–47
And the veil of the temple was torn in two from top to bottom. When the centurion, who was standing right in front of Him, saw the way He breathed His last, he said, "Truly this man was the Son of God!"	And Jesus, crying out with a loud voice, said, "Father, into your hands I commit my spirit." Having said this, He breathed His last. Now when the centurion saw what had happened, he began praising God, saying, "Certainly this man was innocent."

Again, any supposed problems arise only because there are multiple Gospels, which *inevitably* will reveal differences. In fact, some of the most interesting cases of difference actually arise from the fact that the Synoptic Gospels share *so many similarities*. 4.2

Handling Gospel Differences in the Early Church

Some of the anxieties over Gospel differences appear in the first few centuries of the Christian church, where we see temptations to select one Gospel only, produce Gospel harmonies, or write works that harmonize the Fourfold Gospel.

The archheretic Marcion (85–160 CE), for example, rejected Matthew, Mark, and John and selected only a version (one purged of particularly Jewish elements) of Luke's Gospel.[1] Marcion is famous for his theological beliefs that the Creator God of the Old Testament was different from the superior God of Jesus Christ. Marcion's hermeneutic set up a binary, antithetical opposition between Christianity and the practices of Judaism. Marcion, therefore, selected one Gospel, a revised edition of Luke, as the only true and reliable account of Jesus.

Tatian, a student of Justin Martyr who worked toward the latter part of the second century, is best known for his production of a work called the *Diatessaron*. This work is fascinating in that it demonstrates the authority of the Fourfold Gospel, precisely because it uses the four Gospels as its sources *and* in its harmonizing, synthesizing manner of conflating these Gospels into a single rewritten text. We don't know exactly why Tatian produced the harmonization, and the reason may not reflect any apologetic attempt to smooth over contradictions; rather, at minimum, Tatian's *Diatessaron* "bears eloquent witness both to the acceptability of textual conflation and yet to the authority of the gospels that went on to become canonical."[2]

We have briefly noted already in an earlier chapter that Augustine produced a work titled *On the Harmony of the Gospels*. Like Tatian, Augustine assumes the authority of the Fourfold Gospel, although, unlike Tatian, he is not attempting to create a new harmonizing composition. Both Porphyry, the Platonist critic of Christianity, and the Manichaeans had argued that the four Gospels offer up contradictory details on the life of Jesus.[3] Augustine says that he is writing the work in response to pagan critics who have used the apparent contradictions of the Gospel stories in order to

SIDEBAR 4.2

Francis Watson on Gospel Writing

"If there are to be four gospels at all, they must differ from one another. Without differences they would simply be four copies of a single gospel. But if they together constitute the one canonical gospel, they must also be similar, variations on a common theme rather than disparate and unrelated. Difference and similarity belong together. Where there is difference there will also be similarity, if the canonical gospel is indeed singular. Where there is similarity there will also be difference, given that the canonical gospel is also plural."[a]

question "the veracity of their account" (*On the Harmony of the Gospels* 1.10). Based on these contradictions, Porphyry had argued that the Gospel writings were fabrications and inventions by the disciples. Thus, Augustine argues that Matthew and John were apostolic eyewitnesses and Mark and Luke base their Gospels on received eyewitness testimony. Furthermore, Augustine works hard to explain apparent contradictions such as, for example, Matthew's and Luke's genealogies, the differences in the accounts of the Last Supper, and why Mark 1:2–3 presents a mixed citation of Isaiah and Malachi but attributes both quotations to Isaiah. Augustine does not choose one single Gospel nor does he rewrite the Gospels into a new harmonious composition, but by working to show how the Gospels do not contradict one another he postulates the possibility of producing "a single comprehensive text that might be reconstructed out of the fourfold canonical gospel."[4] Some also think that Eusebius of Caesarea produced his "Gospel canons"—a system for tracking parallel Gospel passages—as a response to the criticisms of Porphyry. Rather than rewriting the four Gospels, Eusebius's table of canons assists the reader in making chronological harmony out of their accounts.[5]

Handling Gospel Differences Today

Similar anxieties are with us today as we attempt to make sense of how to read four *different* Gospels that, nevertheless, show considerable overlap in terms of the specific content of the saying and stories of Jesus as well as the larger pattern of his identity and life. There are different options today for how one handles the similarities and differences. One might engage in what some refer to as "maximal harmonization," whereby one attempts to smooth out every single difference into a coherent whole.[6] So, for example, at Jesus's crucifixion the Roman centurion said, "Truly this man was the Son of God" (Mark 15:39), and he then also said, "Truly this man was innocent" (Luke 23:47). Where there are discrepancies in terms of the reportage of Jesus's actions, this view suggests that Jesus performed the activity twice. For example, Jesus cleansed the temple twice, once at the beginning of his ministry (John 2:13–22) and on a second occasion near the very end of his life (Matt. 21:12–13; Mark 11:15–17; Luke 19:45–46). Likewise, Jesus healed Bartimaeus as he was leaving Jericho (Mark 10:46), and he also healed another blind man as he entered into Jericho (Luke 18:35). These attempts at harmonization are obviously motivated by considerable anxiety that even the hint of potential discrepancies could call the veracity of the Gospels into question.

There are, however, more moderate and reasonable versions of harmonization. For example, Luke's and Matthew's differences regarding the number of Gerasene demoniacs (two according to Matthew, one according to Luke) need not imply any kind of contradiction. When one allows for the simple reporting of events based on different perspectives and memories, there is no problem in one account having a different emphasis and with the reportage of different details. The same event can be understood as having been told accurately and truthfully but also told from different perspectives, based on different memories, and with different details and emphases.

We have seen in an earlier chapter that the Gospels began as orally transmitted stories; that is, the Gospels are examples of collective memory that were retold and performed in the churches. Thus, differences in versions of the Lord's Prayer (Matt. 6:9–13; Luke 11:2–4), healing stories (Matt. 17:14–20; Mark 9:14–27; Luke 9:37–42), the divine words uttered at Jesus's baptism (Matt. 3:16–17; Mark 1:9–11; Luke 3:21–22), and many more—all of the slight differences can be explained, in part, as deriving from different oral performances in the churches. Furthermore, we should note that orthodox doctrines regarding Scripture invariably emphasize God's communication *through real human persons and all that this entails*.

In our following chapters we'll examine how each evangelist writes, how he tells his story and communicates the Gospel message. Matthew tends to abbreviate his stories. Luke prefers shorter units of Jesus's teaching as opposed to lengthy sermonic discourses. John portrays Jesus as one who draws on riddles, irony, and misdirection to reveal heavenly truth. We should also emphasize that our Gospel writers do not purport to give us the *exact transcript* of what Jesus said; rather, we have Jesus's *voice* as represented by the evangelist—that is, the basic message of what he said. Jesus almost certainly spoke in Aramaic, and we see this in certain Aramaic words and phrases preserved in our Gospels (see sidebar 4.3). The Gospel texts, however, present Jesus communicating through the Greek language; thus, even here our access to Jesus's teaching is presented *in a translation*. Jonathan Pennington states this well: "The evangelists provide us with a paraphrase of Jesus's words. We can be confident that the Gospels, as inspired, canonical documents, accurately reflect Jesus's teaching, but we need not (and cannot) insist that they always contain the *exact words* of Jesus (or any other character in the story). This is to demand too much and goes beyond what is required in historical discourse."[7] In our study, we will continually see that the evangelists have the freedom of the preacher to represent Jesus's message in their own language and style. Thus, when we encounter one Gospel representing the centurion calling Jesus "the Son of God" (Mark) and another calling him "innocent" (Luke), or when we find Jesus, in the same saying, speaking of the Father giving "good things to those who ask him" (Matt. 7:11) and giving "the Holy Spirit to those who ask him" (Luke

11:13), we need not choose which one is the truthful, accurate account, nor do we need to harmonize the accounts; rather, we can simply recognize that each evangelist is communicating the basic voice and gist of Jesus's teachings.[8] 4.3

SIDEBAR 4.3

Two Aramaisms in the Gospels

Mark 5:41	And while taking the hand of the child, he said to her, "*Talitha koum*," which is translated, "Girl, to you I say, wake up."
Mark 15:34	And in the ninth hour, Jesus cried out with a great voice, "*Elōi, elōi, lema sabachthani*," which is translated, "My God, my God, why did you forsake me?"

What we have, then, are four stories that depict the same Jesus, albeit drawing on their own versions of collective memory with different ways of writing and viewing their subject matter.

What about differences with respect to chronology? Most scholars today find it neither necessary nor convincing to engage in "maximal harmonizing" tendencies to account for apparent chronological discrepancies such as the timing of Jesus's cleansing of the temple, of Jesus's baptism by John the Baptist, or of Jesus's healings (e.g., Jairus's daughter, the blind man in Jericho). Rather, the nature of ancient biographies is such that they expect a coherent ordered treatment of one's subject matter but are flexible enough so as to allow the author to arrange the material as he sees fit.[9]

Of course, recognizing and dealing with differences in our Gospels is simply inevitable with the canonization of *four* Gospels; the only way around this would have been for the church to select one Gospel only (as with Marcion) or a rewritten harmonization (Tatian). And on occasion, some of the differences are at the macrolevel. Mark consistently portrays Jesus as a secretive figure who does not reveal his identity openly and publicly, who often silences those who know his identity, and who retreats from the crowds at the height of his popularity (i.e., the so-called messianic secret). How does Mark's characterization of Jesus cohere with John's Jesus, who frequently and publicly declares his divinity and his personal relationship with God the Father? Or, in Mark's Gospel we see Jesus going to his death distraught and filled with troubling emotions as he cries out, "My God, my God, why have you forsaken me?" (Mark 15:34); but how does this cohere with Luke's portrait of Jesus as one who is almost Stoic-like, comforts others on his way to the cross, and who cries out, "Father, into your hands I commit my spirit" (Luke 23:46). The interpreter should attend to these differences without the anxieties or fears that often result in explaining them away. Again, Francis Watson provides some sage advice: "In its fourfold form, the canonical gospel actually *prescribes* difference. It represents the recognition that no single telling of Jesus's story can be final and definitive, and that the same story must be told and retold in variant forms."[10] The church's decision to continue to read four Gospels confirms the truth that multiple perspectives and vantage points are required to do justice to Jesus's identity and life. In our engagement of the Gospels we will primarily attend to each evangelist's take or telling of the Jesus story without smoothing out or ignoring their differences; at the same time we will also, on occasion, look for ways to show how each Gospel and its distinctives provide points of convergence with the others.[11]

The Fourfold Gospel

We have explored some of the challenges involved in the canonization of the Fourfold Gospel, but we have not asked yet about the nature of its origins. In fact, one will often hear that the selection of these four Gospels was a political act imposed on Christendom by those who just happened to have the power to enforce such a canonization, which then also resulted in the exclusion of other Christian voices and Gospels. Sometimes, the emperor Constantine is invoked as responsible for using his power to close the canon and thereby exclude the other competing Gospels. While there are differences in terms of the details, the basic story is often told in a way that emphasizes *political* conflict between the orthodox (or often "proto-orthodox") Christians and all of the other Christians, who, it is emphasized, had their own passionate convictions about Jesus and wrote their own Gospels. History is written by the winners (a.k.a. the orthodox), but simply "because one side emerged as triumphant, we should not assume that its victory was assumed at the outset or that its opponents were easily defeated."[12] On this view, the defeated "opponents" are sometimes referred to as lost and forgotten Christianities, which, of course, lends itself well to a conspiracy story or a plot that focuses on intentional suppression.[13]

The origins of the Fourfold Gospel are actually a story that is much more mundane than some of the conspiratorial popular narratives perpetuated by scholars and novelists alike. In what follows, I'll offer a few reasons that help us understand the organic and largely unsurprising origins of the Fourfold Gospel.

The Four Canonical Gospels Are the Earliest Written Gospels

We've already looked at some of the evidence that suggests that the four canonical Gospels derive from both the social memory of the earliest churches and the testimony of eyewitnesses of Jesus's ministry. While there are many possible reasons for writing a Gospel, we have seen that one of the main reasons was to provide a legitimate and authoritative take on the

Gospel tradition as the eyewitnesses were beginning to pass away. Thus, these four books are organically rooted in the eyewitness testimonies and collective memories of the earliest churches. While dating each of the four Gospels is difficult, most scholars would offer the date of 100 CE as the latest for the writing of the four Gospels. The Gospels of Matthew, Mark, and Luke are almost always dated to, again at the latest, somewhere between 70 and 90 CE. In contrast, most scholars believe that even the earliest noncanonical Gospels cannot be dated before 125 CE; and most of them are, in fact, dated much later.[14] While it is certainly possible, though by no means certain, that some noncanonical Gospels preserve a few authentic sayings and memories of Jesus, very few scholars would argue that texts like the Gospel of Thomas were in existence and circulation in the first century or that the Gospel of Thomas stems from eyewitness testimonies about the historical Jesus.

The Canonical Gospels Have Early and Extensive Attestation by Other Early Christian Writings

We have seen in an earlier chapter that early New Testament writings demonstrate awareness of the oral Gospel tradition. In other words, while texts such as 1 Corinthians, James, and 1 Peter may not know the literary text of the Gospels, these writings demonstrate clear engagement with the oral sources that later were textualized into the written canonical Gospels. And there are some instances where we have good reason to see explicit literary attestation of the Gospels. For example, Paul's statements that "the worker is worthy of their wage" (1 Tim. 5:18) and "the Lord commanded that those who proclaim the gospel should get their living by the gospel" (1 Cor. 9:14) seem to demonstrate explicit awareness of the Lukan Jesus's teachings (Luke 10:7).[15] The Didache demonstrates obvious awareness of the Gospel of Matthew as it reproduces its version of the Lord's Prayer (Didache 8:2; cf. Matt. 6:9–13) and sayings found in the Sermon on the Mount (Didache 9:5; cf. Matt. 7:6). In an earlier chapter we noted the testimony in the early second century of Papias as it pertained to his preference for "the living voice" as the sources of his own writings. But Papias is also important in that he explicitly provides an explanation for the origins of both Matthew's and Mark's Gospels—Gospels that he explicitly identifies by name (Eusebius, *Ecclesiastical History* 3.39.15–17). And most think that there is strong evidence that he also knew John's Gospel.[16] We could continue to work our way through authors and writings such as Ignatius of Antioch, the *Epistula Apostolorum*, and Justin Martyr, among others, to establish the literary attestation of the canonical Gospels, but the words of

Charles Hill can present us with a helpful summary: "Each of the canonical Gospels is used or named in ecclesiastical authors from a very early time, and the attestation for each far outstrips that of any other Gospel. Moreover, by the last two decades of the second century, testimonies to a fourfold Gospel converge from widely divergent geographical areas: Alexandria, Antioch, Italy and Gaul."[17]

The Collection of the Four Gospels into One Book Validates the Church's Consensus That These Gospels Best Narrate the Church's Traditions about Jesus Christ

The rise of the Fourfold Gospel makes better sense as an organic development from "the bottom up" whereby Christians in a variety of locales assent that *only these four Gospels* rightly preserve the traditions, stories, and sayings of Jesus that were transmitted in their churches. When sifting through the evidence, we find it much more historically plausible that a consensus was established precisely because the majority of the earliest Christians could affirm that their faith in Jesus was nourished and nurtured by the traditions found in these four Gospels. Francis Watson states this well: "[The Fourfold Gospel] took the form it did not because some bishop or council forcibly imposed it on an unwilling or unthinking majority but because of countless small-scale decisions about which texts were to be copied and used and which were to be passed over."[18]

We have already seen that texts from the first and second centuries provide testimony that our four canonical Gospels were being read and interpreted as authoritative *and*, in some instances, were being read together. Some of the earlier writings here (the New Testament Epistles and the Apostolic Fathers) do not explicitly speak of four *and only four* Gospels, but they draw on and allude to Synoptic and Johannine traditions about Jesus as authoritative in a way that they do not with noncanonical Gospels.

In the second century CE we begin to find more explicit discussion of which Gospels are to be read within the church. Part of the reason for this concern is obviously that there are other Gospel writings and other traditions about Jesus circulating. Indeed, there were questions about whether one could and should read the Gospel of Peter or the Shepherd of Hermas within the Christian churches. It would be silly to assume that all Christians agreed about what constituted authoritative and legitimate Gospel writings, given the plurality of Gospel writings and the geographical diffusion of the Christian church; however, there is no evidence that would support the belief that any noncanonical Gospels were as popular or considered authoritative by the majority compared to the Fourfold Gospel.[19]

Important testimony for the origins of the Fourfold Gospel in the second century is the so-called Muratorian Fragment. This fragment was discovered in 1700 as part of a codex containing other patristic writings; the text functions as something like an "Introduction to the New Testament Writings" and provides a canon list of the New Testament. The significance of the Muratorian Fragment is that it is the only second-century canon list from the Western church, and that its testimony to a canon of New Testament books is remarkably close to our contemporary notion of twenty-seven New Testament writings. While the traditional date for the Muratorian Fragment is the second century, written from Rome, some have recently argued that it was written in the fourth century. For our purposes, its significance is seen in its affirmation that the church has, and should read, only the four canonical Gospels.[20] The fragment picks up with its discussion of Luke as the *third* Gospel, then moves to John's Gospel as the *fourth* Gospel; therefore, most agree that the first two Gospels are Matthew and Mark. 4.4

SIDEBAR 4.4

Excerpt from the Muratorian Fragment

". . . at which nevertheless he [probably Peter] was present, and so he [probably Mark] placed [them in his narrative].[b] And so, though various elements may be taught in the individual books of the Gospels, nevertheless this makes no difference to the faith of believers, since by the one sovereign Spirit all things have been declared in all [the Gospels]: concerning the nativity, concerning the passion, concerning the resurrection, concerning life with his disciples, and concerning his twofold coming; the first in lowliness when he was despised, which has taken place, the second glorious in royal power, which is still in the future" (Muratorian Fragment 17–24).[c]

While the simplistic notion of a top-down decision from an emperor or powerful bishop regarding what constitutes the canon may make for a good story, it's historically unlikely that a single decision from a powerful individual could bring wide consensus and unity to what constituted the church's Scriptures. Irenaeus, the late-second-century-CE bishop of Lyons, is often invoked as the supposed inventor and innovator of the notion of the Fourfold Gospel as the singular collection of Gospel writings for the church at large. More likely, however, is the view that his arguments for the Fourfold Gospel assume that the church at large is already engaging in public and liturgical reading of these Gospels. 4.5

Some have seen Irenaeus's argument here as weak or contrived. Is it really convincing to argue that we need four Gospels to correspond to the four zones of the world, the four principal winds, and four-faced cherubim? I think that the argument should be exactly the reverse. Irenaeus does not need to make detailed arguments for the Fourfold Gospel, since he expects the majority of those within the Christian churches to already believe and assent to this. Irenaeus refers to these four Gospels "naturally, organically and unapologetically, with every confidence that his audience is familiar with them. There is no indication that he is pushing a new scriptural collection of books onto an audience that did not previously have one."[21] And

SIDEBAR 4.5

Irenaeus on the Fourfold Gospel

"It is not possible that the Gospels can be either more or fewer in number than they are. For, since there are four zones of the world in which we live, and four principal winds, while the Church is scattered throughout all the world, and the 'pillar and ground' [1 Timothy 3:15] of the Church is the Gospel and the spirit of life; it is fitting that she should have four pillars, breathing out immortality on every side, and vivifying men afresh. From which fact, it is evident that the Word, the Artificer of all, He that sits upon the cherubim, and contains all things, He who was manifested to men, has given us the Gospel under four aspects, but bound together by one Spirit. As also David says, when entreating His manifestation, 'You that sits between the cherubim, shine forth.' For the cherubim, too, were four-faced, and their faces were images of the dispensation of the Son of God. For, [as the Scripture] says, 'The first living creature was like a lion,' [Revelation 4:7] symbolizing His effectual working, His leadership, and royal power; the second [living creature] was like a calf, signifying [His] sacrificial and sacerdotal order; but 'the third had, as it were, the face as of a man,'— an evident description of His advent as a human being; 'the fourth was like a flying eagle,' pointing out the gift of the Spirit hovering with His wings over the Church. And therefore the Gospels are in accord with these things, among which Christ Jesus is seated" (*Against Heresies* 3.11.8).[d]

this is further supported by the frequency with which not only Irenaeus but also others cite these four Gospels as authoritative texts. For example, Clement in Alexandria (Egypt) and Theophilus and Serapion in Antioch, among others, provide testimony that the church considers the four canonical Gospels as their authoritative texts.[22] C. E. Hill puts it succinctly: "The less sensational truth . . . is that, even apart from the considerable efforts of Irenaeus, a four-Gospel canon appears to be secure in the church in the final decades of the second century. Irenaeus evidently had less to do with the further success of this four-Gospel canon than many have thought. This is because its acceptance must even have pre-dated him from the wide geographical separation of [authors such as Clement, Theophilus, Serapion, etc.]. The testimony of these authors is that the four Gospels were not recently foisted on them, by Irenaeus or anyone else, but had been passed down to them from their forebears in their local Christian communities."[23]

We remember Marcion's preference for one Gospel: the revised ("mutilated") version of the Gospel of Luke. Tertullian wrote a response *Against Marcion*, wherein he argues for all four Gospels as authoritative. Michael Bird is right to note here that this makes it difficult "to imagine that Irenaeus, out in lonely Lyons, could command such currency for his innovative views on a fourfold Gospel by authors spread as far as Alexandria [Clement], Antioch [Theophilus], Carthage [Tertullian], and Rome [Muratorian Fragment] within a few decades. It is more likely that he represented what was already happening on the wider scene as the Gospels were already known and highly regarded as a collection of sacred writings for diverse Christ-believers."[24]

Again, this is not to say that all Christians believed the same thing with respect to the four Gospels, that they used them equally, or that they didn't read other Gospels; however, it does support the claim that these four Gospels were not imposed as a collection on the church but rather that there was a broad consensus that these four Gospels most faithfully reflect the true traditions of the churches about Jesus of Nazareth.

The Four Canonical Gospels Narrate the Story of the Same Jesus through Their Individual Accounts

The four canonical Gospels exhibit plenty of diversity in terms of audience, literary style, theological agenda, and so forth; we'll explore this diversity in the second part of the book as we focus on the distinct contributions of each evangelist with attention to his particular way of telling the story of Jesus. And yet the four Gospels provide a recognizably unified portrait of the identity and life of Jesus. By "unified portrait" I do not mean that they are homogeneous; rather, it is clear that they narrate the story of the same recognizable person. We could flesh out each of these in much more detail as well as provide many more examples, but notice the following five ways in which the four Gospels converge to narrate the significance of the same person Jesus, albeit through their different stories. 4.6

Israel and the Old Testament. The four Gospels agree that the appropriate context within which to understand Jesus is God's electing and saving work within Israel. Jesus affirms the goodness and validity of the Torah and the prophets. The God of Jesus is the God of Israel. Jesus is the Messiah of Israel. Jesus does not disobey the commandments of the law, and he rightly interprets them.

Kingdom and eschatology. The four Gospels portray Jesus as proclaiming the presence of the kingdom of God. All of them also show Jesus to be one who anticipates an eschatological consummation of the kingdom when the Son of Man returns in final judgment and salvation.

Discipleship. Each of the four Gospels supposes that salvation and the meaning of human life are found in discipleship—that is, in terms of following Jesus's pattern of humility, obedience to the Father, hospitality and mercy, and love and sacrifice for others.

Human and divine. The four Gospels agree that Jesus was a real human. He was born from a woman, experienced emotions, and truly suffered and tasted death. The Gospels also manifest a "high Christology" in that they depict Jesus as a divine figure or, at very minimum, as one who shares an utterly unique relationship with the God of Israel.

Saving necessity of Jesus's acts. The four Gospels agree that Jesus's birth, life, sufferings, death, resurrection, and exaltation to the right hand of the

SIDEBAR 4.6

Michael Bird on the Joys of Having Four Gospels

"The four Gospels exhibit a plurality and unity that both encourages and restricts Christological reflection. As a plurality, they demonstrate that no single Gospel, no one narration, and no solo story possesses a monopoly on describing who Jesus is. It takes the richness and diversity of four different accounts to come close to penetrating into the mystery of the man and his mission. In fact, the plurality of the Gospels stimulates us to write, preach, teach, paint and sing about Jesus in ways that are far from monolithic but celebrate the diverse ways that Jesus Christ quickens our hearts, fills us with joy, drives us to Godward devotion, and inspires us to love others. At the same time, as a unity the four Gospels are in a sense constricting, setting the boundaries as they do for all Christological discourse."[e]

Father are necessary for the salvation of God's people. The Gospels affirm the necessity of Jesus's sufferings and death as providing atonement for sins.

The rise of the Fourfold Gospel, then, has its roots in the early church's broad attestation that these Gospels have apostolic roots that preserve the traditions on which their faith in Jesus is based. These four Gospels are the ones that converge to narrate the same person and story of Jesus of Nazareth. But what about the other Gospel writings? Do they narrate another Jesus? Were they intended to supplant or supplement the canonical Gospels?

Reading Noncanonical Gospels

It may surprise you to find out that there are more than four Gospels; in fact, there are many different ancient Gospels that are not in the Christian canon. Sometimes these Gospels are referred to as the "apocryphal Gospels"—the first term, taken from Greek, meaning something like "hidden" or "secret." And while a few of these Gospels do present Jesus as offering a secret wisdom to his followers, I will refer to these other Gospels simply as noncanonical. These Gospels do not all uniformly present Jesus offering hidden wisdom, nor do they make up a group of writings intended to be read as a collection. And while some are clearly outside the boundaries of mainstream orthodox Christianity, many of the writings are entirely orthodox in their theology and are likely intended to supplement, rather than critique or replace, the accounts in the canonical Gospels.

For example, the Infancy Gospel of James transmits stories and traditions about the birth of Jesus and especially provides supplementary information about his mother, Mary. The text emphasizes Mary and her family's piety, her Davidic lineage, her upbringing (like Samuel) in the temple from an early age, her visit to her cousin Elizabeth, and Joseph's obedience to the angel's command to show fidelity to his wife. Most scholars have demonstrated that the text is dependent on the Gospels of both Matthew and Luke, and there are numerous places where there are exact quotations from Matthew and Luke (e.g., 11:1–3 is clearly dependent on Luke 1:28–42).[25] But while literary dependence is likely in some places, the Infancy Gospel of James also has more fantastical elements, such as the belief in Mary's perpetual virginity and other highly exalted claims about Mary. But, again, the Gospel is more likely intended to supplement the canonical Gospels, and its teaching is by no means heretical. In fact, many have shown the enormous influence this work has had on contemporary

Christian imagination and celebration of Christmas.[26] On the other hand, the Infancy Gospel of Thomas, while also filling in some of the gaps in Jesus's childhood left by the canonical Gospels, transmits stories that are utterly fantastical and presents an adolescent Jesus who is full of power and intellect but is also capricious, defiant, and arrogant (see sidebar 4.7). He treats his fellow playmates with anger and malice, and he is remarkably arrogant toward his teachers. The text is not necessarily "heretical," in part because it's largely devoid of theology, but it's obvious why a text like this would not be included in the Fourfold Gospel. In other words, no one suggests that a text like this authentically preserves the remembrances of Jesus or that its portrait of the character of Jesus in any way coheres with the canonical Gospels. 4.7

In addition to infancy Gospels, there are also writings that center on Jesus's sufferings and death, the foremost of significance here almost certainly being the Gospel of Peter. Again, the writing often supplements and expands traditions found in the New Testament writings, especially the Gospel of Matthew. For example, the Gospel of Peter expands Matthew's account of the Roman guards at the tomb of Jesus (see sidebar 4.8). Here we find the named figure of Petronius, the centurion put in charge by Pilate (8:28–33). The guards actually witness the angels moving the great stone at the entrance to the tomb (9:34–37). 4.8

The text clearly expands on the Matthean account of the guards at Jesus's tomb (Matt. 28:11–15). The features of the account are obviously more expansive and fantastical; thus, it strikes most as obviously fictional and unbelievable. The text also heightens and enhances anti-Jewish sentiment in that the Jewish leaders and priests are almost solely responsible, while Pilate bears little of the responsibility for Jesus's death.[27] Certainly the image of the moving and speaking cross in the Gospel of Peter 10:38–42 is provocative, though it is by no means clear how the reader is to understand its significance. It seems most likely that the Gospel of Peter is, like the Infancy Gospel of James, a secondary account of the events surrounding Jesus's sufferings, death, and resurrection and is intended primarily to offer a popular, edifying, and entertaining account of already familiar Gospel traditions.

SIDEBAR 4.7

Infancy Gospel of Thomas 2:2–5

"When this boy Jesus was five years old he was playing at the ford of a brook, and he gathered together into pools the water that flowed by, and made it once clean, and commanded it by word alone. He made soft clay and fashioned from it twelve sparrows. And it was the sabbath when he did this. And there were also many other children playing with him. Now when a certain Jew saw what Jesus was doing in his play on the sabbath, he at once went and told his father Joseph: 'See, your child is at the brook, and he has taken clay and fashioned twelve birds and has profaned the sabbath.' And when Joseph came to the place and saw (it), he cried out to him saying: 'Why do you do on the sabbath what ought not be done?' But Jesus clapped his hands and cried to the sparrows: 'Off with you!' And the sparrows took flight and went away chirping. The Jews were amazed when they saw this, and went away and told their elders what they had seen Jesus do."[f]

By far the most popular noncanonical Gospel is the Gospel of Thomas. Even before the discovery of the Coptic text around 1900, scholars were aware that a writing such as this existed because of a handful of early Christian authors who refer to it by name. Some contemporary scholars have even gone so far as to argue for a first-century dating and suggest that it provides an important source for understanding the historical Jesus. But most now agree that the Gospel of Thomas demonstrates literary dependence on the Synoptic Gospels (or Synoptic traditions) and should be dated no earlier than the early second century CE.

SIDEBAR 4.8

Gospel of Peter 10:38–42

"When now those soldiers saw this, they awakened the centurion and the elders—for they also were there to assist at the watch. And whilst they were relating what they had seen, they saw again three men come out from the sepulcher, and two of them sustaining the other, and a cross following them, and the heads of the two reaching to heaven, but that of him who was led of them by the hand overpassing the heavens. And they heard a voice out of the heavens crying, 'Has thou preached to them that sleep?,' and from the cross there was heard the answer, 'Yea.'"[g]

SIDEBAR 4.9

The Gospel of Thomas and Judaism

- "Jesus said to them: If you fast, you will put a sin to your charge; and if you pray, you will be condemned; and if you give alms, you will do harm to the spirits" (logion 14).
- "His disciples said to him: On what day will the rest of the dead come into being, and on what day will the new world come? He said to them: What you await has come, but you do not know it" (logion 51).
- "His disciples said to him: Twenty-four prophets spoke in Israel, and they all spoke of you. He said to them: You have abandoned the living one before your eyes, and spoken about the dead" (logion 52).
- "His disciples said to him: Is circumcision useful or not? He said to them: If it were useful, their father would beget them from their mother (already) circumcised. But the true circumcision in the Spirit has proved useful in every way" (logion 53).
- "His disciples said to him: On what day will the kingdom come? <Jesus said:> It will not come while people watch for it; they will not say: Look, here it is, or: Look, there it is; but the father of the kingdom is spread out over the earth, and men do not see it" (logion 113).[h]

The conversations are complex and unwieldy, but let's take a quick look at what we find in this Gospel writing. First, the Gospel is entirely composed of 114 logia, or "sayings," of Jesus and contains no narrative whatsoever. The writing begins, "These are the secret words which the living Jesus spoke and which Didymus Judas Thomas wrote down. And he said: He who shall find the interpretation of these words shall not taste death" (prologue–1). Readers of the text, it would seem, are intended to mull over and meditate on Jesus's secret words. Thus, the entire Gospel is filled with ambiguous and difficult-to-interpret sayings of Jesus; it's notoriously difficult to provide a summary, theology, or structure of the text.[28] The portrait of Jesus in the Gospel of Thomas is strikingly different from that of the canonical Gospels. In the Gospel of Thomas, Jesus is characterized as a wise sage whose words enable those who listen to attain knowledge. There is no hint that Jesus is the Jewish Messiah who suffers, dies, and is raised from the dead in order to save humanity. In fact, often Jesus's teachings contradict his teachings in the canonical Gospels. In the Gospel of Thomas Jesus rejects the prophets of Israel as providing testimony to his coming; overturns the necessity and importance of Torah practices such as circumcision; rejects the practices of prayer, fasting, and almsgiving; and denigrates the notion of resurrection from the dead. 4.9

Instead of a Gospel that centers on Jesus as the Messiah of Israel, sent by God in the fulfillment of his Scriptures, who calls humanity to follow him through patterning their lives after him, and who dies on the cross to save humanity from their sins, the Gospel of Thomas presents a radically different construal of Jesus. Here, Jesus the wise teacher attempts to lead people to an inner knowledge and awareness of who they are and from whence they came (see sidebar 4.10). Jesus often speaks of this in such a way that a human resolves plurality in favor of unity; stated differently, the goal is that humans overcome the world and their body so as to overcome division and obtain knowledge of their true selves that comes from the light. 4.10

SIDEBAR 4.10

The Gospel of Thomas on Self-Knowledge

- "Jesus saw some infants who were being suckled. He said to his disciples: These infants being suckled are like those who enter the kingdom. They said to him: If we then become children, shall we enter the kingdom? Jesus said to them: When you make the two one, and when you make the inside as the outside, and the outside as the inside, and the upper as the lower, and when you make the male and the female into a single one, so that the male is not male and the female is not female, and when you make eyes in place of an eye, and a hand in place of a hand, and a foot in place of a foot, an image in place of an image, then shall you enter [the kingdom]" (logion 22).
- "His disciples said: Teach us about the place where you are, for it is necessary for us to seek it. He said to them: He who has ears, let him hear! There is light within a man of light, and he lights the whole world. If he does not shine, there is darkness" (logion 24).
- "Jesus said: If the flesh came into existence because of the spirit, it is a marvel. But if the spirit (came into existence) because of the body, it is a marvel of marvels. But as for me, I wonder this, how this great wealth made its home in this poverty" (logion 29).
- "Jesus said: Blessed are the solitary and the elect, for you will find the kingdom, for you came forth from it, (and) you will return to it again" (logion 49).
- "Jesus said: He who knows the all, (but) fails (to know) himself, misses everything" (logion 67).
- "Jesus said: Wretched is the body which depends on a body, and wretched is the soul which depends on these two" (logion 87).[i]

These texts are worthy of further study for a variety of excellent reasons. But a careful study of these Gospels reveals that there are good reasons for Christians—both then and now—to hold to our current Fourfold Gospel. First, many of the noncanonical Gospels are dependent on the canonical Gospels; they, in fact, often seem to intentionally supplement the canonical Gospels. Relatedly, we have seen that they are almost unanimously dated later than all of the four Gospels. Second, through our look at the Gospel of Thomas we have seen that its portrait of Jesus is frequently at odds with the Jesus of the Fourfold Gospel. While there are some overlaps, there are aspects of his person and identity propagated by the Gospel of Thomas that are irreconcilable with those of the Fourfold Gospel. A collection of Gospels that included both the Gospel of Thomas and the Gospel of Matthew would simply result in obvious and irreconcilable contradictions in its characterization of Jesus, understanding of the importance of Israel's history and people, and articulation of human salvation.

Summary

We have explored now some of the major questions pertaining to the origins of the canonical Fourfold Gospel as well as some of the joys and challenges involved in having four different but similar sacred Gospel writings. More specifically, in this chapter, we have seen the following:

1. The differences between the Gospels are inevitable and stand out precisely because there are so many similarities. In other words, canonizing four different Gospels will inevitably result in differences between the four.
2. Some of the earliest Christians demonstrated some concerns over these differences and responded in different ways. Some chose one Gospel above all others, while some produced Gospel harmonies, and others attempted to show how the four Gospels could be harmonized. The orthodox response was to insist on all four Gospels as authentic accounts of the life and teachings of Jesus of Nazareth and as canonical scriptural writings.
3. Maximalist attempts at harmonization are unconvincing to most scholars, although some level of harmonization is certainly reasonable in some instances. But the main truth to be affirmed is that the church's decision to continue to read all four Gospels together as canonical Scripture reveals the important insight that multiple perspectives and vantage points are required to do justice to Jesus's identity and life.
4. Despite the more adventurous and exotic claims that the "proto-orthodox" church suppressed other Gospel writings as a political power play, there are actually very sensible reasons for the rise of the Fourfold Gospel. The canonical Gospels are, for example, almost certainly the earliest writings and best sources for understanding the historical Jesus, and they were the Gospel writings most extensively engaged by early Christians.
5. The most famous of the noncanonical Gospels, the Gospel of Thomas, though a fascinating and important text, would create irreconcilable differences and contradictions were it to be set next to the Fourfold Gospel.

PART 2

How Should We Read the Gospels?

In the preceding chapters we have explored many of the most important matters related to the questions and challenges involved in moving from the historical person of Jesus of Nazareth to the collection of the Fourfold Gospel. The next three chapters are transitional in that I will continue to introduce some necessary background material regarding the nature of the Gospels, but we will start to make a more explicit turn toward focusing on how this information will aid us in our actual reading of each of the four Gospels. There are many and diverse ways in which the Gospels have been read—and many of them are good! The Gospels can be, and have been, read in order to settle dogmatic disputes, as spiritually formative devotional guides, for ethical instruction, to inspire activist movements, for worship in liturgical settings, as historical witnesses to the world of first-century Judaism, and for many other purposes. In fact, the influence of the Gospels on church, culture, and politics throughout global history is extensive and can play an important role in our reading of the Gospels. While there are many good ways to read the Gospels, I will propose three major principles that I will employ in our reading of each Gospel writing. These are not the only ways to read the Gospels, but they are, in my view, principles that best honor the intentions and purposes of the writings and attend to their influence within Christian history. In what follows, I'll unpack three primary claims that will help us read the Gospels. These claims take the Gospels seriously as first-century Jewish texts (i.e., history), as narrative renderings of the person of Jesus (i.e., narrative), and as theologically transformational (i.e., discipleship).

Reading the Gospels in Their First-Century Historical Context

The Gospels are written for an audience familiar with what we might refer to as first-century Judaism. Rightly reading these texts requires, then, some basic familiarity with the ancient history, culture, religion, and economics of which the Gospels speak and often simply presume. They require awareness additionally, then, of God's sacred words to his people in what Christians refer to as the Old Testament. Everything within our Gospels constantly reminds us that Jesus was a Jew whose identity and mission can be understood only within the Hebrew Scriptures and God's election of Israel as the means whereby he would fulfill his purposes for the world.[1] All kinds of fallacies and mistakes await the reader who simply assumes that our world is in most ways the same world that we find in the Gospels. Most of us are familiar with democracy; Jesus knew a world dominated by foreign imperial powers. Most of us are familiar with capitalism and an economy that operates through markets; Jesus's world was an agrarian society that was heavily taxed by the rich. Many of us live in a world where individual freedom and human rights are ingrained within us; Jesus lived in a society where shame and honor and collective values dominated.

What Is Judaism?

Giving a definition of first-century Judaism is impossible, though we can list some of its major characteristics. We do well to think here of Judaism as an ethnicity rather than a "religion" (in our modern sense of the term).

Ancient notions of ethnicity typically centered on shared ancestral customs, family/lineage, education/culture, land, language, and the worship of God/gods.[2] Thus, in the time of Jesus, Judaism was often marked by the characteristics described in sidebar 5.1. 5.1

The Gospels as First-Century Jewish Writings: Three Examples

Our reading of the Gospels will frequently attend to specific aspects of first-century history, culture, religion, and economics; but here I want to very selectively exemplify the importance of taking the Gospels as first-century Jewish writings as an essential principle for reading the Gospels, even as I introduce some of the guides and practical aids we can draw on as we grow in our understanding of Jesus's world. Again, our studies here are illustrative and could be fleshed out in much more detail; I advise you, then, to use the following examples as opportunities to stimulate further study and investigation.

SIDEBAR 5.1

Judaism in the Time of Jesus

The true God is the God of Israel. This God is the creator of everything (Gen. 1–2). Whether the gods of the nations are angels, demons, or idols with no true existence, it is only the Creator God, the God of Israel, who is worthy of worship. This belief is enshrined in what is called the Shema, in Deuteronomy 6:4: "Hear, O Israel: The Lord is our God, the Lord alone."

God has elected Israel to be his people. God called Abraham and the patriarchs, as the ancestors of Israel, to be the people through whom he would work his purposes to bless "all the families of the earth" (Gen. 12:1–4; cf. 22:15–18; Deut. 4:35–39). Israel is God's treasured possession, his holy people on whom he has set his love (Exod. 19:5–6).

God has given the Torah at Sinai to guide his people in wisdom, justice, and love. After God liberates Israel through the exodus event, he bestows on them the covenant charter of the law of Moses at Sinai. Among other things, the Torah expresses God's will and wisdom for a just society that enacts love for God and love for neighbor (Exod. 19:4–6; 24:1–18; Lev. 19:18). The Torah also calls God's people Israel to a distinctive way of life marked by prayer, almsgiving, and holiness. In the first century God's people often met in synagogues in order to pray and read Torah. The covenant is marked by distinctive observances such as Sabbath keeping, circumcision, and food laws.

God has promised his people the blessings of land and temple. One of God's primary promises to Israel is that he will be their God and that his presence will dwell with them. God's gift of the promised land to his people is for the purpose of offering a place for them where he will walk among them (e.g., Lev. 26:9–13). The temple, and before it the movable tabernacle (Exod. 25–40), is also a place where God's presence dwells (Deut. 12:5–14; 1 Kings 8). God institutes repentance and sacrifice as the means whereby he promises to atone for Israel's sins. Many of the Jewish feasts and festivals, such as the Day of Atonement (Lev. 16) and Passover (Exod. 12), were associated with sacrifices and celebrations at the Jerusalem temple.

God has promised to rule his people with a righteous Davidic king. The origins of Israel's monarchy are complex (see 1 Sam. 8–12), but the result is that God makes a covenant with David and his dynasty such that God will establish David's throne forever (2 Sam. 7:12–16; see also Gen. 49:8–12). Many of the psalms and prophetic oracles reaffirm God's promise to provide a good Davidic ruler who will lead God's people in peace and justice (e.g., Pss. 72; 89; Isa. 11; Ezek. 34).[a]

Jesus Navigated the Tense Relationship between God's Covenant Promises and Israel's Experiences of Subjugation by Foreign Powers and Rulers

Readers of the Bible remember that God had called Abraham and made promises to him that he would give him land and descendants, make a great nation out of him, and use his family to bless the world (Gen. 12:1–3; 15:5–16; 17:1–8, 15–22; 22:15–18). God works, in part, to fulfill these promises through the royal Davidic dynasty that rules over Israel (Abraham's descendants) in the land of the promise (2 Sam. 7:2–16). Bound up in God's promises to Abraham and David is the hope that Israel will live peacefully and flourish in their land as they experience God's presence in the land through their sacred cultic institutions and through the just and righteous rule of their rulers/kings. The Scriptures, however, repeatedly indicate that despite God's blessings and promises made for the good of his people, their idolatry, sin, and failure to obey God's law set up roadblocks that stand in the way of God's blessings (e.g., Deut. 32:1–47). Israel's idolatry and disobedience to God lead

SIDEBAR 5.2

Foreign Empires Ruling over Israel

Empire	Dates
Assyria	721–605 BCE
Babylon	605–539 BCE
Persia	538–332 BCE
Macedonia/Greece	332–166 BCE
Jewish Maccabean/Hasmonean Rule	166–64 BCE
Rome	64 BCE–135 CE

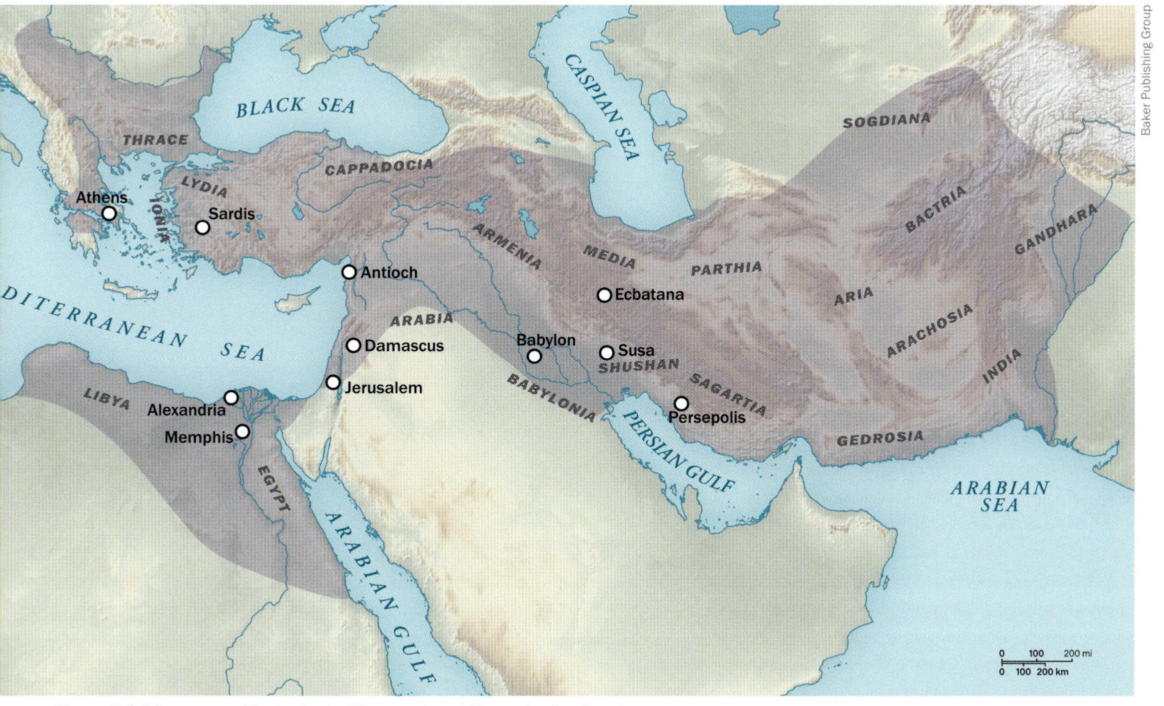

Figure 5.1. The geographical extent of the empire of Alexander the Great

to a situation where God's people are exiled from their own land. The Northern Kingdom (Israel) undergoes exile by the Assyrian Empire in 722 BCE, and the Southern Kingdom (Judah) is deported by the Babylonian Empire in 586 BCE. The historical records are much more detailed and richer than we have time for here, but we can note that the Persian ruler Cyrus allows some of the Jewish people to return to their homeland (see the books of Ezra and Nehemiah) but that God's people are now ruled by one empire after another: Assyria, Babylon, Persia, Macedonia/Greece, Rome. 5.2

Even within the Old Testament, we find evidence that God's people are wrestling with reconciling God's covenantal promises and their experiences of being ruled by foreign empires. Psalm 89, for example, reflects on God's promises to David and God's covenantal trustworthiness and love in light of Israel's experience of exile, shame, and no Davidic king. 5.3

We cannot say, "All of the Jewish people were ______" (fill in the blank). Our sources are too diverse and give the lie to almost any hegemonic claim like that. We can say, however, that there are significant Jewish writings that continue the trajectory of Psalm 89 in anticipating that God's sending of a messiah would, among other things, result in a situation where his people are self-governed by God and his messianic ruler (rather than foreign powers). The Psalms of Solomon, written most likely in response to the Roman general Pompey's invasion of Judea in 63 BCE, testify to this hope. 5.4

SIDEBAR 5.3

Psalm 89: The Question of the Davidic Monarchy in the Time of Exile

Psalm 89:1–4, 38–52

I will sing of the lovingkindness of the LORD forever;
To all generations I will make known Your faithfulness with my mouth.
For I have said, "Lovingkindness will be built up forever;
In the heavens You will establish Your faithfulness."
"I have made a covenant with My chosen;
I have sworn to David My servant,
I will establish your seed forever
And build up your throne to all generations." Selah.
. . . .
But You have cast off and rejected,
You have been full of wrath against Your anointed.
You have spurned the covenant of Your servant;
You have profaned his crown in the dust.
You have broken down all his walls;
You have brought his strongholds to ruin.
All who pass along the way plunder him;
He has become a reproach to his neighbors.
You have exalted the right hand of his adversaries;
You have made all his enemies rejoice.
You also turn back the edge of his sword
And have not made him stand in battle.
You have made his splendor to cease
And cast his throne to the ground.
You have shortened the days of his youth;
You have covered him with shame. Selah.
How long, O LORD?
Will You hide Yourself forever?
Will Your wrath burn like fire?
Remember what my span of life is;
For what vanity You have created all the sons of men!
What man can live and not see death?
Can he deliver his soul from the power of Sheol? Selah.
Where are Your former lovingkindnesses, O Lord,
Which You swore to David in Your faithfulness?
Remember, O Lord, the reproach of Your servants;
How I bear in my bosom the reproach of all the many peoples,
With which Your enemies have reproached, O LORD,
With which they have reproached the footsteps of Your anointed.
Blessed be the LORD forever!
Amen and Amen. (NASB)

SIDEBAR 5.4

Messianic Hope in the Psalms of Solomon

Psalms of Solomon 17:22–37

Undergird him with the strength to destroy the unrighteous rulers,
to purge Jerusalem from Gentiles
who trample her to destruction;
in wisdom and in righteousness to drive out
the sinners from inheritance;
to smash the arrogance of sinners
like a potter's jar;
To shatter all their substance with an iron rod;
to destroy the unlawful nations with the word of his mouth;
At his warning the nations will flee from his presence;
and he will condemn sinners by the thoughts of their hearts.

He will gather his holy people
whom he will lead in righteousness;
and he will judge the tribes of the people
that have been made holy by the Lord their God.
He will not tolerate unrighteousness (even) to pause among them,
and any person who knows wickedness shall not live with them.
For he shall know them
that they are children of their God.
He will distribute them upon the land
according to their tribes;
the alien and the foreigner will no longer live near them.
He will judge the peoples and nations in the wisdom of his
righteousness.
Pause.
And he will have gentile nations serving him under his yoke,
and he will glorify the Lord in (a place) prominent (above) the
whole earth.
And he will purge Jerusalem
(and make it) holy as it was even from the beginning,
(for) the nations to come from the ends of the earth to see his glory,
to bring as gifts her children who had been driven out,
and to see the glory of the Lord
with which God has glorified her.
And he will be a righteous king over them, taught by God.
There will be no unrighteousness among them in his days,
for all shall be holy,
and their king shall be the Lord Messiah.
(For) he will not rely on horse and rider and bow,
nor will he collect gold and silver for war.
Nor will he build up hope in a multitude for a day of war.
The Lord himself is his king,
the hope of the one who has a strong hope in God.

He shall be compassionate to all the nations
(who) reverently (stand) before him.
He will strike the earth with the word of his mouth forever;
he will bless the Lord's people with wisdom and happiness.
And he himself (will be) free from sin, (in order) to rule a great
people.
He will expose officials and drive out sinners
by the strength of his word.
And he will not weaken his days, (relying) upon his God,
for God made him
powerful in the holy spirit
and wise in the council of understanding,
with strength and righteousness.[b]

Although there was a brief period of Jewish independence under the Hasmonean dynasty (166–63 BCE), those who ruled over Israel during this period often acted like Hellenistic kings and provoked sharp disagreements over the legitimacy of their rule. The revolt began when the Seleucid king Antiochus IV set up an altar to Zeus for sacrifices to pagan gods. He installed a gymnasium and outlawed circumcision, food laws, and Torah obedience. Thus, the revolt began as an attempt to resist a tyrannical ruler who wanted to impose Hellenistic culture on his subjects. As the story is recounted in 1–2 Maccabees, some Israelites wanted to collaborate with the Hellenistic king and engage in what we might call assimilation. But some were entirely resistant and, out of their allegiance to the God of Israel and the Torah, engage in guerrilla warfare, whereby they remarkably establish their independence. 5.5

SIDEBAR 5.5

The Maccabean Fight for Freedom

But Mattathias answered and said in a loud voice: "Even if all the nations that live under the rule of the king obey him, and have chosen to obey his commandments, every one of them abandoning the religion of their ancestors, I and my sons and my brothers will continue to live by the covenant of our ancestors. Far be it from us to desert the law and the ordinances. We will not obey the king's words by turning aside from our religions to the right hand or to the left." (1 Macc. 2:19–22 NRSVue)

By the time of Jesus's birth, the Jewish people have been ruled by Rome's client king Herod the Great (37–4 BCE). Herod was notorious for building projects that included pagan cities in the land of Israel, imposing heavy taxes, and murdering family members. His rule was dependent on the imperial power of Rome, and his lifestyle did not manifest the commitment to God's Torah that Israel's Scriptures prescribed.

Reading through our four Gospels will reveal continuing tensions between God's covenantal promises to Israel and the reality of imperial domination. For example, Matthew's birth narrative sets up a contrast between the messianic child who receives worship from the magi and the tyrannical and murderous intent of Herod the Great (Matt. 2:1–12). The Herodians and Pharisees attempt to trick and trap Jesus through a difficult question regarding paying taxes to Rome, to which Jesus cryptically replies, "Give to Caesar the things that belong to Caesar, and to God the things that belong to God" (Mark 12:17). Mark's Gospel shows how Herod Antipas (ruler/tetrarch over Galilee and son of Herod the Great) kills the prophet John the Baptist, giving us an example of a conflict between the kingdom of God and the kingdoms of this world (Mark 6:17–29). Luke's Jesus contrasts his lifestyle with the practices of the Hellenistic kings and rulers with respect to leadership practices (Luke 22:24–27). And the trial scenes in the Gospel of John contain one of the most aesthetically and theologically rich contrasts between Pilate/empire and Jesus/Messiah (John 18–19). Much could be said about these texts, and more will be said later, but for now I simply want to highlight that a basic understanding of Israel's history—here as it pertains to Israel's negotiating the rule of imperial powers—is necessary for a robust reading of our Gospels.

Jesus Navigated the Difficult Relationship between God's Sacred Teachings on Economics and an Agrarian Society Whose Economy Was Controlled by the Wealthy and Powerful Elite

The Gospels are by no means devoid of economic concerns. Jesus frequently teaches about wealth and possessions; tax collectors like Levi and Zacchaeus seem to carry a negative stereotype based on their vocation; the question of whether Jesus and the disciples should pay the temple tax and taxes to Caesar is raised; and Jesus tells stories about debt, debtors' prison, inheritance disputes, and greedy landowners. Knowing something about the ancient economy is therefore necessary for our understanding of significant texts in the Gospels.

The ancient economy and the creation of wealth were driven not primarily by market mechanisms but rather by the politically powerful and elite who owned the majority of arable land. The economy was a social institution that was embedded within the broader value systems and political relations that privileged the wealthy and elite. The ancient economy was not an institution or sphere of life that was separable, then, from family and marriage, slavery, religion, politics/governance, and, most importantly, social status and political power. Agriculture was the centerpiece of wealth, as the vast majority of the population made their living off of the land, but these societies were also usually in the hands of a small group of wealthy rulers.[3] Although the great majority of the population made its living off of

SIDEBAR 5.6

Economic Legislation in the Torah

Jubilee: Leviticus 25:23–28

The land, moreover, shall not be sold permanently, for the land is Mine; for you are but aliens and sojourners with Me. Thus for every piece of your property, you are to provide for the redemption of the land.

If a fellow countryman of yours becomes so poor he has to sell part of his property, then his nearest kinsman is to come and buy back what his relative has sold. Or in case a man has no kinsman, but so recovers his means as to find sufficient for its redemption, then he shall calculate the years since its sale and refund the balance to the man to whom he sold it, and so return to his property. But if he has not found sufficient means to get it back for himself, then what he has sold shall remain in the hands of its purchaser until the year of jubilee; but at the jubilee it shall revert, that he may return to his property. (NASB)

Kings: Deuteronomy 17:14–17

When you enter the land which the LORD your God gives you, and you possess it and live in it, and you say, "I will set a king over me like all the nations who are around me," you shall surely set a king over you whom the LORD your God chooses, one from among your countrymen you shall set as king over yourselves; you may not put a foreigner over yourselves who is not your countryman. Moreover, he shall not multiply horses for himself, nor shall he cause the people to return to Egypt to multiply horses, since the LORD has said to you, "You shall never again return that way." He shall not multiply wives for himself, or else his heart will turn away; nor shall he greatly increase silver and gold for himself. (NASB)

Strangers, Widows and Orphans: Exodus 22:21–24

You shall not wrong a stranger or oppress him, for you were strangers in the land of Egypt. You shall not afflict any widow or orphan. If you afflict him at all, and if he does cry out to Me, I will surely hear his cry; and My anger will be kindled, and I will kill you with the sword, and your wives shall become widows and your children fatherless. (NASB)

Widows and Orphans, Aliens: Deuteronomy 10:17–19

For the LORD your God is the God of gods and the Lord of lords, the great, the mighty, and the awesome God who does not show partiality nor take a bribe. He executes justice for the orphan and the widow and shows His love for the alien by giving him food and clothing. So show your love for the alien, for you were aliens in the land of Egypt. (NASB)

Loans: Exodus 22:25–27

If you lend money to My people, to the poor among you, you are not to act as a creditor to him; you shall not charge him interest. If you ever take your neighbor's cloak as a pledge, you are to return it to him before the sun sets, for that is his only covering; it is his cloak for his body. What else shall he sleep in? And it shall come about that when he cries out to Me, I will hear him, for I am gracious. (NASB)

agriculture, the masses lived close to subsistence level, as their production was aimed primarily at self-sufficiency; the majority of wealth production benefited the elite and wealthy landowners instead.[4]

Israel's Scriptures consistently speak of an alternative way of using wealth, land, and resources. Israel's economy was not necessarily focused on everyone having the exact same amount, but it certainly was deeply concerned with equity, fairness, and provision with the goal that no one was exploited or went without what they needed to flourish and live well. One can see this concern in central institutions and practices such as the Jubilee, which called for a cancellation of debts and return of land; kings who practiced justice instead of extortion; and legislation for justice and charity for widows, orphans, and immigrants. 5.6

During the monarchy Israel's prophets testify to a situation where a few rich landowners begin to engage in a process of acquisition of the land, a situation that results in the displacement of landless tenants and the impoverishment of subsistence farmers.[5] The prophetic oracles of the eighth-century prophets Amos and Micah indicate a concern that the elites' practice of acquiring the majority of the land is destroying the lives of subsistence farmers. The prophets condemn the elites for their arrogance and devotion to luxury and self-indulgence (Isa. 2:5–22; Amos 6:4–7). Isaiah pronounces woes on those "who add house to house and join field to field until there is no more room and you alone are left in the land" (Isa. 5:8). The wealthy landowners give free reign to the greedy acquisition of the land of others that thereby results in the oppression of the poor (Mic. 2:2). The wealthy landowners furthermore use unjust and violent means of acquiring people's land and wealth: "For the wealthy of the city are full of violence, and its residents speak lies; the tongues in their mouths are deceitful" (Mic. 6:12). They take bribes (Mic. 7:3), extract material resources from the poor (Amos 5:10–12), use dishonest scales to cheat the poor (Amos 8:4–8), and prey on widows and orphans (Isa. 1:23; 10:1–3).[6]

During the period when Judea was under Persian rule (558–331 BCE), Persian overseers collaborated with a very small group of elite members of the Judean ruling class as a means of collecting taxes from the ordinary laborers and peasant farmers. This often led to a situation where many of the Jewish farmers lived with, and feared, significant debt; economic debts would then reinforce both a level of economic hierarchy and poverty for many. Thus, a consistent feature of Israel's postexilic history is the distinction between the imperial power, the local aristocracy or governing class, and the usually impoverished subsistence-level workers (Neh. 5:1–15).[7]

Skip ahead a few hundred years and closer to the time of Jesus when Herod the Great is ruling over Palestine (37–4 BCE). The economic situation remains similar: pro-Roman aristocrats localized around the temple (e.g., the Sadducees and the Sanhedrin), the few wealthy landowners, and the vast majority who lived at or below subsistence level.[8] This pattern resulted in small farmers increasingly being pushed off of their land due to extreme indebtedness and the attending confiscation or appropriation of their land by the wealthy. Lack of land, oppressive demands for taxation and tribute, and increasing indebtedness resulted in incredible wealth disparities in ancient Palestine. 5.7

Knowing even a little about both the Torah's teaching on economics and Israel's historical experiences of navigating taxation by imperial elites, local aristocratic rulers who aided the imperial elites, and the common person's experience of subsistence farming, taxation, and debt can help us understand Jesus's frequent teachings on economics in the Gospels.

The Gospel of Luke is filled with Jesus's criticisms of the Roman economy and its operations in ancient Palestine as being something exploitative, extractive, hierarchical, and predicated on greed. From the beginning of Luke's Gospel, we see that Jesus's presence will mean the inauguration of *another kind of king and kingdom* that will challenge the current operations of Rome and Roman Palestine.

Mary the mother of Jesus interprets God's miraculous act to make her virgin womb pregnant with this coming Messiah as the means whereby he will "scatter the proud . . . and topple the mighty from their thrones and exalt the lowly" (Luke 1:51b–52). Mary praises God's act as the means whereby he will give food to the hungry and will send the rich away with nothing (1:53). In accordance with Mary's prophetic anthem, Jesus is born far away from the rich and powerful who oppress and exploit, such as the Caesars and governors of Rome (2:1–7). This is undoubtedly why John the Baptist's simple message of repentance is focused exclusively on the use of possessions. Those who will be ready to embrace the coming act of God will be those who share their surplus of resources and possessions with others, turn away from exploitative and acquisitive forms of wealth generation, and refrain from using their power to extract from the vulnerable (3:10–14).[9]

SIDEBAR 5.7

The Multiple Herods in the Gospels

Keeping track of the different rulers named "Herod" and the Herodian family is a tricky and difficult task. The following list can help you keep track of those named "Herod" in the Gospels (note that there are two more in the Acts of the Apostles!).

- **Herod the Great** (37–4 BCE) was a client king for Rome. He killed Jewish boys under two years of age in an attempt to eliminate the infant Jesus (Matt. 2:1–18).
- **Herod Archelaus** (4 BCE–6 CE) was a son of Herod the Great who ruled over Samaria, Idumea, and Judea. Even after Herod the Great's death, Jesus's father Joseph was afraid to move back to Judea when he heard that Archelaus was the ruler (Matt. 2:22).
- **Herod Antipas** (4 BCE–39 CE) was a son of Herod the Great who ruled over Galilee and Perea. After being castigated by John the Baptist for divorcing his wife to marry Herodias (his brother Philip's wife), Herod is involved in putting John to death (Matt. 14:1–12). Herod also takes part in the trial of Jesus (Luke 23:1–12).
- **Herod Philip** (4 BCE–34 CE) was a son of Herod the Great who ruled over Iturea and Trachonitis (Luke 3:1). As noted above, his wife Herodias married Herod Antipas.

The text that most clearly sets forth Jesus's teaching on the dangers of greed and excessive consumption is Luke 12:16–21, the parable of the wealthy landowner. This text takes on deeper meaning when we remember that most people survived through subsistence agriculture, that cities were primarily places of consumption and extraction, and that wealth and power were generated from the land and those who owned and controlled the land. In this parable there is a man whose land produces a fabulous yield. So extraordinary is the man's surplus that he has to decide how to best steward his incredible wealth, and he chooses to put it all away in barns and save it for himself. Jesus portrays the man as a symbol of the exploitative, extractive, consuming landowners who unjustly control the majority of the land. In an economy where most people live at a subsistence level, the man's decision to use his surplus for his own protection and security instead of sharing with the hungry demonstrates that he simply does not care about the poor and hungry who surround him.

Within the Gospels, we will find Jesus appealing to Israel's sacred economic teachings to explain how God's people should live, parables centering on debt, parables depicting the contrast between wealthy landowners and the impoverished, and characters whose primary identity is their tax-collecting. Jesus's teachings and parables will require that we have some background information about Jewish history and the Scriptures of Israel.

Jesus and His Followers Were One of Many Groups That Advocated for a Particular Purpose and Vocation for Israel

Jesus proclaimed the coming of the kingdom of God. John the Baptist engaged in a ministry of baptism in the Jordan River to prepare Israel for the coming kingdom. Jesus called twelve disciples to follow him. He interpreted God's will and laws with unparalleled authority. He promised his followers that they would reign with him when God renewed all things. Throughout the Gospels we see that Jesus initiated a movement, within Judaism, around himself that centered on God's ultimate purposes and plans for his people.

But Jesus was not the only individual (nor was his messianic community the only sect or group) who had a vision for how Israel could rightly follow God even in the midst of imperial dominance. In fact, Judaism of the first century was "dynamic and diverse."[10] We should not make the mistake here of assuming that every person within Israel—even a large percentage of people—belonged to a Jewish sect. The majority of Jewish people, while not belonging to a sect, sought to observe the Torah apart from an allegiance to a particular sect. Still, there are a variety of groups that dot the landscape of the Gospels and that we need to know something about if we're going to correctly read the Gospels.[11] E. P. Sanders, one of the greatest twentieth-century scholars on first-century Judaism, noted four primary questions that the Jewish groups described below responded to: (1) Hellenization: How much assimilation and what kind of contact with non-Jews was appropriate? (2) The law: How would the law of Moses be interpreted? And were gentiles living in Palestine expected to observe it? (3) The high priesthood: Could only descendants of Zadok hold the office? How was the high priest to respond to Hellenistic culture? (4) Military control: Should Israel accept foreign rule for the sake of peace?[12] If so, how should the Jewish leaders relate to the imperial authorities? Many of these questions form the background for episodes in the Gospels.

Hellenistic reformers. I mentioned earlier that although Israel was dominated by imperial powers for much of its postexilic history, there was about a one-hundred-year period of Jewish independence when the Hasmonean dynasty ruled Judea (167–63 BCE). Israel won its independence from the Seleucid tyrant Antiochus IV, but what students often forget here is that there was an important group of Jewish "renegades" who wanted to transform Jerusalem into a Greek city with a gymnasium and impose "the ordinances of the Gentiles" (1 Macc. 1:13–14). We get a window, at least from the perspective of the author of 1 Maccabees, into their reasoning of this Jewish group: "Let us go out and make a covenant with the Gentiles around us, for since we separated from them many disasters have come upon us" (1 Macc. 1:11 NRSVue). Joining the Maccabeans are a group referred to as the "Hasideans," who fight for the sake of the law (1 Macc. 2:42; 2 Macc. 14:6). Thus, the Maccabean revolt creates a conflict between the Seleucid king Antiochus and Jewish allies sympathetic to his Hellenistic reforms and those who, according to 1–2 Maccabees, want to remain faithful to God's Torah and covenant and thereby resist the Hellenistic reforms.

Pharisees. The most well-known group to readers of the Gospels is, of course, the Pharisees. The origins—both with respect to when and why—of the Pharisees are controversial. Many have argued that the Pharisees developed sometime soon after the Babylonian exile when study of the Scriptures became central as a replacement for temple worship. In addition to the written laws of Moses, they propagate their oral ancestral traditions about Moses as authoritative. We see Jesus criticize their "tradition of the elders" harshly for failing to understand the intent of God's law (e.g., Matt. 15:1–11). Some have argued that the Pharisees sought to extend the priestly purity laws into everyday facets of life. The Pharisees were the group that interpreted the laws for the broad populace. Most did not have access to priestly power (some may have been priests), and at times they criticize the current priestly regime as corrupt. While some historical sources present the Pharisees as politically engaged at a national level especially with respect to navigating Roman rule, the Gospels portray this group as focused on Jewish piety and Torah observance. The Pharisees were not priests and seem to have been drawn largely from the middle class and often to have had a good reputation among and support from the people. 5.8 5.9

In the Gospels the Pharisees are frequently a foil for, and opponents of, Jesus. Their primary disagreement often centers on how to interpret the Torah, with Jesus insisting on a hermeneutic that reads Torah as centering on love for neighbor (e.g., Matt. 23; Luke 11:37–54). Although Jesus shares meals with the Pharisees in Luke's Gospel (7:36–50; 11:37–54; 14:1–6), they are unable to find common ground in their vision for how Israel is to follow God and obey the Torah.

SIDEBAR 5.8

It's Time to Stop Denigrating Other People or Groups with the Term "Pharisee"

I would guess that almost every one of my readers has heard someone or some group denigrated by being called a "Pharisee." It's time to stop doing this. There are at least two reasons why Christian readers of the Gospels should be sensitive here. First, it is not the case that the Gospel texts cohere with the contemporary claims that the Pharisees were self-righteous, money-loving, legalistic, arrogant, and hypocritical. The apostle Paul, Nicodemus, and Gamaliel were all Pharisees, and they do not fit the negative stereotypes often advanced about Pharisees. The New Testament texts themselves, then, indicate that not all Pharisees were hypocritical or money-loving. It is true that the Gospels depict Jesus and the Pharisees as having rival or different views of how to interpret the Torah and of God's vision of Israel's future and restoration. Undoubtedly, the Gospels' authors want their readers to identify with Jesus's interpretation. But this should not result in a complete vilification of the ancient Pharisees. Second, and perhaps more importantly, in the minds of many contemporary Christians there is a virtual equivalence between "Pharisee" and "Jew," and this often results in anti-Jewish stereotyping, which has been used to perpetuate anti-Semitism. A frequent refrain of this textbook is that good readings of the Gospels situate Jesus within Judaism and God's election of Israel, and thus contemporary Christians must reject anything that smacks of anti-Judaism. Living out Jesus's teachings on hospitality, nonviolence, and love demands that faithful followers of Jesus interrogate any manner in which their language has harmed or continues to harm others.[c]

Sadducees. The Sadducees are a group made up of some priestly and aristocratic families. They often show up in the New Testament writings as connected to the Sanhedrin and temple complex. They have Roman support and therefore have a vested interest in maintaining peace and the status quo as the best path for Israel. In many ways the Sadducees are even further from Jesus's vision for Israel than are the Pharisees. We're told that this group denied the resurrection (or immortality of the soul) and angels (Acts 23:8; Josephus, *Jewish War* 2.164–65), divine providence (Josephus, *Jewish Antiquities* 13.173), and the Pharisaic traditions of the elders (Josephus, *Jewish Antiquities* 13.297).

Essenes / Qumran community. Josephus, among other writers, describes the Essenes as a group that withdrew to the Judean wilderness as a small, intentional community. Most now (not all) identify this group with the community responsible for the Dead Sea Scrolls (discovered in the middle of the twentieth century). Shaye Cohen summarizes the separatist impulses of the Essenes: "The Essenes attacked the legal practices of their fellow

Jews (esp. their observance of the law governing marriage; Sabbath, festivals, and calendar; and purity), denied the sanctity of the Jerusalem temple, and interpreted the Bible in their own peculiar fashion (and accepted certain books known only to themselves)."[13]

SIDEBAR 5.9

Josephus on the Pharisees as a Philosophical School

"Of the two first-named schools, the Pharisees, who are considered the most accurate interpreters of the laws, and hold the position of the leading sect, attribute everything to Fate and to God; they hold that to act rightly or otherwise rests, indeed, for the most part with men, but that in each action Fate cooperates. Every soul, they maintain, is imperishable, but the soul of the good alone passes into another body, while the souls of the wicked suffer eternal punishment" (Josephus, *Jewish War* 2.162–63).

Like Josephus's Essenes, the Qumran community describes its origins as a group centered on a rigorous interpretation of the Torah that is at odds with other interpreters of the law. In fact, their "Teacher of Righteousness" appears to have been a Jerusalem priest who was exiled from Jerusalem; as a result, the group considered the Jerusalem temple and its sacrifices to be corrupt, and they offered, in its stead, spiritual sacrifices. Their documents are rich and diverse, but one highly significant component of these writings is their biblical exegesis whereby they interpret the Scriptures as revealing their own historical experiences (often referred to as *pesher* interpretation). Apocalyptic in orientation, with plenty of emphasis on a dualism consisting in light/darkness and angels/demons, the community expected God to wage a war whereby they would be rescued from their wicked enemies.

Sign prophets and freedom fighters. If one reads Josephus's writings, one will quickly notice individuals and groups who might be described as revolutionaries. Some of them, whom we can call "sign prophets," would gather a group and promise to show signs that would lead to the freedom of the Jewish people from the Roman Empire. For example, Josephus mentions a figure who, in the vein of Moses and Joshua, takes a group of people into the wilderness to show them signs and wonders that demonstrate his ability to liberate them from Rome (*Jewish Antiquities* 20.167–68). On another occasion Josephus tells about Theudas, a man who convinces a crowd of people to follow him to the Jordan River, where he promises to divide the river (*Jewish Antiquities* 20.97–99). Josephus reports on another figure who, pretending to be a prophet, leads his followers to the Mount of Olives and promises to breach the walls of Jerusalem and conquer the Roman garrison (*Jewish War* 2.261–63; cf. Acts 21:38). There are a variety of Jewish freedom fighters who use violent force and other forms of resistance, perhaps the most famous being the group that Josephus refers to as the Zealots, to directly counter Roman rule.

If we were aiming for completeness in scope, we could add more Jewish groups (e.g., Samaritans, the Therapeutae, the Herodians), but I hope that this short sketch of a few of the groups within Israel will help us in at least two ways. First, in our reading of the Gospels we'll encounter Pharisees, Sadducees, and Romans. We'll see that John the Baptist's activity of baptizing a great group of people in the Jordan River is reminiscent of the sign prophets who dot the landscape of Josephus's histories. In order to understand the Gospels, we'll need to have some basic information about these groups, their activities, and their theological convictions. Second, it reminds us that there were different visions for Israel and how to navigate God's covenantal promises and the current difficult realities that Israel faced. Not all had the same beliefs, convictions, practices, and strategies; in fact, many of them were directly opposed to one another. But we should also remind ourselves that most Israelites did not belong to a sect or group. Most of them, sometimes referred to as "the people of the land," were concerned with providing for the needs of their family, considered rebellion against Rome or refusal to pay taxes to be too risky and absurd, and were dependent on their teachers of Torah and their priests to lead them in their obedience to God.

The Gospels are first-century Jewish writings, and as such they presume readers who will read and interpret the writings with sympathy and awareness of the world in which they were written. I have highlighted only three important pieces of historical information as a means of introducing some important information on which we will rely in our reading of the Gospels and as a means of highlighting the important principle of studying the first-century-Jewish context of the Gospel writings.

Reading the Gospels as Narratives

The Gospels Are Narratives

In an earlier chapter we saw that the gospel is the story of what God has done in the life, death, and resurrection of Jesus Christ, in faithfulness to his promises to his people Israel, to save and rescue a people for himself. Frequently, many of us like to take a piece of the gospel and turn it into a short propositional, devotional, or creedal statement. And there are understandable reasons for this. Jesus is, after all, a wisdom teacher, and his words justifiably provide guidance in a variety of situations and circumstances. "Do not worry about tomorrow, for tomorrow will bring worries of its own. Today's trouble is enough for today" (Matt. 6:34 NRSVue). Additionally, Paul (among others) summarizes the gospel with propositional statements rather than telling a story: "Christ died for our sins according to the Scriptures, he was buried, he was raised on the third day according to the Scriptures" (1 Cor. 15:3–5). But these statements require a broader narrative within which they make sense. This broader narrative is, in fact, the stories of Jesus as recounted by the four evangelists. While we might abstract a portion of Jesus's teaching to provide comfort, or isolate one episode to be read devotionally, or use select verses as the raw materials for our doctrines—all of which are perfectly justifiable—the Gospels are best honored first and foremost as stories or narrative depictions of Jesus's life. Meaning and form are interdependent; therefore, to read any text well requires familiarity with the basic workings of its genre. As Jonathan Pennington notes, "To wisely read any narrative or story we must be sensitive to the form that stories take and how they function."[1] Furthermore, narratives have an experiential and self-involving quality that can enrich not only our reading experiences but also our faith.

SIDEBAR 6.1

Story and Discourse

Reading narrative criticisms requires some familiarity with the distinction between the "story" and "discourse" levels of the narrative. While a strict distinction is sometimes difficult to maintain, the story refers to *what* happens in the text (i.e., actual events), while discourse refers to *how* the story is told. This might include the point of view of the author, the selection of events, the timing and pacing of the story, and more. The distinction between story and discourse was popularized by Seymour Chatman, *Story and Discourse: Narrative Structure in Fiction and Film*.[a]

Narrative criticism, in the words of Jeannine Brown, "attends to the literary and storied qualities of a biblical narrative, like a Gospel."[2] This means that we read each Gospel attentive to how each particular evangelist *tells his story about Jesus*. Many of us intuitively adopt a synthesizing, harmonizing approach whereby the four Gospels blend together in order to create something like a "life of Jesus." But each Gospel has a distinctive take on how to select, arrange, order, and theologize the Jesus traditions. When we read each individual Gospel episode within the larger literary framework of that Gospel as a whole, we are better equipped to construct a fuller portrait of the evangelists' aims and purposes, and therefore better able to understand what they are telling us about Jesus. For example, Jesus's three parables in Luke 15 (lost sheep [vv. 3–7]; lost coin [vv. 8–10]; lost son [vv. 11–32]) work together as stories interpreting Jesus's consistent act of eating with sinners and tax collectors (vv. 1–2). The parables explain Jesus's activity as enactments of God's searching and rescuing those who are lost. Examples could be multiplied to show how each evangelist intentionally connects each episode to what precedes and what comes after, but the basic point to note here is that Jesus's teachings and actions are enriched and more deeply understood when read within their literary context. When we do this, we are able to see how Luke is concerned to highlight Jesus's ministry of table fellowship as breaking down boundaries and creating space for the lost to encounter God's kingdom. Rather than continuing to look at examples here, we will work through this principle in great detail in our examinations of the four Gospels. 6.1

As opposed to other methods such as source criticism, which uses a Gospels synopsis to engage in "horizontal readings" and looks at parallels and differences between distinct Gospel writings, narrative (or literary) readings are primarily attuned to making sense of each Gospel's literary framework, devices, and theology on its own terms.[3] 6.2

The Primary Elements of Biblical Narrative

If we want to understand how to read the Gospels as narratives, it's incumbent on us that we understand the basic building blocks of biblical narrative that will guide us in our reading of the Gospels in the next section.

1. *Plot*. The authors of *Mark as Story* note, "Plot has to do with events: how they are arranged, how they are connected, and what they reveal." Focusing on a story's plot "enables us to see the design of events that gives a narrative its meaning and direction."[4] As is true with many stories, conflict plays a major role in the plot of the Gospels. Each Gospel alerts us immediately to the fact that Jesus is God's beloved Son and the one upon whom the Spirit dwells (e.g., Mark 1:9–11; John 1:32–34). Jesus is favored and loved by God, but he is in conflict with much of the rest of society. Jesus is in conflict with the powers of Satan through exorcisms; Jesus is in conflict with many of the Jewish leaders; on occasion there is even conflict between Jesus and his disciples; and Jesus ultimately comes into conflict with the imperial authorities. As one works through each of the Gospels, one notices *rising tension* as the conflicts increase. The reader wonders, Will the disciples ever understand Jesus's teachings? Will the leaders of Israel accept his message or will they succeed in silencing him? For each Gospel narrative, the rising tension is evident during Jesus's final week, when, for example, Peter denies him and Judas betrays him, when Jesus's temple cleansing provokes the anger of the leaders, and when Jesus prays to his Father in the garden. The plot comes to a climax at Jesus's death, where the Jewish leaders, the imperial authorities, and Satan are involved in crucifying him. The narrative resolution is largely found in the stories of Jesus's empty tomb, resurrection, and appearances to the disciples, where many of the Gospels' story threads are finally resolved.
2. *Setting*. Setting refers to the geographical locations, social and political institutions, constructed places such as households and temples, and the temporal and spatial markers within which the plot of the story takes place. The setting is easily overlooked, but frequently it is central to the plot of the story and, in the Gospels, often carries theological significance. Mark's Gospel, for example, often seems to work with a contrast between synagogue and household in terms of receptivity to Jesus's teaching. In John's Gospel, the Jewish feasts almost always bear theological significance in communicating something significant about Jesus's identity. Jesus's teaching carries further revelatory significance on Matthew's Gospel when we observe the significance of the location of

SIDEBAR 6.2

Narrative Resurgence in Reading the Gospels

"Horizontal readings" (source, form, and redaction criticism) dominated twentieth-century scholarship on the Gospels. In the 1980s, however, a major resurgence in reading the Gospels as narratives took place. The most foundational are the following: Jack Kingsbury, *Matthew as Story* (1988); David Rhoads, Joanna Dewey, and Donald Michie, *Mark as Story* (1982); Robert Tannehill, *The Narrative Unity of Luke-Acts* (1986–90); Alan Culpepper, *The Anatomy of the Fourth Gospel* (1983).[b]

the mountain as a site for his teaching. The contrast, or relationship, between heaven and earth also plays a crucial role in the Gospels. In Mark's Gospel, it is significant that God "breaks open" the heavens in order to send his Spirit on Jesus and declare that Jesus is his beloved Son (Mark 1:9–11). The authors of *Mark as Story* summarize: "The arrival of God's rule changes cosmic space, because the power of God from above is now available on earth for healing and exorcism. The power of God's rule breaks out of local, national, and natural boundaries to make all space God's space."[5] A careful reading of Matthew's Gospel also shows a consistent cosmological contrast between heaven and earth, and this contrast reveals "the tension that currently exists between heaven and earth, between God's realm and ways and humanity's, especially as it relates to God's kingdom . . . versus humanity's kingdoms."[6]

3. *Characterization.* "Characterization is the art of bringing to life the characters in a story through what they say and do and in relation to other characters in the story."[7] The narrator plays a key role here in either *telling* or *showing* the reader the characterization of individuals and groups. For example, Luke shows us that Jesus is a journeyer when, in the so-called travel narrative (Luke 9:51–19:44), he is depicted as journeying on the way to Jerusalem like an itinerant wanderer; Luke tells us almost nothing about the actual geographical locations of Jesus, and this reveals that Luke is more concerned to show us something about Jesus's character. Luke can also simply tell his audience that the reason why the Pharisees rejected Jesus's teaching on wealth and possessions is that they loved money (Luke 16:14). Luke shows more directly their characterization as rejecting Jesus's ministry of hospitality when he portrays them as inviting Jesus to meals and treating him as an enemy. Jesus, conversely, is often described before a miracle as "having compassion" (7:11–13), and therefore his acts of healing are ultimately acts of his mercy. Titles and honorifics such as Son of Man, Messiah, Son of God, and Teacher are another important way in which the Gospels characterize Jesus (and others). These designations almost invariably have scriptural resonances, and determining their meaning involves a complex interplay between those resonances and the way the evangelists depict Jesus's activities. In Mark's Gospel, for example, Jesus consistently speaks of himself as the Son of Man, whereas other characters identify him as the Messiah and the Son of God. What do these titles mean? And what does it say about Jesus that he adopts "Son of Man" to describe himself? We can also learn about characters based on their place in society. Are they male or female?

Rich or poor? Jewish or gentile? Attending to whether they conform to societal expectations or act in exceptional ways will shed light on their role in the story.[8] We also learn about characters by paying attention to their motives, emotions, and character traits. Are they motivated by compassion, fear, love of honor? In what ways are their character traits and emotions related to the author's evaluative standpoint?

4. *Intertextuality.* Intertextuality most simply refers to the act whereby one written text cites or evokes another text. The Scriptures of Israel provide the framework and background for each of the four Gospels as they repeatedly narrate the story of Jesus within the context of God's election of Abraham and covenant with Israel. Sometimes the Gospel authors explicitly cite an Old Testament text to provide the lens for their story. For example, each of the four Gospels cites Isaiah 40 as the lens for interpreting the ministry of John the Baptist (Matt. 3:3; Mark 1:3; Luke 3:4–6; John 1:23). By evoking Isaiah 40 and its call to "prepare the way for the Lord," the evangelists interpret John's ministry as one of readying Israel for God's climactic act whereby he would come to be with his people, forgive their sins, provide salvation, and restore Jerusalem. Matthew's Gospel repeatedly engages in direct citations in order to frame the meaning and significance of Jesus's ministry (e.g., Isa. 7:14 in 1:23; Mic. 5:2, 4 in 2:6; Hosea 11:1 in 2:15; Jer. 31:15 in 2:18). Matthew's consistent narration of the events surrounding Jesus's birth through these Old Testament intertexts enables the reader to see that Jesus fulfills God's covenantal promises to be with his people, rule them as a good shepherd, and rescue them through a new exodus. On another occasion, a Gospel story may simply (but clearly) evoke a biblical precedent. For example, Luke's story of Jesus's transfiguration does not explicitly cite an Old Testament text, but the descriptive details of a high mountain; a transfigured face; a conversation between Moses, Elijah, and Jesus about his exodus; and the cloud clearly resonate with stories of Moses and Sinai (Luke 9:28–36). Often, as we saw briefly above, the settings of the biblical stories carry intertextual significance. Mountains, sea, wilderness, Jewish feasts, the Jerusalem temple—these settings are not incidental details but rather evoke Israel's Scriptures in order to frame Jesus's activities.[9] 6.3

SIDEBAR 6.3

Characterization and Intertextuality

The Gospels often use intertextuality in order to characterize Jesus. For example, each Gospel writer characterizes Jesus as the suffering Messiah by frequently invoking the Davidic psalms to portray Jesus as faithful to God in the midst of his sufferings and as one who confidently trusts God for his vindication. For example, Mark depicts Jesus praying the words of David's lament in his trials in the garden (Pss. 42:6, 11; 42:5 in Mark 14:34). Luke and John show how Jesus's persecutors play the role of the enemies of the Davidic king (Ps. 22:17 in Luke 23:35a; Ps. 22:18 in Luke 23:34b; Ps. 69:21 in Luke 23:36; Ps. 69:9a in John 2:17; Ps. 69:21 in John 19:28–29). And Luke shows Jesus praying the psalms in confident expectation of his resurrection (Ps. 31:5a in Luke 23:46a).

5. *Sequencing and arrangement*. The evangelists do not simply stitch together their stories as random collections of important material. Rather, careful study of the Gospels shows that they select and arrange their stories carefully. Matthew, for example, arranges his material in such a way that it alternates back and forth between story and discourse with the result that Jesus gives five great speeches (Matt. 5–7; 10; 13; 18; 23–25). The sequencing of his material in this way obviously contributes to the characterization of Jesus as the great teacher of wisdom to Israel along the lines of Moses. Or, in Mark's Gospel we find Jesus "on the way" and on three occasions teaching his disciples that the Son of Man must suffer and die in Jerusalem (Mark 8:27–32a; 9:30–32; 10:32–34). On each occasion, the disciples misunderstand Jesus's teaching about the necessity of his death (8:32–33; 9:33–34; 10:35–40), to which Jesus responds with a corrective teaching on discipleship (8:34–9:1; 9:35–50; 10:41–45). We are able to see Mark's distinctive way of showing us that discipleship is rooted in the confession and following of a Messiah who laid down his power and authority in order to suffer in obedience to God's purposes.
6. *Narrator*. The narrator is a literary device that the author uses in order to tell a story. In our four Gospels, the narrator is not a character *within* the story but rather is an invisible and omniscient storyteller who speaks from *outside* the narrative.[10] As a result, sometimes the narrator engages in explaining the feelings or emotions of characters, shares short asides in order to explain customs or the meaning of words, and provides the theological context for interpreting Jesus's ministry (e.g., Mark 1:1–15; John 1:1–18). The narrator also employs literary devices to tell his story such as poetry, hymn, irony, *inclusio* (a bookend or bracket), and foreshadowing. 6.4

SIDEBAR 6.4

The Narrator and the Audience

The narrator often provides privileged information only to the reader. This can create a reading experience where the drama is found in watching to see how the characters in the story respond to Jesus and whether it aligns with the narrator's point of view. For example, in the Gospel of Mark, the narrator gives a prologue that provides crucial information about Jesus to the reader. Mark tells the reader right away that Jesus is the Messiah, the Son of God, the one stronger than Satan, and the one who will baptize with the Spirit (Mark 1:1–15). Much of the drama of Mark's story, then, will consist in how the story's characters respond to Jesus's true identity as revealed in the prologue.

Narrative and Theological Meaning

But how does biblical narrative "make meaning"? How do we understand the relationship between narrative and theological meaning?

First, narratives construct and project possible worlds.[11] Through its construction of a plot, narrative imitates reality and thereby creates new worlds, a certain ordered way of seeing reality, including human life and experience.[12] Narrative makes meaning, then, not through setting forth timeless doctrinal concepts or propositions; rather, narrative creates a new world, a new way of interpreting the world through its representation of time, characters, and action. As Jeannine Brown says, "Stories not only represent our reality, but they also help us to understand and speak of our lived experience coherently."[13] Furthermore, narrative is intrinsically moralizing in that it produces an ordered world, in conformity to the author's viewpoint, and thereby confers meaning on reality. The same is true for all narrative representations of history, for before the creation of the work the author has selected the narrative strategies, construction of plot, closure of story, and meaning of the events that will make up the narrative.[14] Thus, narratives do not only describe what happened; they also explain why it happened. Every narrative, then, has a "moralizing impulse" in that it claims something like "this is what the world is like" or "imagine if the world was like this."[15]

Second, a true understanding of a narrative occurs only when the reader understands their world in light of the narrative. Narratives have a mediating role in that they reconfigure the "real world" for the purpose of transforming "the world of the reader."[16] Narratives are inherently participatory in that they redescribe the world and invite the reader to inhabit this new world, to accept its premises as true, and to be addressed and transformed. Narrative makes meaning when the reader enters into a dialogue with the text and considers the fit (or not!) between the story and the world of the reader. 6.5

The Gospels, however, are different from a novel in that their vision claims to constitute the very world of the reader. Given that their subject matter is the one God, who has intervened within history through Jesus to

SIDEBAR 6.5

Narrative and Meaning

The meaning of a narrative is found in the relationship between the story world of the text and the real world of its reader. For example, I can claim to understand Dostoevsky's *The Brothers Karamazov* when I reflect on what it would mean for me to live in a world where there is no God and, therefore, where murder and all else are permitted and go unpunished. I thereby participate in the narrative by understanding myself, my situation, and the world in the light of the author's projected world. To give another example, one of my favorite novels is *A Man in Full* by Thomas Wolfe. When I read the story, I enter into the world the author has constructed about late-twentieth-century Atlanta, about race relations, about the social life of upper-class corporate moguls. I enter into a world where life circumstances and the rise and fall of characters are due to their obsession with wealth, status, and luxury. I encounter an imprisoned man who, however, discovers that Stoic philosophy can counter the fleeting circumstances of life and experiences a transformed life despite difficult outward circumstances. Narratives construct possible worlds for me to enter into and consider; they allow me to align myself with—or reject—the attitudes and behaviors of the characters. The meaning of these novels resides in my reflection on the relationship between the world of the story and my own world. Narratives are, then, inherently formational and press the reader to make decisions, to accept or reject their premises regarding how the world works, to identify with characters, and so on. Narrative invites readers to "a fundamental acceptance of its premises, an adjustment of vision according to its perceptions, and a decision to act as though these premises and perceptions were not only real but valid."[c]

fulfill the promises he made to Israel and for the salvation of the world, the Gospels make totalizing claims on their readers. "These stories claim to offer a framework—a beginning, an end, a center—for all of history, and they propose that our lives and all other events have meaning only to the extent that they fit into that framework."[17] In a sense, the reader is included within the world projected by the Gospels. Thus, readers are to evaluate their very lives, beliefs, and behaviors in light of the Gospel narratives and to draw on them as scripts to perform in their very lives.[18] As we read the Gospel narratives, we will be attentive, then, to both the particular elements of the narrative and how each author tells his story as well as how each Gospel story works to draw its readers into the text such that they are drawn into a relationship with God. Readers will find that they, too, are implicated within the same problems and vices that plague the characters of the Gospel narratives, and conversely they are invited to identify with Jesus and those characters who identify with God's plan.

Learning the concrete elements of biblical narrative along with reflecting on how narrative relates to theological meaning is important, but there is one concrete practice that is nonnegotiable for growing in one's ability to read the Gospels well: simply the habitual practice of reading and rereading. Good readers of the Gospels will read both the discrete pericopes and the entirety of each Gospel multiple times. By reading a Gospel repeatedly, one is able to discern its overarching structure and come to "an understanding of a Gospel in its totality—as a narrative unity."[19] One can discern the Gospels' structures, distinct literary motifs, characterization of individuals and groups, and particular theological aims. Further, we should appreciate the gift that God has given his people in terms of the storied nature of our Gospels. Stories hold great power as they draw us into their world and allow us to experience Jesus's compassion for the sinner and the outcast, his unrelenting obedience to his Father, and his suffering during the crucifixion. The Gospel stories hold incredible power as we reflect on whether we identify with the humble tax collector ashamed to lift his head to God during his prayer *or* with the proud Pharisee who is confident of his standing with God and looks down on others (Luke 18:9–14). Attending to these Gospel stories in a way that reflects on the relationship between them and our own lives has untold power to produce a transformed life.

Reading the Gospels for Transformative Discipleship

The Gospels are the revelatory Word of God that show us who God is and how he has acted through the Son and the Holy Spirit to accomplish salvation and to form a holy people for himself. We read them well not by holding them at arm's length, pretending that we can give an "objective" account about what they say; rather, we recognize as we read God's Word that the Gospels were written and are used by God for theological transformation. That is, they call us to enter into a certain way of life.

As I argued in the preceding chapter, the very self-involving nature of narrative means that when we read a Gospel, we are involved in reflecting on the relationship between its story and our own lives. "We as readers become part of the story we are reading, and thereby the world of the story and our world merge."[1] Will we accept or reject the claims that Jesus is the Son of God (Matt. 3:16–17), God's very salvation (Luke 2:28–30), and the Word who was with and is God (John 1:1–2)? We are forced to choose whether we will align ourselves with the characters we are confronted with or reject their behavior and beliefs. Will we agree with the Pharisees and scribes that Jesus's indiscriminate table fellowship with sinners reveals that he is a drunkard and a glutton, or will we see Jesus as the great shepherd-king who searches for and rescues the lost among God's people (Luke 7:34; 15:1–32)? Will we agree with Jesus that one can confess him to be the Messiah but have no true understanding of what this means unless we understand the cross (Mark 8:27–33)? A community of believers who read these

Gospels should find themselves communally reflecting on what they believe, how they behave, and the entirety of their lives as they encounter God's word in these writings. In what follows I make four brief calls for how we should approach the Gospels as the Word of God that aims to transform us into faithful disciples of the living Christ.

A Call to Humility and Prayer

The subject matter of the Gospels is God as revealed in the person of Jesus Christ. The goal of reading is fellowship with God and transformation into the image of Jesus Christ. Therefore, to rightly read these texts requires an appropriate posture as we read. Jesus Christ is the teacher, and we are the disciple-learners. We do not read the Gospels with the hope of mastering the texts or pridefully using them in the service of our theological agendas; rather, we read them with a posture of humility, knowing that they critique, convict, and challenge us to repent—that is, to change our lives in humble obedience to the Christ of the Gospels. Techniques, methods, and skills for reading the Gospels are important. But they cannot replace the necessity of coming to the Gospels with attention, humility, trust, and openness to receive God's revelation.[2] 7.1 7.2

Here I will highlight one disposition and one practice in particular that are necessary for rightly reading the Gospels.[3] First is the disposition of humility. Jesus repeatedly holds up humility as a central characteristic of his followers. We might think of his beatitudes in the Sermon on the Mount: "Blessed are the poor in spirit, for theirs is the kingdom of heaven" and "Blessed are the meek, for they will inherit the earth" (Matt. 5:3, 5). Jesus's call for humility is rooted in his own character, as he calls his followers to learn from his way of life as one who is "gentle and humble in heart" (Matt. 11:29). Throughout the Gospels those who draw Jesus's ire and strong rebuke are the prideful and arrogant. We might think again of Luke's parable of the tax collector and the Pharisee. One embodies a disposition of humility and remorse over sin, while the other is pleased with himself and looks down on others in arrogance (Luke 18:9–13). The story concludes with Jesus's pronouncement, "I tell you, this man [the humble tax collector] went down to his home justified rather than the other, for all who exalt themselves will be humbled, but all who humble themselves will

SIDEBAR 7.1

Thomas à Kempis on Humility

"All naturally desire knowledge, but what good is knowledge without the fear of God? Surely humble peasants who serve God are better than proud philosophers who strive to understand the ways of the universe and neglect their own souls. If you know yourself well you will become lowly in your own sight and not delight in the praises of others. If I understood all things in the world and had not love, what help would that be to me in the sight of God who will judge the things that I do?"[a]

be exalted" (18:14 NRSVue). The parable enables us to evaluate numerous characters within the Gospels who, due to their pride, fail to respond rightly to Jesus's teachings. For Jesus, then, a flourishing life requires the ability to take the humble posture of disciple who can learn the way of Jesus and embrace his teachings. As we read the Gospels, we too must approach them with the humble expectation that God wants to teach us, to turn us away from sinful desires and practices, and to give to us the life that can be found only in Jesus.

Second is the practice of prayer. If the goal of reading the Gospels is communion with God, then prayer is a divine gift that enables God's people to rightly read and respond to the Gospels. Jesus declares that for those who ask, search, and knock, God gives the Spirit of illumination and wisdom (Luke 11:9–13). In John's Gospel, Jesus declares that he will answer the prayers of those who pray in his name and that he will send them "the Spirit of truth" (John 14:13–17). Though Jesus has ascended to heaven, the Spirit whom he sends them will teach and remind the disciples of his teachings (John 14:25–26; 15:26–27). We could add more character traits and dispositions to our list. For example, the person who has already made progress in financial generosity and simplicity of lifestyle will be able to understand *and follow* Jesus's frequent teachings on self-renunciation (e.g., Mark 8:34–38; Luke 6:20–36). We read the Gospels well when we approach them as divine revelation and when we seek a posture of humble submission and through prayer seek God's Spirit to illuminate our hearts and minds in order to lead us into the path of truth. 7.3

SIDEBAR 7.2

Moral Virtue as Necessary for Biblical Interpretation

Many of the early church fathers recognized that practices and dispositions such as prayer, fasting, and purity were necessary for right reading of the Gospels. Augustine, for example, states, "The mind should be cleansed so that it is able to see the divine light and cling to it once it is seen" (*On Christian Doctrine* 10).[b] Athanasius of Alexandria holds up the ascetic Antony as one who, despite being illiterate, understands the Scriptures better than the learned due to his moral purity and virtue. Irenaeus's critique of the Gnostic interpreters often emphasizes their moral corruption, as Irenaeus could assume the relationship between doctrinal error and immoral character. Proper interpretation of the Scriptures requires proper moral formation and the appropriate posture of humility when reading them. Stated simply, the church fathers believed that "lives that mirrored the message were best disposed to see that message."[c]

A Call to Worship the Living Risen Christ

Jesus is the definitive revelation of God. Jesus brings God's purposes and plans to their fulfillment. The Scriptures of Israel anticipate his incarnation, life, death, and resurrection. Thus, we read the Gospels rightly when we expect them to reveal who God is for us in the person of Jesus Christ; as such, worship is consistently the right response when we read the Gospels.[4] John's Gospel makes crystal clear to us that Jesus is the supreme revelation

SIDEBAR 7.3

Dietrich Bonhoeffer on Prayer and Scripture

"Prayer means nothing else but the readiness and willingness to receive and appropriate the Word, and, what is more, to accept it in one's personal situation, particular tasks, decisions, sins, and temptations. . . . And we may be certain that our prayer will be heard, because it is a response to God's Word and promise. Because God's Word has found its fulfillment in Jesus Christ, all prayers that we pray conforming to this Word are certainly heard and answered in Jesus Christ."[d]

of God: "No one has ever seen God. It is God the unique Son who is in the bosom of the Father who has made him known" (John 1:18). John's Gospel repeatedly identifies Jesus as the way to the Father and the one who makes the Father known (e.g., 14:1–14). The testimonies of the four Gospels are unified in their proclamation that Jesus has been raised from the dead and exalted to God's right hand. Jesus is the living and risen Christ who shares God's throne. As such, the New Testament writings show us that he is worthy to receive worship (Col. 1:15–20; Rev. 4–5). Matthew's Gospel gives us character portraits of those who rightly recognize Jesus's identity and bow down before him to give him worship (Matt. 2:11; 28:9).

There are many Gospel passages where our primary response is not one of imitation of Jesus or character transformation but rather one of worship of the living Christ. I think that this is obvious for certain passages where Jesus is shown to have power and authority that transcend that of even heroic humans. When Jesus calms the storm and the disciples are filled with amazement and ask, "Who then is this that he commands the winds and the water and they obey him?" (Luke 8:25), the right response of the reader is something along the lines of, "No one can do this except God!" The appropriate response to this text, then, is worship of Jesus. Or, note the story of when Jesus walks on water and calls Peter out of the boat to come to him (Matt. 14:22–33). It seems that we too should respond as do the disciples: "And those in the boat worshiped him, saying, 'Truly you are the Son of God'" (14:33). When Jesus declares forgiveness of a paralytic's sins, the scribes ask, "Who can forgive sins but God alone?" (Mark 2:7). Jesus then demonstrates his authority by healing the man. Mark notes, "Everyone was amazed and glorified God, saying, 'We have never seen anything like this!'" (2:12b).

Luke's Gospel frequently shows how humans respond to Jesus's mighty acts of healing, teaching, and exorcisms with the language of rejoicing and praising God. When a woman with a bent back is healed, her first response is to give glory to God (Luke 13:13), and this results in the "entire crowd rejoicing over all the glorious things he was doing" (13:17b). When ten Samaritan lepers are healed, only one returns to Jesus "to give glory to God" (17:18). Jesus's healing of a blind man near Jericho nicely encapsulates this motif. Jesus's granting of sight to the blind man results in the man's "giving glory to God," and the crowd in turn "gives praise to God" (18:43). We'll look at this theme in detail later, but for now we can simply note that Luke is working hard to align his reader with those characters who respond to the activities of Jesus with worship.

Wikimedia Commons

Figure 7.1. Rembrandt van Rijn, *Christ in the Storm on the Lake of* Galilee

Many know that John's Gospel has Jesus repeatedly making "I am" statements. Some of them have a predicate: "I am the bread of life that came down from heaven" (John 6:51) and "I am the good shepherd" (10:11). Sometimes Jesus simply declares, "I am" (6:20; 18:5). The "I am" statements reveal the identity of Jesus as they also draw on the statement of the God of Israel to Moses at the burning bush where God reveals his special name: "I AM WHO I AM" (Exod. 3:14–15).

When we read the Gospels, we are brought face-to-face in a personal encounter with the living and risen Jesus Christ. While these texts have untold transformative potential, our first response should be one of worship. In other words, "We must first receive Jesus as gift before we can have him as example. . . . We must first read and receive the Gospels as a revelatory act of God on our behalf in which we are given Jesus himself."[5]

A Call to Faithful Discipleship

In an earlier chapter we saw that one of the main reasons for writing a biography is the desire to hold up a character who is worthy of admiration and emulation. And, in fact, in all four Gospels, Jesus consistently calls his disciples and all who listen to his message to follow his teaching and his manner of life. Jesus is a wise teacher who rightly interprets God's will for his people. Jesus is emphatic that his words are of the utmost seriousness and must be followed (Matt. 7:21–29). In his words are "spirit and life" (John 6:63). And so, Jesus's disciples will pursue peace, reconciliation, marital fidelity, honesty, and love of their enemies (Matt. 5:21–48). As they attempt to follow Jesus's teachings, they have Jesus's very life as the

SIDEBAR 7.4

The Church in the Gospels

The apostle Paul is the one who most frequently emphasizes followers of Jesus as "the church" or as "the body of Christ" (1 Cor. 12:12, 27). But the Gospels also show Jesus calling a community into existence that will, in fact, embody his teachings and his ministry. Before Jesus delivers his Sermon on the Plain, in Luke's Gospel, he prays on a mountain, calls twelve apostles, and delivers his teaching at the foot of the mountain to his disciples and the crowd (Luke 6:12–19). This is the covenant community that will implement his teachings; they are his true family "who hear the word of God and do it" (Luke 8:21). In Matthew's Gospel, Jesus declares that he will build his church upon Peter and the confession that Jesus is the Christ, and this church will embody his teachings of mercy, forgiveness, and reconciliation (Matt. 16–18). Matthew concludes, of course, with Jesus's commission to the disciples to go into all the world and make disciples by teaching everything that Jesus himself had taught them (Matt. 28:18–20). In John's Gospel, the Spirit will empower the disciples to testify to the world about Jesus and his teachings (John 16:1–15).

pattern to follow.[6] Jesus himself embodies humility and meekness (Matt. 11:28–30); he dispenses mercy to the needy and afflicted (Matt. 9:27; 15:22); he suffers as the innocent and righteous one (Luke 23:1–5, 39–47); when persecuted, he doesn't retaliate (Matt. 26:67; 27:30); he prays privately (Mark 1:35–37); and he sacrificially serves and loves his disciples and those around him (Luke 22:24–27; John 13:1–20). 7.4

The Gospels repeatedly make it clear that Jesus's life *is the very pattern of God's intended shape for human life and behavior*. One of the ways the Gospels do this is through showing how the disciples, albeit very imperfectly, emulate the teaching and behavior of Jesus. This is seen clearly in those accounts where Jesus commissions the disciples for ministry in Matthew 10 and Luke 10. The disciples share in Jesus's authority in order to continue his mission (Matt. 10:1). Thus, like Jesus, they proclaim the gospel to the lost sheep of Israel (Matt. 10:5–6; cf. 15:24), proclaim the good news of the kingdom of heaven (10:7; cf. 4:17), perform merciful healings and exorcisms (10:8; cf. 9:32–33; 12:15), raise the dead (10:8; cf. 9:18–19, 23–26), appear before the Sanhedrin (10:17; cf. 26:57–68), and are dragged before governors (10:18; cf. 27:1–2, 11–26).[7] Jesus's very life provides the pattern, then, that his disciples are called on to emulate. 7.5 7.6 7.7

The testimony of the Gospels and the entire New Testament is that Jesus is the living, risen Christ. As such, we do not approach him simply as a great historical figure whose teaching holds historical interest; rather, we approach him as the living resurrected Christ, whom we are called to follow, obey, and learn from. Luke Timothy Johnson states this well: "If Jesus lives, then it must be as life-giver. Jesus is not simply a figure of the past in that case, but a person in the present; not merely a memory that we can analyze and manipulate, but an agent who can confront and instruct us. What we learn *about* him must therefore include what we continue to learn *from* him."[8] Thus, as we read the Gospels, we should consistently be asking the question of what "faithful discipleship" looks like in our context based on Jesus's teachings and pattern of life. We live in another time and location than that of Jesus and the first disciples. Thus, faithful discipleship and learning

SIDEBAR 7.5

Gerard Manley Hopkins, "As Kingfishers Catch Fire"

Gerard Manley Hopkins's poem calls forth different aspects of creation living into their particular vocation. A kingfisher exposes its orange beauty as it dives for its prey; a dragonfly beats its wings; a rock makes a sound when thrown into a well. "Selves—goes its self; *myself* it speaks and spells, Crying *What I do is me: for that I came*." But notice the second stanza's emphasis on humanity, transformed by Christ and thereby enabled to embody Christ's presence "in ten thousand places."[e]

As kingfishers catch fire, dragonflies draw flame;
  As tumbled over rim in roundy wells
  Stones ring; like each tucked string tells, each hung bell's
Bow swung finds tongue to fling out broad its name;
Each mortal thing does one thing and the same:
  Deals out that being indoors each one dwells;
  Selves—goes its self; *myself* it speaks and spells,
Crying *What I do is me: for that I came.*

I say more: the just man justices;
  Keeps grace: that keeps all his goings graces;
Acts in God's eye what in God's eye he is—
  Christ. For Christ plays in ten thousand places,
Lovely in limbs, and lovely in eyes not his
To the Father through the features of men's faces.[f]

SIDEBAR 7.6

Major Gospel Texts on Discipleship

Matthew 11:28–30

Come to Me, all who are weary and heavy-laden, and I will give you rest. Take My yoke upon you and learn from Me, for I am gentle and humble in heart, and YOU WILL FIND REST FOR YOUR SOULS. For My yoke is easy and My burden is light. (NASB)

Mark 8:34–38

Then he called the crowd to him along with his disciples and said: "Whoever wants to be my disciple must deny themselves and take up their cross and follow me. For whoever wants to save their life will lose it, but whoever loses their life for me and for the gospel will save it. What good is it for someone to gain the whole world, yet forfeit their soul? Or what can anyone give in exchange for their soul? If anyone is ashamed of me and my words in this adulterous and sinful generation, the Son of Man will be ashamed of them when he comes in his Father's glory with the holy angels." (NIV)

Luke 22:24–27

And there arose also a dispute among them as to which one of them was regarded to be greatest. And He said to them, "The kings of the Gentiles lord it over them; and those who have authority over them are called 'Benefactors.' But it is not this way with you, but the one who is the greatest among you must become like the youngest, and the leader like the servant. For who is greater, the one who reclines at the table or the one who serves? Is it not the one who reclines at the table? But I am among you as the one who serves." (NASB)

John 13:13–15

You call Me Teacher and Lord; and you are right, for so I am. If I then, the Lord and the Teacher, washed your feet, you also ought to wash one another's feet. For I gave you an example that you also should do as I did to you. (NASB)

SIDEBAR 7.7

Imitating Christ's Character in the New Testament

Along with the four Gospels, the rest of the New Testament writings share the theme of the imitation of Christ in that they assume and argue for Jesus as the supreme revelation of God's intent for human life. Paul, for example, exhorts the church in Philippi to have "the same mind in you that was in Christ Jesus" (Phil. 2:5). To the church in Corinth he commands, "Be imitators of me, as I am of Christ" (1 Cor. 11:1). To the author of Hebrews, Jesus is "the author and perfecter of our faith" who has finished the race we are currently still running (Heb. 12:2). First Peter says that Christ's faithfulness in the midst of suffering has left behind "an example so that you should follow in his footsteps" (1 Pet. 2:21). First John consistently roots our love for one another in Jesus's example of love: "We know love by this, that he laid down his life for us—and we ought to lay down our lives for one another" (1 John 3:16).

from Jesus will not be a simple matter of rote repetition; rather, knowing how to follow the Jesus of our Gospels will require communal discernment together as God's people, a commitment to prayer and expectation of Spirit-illumination, and a constant and close attentiveness to the person of Jesus in the Gospels. Our fourth call, which we will explore next, can also stimulate our imaginations as we seek to learn from others the way of discipleship.

A Call to Learn about Jesus from World Christianity

Churches in many different places, speaking in different languages, and throughout the centuries have read the Gospels to learn what it means to follow Jesus. The impact that the Gospels, and those communities that have read them, have had on history, culture, and church life is immeasurable. Paying close attention to how the Gospels have been read in other cultures, time periods, and theological traditions can allow us to see the important relationship between the reading of the Gospel writings and the communities that seek to live out their meaning. Prior readings of the Gospels can broaden "our horizon by mediating a great treasury of experiences which other Christians have found."[9] Often the sources for these readings of the Gospels include hymns, liturgies, sermons, art, and books. While we can never know even a fraction of the many ways in which the Jesus of the Gospels has transformed societies, cultures, and individuals, our own reading of the Gospel writings can be sharpened and challenged when we have the curiosity to learn from other Christian communities.

We can learn from the early church fathers, for example, the role the Gospels play in articulating orthodox Christology. The church fathers provide significant help in clarifying the importance of Jesus's real humanity and divinity, the relationship between the Spirit and the Son, and the saving necessity of the incarnation of the Son of God. The church fathers are often involved in clarifying the grammar of the Christian faith as found in the four Gospels. Cyril of Alexandria (ca. 376–444), for example, provides a wealth of exegetical and theological knowledge for readers in his commentaries on the Gospel of John. Let's look briefly at one of his important theological conclusions. Many readers of the Gospels may find themselves perplexed—just as John the Baptist was!—when Jesus is baptized. If Jesus is sinless and divine, why would he need to undergo a baptism of repentance for the forgiveness of sins (Matt. 3:6)? Cyril notes that Jesus is the Messiah, the Son of God, and this indicates that he is humanity's representative. Cyril observes that in John 1:32–34, when Jesus receives the Holy Spirit at his baptism, the Spirit *remains* on Jesus. The Son of God receives the Spirit and preserves the Spirit to human nature. In this way, the Son becomes both the giver of the Spirit and its representative recipient. Jesus's baptism is thus emphasized by Cyril as the decisive event within salvation history, for it is here that the image of God is restored and the Spirit returns to transform and sanctify human nature. But human nature is not completely transformed, Cyril argues, until the resurrected Jesus anoints his disciples with the Spirit (John 20:22–23).

We can learn from African American readings of the Gospels how Jesus's teaching in the Sermon on the Mount and his consistent call to love "the other" provided fuel for the philosophy of nonviolence found in many of the leaders of the civil rights movement (Matt. 5:38–48; Luke 10:25–37). We can see how Black theologians found in Jesus the revelation of God's purposes to bring about justice and equity, and how Jesus called forth a movement in which people would join Christ in bringing about freedom and liberation.

From Latino/a theologians we can learn more fully about how Jesus's consistent identification with the poor and oppressed challenges the political and structural oppression of the weak and marginalized. We see how Jesus's vocation to bring good news to the poor, provide release for the captive and oppressed, and restore sight to the blind is part and parcel of the gospel of Jesus Christ (Luke 4:16–18). This Jesus is one who does not simply speak of an otherworldly future but rather calls forth economic justice, an end to racism, and judgment on the wealthy and powerful upholders of the status quo. For many of us, a Jesus who focuses on our praxis—behavior and lifestyle—as opposed to merely wanting us to believe certain facts about God is a Jesus who will challenge some of our most deeply held convictions and ways of seeing the world.

Pentecostal groups show us the central role the Holy Spirit plays in Jesus's ministry as well as how the same Spirit who anointed Jesus now empowers the church to continue to live out the story of Jesus in the Gospels. Anabaptists (and other peace traditions) hold up for us a Jesus who creates an alternative society that values peace, justice, and sacrificial love at all costs.

We could continue to add to our list as well as flesh out the ways in which we can learn about the Jesus of the Gospels from different peoples and from different time periods. But here my purpose is simply to suggest that our reading of the Gospels will be even richer when we listen to and learn together about Jesus from our fellow brothers and sisters in the faith. We do not necessarily need to adopt or agree with every interpretation and image of Jesus that is set forth, but often we will find some of our blind spots overcome as we learn from the global church, from ancient interpreters, and from other Christian traditions.

Summary of Part 2

I have set forth three broad claims that can guide us in our reading of the Gospels.

1. We read the Gospels recognizing that they are first-century Jewish literature. Therefore, one of the horizons within which we interpret them must be the ongoing history of God's relationship and dealings with his people Israel. This requires knowledge of the Old Testament Scriptures, which are so very frequently assumed or explicitly engaged as the appropriate context for understanding the identity and activities of Jesus. We explored a few examples whereby Jesus addressed his particular first-century Jewish context as it pertains to relating to foreign imperial powers, economic practices, and his vision for Israel. Understanding something about Israel's history functions as an important guide to us as we attempt to read the Gospels well.
2. The Gospels are narratives, and as such they are rightly read *in the first instance* as stories rather than as doctrinal treatises or devotional writings. This means that we need to have a basic understanding of the elements of biblical narrative, including plot, setting, characterization, intertextuality, sequencing and arrangement, and narrator. Each Gospel is its own self-contained story with its own particular way of telling the story of Jesus; as a result, our reading of the Gospels will give detailed attention to each Gospel on its own terms. We also explored how narratives "make meaning." They construct possible worlds for the readers to enter, but the Gospels are unique in their claim that this story *is* the real world. As such, they invite their readers to evaluate their own lives, beliefs, and behaviors as they encounter the Jesus of the Gospels.
3. The Gospels aim to produce theological transformation on the part of their audience. As such, while method and information are indeed important, nothing can replace the necessity of readers approaching the Gospels with prayer and humility. The Gospels are divine revelation as they depict the living and risen Jesus, who is meant to be worshiped, loved, and obeyed. Additionally, the Gospels call us to consider Jesus as the supreme and definitive revelation of God's pattern for human life. Thus, the Gospels are to be read as calling forth the imitation of Christ and the submission to his teaching on the part of the disciple who would follow him. Finally, theological transformation can take place when we learn about Jesus from other peoples, cultures, and periods of Christian history.

PART 3

Reading the Gospels

Now that we have explored the origins of our Gospels and their relationship to the historical Jesus of Nazareth (part 1) and have set forth three principles for how to best read the Gospels (part 2), we are ready to read each of the four canonical Gospels. I cannot emphasize enough the importance of reading each Gospel both on your own and in community. My hope is that the following chapters will be a fruitful guide as they let you see what I take to be some of the most important historical, literary, and theological themes of these texts. You will see that four chapters are devoted to each Gospel. One chapter examines some of the major questions related to the historical background of the Gospel. So, for example, we'll look at who authored the Gospels, for what reason they wrote, and how they composed their Gospel writing.

The next two chapters are the most extensive as they look at the literary or narrative artistry of each Gospel. A more predictable method, and one that I have rejected, is that of simply making a few comments about each Gospel sequentially—that is, working through the Gospel chapter by chapter. Instead, I try to show you how to read the Gospel well by looking at three key features. First, we look at the structural and narrative features of each Gospel. What narrative devices are used to tell the story? What is the structure of each Gospel, and how does the structure of the text work together with the plot? Second, I set forth a few key words and phrases of each Gospel writing. Each Gospel uses distinctive terms and phrases that often highlight an important literary aspect or theological truth of the text. Third, we take a more extended look at some of the main narrative threads of each Gospel.

The final chapter about each Gospel is focused on discipleship. As I've noted, the Gospels call us to live a certain way of life in worship of and obedience to the living Jesus. And Christians have been doing just this for centuries! So, in these chapters I briefly look at how the story and teachings of Jesus encourage us to be a certain kind of people, living a specific way of life. And, as I do this, I draw on wisdom from other faithful disciples who have sought to follow Jesus in their time and place through their own reading of the Gospels. I hope that these chapters on discipleship will also stimulate your prayers and imaginations as you seek to reflect on how the Spirit of the living Jesus is calling you to love him and to love others.

Matthew and History

Despite the scholarly consensus, which I have also argued for, that Mark's Gospel was both written first and used as a source for later Gospel writings, we will follow the order of the Christian canon, as well as the unanimous ordering of the Gospels in the earliest manuscripts, by beginning our study with the Gospel of Matthew. Many studies of the four Gospels begin with Mark because this allows them to show how Matthew uses Mark as a source and makes editorial changes and additions, but we will respect the church's canonical arrangement of the four Gospels.

While making strict distinctions between history, exegesis, and theology is impossible, in this chapter we'll focus on some of the major questions pertaining to Matthew's Gospel and history. For example: What role did Matthew play in the early church? What is its relationship to the other Gospels? Did someone named Matthew actually write this Gospel? What is the Gospel's perspective on the relationship between Jesus and Judaism?

Matthew and History

Matthew's Place in the History of Early Christianity

When we look at the earliest canon lists, early codices (ancient books), and testimony from church fathers, we find that there is a near unanimous consensus that Mathew comes first in order.[1] Sometimes the arrangement is the traditional one: Matthew, Mark, Luke, John; in some instances, the order is Matthew, John, Luke, Mark. The priority of Matthew in the canonical ordering coheres with what we saw in a previous chapter regarding the fact that sayings of Jesus in the General Epistles and the apostolic fathers most closely align with the wording as found in Matthew's Gospel. An examination of the relationship between Matthew and the earliest postapostolic Christian writings shows us that "it was Matthew which quickly established itself as *the* gospel par excellence, the natural place from which to expect to derive the authoritative account of the words and deeds of Jesus."[2] We can illustrate this by noting that almost all of us today know the version of the Lord's Prayer in Matthew's Gospel (Matt. 6:9–13) rather than the version in Luke's Gospel (Luke 11:2–4). The same was true of the early church: it was Matthew's version of the Lord's Prayer, among other sayings, with which the majority were most familiar. The popularity and preeminence of Matthew's Gospel, among the four, was almost certainly the primary factor leading to the early belief that Matthew was also the *first written Gospel*—a fact we noted in the discussion on the Synoptic problem in chapter 3. R. T. France summarizes what we will see: Matthew's Gospel "met more directly than the other gospels some of the deep-seated needs of the church; as a teaching document it provided, both in form and in content, what the church and its leaders wanted."[3]

What accounts for Matthew's apparent preeminence in the early centuries of the church? I can offer at least three suggestions. First, we can easily account for why Mark, despite being the earliest written Gospel and source for Matthew, would not (and did not) attain the same popularity as Matthew. Many important sayings and deeds of Jesus that were known orally by the earliest Christians were not passed along in Mark. And while some certainly believed that the disciple Peter stood behind the traditions of Mark's Gospel, it was not considered to have been written by an eyewitness of Jesus's ministry.

Second, and perhaps most importantly, is Matthew's depiction of Jesus as a wise teacher who engages in lengthy discourses instructing his followers about the law and righteousness (chaps. 5–7), preparing disciples for mission (chap. 10), expounding on the kingdom of God (chap. 13), declaring the origins and nature of the church (chap. 18), and preparing his followers for the final judgment (chaps. 24–25). These long blocks of Jesus's teaching provide essential wisdom for the ecclesial concerns of the earliest Christians. Some of the sayings of Jesus, as noted above, also have a liturgical quality to them, most notably the Lord's Prayer (6:9–13). For these reasons and more, some have supposed that Matthew's Gospel was composed in order to have a catechetical function, and others have noted that one of its main functions is to be an aid for Christian teachers.[4] Luke Timothy Johnson speaks to the catechetical character of Matthew's Gospel: "Matthew provides instructions for missionaries, discipline in the community, and forms of piety in a way that anticipates later church writings called church orders, the earliest of which is the *Didache* (usually dated ca. 90)."[5] As we will see in more detail, Matthew's Gospel sets out Jesus's teaching in a way that is much more systematic in its arrangement than what we find in the other Gospels. Thus, the content as well as the structure of Matthew make this Gospel's preeminence in the early church entirely understandable. And, in fact, some have noted that the best explanation for the Gospel author's goal in his composition is found in Jesus's statement about a "scribe who has been trained for the kingdom of heaven who brings out of his treasure what is new and what is old" (13:52).[6] Matthew, in other words, is a disciple of Jesus who functions like a wise scribe who produces a narrative explaining both the surprising and new work of God in Jesus but within the context of his Jewish heritage and Scriptures.

A third reason for the popularity of Matthew within the early church is the specific application it has to the social setting of the earliest Christians. Despite the frequency and popularity of the claim, it's not quite true to say that Matthew is "more Jewish" than the other Gospels. We'll see that Mark, Luke, and John are no less "Jewish" than Matthew; nevertheless, it is the case that the First Gospel is directly concerned with the difficult relationship between the Jewish followers of Jesus and the Jewish synagogue out of which the church emerged. As such, there is much "intra Jewish" argumentation that takes place in Matthew, and the author assumes that the readers are familiar with matters such as halakic disputes (i.e., how to interpret Torah; 5:20–48), food laws and ceremonial washings (15:1–20), and the temple tax (17:24–27). Jesus is a Jew making Jewish arguments about Torah, God's will, Israel's future, the Jewish temple, and so forth. Later gentile readers will read the text in new ways that will have significant ramifications for how Christians understand the relationship between Christianity and Judaism, but within Matthew's Gospel—despite all that is new and surprising—there is no evidence that Jesus (or his community) is rejecting Judaism or seeking to supplant it.

While Matthew does use the word "church" (Greek: *ekklēsia*) to describe the community that confesses Jesus as the Messiah (16:13–20), we need to be careful that we do not anachronistically set up a contrast between "church" and "synagogue" or, worse, between "Christianity" and "Judaism." Matthew narrates an intense conflict between Jesus (and his followers) and the Pharisees, scribes, and Jerusalem authorities, but we do well to note that the passionate differences occur *within Judaism*. One of Matthew's agendas is to narrate how Jesus fulfills the Torah (chaps. 1–2), rightly interprets Israel's Scriptures in strong contradistinction to the scribes and Pharisees (11:25–12:14; 23:1–39), is the embodied presence of Israel's God (1:23), and is the only one whose life and death can save God's people from their sins (1:21; 20:28; 26:28). Matthew's Gospel suggests that it was written in order to explain and justify the conviction that Jesus is the incarnate Messiah of God whose appearance results in a new and powerful understanding of Israel's Scriptures and the symbols, rituals, and institutions of the broader Judaism within which the movement took root. This Gospel strongly and exclusively identifies Israel's God with a final and singular messianic ruler who offers his life as *the sacrifice* for the sin of his people, is raised from the dead, and is enthroned to God's right hand as the universal and cosmic Lord. These convictions lead to a strong disagreement about who are the true worshipers of the God of Israel. Are they Jesus and his followers or are they the scribes and Pharisees?

The challenge of defining the relationship between the burgeoning Christian movement (the church) and those Jewish communities that did not recognize Jesus to be the Messiah pervaded the writings of second-century Christians (e.g., Ignatius of Antioch, Justin Martyr, and Melito of Sardis). Thus, Matthew's Gospel is the one that most directly addresses these challenges and thereby provides resources to help explain Jesus's interpretation of the Torah, how to rightly read the Old Testament writings, and how to understand the developing relationship between the earliest Christ-followers and the synagogues. Whether they did this well is another matter, but the simple point is that Matthew's popularity in the early church stemmed in part from its ability to meet early Christians' needs to explain their relationship with Judaism.

What we refer to today as Christianity had its origins within Judaism. One of the tragic features of the history of Christianity, however, is the way in which later followers of Jesus often tried to supplant and demonize the very people of God out of which the church originates. Since Israel rejected Jesus, the claim is often sadly made, God rejects his people Israel in favor of the church. We refer to this as supersessionism—that is, the view that the church replaces historical Israel, thereby rendering it obsolete (see sidebar 8.2).[7] This is a very long and complicated story with many winding paths. But good readers of the Gospels will try to grow in their knowledge and skills in at least three ways as it pertains to the complicated history of Christianity's relationship to Judaism. First, we should recognize that the reading of biblical texts has had, and continues to have, real-world consequences. Followers of Jesus need to be accountable for their readings of their sacred texts.[8] I'm not so much saying that we are culpable for *every* poor reading that has negative consequences as much as I'm encouraging us to take seriously the fact that readings of authoritative texts can also have damaging and oppressive consequences. We may think that anti-Judaism was a problem only during Hitler and Nazi Germany's violent reign of terror. While we should never underestimate the extent of the violence and evil perpetuated against the Jewish people during the Holocaust, we would be greatly mistaken if we fail to see that anti-Judaism has been pervasive in many cultures influenced by Christianity and in much of the history of biblical scholarship.[9] 8.1

Second, many poor readings, readings that refer to Matthew's Gospel as rejecting and replacing Israel with the church, stem from anachronistic assumptions or negative stereotypes that fail to make good historical sense. Whereas the Old Testament consistently refers to God's law as good and holy, many anti-Jewish interpretations assume the opposite: the law leads to prideful and legalistic works-righteousness. Supersessionist readings fail to recognize that Matthew's Gospel reflects a Jewish community that is engaging in polemical argumentation with *other* forms of Judaism. Christian readers of Matthew can work to avoid problematic historical, and potentially anti-Jewish, readings of Matthew by carefully reflecting on whether they are making unwarranted leaps. For example, in Matthew 23 Jesus certainly critiques the practices and manner of law observance of the Pharisees and scribes, but it is entirely unwarranted to thereby claim that he is critiquing "Judaism" or rejecting Torah observance in toto. More specifically, Jesus's parable of the wicked tenants (21:33–43) does not target the vineyard (Israel) but instead the workers of the vineyard (the Jerusalem leaders). In other words, it's the Jerusalem leadership that is replaced by the followers of Jesus; it is not "the church" that replaces "Judaism."[10] Another example: although Jesus does have unparalleled authority to interpret the Torah—often in surprising ways—and although he strongly critiques certain types of Torah observance (e.g., 15:1–20), one cannot rightly read Matthew's Gospel and affirm that Jesus has abolished or rejected Torah (see 5:17–20; 23:23–26). 8.2

Third, we can work to acknowledge, critique, and reject negative popular portrayals of Jewish people, practices, and history sometimes perpetuated by Christian readings of the Gospels.[11] This may mean interrogating and rejecting even some of the unfortunate readings by gentile church fathers or questioning the portrayal of Jewish people in popular movies (such as Mel Gibson's *The Passion of the Christ*) or even children's story Bibles. Popular portrayals of Christ's death often emphasize the entire Jewish people as responsible for killing Jesus and as therefore deserving retribution. In terms of promoting anti-Semitism, there is probably no more difficult text than Matthew 27:25, where the people plead with Pilate to crucify Jesus: "Let his blood be on us and on our children!" (cf. 23:35). The text indeed

SIDEBAR 8.1

Difficult Texts on "Matthew and Judaism"

Matthew 6:1–18: Jesus repeatedly exhorts his disciples to not be like "the hypocrites," referring to Jewish leaders, particularly the Pharisees.

Matthew 21:43: Addressing the chief priests and Pharisees, Jesus says, "I tell you that the kingdom of God will be taken away from you and given to a people who will produce its fruit."

Matthew 23:1–39: Jesus pronounces "woes" on the scribes and Pharisees.

Matthew 27:25: When Pilate the Roman governor claims to be innocent of shedding Jesus's blood, "All the people answered, 'Let his blood be on us and on our children!'"

SIDEBAR 8.2

What Is Supersessionism?

The word "supersession" is used frequently in New Testament scholarship, but its meaning is not always clear, and it is used by scholars in different ways. It basically means something to the effect of "the church (or Christianity) replacing/supplanting the synagogue (or Judaism)." At minimum, we should insist on recognizing that while the Gospels criticize some of the Jewish leaders for their interpretation of the Torah and for rejecting Jesus as the Messiah, they do not envision a situation where Torah is rejected or critiqued, where God's election of Israel is undone, or where gentiles are privileged over Jews. Throughout our reading of the Gospels, we will return to questions of how to respond to and be accountable for centuries of anti-Jewish readings of the Gospels and of how we can read the texts rightly and ethically.

emphasizes the *Jerusalem people's* culpability for the death of Jesus. But within Matthew's Gospel the cry of the people for the blood of Jesus to be on them and their children functions as an ironic echo and counterpart to the people of Israel in the wilderness who are splattered with the blood of the covenant (Exod. 24:7–8). The call for Jesus's blood thereby affirms *both* the people's culpability for Jesus's death *and* their salvation by means of offering his blood to effect redemption and a new covenant that cleanses God's people from sins.[12] Furthermore, the move from this cry of bloodguilt to the frequently attested early church claim that the Jewish people are cursed by God and have had their election revoked is simply egregious and vicious for any Christian to make.[13]

The Composition of Matthew

In discussing the composition of the Gospel, the first point of order is to note Matthew's relationship to the Gospel of Mark. Perhaps now you're asking, If it's true that Matthew's Gospel was so clearly the most popular of the four, then why not agree with the majority of the early church tradition, which assumed that it was also the first written Gospel? By way of reminder, Matthew's Gospel almost certainly was composed using Mark's Gospel as a source. When they share the same story, Matthew consistently abbreviates Mark's version (e.g., compare Matt. 8:28–9:1 with Mark 5:1–20); Matthew often irons out Mark's theological difficulties or potentially embarrassing statements; and, of course, Matthew contains many beloved and important episodes—foremost of which is the Sermon on the Mount—the absence of which in Mark is difficult to explain if Matthew was written first.

Matthew's plot outline of Jesus's life and ministry follows Mark's storyline quite closely. Most estimate that close to 90 percent of Mark is taken up in Matthew's Gospel. While there are a few scenes from Mark that Matthew omits from his story (e.g., Mark 1:21–27, 35–38; 12:41–44), his Gospel is much longer than Mark's, largely because of the additional episodes it contains. Let's take a look at some of the most important scenes in Matthew that have no counterpart in Mark or Luke. 8.3

This "M" material—material unique to Matthew (see sidebar 8.3)—does not necessarily all originate from one written or oral source, and in fact it is more likely to reflect the ongoing collective memory of the earliest communities on which Matthew's Gospel is dependent. Within the M material we find distinctives such as a heightened prominence for Peter (see especially his prominence in chaps. 16–18), Jesus preaching through many parables distinct to Matthew (e.g., 13:24–30, 36–43; chaps. 22; 25), pairs and doublets (e.g., two demoniacs cured in 8:28–33 instead of the one in Mark 5:1–14; two blind men healed in 20:29–34 instead of the one in Mark 10:46–52), and a complicated view of gentiles (positive in 2:1–12; 8:5–13; 15:21–28; negative in 6:7; 10:5–6, 18; 20:25–26).[14]

SIDEBAR 8.3

"M" Material

Matthew 1:1–2:21; 5:17–20, 21–24, 27–28, 33–38; 6:1–18; 11:28–30; 13:24–30, 36–52; 14:28–31; 16:17–19; 17:24–27; 18:15–35; 20:1–16; 21:28–32; 23:1–39; 25:1–13, 31–46; 27:3–10; 28:11–15, 16–20.[a]

This leads to a second question: Who wrote the Gospel of Matthew? Undoubtedly, it is easier for us to imagine the Gospel as the work of a single creative author. In an earlier chapter we noted that the Gospel writings are technically anonymous; that is, nowhere in the body of the text does the author make a clear reference to his authorial name such as we have in the Pauline and (most) General Epistles. But we also saw that each of our four Gospels receives its title ("The Gospel according to X") at a very early date and there is *no variation* in the titles given to each particular Gospel. In other words, we have no instances of our current "Gospel of Matthew" (or any other Gospel) being referred to by another name. There is no evidence that the Gospels ever circulated anonymously—that is, without *these names* attached to the writings.

The first author to provide information about the authorship of the First Gospel is Papias, who says, "Therefore Matthew put the oracles [*logia*] in ordered arrangement in the Hebrew language [or "dialect"], and each one interpreted them the best they could" (Eusebius, *Ecclesiastical History* 3.39.16). Some will entirely discount the testimony of Papias, as well as the claims made by other church fathers who identify Matthew as the author of the First Gospel, given both the strangeness of some of Papias's claims and the possibility that he is offering a late apologetic justification for the origins of the Gospels. What do we make of Papias's testimony? First, we can state with some confidence, as we have seen, that Matthew used Mark—a Gospel written in the Greek language—as a source. Thus, it is quite difficult to accept that Matthew wrote his Gospel in Hebrew or Aramaic and then had it translated into Greek, given that the text so frequently follows Mark's exact (Greek) wording. It is possible, however, that Papias's statement should be understood as indicating that Matthew wrote with a style and structure characteristic of Jewish writings.[15] Second, whatever we want to make of it, church tradition consistently identifies the First Gospel with

Figure 8.1. Caravaggio, *The Calling of Saint Matthew*

the person of Matthew (e.g., Irenaeus, Tertullian, Origen, Jerome, Augustine). Many of these church fathers appear to be dependent on Papias's statement as they pass on both the claims of Matthean authorship and its (potential) Hebrew origins. Thus, answering the question "Who wrote the Gospel of Matthew?" is not easy. It strikes some as strange to posit Matthean authorship, for why would Matthew, as an eyewitness to Jesus's ministry, rely so heavily on Mark's Gospel as a source? That said, if Mark's Gospel was understood to derive from eyewitness testimony, then Matthew's use of Mark suggests his agreement with its veracity, and so there is no great problem in seeing Matthew as both using Mark and being an eyewitness to Jesus.

Given that the First Gospel circulated very early with the name Matthew attached, the unanimous testimony of church tradition, and the twofold reference to Matthew within the Gospel (9:9; 10:3), I am inclined to accept that Matthew is its author. That said, we probably should not think of Matthew here as a single, solitary author doing the work of a creative genius; rather, Matthew, the follower of Jesus, drawing on and collecting eyewitness testimony *and* the collective memory of the earliest churches, in some way is the source for and associates his name with the written Gospel that comes first in the canonical order of the New Testament. Nevertheless, there is nothing in our reading of the First Gospel that will depend on our understanding of the question of authorship. Matthew's Gospel is an ancient biography that places its subject matter, Jesus, front and center, not the author. Additionally, the author never inserts himself into the story in a way that suggests our interpretation of the Gospel is dependent on information about the author. Any attempts to psychologize about how Matthew's identity (and we don't know much) is an essential aid in reading his Gospel is likely to put us on the wrong track.

The Location and Date of Matthew's Gospel

We are often taught that good interpretation of the Bible must attend to questions such as, When was the text written? From where and to whom was the text written? But with the Gospels not only are such questions difficult to answer with any degree of certainty but also there is little in our readings that hinges on our answers.

Identifying the geographical locale of Matthew's Gospel is a difficult and speculative task, and as one commentator notes, "The numerous hypotheses all have something in common: they are based on very insubstantial indications."[16] Nevertheless, many have argued that Antioch (in Syria, north of Israel) is the most likely place where the Gospel was composed. What can be said for this? Indeed, it is likely that the Gospel was composed in an urban environment; we know that Antioch had a large Jewish population out of which it birthed a prominent Christian community that included both gentiles and Jewish followers of Jesus (Acts 11:19–26; 13:1–4; Gal. 2:1–14); Matthew 4:24 speaks of Jesus's "fame spreading throughout all Syria" (whereas Mark 1:28 speaks only of "the surrounding region of Galilee"); and Ignatius of Antioch is the earliest author to show explicit awareness of Matthew's Gospel. These factors make it highly plausible that the Gospel was written in Antioch. I do not think that one can be much more definitive. And fortunately, we will not find that our reading of the Gospel necessitates our ability to identify the provenance with any certainty. In fact, tying our reading of the Gospel *too closely* to one community would likely be a mistake because the Gospel writings, while certainly bearing the historical features of their setting, are intended for wide circulation.[17]

Figure 8.2. The Mediterranean Basin

What about dating the Gospel of Matthew? Again, it's difficult to be precise. Most would argue for a date between 70 and 80 CE, given that there must be a time gap of a decade or so between Mark's composition and Matthew's, and the belief that Matthew seems to show awareness of the Jerusalem temple's destruction, which took place in 70 CE (22:1–14; 24:1–35).

CHAPTER NINE

Matthew and Narrative (1)

In this chapter we'll take a look at Matthew as narrative and examine its primary literary threads and artistry, focusing mainly on its structure, an overview of the plot, key words and phrases, and four narrative threads that are essential for reading this Gospel well. Let me remind you of what you already certainly know: there is nothing that can offer a substitute for your own careful study and reading of, and meditation on, the Gospel of Matthew.

Key Structural Features and Plot

Matthew's Gospel is filled with important literary devices such as repeated words and phrases, temporal transition markers, foreshadowing, fulfillment-of-Scripture formulas, typology, and more. These literary devices help to provide structure and coherence to Matthew's story. Before I read any book or story, I almost always look to see how the book is divided and structured. How many chapters does the book have? Is it structured by "parts" that help me understand its outline? As I read the text, my ability to pick up on the literary devices helps me provide a mental structure or outline to the story. The four Gospels almost certainly were composed in order to be heard (rather than read), and so multiple stylistic and structural features would likely have aided the one responsible for the oral delivery as well as the listeners.[1] Therefore, we do not need to pick one single feature as the key for the structure (as many commentators often do); rather, we can attend to multiple structural markers and literary devices in order to organize the Gospel. Let's look at three structural elements that will help us read Matthew's Gospel well.

First, in the early chapters of Matthew we find *typology or biblical patterns* employed by the author as a means of framing the significance of Jesus's identity and actions. In other words, Matthew often shows us the meaning and significance of a story by patterning it after important episodes from the Old Testament. In earlier discussion of the role of memory in the oral transmission of the Jesus tradition, I referred to this as "keying"—that is, remembering a recent event or episode through the framework of an older sacred event.[2] For the Gospels, Jesus is frequently remembered through the aid of Old Testament stories.[3] This is often indicated through Matthew's use of the key word "fulfillment." Thus, Jesus's birth (1:22–23; 2:1–6), childhood in Nazareth (2:23), teaching about the Torah (5:17–20), healing ministry (12:17–21), and suffering and death (26:54) fulfill claims made in Israel's Scriptures.

This theme is evident immediately as Matthew begins his narrative with a genealogy that surveys the history of Israel (1:2–17; for Old Testament genealogies, see Gen. 5:3–32; 1 Chron. 1–9). The genealogy offers a summary version of the biblical story of God's history with Israel and situates the birth of the Messiah within God's election of Abraham, the rise of the Davidic monarchy, and the sad event of Israel's exile to Babylon. This makes it clear that Jesus's significance will be rightly understood only within God's broader story of election, kingship, and exile. A second example is found in Matthew 4:1–11, where Jesus's temptations are typologically patterned after the scriptural stories of Israel's time in the wilderness during Moses's leadership. The parallels are clear: both Jesus and Israel are referred to as the Son of God, the setting is the wilderness, and both are tempted to doubt God's goodness and provision. But in Matthew, we see that Jesus is the faithful Son who responds to each one of Satan's tests through quoting portions of Deuteronomy 6–8 and thereby successfully resists testing God. A third example of typology can be found in the introduction to Jesus's Sermon on the Mount (chaps. 5–7), when we are told that Jesus went up on a mountain and opened his mouth to speak (5:1–2). This should remind us of Moses's giving of God's law on Sinai and his promises of blessings and curses depending on the people's response. One final example: when Jesus rides on a colt into Jerusalem and makes his way to the temple receiving royal acclamations (21:1–11), Matthew shows us the scene has been patterned according to the stories of the royal coronation of Israel's kings (e.g., 1 Kings 1:28–53). In writing a Gospel that is so obviously concerned to show Jesus's relationship to Israel, the Old Testament Scriptures, and the events and institutions associated with the people of God, Matthew uses typology as an important literary feature to make associations between Jesus and the Old Testament.

A second structural feature of Matthew's Gospel can be seen when on two occasions the narrator states, "From that time on Jesus began to . . ." (4:17; 16:21).[4] These temporal transitions allow Matthew to move to a new portion of his story; in other words, the markers function to indicate a new stage in the narrative. 9.1

These markers have the benefit of dividing the Gospel according to its three major plot movements. They also nicely focus on the theme of Christology and Matthew's portrait of Jesus's messianic identity as the Son of God.

SIDEBAR 9.1

Matthew's Gospel as Structured by Temporal Markers

1. Matthew 1:1–4:16: Jesus's messianic identity and preparation for public ministry.
2. Matthew 4:17–16:20: Jesus's proclamation of the kingdom to his people: success and rejection.
3. Matthew 16:21–28:20: Jesus's journey to Jerusalem: teaching, suffering, death, and resurrection.

A third illuminating approach recognizes Matthew's consistent alternation between narrative and discourse. On five occasions Matthew uses a formulaic saying to the effect of "And it came about that when Jesus had finished these words . . ." (7:28; 11:1; 13:53; 19:1; 26:1). The formula obviously marks an end to Jesus's teaching and notes a transition into narrative material. This divides Matthew's chapters into the following back-and-forth between Jesus's actions and speech.[5] That there are *five* blocks that alternate between speech and narrative, along with the fivefold formula ("when Jesus had finished these words"), recalls the Pentateuch—the first five books of the Old Testament.

Chapters 1–4: Narrative

Matthew situates Jesus within God's prior election of Israel as his people. Jesus is shown to be the Messiah, Son of God, and God's presence with his people. He will bless his people and the nations as the messianic shepherd who rules with truth and justice. His baptism marks him out as the Son of God who identifies with his people's sin and plight. He is the faithful and obedient Son even in the midst of temptation.

Chapters 5–7: Discourse

Jesus's Sermon on the Mount is his first public speech and shows that the Messiah is a uniquely authoritative teacher of God's will and righteousness. Here he sets forth God's blessings on his covenant people, reaffirms God's Torah as authoritative as well as his own unique ability to interpret its meaning, and offers wisdom and guidance for how to practice righteousness in a way that honors God.

Chapters 8–9: Narrative

Jesus's authority and power are also manifested in his compassionate miracles of healing that establish the presence of the kingdom of heaven and bestow God's blessings on the weak, suffering, and marginalized. This brings him into conflict with the leaders of Israel and foreshadows his eventual rejection.

Chapter 10: Discourse

Jesus commissions his disciples to share in his ministry through healings, exorcisms, and proclamation of the kingdom of heaven. Judgment is pronounced on those who encounter but reject Jesus's and the disciples' announcement of the kingdom.

Chapters 11–12: Narrative

The crisis within Israel over what to make of Jesus's ministry is brought to the fore not only by those who are explicitly against and antagonistic toward Jesus (such as the Pharisees and scribes) but even by John the Baptist, who, through his disciples, questions whether Jesus is the Christ. Jesus's authoritative interpretation of the Torah and his promise to give rest to his followers continue to be major points of contention between Jesus and his opponents.

Chapter 13: Discourse

Jesus teaches with a variety of parables in order to explain why there are both positive and negative responses to him and his proclamation of God's kingdom. He draws on agricultural practices, the testimony and experience of Israel's prophets, and the workings of Satan in order to explain the division within God's people. Despite opposition and small beginnings, however, the kingdom of God will grow and will be finally established.

Chapters 14–17: Narrative

Jesus continues to perform compassionate miracles and interpret God's law, despite more hostility from Israel's teachers. But these chapters also have a special emphasis on Peter and the foundation of the church. Peter walks on water. He finds a coin in the mouth of a fish in order to pay the temple tax. He later confesses that Jesus is the Christ, the Son of God, though he must learn that the Messiah will fulfill God's will through laying down his life on the cross. Peter's confession that Jesus is the Christ is the foundation on which Jesus will build the church.

Chapter 18: Discourse

The identity and practices of the church are set forth here by Jesus. The church will have a special concern for the vulnerable and marginalized; will be marked by humility, mercy, and forgiveness; and will seek reconciliation for those who go astray.

Chapters 19–23: Narrative

Jesus journeys to Jerusalem. He continues to interpret the Torah, teach about the kingdom of heaven, and prepare his disciples for the necessity of his suffering, death, and resurrection. His journey to Jerusalem is marked by his royal coronation as he approaches the temple and engages in a prophetic act of demonstration against it and its leaders. More hostility ensues as Jesus is tested and questioned by Pharisees and Sadducees, and he offers a lengthy polemic against the practices of the scribes and Pharisees.

Chapters 24–25: Discourse

Jesus delivers lengthy teachings about the parousia (the return of Jesus) and the future consummation of the kingdom of heaven. His emphasis falls on preparation through faithfulness and care for the vulnerable as opposed to predicting the timing of his return.

Chapters 26–28: Narrative

The Gospel reaches its climax in the events of the passion: Jesus is handed over by the religious leaders of Israel and betrayed by the disciple Judas, and he is tortured and crucified by the Roman authorities. Jesus is raised from the dead by God, however, and the tomb is empty. Jesus is alive and commissions his disciples to take the gospel and his teachings to all the nations.

Key Words and Phrases

Matthew also has favorite words and phrases that clue us in to some of his most important narrative themes. We need to be careful not to make the mistake of confusing a single word with one concept; the same word can be used in different ways, and a concept can be evoked through a variety of different words and phrases. However, Matthew often does signal important concerns and narrative threads by repeating some of his favorite words.

Let's look at four of them here, which will help us as we start to explore the major themes of Matthew's Gospel: "righteousness," "hypocrisy," "kingdom of heaven/God," and "mercy."[6]

Righteousness. Throughout the Gospel, and especially prominent in Jesus's Sermon on the Mount, Matthew uses the language of "righteousness" to refer to God's will, expectation, and purposes, especially as it pertains to followers of Jesus. If we approach the language of righteousness from a Pauline perspective, where it is often associated with salvation and deliverance (e.g., Rom. 3:21–4:25), we may be surprised at how Matthew's usage "is overwhelmingly concerned with right conduct, with living the way God requires."[7] When John the Baptist balks at Jesus's demand to receive baptism, Jesus declares that the act is fitting "to fulfill all righteousness" (Matt. 3:15). We'll look more at this episode later, but at minimum we can say here that Jesus is discerning and submitting himself to God's will and plan to receive John's baptism. In the Sermon on the Mount, we see disciples of Jesus will "hunger and thirst for righteousness" (5:6), can expect persecution on account of doing righteousness (5:10), and will listen to and obey Jesus's teaching, which sets forth "the greater righteousness" (5:20). Jesus refers to prayer, giving alms, and fasting as expected norms for how his disciples will practice righteousness, though he warns them to do these good deeds only before God, not before other people (6:1–18). The righteous are those who enact God's mercy for the vulnerable (1:19; 10:41; 25:37, 46). They are those who commit themselves to "doing the will of the heavenly Father" as they listen to and follow the teachings of Jesus (7:21–24; cf. 12:46–50).

Hypocrisy. Doing acts of outward righteousness for the wrong reasons is what Matthew means when he uses the term "hypocrisy." Hypocrisy is the exact opposite of righteousness. This theme is stated most clearly throughout Matthew 6:1–18, where the same practices (prayer, almsgiving, and fasting) are performed, but those who do them in order to be seen and approved, honored, and respected before others are termed "hypocrites" (vv. 2, 5, 16). The term frequently shows up as a reference to Jesus's opponents when they disagree over the interpretation of the Torah. Matthew portrays Jesus as interpreting the Torah in a way that leads to love, mercy, and human flourishing, whereas the Pharisees and scribes interpret it in a way that not only burdens others but draws attention to their own authority (e.g., 15:7; 23:13, 15, 23, 25–29). 9.2

Kingdom of heaven/God. The Old Testament frequently speaks of the prophetic hope and anticipation that God will establish his dynamic and sovereign rule on the earth (see especially Isa.

SIDEBAR 9.2

Ellen Charry on Obedience to God in Matthew

"The question of obedience to God goes far beyond what one is to do—it crafts what kind of person one is to be. Matthew turned attention from correct performance to the agent's self-concept, from behavior to character."[a]

40:1–11; 52:7–12; Amos 9:11–15; Zech. 8–13; Dan. 7). In the Synoptic Gospels, Jesus repeatedly proclaims the kingdom of God, and the phrase functions as a primary descriptor of his entire ministry. Instead of "kingdom of God," Matthew most frequently uses the equivalent "kingdom of heaven" (although see 6:33; 12:28; 19:24; 21:31, 43). While the standard view has been, and may still be, that Matthew simply uses "heaven" as a reverential circumlocution for "God," many now rightly observe that Matthew often contrasts heaven (i.e., God's ways and values) with earth (i.e., humanity's ways and values). Thus, when John the Baptist as well as Jesus proclaim the coming kingdom of heaven, they are declaring that God's heavenly reign is coming to earth, and this is why people must "repent" and orient themselves toward God's values and ways (3:2; 4:17). Jesus is the messianic king of the kingdom who teaches God's people how to "enter into the kingdom of heaven" (5:20; chaps. 5–7) and who provides deliverance, forgiveness, and signs of God's salvation (chaps. 8–9). This is why Matthew brackets Jesus's initial teaching and merciful acts with summary references to Jesus "proclaiming the gospel of the kingdom" (4:23; 9:35). Thus, the kingdom of heaven is something that is present now in the ministry of Jesus as he establishes God's reign in this world and destroys the works of Satan (12:22–32). Jesus's healings and exorcisms provide evidence that God's kingdom is breaking into the world through the messianic king (see also 10:1–8). The presence of the kingdom is emphasized as it is something to be sought after now with complete devotion (6:33). Jesus frequently tells his disciples that they must listen to and obey his teachings if they would enter into God's kingdom (5:20; 18:1–4; 19:23–24). Yet God's kingdom is something that is also future oriented as it will bring God's purposes for the world and humanity to its consummation (e.g., 8:11; 25:31–46), and so Jesus's disciples are to pray for God's kingdom to come (6:9–13). 9.3

SIDEBAR 9.3

Jonathan Pennington on Heaven and Earth in Matthew

"By stepping back and analyzing Matthew's rich and varied use of heaven language we can see that behind it all is *an intentional focus on the theme of heaven and earth, specifically highlighting the current contrast or tensive relationship between the two realms, between God and humanity. Yet Matthew does not only emphasize the contrast, but also the fact that this contrast or tension will be resolved at eschaton when heaven and earth are reunited through Jesus (6:9–10; 28:18). In fact, only by recognizing the intensity of the tension that currently exists between heaven and earth can we fully appreciate the significance of the eschaton in which the kingdom of heaven will come to earth.*"[b]

Mercy. Matthew consistently portrays Jesus as one who gives mercy and expects his followers to dispense mercy as well. Since God is kind and loving to both the just and the unjust, Jesus argues that the only right way to understand God's Torah is from the standpoint of mercy and justice (5:43–48). So, in his Sermon on the Mount, Jesus calls his disciples to be persons who refuse vengeance, retaliation, covetousness, and greed and instead embrace honesty and love for neighbors and enemies (5:21–48).

Jesus's "hermeneutic of mercy" as it relates to his ministry and interpretation of Torah is seen clearly in Matthew 12:1–14. When Jesus and his disciples are questioned about breaking the law by picking and eating grain on the Sabbath, Jesus responds with a quotation from Hosea 6:6: "If you had known what this means, 'I desire mercy and not sacrifice,' you would not have condemned the innocent" (12:7). Mercy and sacrifice here "stand for, respectively, a form of piety that focuses on God's compassion toward human needs and a form of piety that focuses on ritual observances."[8] And Jesus declares that God's law *itself* prioritizes mercy and compassion as the proper means of interpreting the commandments of the Torah. The Torah rightly interpreted is not a burdensome or impossible yoke; neither is it something that is rightly used as a means of exalting oneself above one's neighbor (23:11–12). Jesus teaches his disciples to observe the entirety of the Torah, even continuing to tithe mint, cumin, and dill, but they are to understand that the weightier matters of the Torah are found in "justice, mercy, and faithfulness" (23:23).

Mercy is also emphasized in Jesus's compassionate healings of those on the margins of society. Thus, Jesus touches and heals two blind men who cry out, "Have mercy upon us, Son of David!" (9:27). Jesus heals the daughter of the Canaanite woman who was crying out, "Have mercy on me, Lord, son of David!" (15:22). Jesus also responds to a father's request for mercy and healing for his epileptic son (17:15). In Matthew 20:29–34 two blind men cry out, "Lord, have mercy on us, Son of David" (v. 30), and again, "Lord, have mercy on us, Son of David!" (v. 31). Matthew notes that Jesus's "compassion" leads to his healing of the blind men (v. 34).

Jesus's disciples are also to bestow mercy. Jesus pronounces a blessing on the merciful (5:7). In response to Peter's question regarding the extent of forgiveness, Jesus tells a parable that positions disciples as those who have experienced the incredible mercy and compassion of the one who has paid their incredible debt and who are thereby obligated to continue the practice of mercy and debt cancellation for their fellow neighbors (18:33–35).

Matthew and Narrative (2)

Key Narrative Threads

Jesus's Life and Death Pay the Debt for His People's Sins

Paul's propositional claim that "all have sinned and fallen short of the glory of God" (Rom. 3:23) is depicted in narrative form in Matthew's Gospel.[1] God's chosen people Israel are implicated to the very core by sin, and so of course the non-Jewish nations, since they worship false gods, are marked in even more extreme fashion by sin (e.g., Matt. 5:47; 6:7, 32; 18:15–17; 20:25–27). We see this right away in Matthew's genealogy where the Babylonian deportation is mentioned; this event would seem to be an insurmountable obstacle to the fulfillment of God's promises to Abraham and David.[2] Matthew's genealogy tells Israel's story as structured around "promise, kingship, exile, and return" and culminating in Jesus as the messianic savior.[3] Jesus's central identity is "the Messiah"; that is, he is the promised Davidic king, and yet the genealogy shows us that sin and evil have taken root within Israel's kings. For example, Judah, from whose tribe comes the Davidic kings and even Jesus the Messiah (see Gen. 49:8–12), is the one who fathers Perez and Zerah by Tamar; Tamar plays the part of the prostitute and deceives Judah as a means of procuring justice for herself (Matt. 1:3; see Gen. 38; 49:8–12). We must note that it is Judah (not Tamar!) who acts sinfully (see Gen. 38:26), thereby highlighting the sinfulness of Judah! The story of Judah's sin toward Tamar previews King David's own sinful history with Bathsheba and Uriah (Matt. 1:6b). This calls to mind David's wicked acts of greedy lust, adultery, and murder of an innocent man (2 Sam. 11–12). Matthew's recounting of the lineage of David, especially in Matthew 1:6–11, recalls the stories of Judah's kings from the canonical books of 1–2 Kings; for those who can recall these stories, despite some glimmers of hope (e.g., Hezekiah and Josiah), there are sad

SIDEBAR 10.1

Jesus and Salvation from Sins in Matthew

- "You will give birth to a son, and you will name him Jesus, for he will save his people from their sins" (1:21).
- "For even the Son of Man did not come to be served but to serve, and to give his life as a ransom for many" (20:28).
- "For this is my blood of the covenant poured out for many for the forgiveness of sins" (26:28).

remembrances of sons of David who did evil in the sight of the Lord (e.g., 1 Kings 11:6; 14:22), who exploited their own people (e.g., Ahab in 1 Kings 21), and who committed gross acts of idolatry (e.g., 2 Kings 21:1–16). 10.1

Matthew refers four times in Jesus's genealogy to the deportation to Babylon (1:11, 12, 17 [2x]). Thus, in a highly condensed form, Matthew retells Israel's history in such a way that God's scriptural promises for a just and righteous Davidic ruler over God's people appear frustrated as a result of the wickedness and sin of Israel's kings. Exile marks the failure and end of kingship in Israel. While Israel's Scriptures do indeed portray an end to the exile and celebrate God's faithfulness to return the people to the land (e.g., Ezra; Nehemiah; Isa. 45; Jer. 29; Haggai), the postexilic writings still portray Israel as a people marked by sin and lacking a righteous Davidic king. The important point for us here is this: Jesus is born within a prior story of God's promises to rescue and rule his people through a son of David *and* of a people plagued by idolatry, injustice, and sexual infidelity. 10.2

Jesus's birth shows us that he shares the same human flesh and same ancestry as Abraham, David, and the other human figures of the Old Testament. And yet Matthew is clear that the birth of the Messiah is an unprecedented new and climactic act of God that takes place through the Holy Spirit (1:18, 20). As a result, within the infancy narrative Jesus is given the name "Emmanuel, which is translated, 'God with us'" (1:23), and as a child he receives worship from foreign magi who have come "to worship him" (2:2). It is within this context that the angel declares to Joseph, "[Mary] will give birth to a son, and you are to name him Jesus, because he will save his people from their sins" (1:21). The reference to "his people" must indicate Israel—that is, God's covenant people in need of salvation due to their suffering the consequences of sin, injustice, and idolatry, as hinted at in the genealogy.

Matthew's depiction of both Jesus's anointing at his baptism (3:13–17) and his temptations in the wilderness (4:1–11) centers on his messianic vocation as the Son of God to identify with and take on the plight of sinful Israel, *his people*, and to offer faithfulness and obedience to his Father. As such, they preview Jesus's climactic act of saving his people from their sins when he lays down his life on the cross in obedience to the Father.

Jesus's solidarity with Israel is seen in his submission to John's baptism, a ritual explicitly intended to symbolize Israel's repentance for the

Figure 10.1. The Judean wilderness

forgiveness of sins (3:1–2, 6, 11). When John the Baptist hesitates, Jesus responds, "Allow it to be so, for in this way it is fitting to fulfill all righteousness" (3:15). In other words, Jesus says that his baptism for repentance is a righteous requirement, and so he expresses his identification with the sinful people he has come to save (1:21). Jesus's fulfillment of this righteous requirement in standing in solidarity with sinful Israel elicits the descent of the Spirit of God from heaven and the Father's approving response as he declares from heaven, "This is my beloved Son. I am well pleased with him" (3:17). Jesus is designated here as God's Son commissioned to enact God's righteousness for the salvation of his people. Jesus's vocation as the Spirit-anointed Son of God (3:16–17) will consist in his obedience to the Father to save his people from their sins in fully identifying with their plight (3:13–15). As he stands in solidarity with his sinful people, his anointing previews a messianic vocation that will lead to his death.[4]

Jesus's testing in the wilderness by the devil centers on his messianic vocation as the Son of God and presents a typological depiction of Israel in the wilderness with Moses (4:1–11; e.g., wilderness, temptations, Son of God, the number forty). Jesus the Son of God again identifies with Israel, who was unfaithful and disobedient in the wilderness. Jesus is the faithful Son who responds

SIDEBAR 10.2

Penitential Prayers and the History of Israel

The Old Testament and other Jewish literature contain may penitential prayers whereby one of the leaders of Israel recounts God's mercy to Israel in spite of his people's sin and unfaithfulness to the Torah. God disciplines his people so that they will return to him and so that by obeying God they may find life. The prayers often end, however, with a lament and a request for God's ongoing mercy and faithfulness. Read through the following Old Testament prayers to see the pattern of God's faithfulness, Israel's disobedience, and the leaders' call for God's mercy: Nehemiah 9; Ezra 9; Daniel 9.

to each one of Satan's tests through quoting portions of Deuteronomy 6–8. Jesus's commitment to "fulfill all righteousness" (3:13–15) and to offer obedience and faithfulness to his Father (4:1–11) instead of using power for his own purposes previews the way in which Jesus's messianic vocation finds its climax on the cross. 10.3

Jesus himself interprets his death as the event that will save his people by providing the ransom that delivers them from bondage to sin. In Matthew 20:28, Jesus declares that "the Son of Man did not come to be served but to serve, and to give his life as a ransom for many." The word translated as "ransom" refers to a payment offered as a means of redemption or some kind of exchange.[5] Frequently this payment is offered as a means of delivering persons from some kind of debt bondage or captivity.[6] Jesus, as the humble and obedient Son of God, identifies with Israel's sinful plight and offers his own life as the payment that will rescue Israel from their sins. Jesus's primary interpretation of his death occurs at the Last Supper, where he anticipates his impending death and interprets the Passover wine as "the blood of my covenant, which is poured out for many for the forgiveness of sins" (Matt. 26:28). The language "blood of the covenant" recalls the covenant that God made with Israel at Sinai (Exod. 24:8), which was also then ratified with a meal (Exod. 24:9–11). Although the people of Israel promised obedience to the Lord's laws and statutes at Sinai (Exod. 24:7), Matthew's reader knows that Messiah Jesus alone, the one who has stood in solidarity with Israel, has offered perfect obedience and righteousness to God.[7] Thus, the theme of obedience of God's covenant people along with the language of "covenant" and "forgiveness of sins" calls to mind Jeremiah's expectation for a new covenant. Jeremiah anticipates a day when God will bring Israel's exile to an end, write his law on his people's hearts, and put an end to their sin (Jer. 31:31–34).[8] 10.4

When we read of Matthew's addition of the name "Jesus" to the placard on the cross, this makes for the written charge "This is Jesus, the King of the Jews" (27:37), and it reminds the reader of the meaning of Jesus's name in Matthew 1:21, the one who will save his people from their sins (cf. 26:28).[9] This further heightens the irony of those mocking Jesus, who suppose that his identity as "the son of God" and "Israel's King" is manifestly false, given his inability to *save himself* by coming down from the cross. Three times the mockers use the language of "save"

SIDEBAR 10.3

Parallels between Jesus and Israel in the Wilderness

Jesus in the wilderness (Matt. 4:1–11)	Israel in the wilderness (Exod. 17–19)
Tempted by Satan	Tempted
Forty days and nights in the wilderness	Forty years in the wilderness
Jesus is the Son of God	Israel is the son of God
Faithful	Unfaithful

or "salvation" in their taunts of Jesus. Thus, "Save yourself! If you are the Son of God, come down from the cross!" (27:40b); "He saved others, but he cannot save himself! He is Israel's king! Let him come down now from the cross, and we will believe in him" (27:42). The mockery of "if you are the son of God" reminds the reader of the devil's threefold temptation of Jesus and Jesus's demonstration of his true messianic vocation in humble obedience to God. As in the time of his temptations, "Jesus as the Son of God, in obedience to the will of the Father, does not make use of the power he possesses but instead fulfills the will of God."[10] Here Jesus's identity as the Son of God is revealed by his refusal to save himself and by his instead saving his people from their sins through his death on the cross. 10.5

SIDEBAR 10.4

Jesus's Temptations in Fyodor Dostoevsky's *The Brothers Karamazov*

In "The Grand Inquisitor," the most famous scene in Dostoevsky's great novel, the rationalist Karamazov brother Ivan tells his saintly Christian brother Alyosha a parable of Christ's return to fifteenth-century Seville (in Spain). Christ reveals himself through his love and mercy for all and by lovingly raising a girl from the dead. "The sun of love burns in his heart, the beams of light, enlightenment, and power flow from his eyes and, as they stream over people, shake their hearts with answering love." This provokes outrage from the Grand Inquisitor, a cardinal or bishop in the Roman Catholic Church, who has just returned from putting to death a great many heretics. The Grand Inquisitor orders Jesus to be imprisoned, where he lectures Jesus and castigates him for failing to accept the devil's three offers in the wilderness. Humankind wants miracle, mystery, and authority, not love and freedom, says the cardinal. They want bread rather than the bread from heaven, servitude rather than freedom, the miraculous rather than God. Jesus was a fool, says the Grand Inquisitor, to reject the devil's offer. He says, "And yet even back then you could have taken the sword of Caesar. Why did you reject that final gift? Had you accepted that third counsel of the mighty spirit, you would have supplied everything that man seeks in the world, that is: someone to bow down before, someone to entrust one's conscience to, and a way of at last uniting everyone into an undisputed, general and consensual ant-heap." After the cardinal finishes berating Jesus, he anxiously waits for the silent Jesus to respond. "The old man would like the Other [Jesus] to say something to him, even if it is bitter, terrible. But he suddenly draws near to the old man without saying anything and kisses him on his bloodless, ninety-year-old lips. That is his only response."[a]

Jesus Is the Wise and Authoritative Teacher of God's Law

Jesus not only pays the debt for Israel's sins, which inaugurates the new covenant, but also teaches his disciples how to interpret and obey God's will as expressed primarily (though not exclusively) through the Torah. One of the promises of Jeremiah's new covenant was that God's law would be written on the hearts of God's people; thus, there is the expectation that true repentance and obedience to the Torah would be a profound mark of the messianic age (see Deut. 30:11–14; Jer. 31:31–34).[11] Within Matthew's Gospel, Jesus is the wise king who authoritatively interprets Torah and proclaims proper obedience to God's laws. Since he is the one who "fulfills all righteousness" (3:15) and teaches his disciples about a "superior righteousness" (5:20), it makes sense that Jesus consistently upholds Torah obedience throughout the Gospel of Matthew (also 5:18–19; cf. 23:3, 23). While echoes of Jesus as a new Moses are present, Jesus's authoritative teaching often is situated within explicitly royal-messianic terms.[12] Bracketing Jesus's teachings (chaps. 5–7) and merciful healings (chaps. 8–9) is the description of Jesus as "proclaiming the gospel of the kingdom and healing every disease and every sickness among the people" (4:23; cf. 9:35). Two of Jesus's beatitudes center on the promise of sharing in the kingdom of heaven (5:3, 10), and Jesus teaches his disciples to pray for the coming kingdom (6:9–10). Jesus's sage-like teaching and revelation of the hidden mysteries center, especially in chapter 13, on his intimate knowledge of *the kingdom of heaven* and his insight that the kingdom is present in history despite its "hidden, unexpected presence in the world" (e.g., 13:11, 19, 24, 31, 33, 44, 45, 47, 52).[13]

The Torah and the Better Righteousness

Jesus does not overturn or abrogate the Torah, and Matthew makes this point as emphatically as possible when Jesus says, "Do not suppose that I have come to destroy the law and the prophets; I have not come to destroy but to fulfill" (5:17).[14] Whatever "fulfill" means, it cannot mean anything *less* than to observe the teachings of the law and the prophets, as is made clear in verses 18–19, where Jesus declares that the law remains in effect until the end of history *and* that anyone who breaks, and teaches others to break, "one of the least of these commandments" will be least in the kingdom of heaven. Jesus, in fact, calls his community to a "righteousness that exceeds that of the scribes and Pharisees" if they would enter into the kingdom of heaven (5:20). And those who fail to understand and obey Jesus's interpretation of the Torah and his call for a better righteousness will find themselves as eschatological lawbreakers, excluded from the kingdom of God (7:21–27). 10.6

The heart of Jesus's teachings is found in the Sermon on the Mount (chaps. 5–7), where he teaches about the "better righteousness." Jesus's six

SIDEBAR 10.5

The Torah-Observant King

Israel's Scriptures provide helpful context for understanding Matthew's depiction of Jesus as one who teaches, interprets, and obeys God's Torah. One of the primary tasks of Israel's kings and rulers was to take the lead in submitting themselves to and following God's Torah from the heart. Foundational here is the so-called Law of the King in Deuteronomy 17:14–20.

> When he takes the throne of his kingdom, he is to write for himself on a scroll a copy of this law, taken from that of the Levitical priests. It is to be with him, and he is to read it all the days of his life so that he may learn to revere the Lord his God and follow carefully all the words of this law and these decrees and not consider himself better than his fellow Israelites and turn from the law to the right or to the left. Then he and his descendants will reign a long time over his kingdom in Israel. (Deut. 17:18–20 NIV)

While 1–2 Kings recounts how the kings of Israel largely disobeyed and ignored God's law, the paradigmatic good king Josiah is portrayed as not only discovering the law but also implementing Torah obedience.

> [Josiah] read in their hearing all the words of the book of the covenant that had been found in the house of the Lord. The king stood by the pillar and made a covenant before the Lord, to follow the Lord, keeping his commandments, his decrees, and his statutes, with all his heart and all his soul, to perform the words of this covenant that were written in this book. All the people joined in the covenant. (2 Kings 23:2b–3 NRSVue)

SIDEBAR 10.6

Jesus the Philosopher-King?

Christians confess that Jesus is Messiah, Lord, and Savior, but rarely do many think of him as a philosopher. And yet there are good reasons to understand him as supremely wise—even brilliant. Despite popular misconceptions of ancient philosophers as lovers of arcane puzzles, most ancient philosophers were devoted primarily to giving a response to the questions "What is the good life?" and "How can I live a flourishing life?" They devoted their lives to articulating the wisdom required to live the good life *and* to embodying this life for others to see and emulate.[b] We have seen that Jesus's teaching astounds everyone, that those with a scribal education are angered and confused by his abilities, and that he communicates wisdom through unforgettable aphorisms, parables, and riddles. We have also seen that Matthew's structuring of his Gospel into five large blocks of teaching contributes to the depiction of him as a great wisdom teacher who calls others to listen, learn, and follow his way of life. Furthermore, like a good philosopher, Jesus practices what he preaches. He is no charlatan but rather conforms his lifestyle to his teaching (see below). In Matthew, in fact, Jesus is *the only wise teacher* who is deserving of the title "Teacher."[c] The other so-called teachers do not know, and are thereby unable to communicate, God's will for humans; nor do they embody their own teaching (Matt. 23:1–10).

Early church fathers recognized Jesus's Sermon on the Mount as the foundational ethical charter that called all followers of Jesus to live his philosophical way of life. John Chrysostom, for example, preaches on the Sermon on the Mount and consistently shows his readers that Jesus is *the* premier philosophical teacher and that his teaching is superior to other ancient philosophers.[d] Whereas the Greeks saw Plato as a wise teacher but Asclepius as the god of healing, John notes that in the one person of Jesus we have one who heals the body (through healings) and the soul (through his teaching). The Sermon on the Mount provides an all-encompassing philosophy for all of life: ethics, politics, metaphysics, and death. John argues that those who would practice Jesus's teachings (Matt. 5:20–7:29) must first start by attending to the virtues set forth in the Beatitudes (5:3–12). One can love one's enemies, for example, only if one embodies virtues such as humility, mercy, and peacemaking.

The philosopher-theologian Dallas Willard has written what I take to be a contemporary classic, *The Divine Conspiracy*, which sets forth Jesus as the supremely wise teacher who offers all who listen to him God's very life, the path to human flourishing in the here and now.[e] Jesus's teaching in the Sermon on the Mount is not a laundry list of difficult rules that one must perform in order to please God; rather, his teaching shows his disciples how to live the life of God's kingdom—a life of goodness, righteousness, and flourishing here in this world. The Sermon on the Mount is Jesus's call to live "the good life." Notice how well this depiction of Jesus makes sense of what we've seen in Matthew's Gospel. Jesus's Beatitudes are a depiction of flourishing and happiness that is surprisingly seen in the lives of the gentle, righteous, peacemakers, merciful, and pure in heart (5:3–12). Jonathan Pennington, like Willard, shows that the heart of the Sermon on the Mount constitutes "Jesus's epitome on what it means to be truly good. . . . To be good/righteous requires seeing and being in the world in ways that match how God the Father himself is. This means obeying God's commands not just externally but from the heart, in the inner person (Matt. 5:21–48)."[f] Jesus's Sermon concludes by setting up a contrast between the wise and the foolish; the wise are those who listen to Jesus's teachings and devote their lives to his vision of kingdom flourishing (7:24–27).

"But I say to you . . ." sayings all set forth God's will, often focusing on the deeper principles or inner motivations of God's laws. Jesus interprets the Torah with the conviction that God's laws have been written on the hearts of his kingdom people (just as Jer. 31 and Ezek. 36 prophesied).[15] This is explained in detail in Matthew 5:21–48, where Jesus calls his disciples to obey the true intent of God's law and to do so from the heart. The divine intention of the Torah's prohibition against adultery (Exod. 20:14; Deut. 5:18), for example, is ultimately to be found in the inner eradication of illicit desire and lust for what belongs to someone else (5:27–30). The divine intention of the command "do not murder" (Exod. 20:13; Deut. 5:17) is that people refrain from the inner propensity to anger and bitterness (5:21–26). Jesus is not overturning the Torah but rather is *interpreting* the divine intention of God's commandments.[16] Jesus makes it clear that his starting point for understanding God's will for how his people live is rooted in his knowledge of the character of God and the goal of the Torah as conformity to God's holy character (5:48; cf. Lev. 19:2). In other words, Jesus agrees with the scribes and the Pharisees that the Torah is holy, given by God, and reveals his will and righteousness; but Jesus is the *authoritative* interpreter of the Torah who interprets its meaning in a way that aligns with God's perspective.

Thus, in Matthew 22:34–40, when Jesus is put to the test by an expert in the law who asks which commandment is the greatest, Jesus responds with two texts from the Torah that call for love for God (Deut. 6:5) and love for neighbor (Lev. 19:18). Jesus twice declares that the law and the prophets find their meaning in these two commands (22:40; cf. 7:12). The disciples are to observe the entirety of the Torah, even continuing to tithe mint, cumin, and dill, but they are to understand that the weightier matters of the Torah are found in its call for "justice, mercy, and faithfulness" (23:23). One can hardly overstate the importance of this text for Jesus's engagement of Torah: the weightier matters of the Torah—justice, mercy, and faith—take precedence over the lesser commandments.[17] Given that God is merciful and kind to everyone (5:43–48), Jesus believes that God's Torah is rightly interpreted from a standpoint of mercy and justice. This makes good sense of many of Jesus's interpretations of Torah in the Sermon on the Mount. Disciples of Jesus are called to be persons who refuse vengeance, retaliation, covetousness, and greed, and instead embrace honesty and love for neighbors and enemies (5:21–48). Jesus's "hermeneutic of mercy" as it relates to his ministry and interpretation of Torah is seen clearly in Matthew 12:1–14. When Jesus and his disciples are questioned about breaking the law by picking and eating grain on the Sabbath, Jesus responds with a quotation from Hosea 6:6: "If you had known what this means, 'I desire mercy and not sacrifice,' you would not have condemned the innocent" (12:7). And Jesus declares that God's law *itself* prioritizes mercy and compassion as the proper means of interpreting the commandments of the Torah. For this reason, Jesus says that the Sabbath is the appropriate day to demonstrate mercy and compassion in healing the sick (12:9–12). Jesus's interpretation of the Torah does not dispense with *any commandment*, but it does require the proper evaluation and ranking of commandments when they conflict with one another.[18]

Jesus consistently turns to the Torah to articulate God's will for loving relations among his people. So, for example, in his dispute with the Pharisees who wonder why he and his disciples do not follow the traditions of the elders, Jesus accuses them of "breaking God's commandment because of [their] tradition" (15:3). Specifically, their tradition of dedicating their possessions to the temple instead of using it to care for the mother and father results in them breaking the commandment to honor their parents (Exod. 20:12; Deut. 5:16). The point here is that Jesus accuses the scribes of failing to obey God's Torah and invokes Torah as a means of understanding what God demands as righteous behavior for his disciples. In another episode, Jesus responds to the rich young man's question about how to obtain eternal life by listing the second table of the Ten Commandments, along, *once again*, with the summary commandment of Leviticus 19:18 (cf. Matt. 7:12; 22:24–30): "Do not murder; do not commit adultery; do not steal; do not bear false testimony; honor your father and mother; and you shall love your neighbor as yourself" (Matt. 19:18–19). There is nothing facetious here in Jesus responding to the man's desire for life by invoking God's commandments that promised life to those who observed them (Lev. 18:5; Deut. 30:1–14). The man believes that he has kept these laws, but his refusal to give his possessions to the poor (19:20–22) indicates that he has not given himself to the "better righteousness" (5:20) as found in Jesus's central interpretation of the divine law as demanding mercy, compassion, and love for neighbor.

Jesus Practices Righteousness

But Jesus not only interprets the Torah; he also follows it himself and can be seen as the premier example of one who interiorizes God's law. Unlike the Pharisees and scribes, who are repeatedly referred to as "hypocrites" (Matt. 23:13, 15, 28) and do not "practice what they teach" (e.g., 23:3), Jesus is the one who "fulfills all righteousness" (3:15) and is himself a "righteous man" (27:19).[19] And, in fact, in Matthew 11:27–30 Jesus declares that his life is a visible display of Torah obedience: "All things have been handed over to me by my Father, and no one knows the Son except the Father, nor does anyone know the Father except the Son and the one to whom the Son desires to reveal him. Come to me, all who labor and are heavily burdened, and I will give you rest. Take my yoke upon you, and learn from me, for I am gentle and lowly in heart, and you will find rest for your souls; for my yoke is easy and my burden light." Jesus's claim that he and his teaching manifest "meekness" or "gentleness" resonates with Matthew's depiction of Jesus as the "meek" and humble "king" entering into Jerusalem during the triumphal entry (21:5). Jesus's calmness, rejection of anger, and care for his subjects presents a powerful contrast with the angry and tyrannical King Herod (2:13, 16).[20] Jesus's life and his teaching, then, embody this rejection of anger, aggression, and violence (see 5:21–26).[21] And Matthew presents Jesus as embodying his own interpretation of the

Torah precisely by portraying him as doing what he says. Jesus acts, then, as an exemplary model for embodying God's righteousness in one's deeds.

Many interpreters have noted this feature of Matthew's Gospel and compiled an extensive list of how Jesus's character conforms to his own teachings. For example, Jesus's blessing on the meek (5:5) is embodied in his character as one who is meek and lowly of heart (11:29; 21:5). His blessing on the merciful (5:7) is seen in his healings and exorcisms, which enact mercy to the oppressed (9:2–8; 15:22–28; 20:30–34). Jesus is persecuted for the sake of righteousness in his trial and crucifixion (5:10; 27:23). He turns his other cheek to those who mock and beat him (5:39; 26:67; 27:30). He prays in private places (6:6; 14:23). One could find many more examples, but the point is clear enough: Jesus's teaching, often encapsulated in his interpretation of the Torah, is embodied in his own deeds.[22]

Jesus Is the Merciful Shepherd-King

Jesus's primary proclamation, one of the central themes throughout Matthew's Gospel, is the kingdom of heaven/God (e.g., 4:17, 23; 5:3, 10, 19–20; 6:10, 33). Jesus's teaching on the kingdom of *heaven* shows us that there is a contrast with all of the kingdoms of the earth.[23] God's rule is different from human assumptions regarding the meaning and purpose of power, authority, and kingship. This should be no great surprise, as Jesus's temptation by the devil indicates his rejection of the devil's gift of "all the kingdoms of the world and their glory" (4:8) and the trappings of power advanced by earthly kingdoms. This offer from the devil stands as the antithesis to the "kingdom of heaven" in Matthew 3:2 and 4:17. As Jesus proclaims the kingdom of heaven, so Matthew frequently depicts him as a king, the Messiah, and the son of David (e.g., 1:1, 20; 2:2, 6; 9:27; 21:9, 15). And yet Matthew consistently emphasizes the contrast between Jesus's wielding of power as the agent of the kingdom of heaven and all earthly kingdoms. In what follows, we'll see that Jesus portrays Israel as the lost sheep who are afflicted by unjust rulers and even their own shepherds. And we'll also see that Jesus is God's singular messianic shepherd-king who rules with peace and justice over the flock.

The Lost Flock of the House of Israel

The Old Testament often portrays Israel as God's flock of sheep (e.g., Isa. 40:10–11; Jer. 13:17; 23:1–6; Pss. 74:1; 77:20; 78:52), thereby emphasizing Israel's dependence on their shepherds (i.e., their leaders). Matthew presents a portrait of "the people" as the exploited and scattered flock of God in need of salvation, in part, from their wicked leaders. When Jesus sends the seventy-two disciples on mission, he commands them to go only "to the lost flock of the house of Israel" (10:6). In his conversation with the Syrophoenician woman, he declares, "I have been sent only for the lost flock of the house of Israel" (15:24). 10.7

Matthew's portrait of those in positions of leadership over the people of Israel is unrelentingly negative, and this theme further contributes to the opposition of the kingdom of heaven and Jesus the royal Messiah versus every other earthly kingdom and ruler. Matthew's depiction of Jesus as the shepherd-king has as its counterpart a strong critique of Israel's current rulers.[21] Matthew's genealogy depicts Israel as a "sinful people" in need of salvation (1:21) in large part as a result of Israel's kings, whose wickedness, idolatry, and failure to obey the law of Moses are responsible for their current state of exile (1:7–12). Herod the Great is an angry tyrant who uses deception and violence to accomplish his purposes (2:1–16). Herod Antipas, the "tetrarch" (14:1), is another ruler who is marked by excessive fear and superstition (14:2, 5), sexual improprieties (14:3–4, 6), and foolishness (14:7), culminating in his violent and grotesque execution of the righteous prophet John the Baptist (14:4–5, 10–11). Pilate, the Roman "governor" (27:2, 11, 14, 15, 21), knows that Jesus has been delivered to death because of envy (27:18), hears from his wife that Jesus is a "righteous man" (27:19), makes a mockery of the Jewish leaders in washing his hands of responsibility for the fate of Jesus (27:24), and, nevertheless, hands Jesus over to the Roman soldiers to be crucified (27:27–31). The scribes and the Pharisees, likewise, do not rule over the people with justice; instead, Jesus criticizes them for interpreting the Torah in such a way that it places impossible demands on the people (23:3–4). Their ultimate commitments and interpretation of the Torah demonstrate that they love status and honor (23:5–8). They evade God's purpose for

SIDEBAR 10.7

Bad Shepherds Condemned by Israel's Prophets

The language of "the lost sheep" recalls Israel's prophets who often speak a word of judgment against Israel's shepherds.

> You have not strengthened the weak, healed the sick, bandaged the injured, brought back the strays, or sought the lost. Instead, you have ruled them with violence and cruelty. So they were scattered because there was no shepherd, and when they were scattered they became food for all the wild animals. My sheep wandered over all the mountains and on every high hill. They were scattered over the whole earth, and no one searched or looked for them. (Ezek. 34:4–6)

Hear the echoes also from the prophet Jeremiah.

> This is what the Lord, the God of Israel, says to the shepherd who tend my people: "Because you have scattered my flock and driven them away and have not bestowed care on them, I will bestow punishment on you for the evil you have done," declares the Lord. (Jer. 23:2)

> My people have been lost sheep; their shepherds have led them astray, leading them away on the mountains; they have wandered from mountain to hill having forgotten their fold. (Jer. 50:6)

For Matthew, the focus is not so much that the sheep have gone astray but rather that they are lost precisely because they have been led astray by bad shepherds.[9]

humans by insisting on their traditions and human commandments (23:16–24; cf. 15:1–9). The Pharisees, elders, scribes, and priests are portrayed as wanting to destroy and kill Jesus (12:14; 16:21; 17:23; 21:38–39; 27:20). The temple has become a "den of thieves," given their violent intentions for Jesus (21:13). The priests' use of wealth is for the corrupt purpose of destroying Jesus, and they are portrayed as engaging in stealthy conspiracy against him (26:3–5, 14–16; 27:1; 28:11–15).[25]

The Merciful and Compassionate Shepherd-King

In contrast to his portrait of the Roman rulers, and Jewish scribes, priests, and Pharisees, Matthew depicts Jesus as the merciful shepherd-king who establishes the rule of his heavenly Father over his people. We have already seen that Jesus's interpretation of the Torah takes as its starting point the call for mercy, love, and justice as an imitation of the heavenly Father (e.g., Matt. 5:43–48; 11:25–12:14; 23:23). In addition to his call for mercy in his reading of the Torah, one of the primary ways Jesus enacts his rule as the merciful messianic shepherd is through his compassionate healings of those on the margins of society. The Messiah's deeds (11:2) consist in his healings of the oppressed: "The blind receive their sight, the lame walk, the lepers are cleansed, the deaf hear, the dead are raised, and the poor hear the good news" (11:5). Thus, in Matthew 9:27–31 Jesus touches and heals two blind men, who cry out, "Have mercy upon us, Son of David!" (v. 27). Jesus's merciful deeds, exemplified primarily in healings and inclusion of outsiders in Matthew 8–9, are the context for the blind men's invocation of Jesus as the Son of David *and* Matthew's description of Jesus who "upon seeing the crowds, had compassion for them because they were harassed and distressed like sheep without a shepherd" (9:36).[26] The current shepherds of Israel have failed to attend to the needs of the flock and have thereby abdicated their role as Israel's leaders. Jesus's compassion on the "harassed and distressed" flock of God is the context, then, for his sending out the twelve disciples to "the lost sheep of the house of Israel" (10:6a) to cast out demons, heal the sick, and proclaim the kingdom of heaven (10:1–8). The disciples are called, then, to continue the compassionate ministry of Jesus the messianic shepherd.

This contrast between kingdoms is further expanded on in Jesus's ensuing interpretation of his healings and exorcisms, where he asks, "If I drive out demons by *the Spirit of God*, then the *kingdom of God* has come upon you" (12:28). Jesus's mercy and compassion to the distressed and needy continue to be seen in his healing of the man possessed by a demon, who is unable to see or speak (12:22). The healing elicits this question from the crowds: "Could this be the Son of David?" (12:23). Despite his call to go only to the lost sheep of Israel (15:24), Jesus finally responds by healing a gentile woman who is crying out, "Have mercy on me, Lord, Son of David!" (15:22). Two blind men twice cry out, "Lord, Son of David, have mercy on us" (20:30–31), and Jesus, filled with compassion, touches their eyes and heals them (20:34). And as Jesus makes his entrance into Jerusalem and the temple, the crowd confesses that he is "the Son of David" (21:9), and Jesus heals the blind and the lame in the temple (21:14). Matthew notes that the chief priests and scribes were furious when they saw the miracles and heard children shouting, "Hosanna to the Son of David" (21:15). In response to the anger of the priests and scribes, Jesus quotes from Psalm 8:2, "Out of the mouths of babies and infants you have prepared praise for yourself" (Matt. 21:16), indicating that the children rightly understand Jesus's identity when they acknowledge him as the Son of David. Jesus's identity as the Davidic messianic shepherd is embodied in the merciful and compassionate care he provides, signified powerfully in healings and exorcisms, for the distressed and harassed lost sheep of Israel.

Matthew portrays Jesus as embodying his Davidic messianic task even in his sufferings from the hands of his enemies. Jesus has, after all, drawn the deepest connection between his messianic kingship and his sufferings (e.g., 16:21; 17:22–23; 20:18–19). Immediately after Jesus's final meal with his disciples, where he interprets his impending death as a payment for sins (26:26–29), at the Mount of Olives Jesus brings the shepherd motif to a conclusion: "'I will strike the shepherd, and the sheep of the flock will be scattered.' And after I have been raised, I will go before you into Galilee" (26:31b–32). Jesus's works of healing have embodied his mercy and compassion for the sheep, but Matthew portrays the climactic act of the messianic shepherd's mercy as coming in Jesus's death at the hands of the wicked shepherds.[27] Drawing on Zechariah 13:7, Jesus speaks of himself as the Davidic shepherd who is struck down in judgment with the result that the flock (i.e., the disciples) is scattered; but, ironically, it is through this very act of the shepherd's death that the flock is forgiven, restored, and purified. Jesus's embodiment of his messianic task is seen, finally, in his rejection of violence and force in his arrest and ensuing death. Matthew's account of Jesus's prayer in Gethsemane and subsequent arrest (26:36–56) has likely been typologically modeled on David's sufferings and trials during Absalom's revolt (2 Sam. 13–18).[28] For example, after Absalom rebels, King David and his followers leave Jerusalem and go to the Mount of Olives, just as Jesus, the Davidic Messiah, leaves Jerusalem and goes to the same mountain (2 Sam. 15:15–30; Matt. 26:30–31). David and his followers are described as mourning and weeping, just as Jesus, accompanied by his disciples, is in emotional distress and praying to God with the lament psalms of David (2 Sam. 15:23, 30; Matt. 26:36–44; cf. Pss. 42:5, 11; 43:5 [these psalm verses in the Greek Old Testament speak of "deep grief" and "confusion"]). As David is betrayed by Ahithophel, who leads a group of the king's enemies against David during the night while he is tired, so does Jesus's "friend" Judas betray him while he is in distress during the night (2 Sam. 17:1–4; Matt. 26:47–50; cf. Ps. 55:12–21). Both Ahithophel and Judas commit suicide by hanging (2 Sam. 17:23; Matt. 27:5). These are just a few of the many parallels one can adduce, but the function of Matthew's portrait of Jesus as typologically undergoing David's sufferings is to depict Jesus's kingship as embodied in the rejection of violence and force, a refusal to seek retribution against his enemies, and a faithful reliance on God for his vindication.[29] And this is why the flurry of references to Jesus as Messiah, Son of God, and King of Israel are, in a deeply ironic manner, found in the mouths of Jesus's enemies as Jesus dies on the cross (27:36–44).

The Return of the Son of Man and Final Judgment

Of the four Gospels, Matthew's speaks most frequently about an eschatological judgment based on true discipleship. And being his disciple is, of course, based on whether one listens to, follows, and obeys his teachings. Matthew's Gospel often evinces an apocalyptic-eschatological framework whereby a coming final judgment will divide all people into two groups: the saved and the damned.[30] Jesus's parables often emphasize that the kingdom is something that starts out in a hidden and small manner but grows surprisingly into something great (e.g., 13:31–39). Jesus tells and explains a parable in which the kingdom of heaven is like a field sown with both good seed and weeds (13:24–30, 36–43). The Son of Man sows the good seed, and the evil one sows weeds. Only at the final judgment, however, will it be revealed who are "the children of the kingdom" and who are "the children of the evil one" (13:38, 40–43a). One's behavior and righteousness must be congruent with what one professes.

For most Protestants this may seem surprising and perhaps may even strike some as conflicting with the first thread stated above, that Jesus's life and death pay the debt for our sins. But Matthew shows us that we must hold together both *Jesus's ransom for humanity's sin* and his clear teaching that *there is no salvation apart from discipleship*. Although this is not much in vogue today, Jesus repeatedly speaks of a coming judgment as a means of motivating his disciples to listen to and obey his teachings. While we should not forget the depictions of Jesus as offering his life for the forgiveness of sins and Jesus the merciful shepherd king, Matthew's Gospel emphasizes that disciples cannot take advantage of God's mercy by living lives of wickedness and sloth.[31] 10.8

Figure 10.2. *Descent into Hell*, icon from the Ferapontov Monastery

That one's life must manifest repentance and obedience in order to evade the coming wrath is previewed as early as John the Baptist's proclamation. It is only by producing "fruit worthy of repentance" that one can avoid "the coming wrath" (Matt. 3:7–9). Jesus says as much in the Sermon on the Mount when he declares that many will seek entrance into the kingdom of heaven who proclaim their successful prophecies, exorcisms, and miracles of healings but who did not do "the will of my Father in heaven" (7:21–22). Jesus's response will be, "I never knew you. Depart from me, you workers of lawlessness" (7:23). Again, later Jesus defines his true family not as his flesh and blood but rather as "whoever does the will of my Father in heaven" (12:50).

SIDEBAR 10.8

Images of Eschatological Judgment in Matthew

- Outer darkness and weeping and gnashing of teeth (8:12; 22:13; 25:30)
- Unquenchable or eternal fire (3:10–12; 18:8–9; 25:41)
- Gehenna (5:22; 18:9)
- Handing over to torment (18:34; 24:51)

Matthew gathers together three parables that emphasize the necessity of obedience and fruit-bearing as a prerequisite for entering into the kingdom of God (21:28–22:14). The literary setting of the parables shows that they are directed to Israel's religious leaders who have rejected John the Baptist's and Jesus's message (21:23–27, 31–32). The parable of the two sons describes a father who asks both sons to work in the vineyard (21:28–32). One professes to go to work but never does; the other says he won't go to work but changes his mind. Jesus asks, "Which of the two did the will of the father?" (21:31a). The parable of the vineyard previews the judgment that will come for those entrusted with the master's vineyard but who never deliver any fruit (21:33–46). And the third parable tells the story of one who shows up to a king's wedding feast but is unprepared and has no appropriate garments to wear. When the king sees him, he casts him out "into the outer darkness with the weeping and gnashing of teeth" (22:13). Clothing here, as elsewhere in the New Testament (e.g., Gal. 3:27; Eph. 4:22–24; Rev. 3:4–5; 19:8), likely symbolizes righteous and pure character—something that the man in the parable lacks. The three parables emphasize what God demands of his disciples if they are to enter into the kingdom of heaven and avoid judgment: doing the will of the Father, fruit-bearing, and righteousness.[32]

Jesus's eschatological discourse in Matthew 24:1–25:46 again emphasizes the final judgment that takes place when the Son of Man returns. Jesus exhorts his disciples to "stay awake" because they do not know when he will return. The "faithful and wise servant" is the one who is occupied with *doing* Jesus's work (24:42, 45–46). This one will be rewarded by being placed in charge of the master's possessions; but the wicked and lazy servant will be cut into pieces and thrown into the place of weeping and gnashing of teeth (24:50–51). Three more parables follow that effectively make the same point: the parables of the ten virgins (25:1–13), the talents (25:14–30), and the sheep and the goats (25:31–46). Notice in the parable of the talents that when the master returns after his delay, he extravagantly rewards the two servants who have "been faithful with a few things" by putting them in charge of *many things* (25:21, 23). The servant who is judged is the *one who didn't do anything*. He heard the commands of the Lord but did nothing. And this is what merits eschatological judgment (25:30). Some did more "work" than others, but even the servant who was faithful with less still gets payment.[33] In the parable of the sheep and the goats, when the Son of Man returns, he will make the division based on whether his disciples cared "for the least of these" (25:40, 45)—that is, whether they practiced Jesus's teachings about dispensing mercy and hospitality to one another (10:40–42; 18:1–14).

To summarize: Jesus will return as the Son of Man in eschatological judgment. Jesus's gifts of mercy and payment for sins do not license willful disobedience or sloth. More than the other Gospels, Matthew emphasizes Jesus's teaching that he expects his people not only to listen to his words but also to practice them. For those who persist in unrighteousness or who deceive themselves by living lives of hypocrisy, the final judgment will consist in eternal destruction.

Matthew and Discipleship

Given my conviction that the Gospels are Christian Scripture, I do not hesitate to approach them as God's Word given to us for our salvation, wisdom, and edification. For each Gospel, then, I will offer a short chapter that introduces a few more themes from each Gospel in a manner that also unpacks Jesus's call for a life of discipleship. I hope that readers of the Gospels will engage in their own prayerful reading and reflection and add to my short list, which offers four aspects of disciples of Jesus.

Disciples of Jesus Practice Righteousness without Hypocrisy

Jesus knows that hypocrisy when we "practice righteousness" (Matt. 6:1) is a temptation for all people who seek to obey God. Hypocrisy is the outward appearance of pursuing God but the inward preoccupation and obsession with ourselves. In Matthew 6:1–18 Jesus gives three examples of what this hypocrisy looks like. In each instance, the desire that stands behind the religious act has moved from wanting to love God and please him to the hope that religious acts would be seen by others so as to win some kind of recognition, honor, and approval *from other humans*. Almsgiving (vv. 2–4), prayer (vv. 5–8), and fasting (vv. 16–18) should be performed, but as concrete acts of worshiping God and not as attempts to earn approval from others. Notice how Jesus describes God here (and throughout the Gospel). God is "your Father, who sees the things that are done in secret" (v. 4); disciples are told to enter a room, shut the door, and pray "to your Father, who is in secret, for your Father sees the things done in secret" (v. 6b); "your Father already knows your needs before you ask him" (v. 8). God is not fooled or deceived, since he knows and sees the hearts of humans. Jesus teaches that the kind of piety the Father desires is the simple prayer of the humble in heart who quietly close the door and pray to him as if God alone is the object of devotion and affection. God loves those who show genuine concern and care for the vulnerable and needy and do not seek honor for themselves from others. 11.1

SIDEBAR 11.1

Mary Oliver, "Praying"

Mary Oliver was a twentieth- and twenty-first-century American poet whose themes often centered on the experience of the transcendent within nature and the mundane. Oliver writes, "Attention is the beginning of devotion."[a] For Oliver, turning our eyes to the world is key for experiencing the wonders of creation and the mystery of the divine. In her poem "Praying" Oliver invites the reader to observe the ordinary and let it bring them into a posture of prayer. She writes, "just / pay attention, then patch / a few words together."[b] But prayer doesn't end with our words. Prayer is communication with God, and her poem ends by reminding the reader (or pray-er) to listen to the voice of God.

Notice here how the Lord's Prayer (6:9–13) functions in the midst of Jesus's teaching on righteousness. Matthew sets forth three practices: giving to the poor (vv. 2–4), prayer (vv. 5–8), and fasting (vv. 16–18). Each one has a warning attached about not performing them to be seen by others, and each one speaks of the Father in heaven who sees in secret. Interrupting this neat structure is Jesus's antidote to hypocrisy: the Lord's Prayer. The prayer invites the disciples to come into God's presence and to order their desires in light of God's kingdom. In effect, Jesus tells his followers that the only way they can avoid the deceptive pull toward hypocrisy is by coming into the presence of God and having their desires oriented toward true worship of him.

Much has been said about the Lord's Prayer, so let's just look at three important aspects of it. First, the prayer teaches the disciples to approach God as a good and loving Father. The prayer is directed to "our Father in heaven" (6:9). If God is the Father, then the disciples are beloved sons and daughters. The language of "Father" is what Jesus used throughout his time here on earth to speak of God. One of Matthew's favorite titles for Jesus is "Son of God," and God is his loving Father. The Father shows intimate love and care for his children (6:25–34). Obedience to the Father's will as taught by Jesus *and* the rejection of being religious to win human approval can come only out of the recognition that God is a loving Father who invites his followers to embody his will and righteousness.

Second, Jesus teaches the disciples to pray that God's name and his kingdom—not their own—will be honored and glorified (6:9–10). The travesty of hypocrisy is that one's good deeds are ultimately serving oneself. So Jesus teaches his followers to pray for God's glory and kingdom. Notice how the next three petitions are all about God receiving praise and glory: "hallowed be *your name*; let *your kingdom* come; let *your will* be done."

Third, Jesus teaches his followers to affirm total dependence on him for all of life. Notice that the rest of the petitions center on God's loving care and protection of his people (6:11–13). Followers of Jesus pray that he will provide today the food that is needed. They humbly trust that when sins are confessed, the Father will cleanse and forgive. And when followers of Jesus pray "Don't let us enter into temptation, but instead deliver us from evil," they are praying that God will protect them from apostasy, from turning away from God when trials and difficulties come.

Disciples of Jesus Practice Peace and Nonviolence

We have seen that Matthew turns power on its head in surprising ways! In Matthew's infancy narrative we see the conflict between the designated messianic "child" (2:2, 8, 9, 11, 13, 14) and "king" Herod (2:1, 3, 9). One kingdom operates according to peace and mercy, whereas the other works with violence, deception, and coercion. And throughout the Gospel, Matthew attempts to show us the difference between the peaceful and just kingdom of heaven inaugurated by Jesus the Messiah and every other worldly king and kingdom.[1] Jesus will not accept Satan's offer of a kingship predicated on using power in a self-serving way (4:1–11). The lesson for disciples of Jesus is critical here. For Jesus, the ends do not justify the means. Jesus refuses to obtain power or to use it in ways that would exalt himself at the expense of his obedience to his Father. Christ's kingship instead witnesses to a form of power that is not like the way of the world but rather is revealed in love, suffering, and truth. Jesus rejects the ways of Herod, Pilate, and others and, instead, calls his people to lives of peace, nonviolence, and gentleness.

In the Beatitudes—blessings that Jesus pronounces on those who follow his way of life—Jesus declares, "Blessed are the peacemakers, for they will be called sons of God" (5:9). Peacemakers are God's children because their heavenly Father's character is one of peace, love, and mercy toward the righteous and the wicked (5:43–48).[2] As God's messianic king, Jesus himself is the Prince of Peace (Isa. 9:6–7; 11:6–9). As Esau McCaulley notes, "Jesus calls his people to be *peacemakers* because the kingdom of the Messiah is one of peace."[3] This call for peace is embodied in actions that intentionally work to reject vengeance and retribution against one's enemies and, instead, seek out reconciliation and an end to hostilities. This kind of peacemaker will not only embody this beatitude but will also be a person marked by gentleness, righteousness, and mercy (5:5–7). The peacemaking activity that Jesus has in mind is spelled out explicitly in his further teachings in the Sermon on the Mount. Disciples of Jesus not only reject murder; they also reject the passion of anger against fellow humans (5:21–26). Disciples of Jesus do not live by the principle of "an eye for an eye, a tooth for a tooth" (5:38)—the so-called *lex talionis*; rather, they are to "resist an evildoer" through nonviolent means such as turning the other cheek (5:39–42). Is Jesus asking for those who are already oppressed and marginalized to simply act passively in response to those who would inflict violence and shame? On the one hand, Jesus does emphatically reject violence as an option for disciples of Jesus. But, on the other hand, Jesus uses a variety of active verbs to describe the response of peacemakers. Peacemakers *turn* their cheeks; they *go* the extra mile; they *give* to those who demand. Thus, "Jesus's call to nonresistance is in fact a call to active response."[4] And the responses are surprising and strange, suggesting that they are creative responses to evil that "bring the evil itself into clear focus and confront the evil one with the implications of their action."[5] The acts of turning the other cheek and giving one's tunic and cloak to the "evil person" highlight the shamefulness and wickedness of that person's actions. The refusal to meet violence with more violence is summed up in Jesus's teachings in Matthew 5:43–48, which call his disciples to "love your enemies and pray for those who persecute you" (5:44). Again, this is

SIDEBAR 11.2

Peacemaking and Nonviolence in the African American Church

Jesus's call for nonviolent resistance might sound abstract, but we are fortunate to have historical examples of individuals and communities who have embodied Jesus's teaching in powerful ways. The fight for civil rights for African Americans in the United States is the struggle for racial justice and equality that so often have been denied to Black persons. Martin Luther King Jr. is, of course, the best-known representative of this movement, though it is important to recognize that he and the Southern Christian Leadership Conference had many predecessors and contemporaries all working together for racial justice.[c] King and the majority of the Black church advocated active nonviolent resistance out of a deep commitment to the life and teachings of Jesus. The Montgomery bus boycotts, John Lewis (of the Student Nonviolent Coordinating Committee), the Freedom Riders in the Deep South, and the Selma-to-Montgomery march for voting registration mark major examples of African Americans working in nonviolent ways for peace. The goal of nonviolent resistance, as Albert Raboteau has noted, is

> to convert, not to defeat, the opponent; it was directed against evil, not against persons; and it avoided internal violence, such as hatred or bitterness. . . . [Nonviolent resistance] was based on loving others regardless of worth or merit; it was premised on the realization that all human beings are interrelated; and it was grounded in the confidence that justice would, in the end, triumph over injustice.[d]

King drew on a variety of biblical images, perhaps foremost of which were God's deliverance of his people and provision of freedom during the exodus, and the kingdom teachings of Jesus of Nazareth. The latter offered an opportunity for the oppressed and marginalized to both actively resist and love their enemies by holding up a mirror directly before the faces of those white persons who wished them harm. Pervading King's sermons is a conviction that society and all of humanity are interrelated, caught up together in an "inescapable network of mutuality."[e]

Esau McCaulley notes that peacemaking cannot be divorced from prophetic truth-telling. In other words, it would be a gross mistake to weaponize Jesus's call for nonviolent resistance by asking African Americans to passively accept unfair and unjust racism and discrimination.

> Housing discrimination has to be named. Unequal sentences and unfair policing has to be named. Sexism and the abuse and commodification of the Black female body has to end. Otherwise any peace is false and nonbiblical. Beyond naming there has to be some vision for the righting of wrongs and the restoration of relationships. The call to be peacemakers is the call for the church to enter the messy world of politics and point toward a better way of being human.[f]

Confronted with the evils of racism and injustice, both McCaulley and King reject complacency as well as violent hatred. Instead, King argues in his "Letter from a Birmingham City Jail" that there "is the more excellent way of love and protest."[g]

rooted in the character of God, who is good to all (5:45). This is a remarkable ethic, as Jesus's disciples are called to see as fellow objects of God's love and mercy even their so-called enemies and those who wish them harm and seek to shame them. 11.2

The civil rights movement *and* the teachings of Jesus testify that those who work for peace and refuse to wield violence will receive violence from others. Jesus commissions his disciples to a mission of proclaiming the kingdom, healings, mercy, and peace (Matt. 10:1–13), but this kingdom is the same one that "has been subjected to violence, and violent people have taken it with force" (11:12). Herod, Pilate, and others respond to John the Baptist, Jesus, and the disciples with violence and even murder (2:1–15; 14:1–12; 26:1–5, 14–16, 47–68; 27:11–44). Those who respond to violence with peace do so with the knowledge that God has promised to vindicate and resurrect them for their faithful prophetic testimony in the face of evil (16:24–28).

SIDEBAR 11.3

What Is Forgiveness?

Christian psychologists have often made a distinction between decisional and emotional forgiveness. Decisional forgiveness refers to our thought process that resolves that it is right for us to seek the transgressor's welfare and forgo vengeance. Emotional forgiveness is what happens when our feelings, desires, and motivations conform to our hope for the offender's flourishing as opposed to retribution.[h] Jesus's teaching is strongly on the side of calling the offender to forgo retaliation and revenge, regardless of whether one "feels" positively toward the offender and the wrong that he or she has inflicted. In this regard, I find the following definition of "forgiveness" to be helpful: "Rather than a determination never again to feel rancor or resentment in perpetuity, 'forgiveness' is simply a promise not to act with retaliatory violence when those painful emotions and vengeful desires inevitably and repeatedly arise."[i]

Disciples of Jesus Practice Mercy and Forgiveness

Closely connected to the practice of peacemaking is the call to Jesus's disciples to extend mercy. The relationship between divine mercy and our extension of mercy to one another is highlighted in a beatitude when Jesus says, "Blessed are the merciful, for they will receive mercy" (Matt. 5:7). Twice in Matthew, Jesus draws on Hosea 6:6 to interpret God's will as requiring humans to extend mercy to one another (9:13; 12:7). We have seen that Jesus interprets God's will and the Torah from the right standpoint: the Torah is an expression of God's justice, love, and mercy (23:23). Thus, we reject vengeance and retribution in our dealings with one another and are measured and gentle in our judgments (7:1–5). 11.3

We have seen already that Jesus's messianic shepherding ministry of extending mercy to the "distressed and harassed" flock of God (9:36) is extended to his disciples, who share in the shepherd's ministry to "the lost sheep of the house of Israel" (10:6).[6]

The disciples share in Jesus's ministry of mercy by freely offering healings, exorcisms, and proclamation of the kingdom of heaven (10:1, 7–8).

SIDEBAR 11.4

The Destructive Futility of Revenge in Shakespeare's *Hamlet*

Shakespeare's famous tragedy *Hamlet* touches on some of the greatest themes of life and literature: identity, gender and sexuality, grief, family relationships, and, perhaps most notably, the question of revenge.

The plot is complex. Suffice it to say that Prince Hamlet is justly angry at the murder of his father, King Hamlet of Denmark, by his uncle King Claudius, who was involved in an illicit affair with Prince Hamlet's mother, Queen Gertrude, and has now married the queen. A ghost, perhaps the ghost of King Hamlet, appears to the prince and exhorts him to take revenge on King Claudius. Throughout the play, young Hamlet is thoroughly enraged and consumed with a desire for revenge. One potential lesson of the play is that revenge is futile, for Hamlet's pursuit of revenge leads to the destruction of himself and all he holds dear. After his rage against Claudius results in Hamlet, intending to kill him, mistakenly killing the beloved lord Polonius, there is great irony in Hamlet referring to himself as God's "scourge and minister" (act 3, scene 4). Hamlet, in other words, sees himself as playing the role of ministering divine vengeance. But by the end of the play, Hamlet's desire for revenge results not only in his death but also in the death of those he loves and in the conquering of Denmark by Fortinbras the prince of Norway.

Perhaps the central moral of the story is found in what Paul says to the church in Rome: "Do not take revenge, my friends, but leave room for the wrath of God" (Rom. 12:19).

One of the primary ways the messianic community continues to embody Jesus's shepherding ministry is through forgiveness, reconciliation, and extending mercy to the needy. Disciples pray to the Father, "Forgive us from our debts, even as we forgive those who have debts to us" (6:12). Those who have received Jesus's merciful forgiveness of their sins (1:21; 20:28; 26:28) must engage in the cancellation and forgiveness of the debts of others. This makes sense of the otherwise challenging statement "If you forgive people their trespasses, so will your heavenly Father forgive you too; and if you do not forgive people, then neither will your father forgive you of your trespasses" (6:14–15). God's mercy, forgiveness, and debt cancellation for those who were in captivity and bondage to sin *must* have as their logical outcome disciples who continue to forgive and extend mercy to their debtors. This theme is powerfully articulated in the parable of the unmerciful slave in Matthew 18:21–35, which functions as an interpretative commentary on Matthew 6:12, 14–15. In response to Peter's question regarding the number of times he must forgive the same offender, Jesus's parable positions disciples as those who have experienced the deep mercy and compassion of the one who has paid their incredible debt, and who are thereby obligated to continue the practice of mercy and debt cancellation for their fellow neighbors (18:33–35). Disciples continue Jesus's ministry as the messianic shepherd when they embody the humility or downward mobility of children (18:1–4), when they give no offense (18:6–7), and when they do not look down on any of God's "little ones" (18:10). Jesus calls his disciples to restore any of God's "lost sheep" who have gone astray (18:12–13) and reconcile with and forgive any brothers or sisters who have sinned (18:15–20). 11.4

Mercy can take the form of actions that attend to caring for the broken and needy. In Jesus's parable of the sheep and the goats, with the imagery of Daniel 7:13–14, Jesus is the eschatological judge over all the peoples (Matt. 25:31–46). Here we should remember that the literary context of the parable is one where the theme of lifestyle "readiness" for Jesus's second return has been emphasized (24:36–25:30).[7] The enthroned Son of Man declares that his disciples will be publicly vindicated as his sheep at the final judgment based on whether they have extended mercy and hospitality and provided food, drink, and clothes for "the least of these brothers and sisters of mine" (25:40, 45). One of the most striking aspects of this parable is the fact that the sheep declare that they did not know that their acts of compassion and hospitality were performed for Jesus: "Then the righteous will answer him, 'Lord, when did we see you hungry and feed you, or when were you thirsty and we gave you something to drink?'" (25:37 [cf. the response of the accursed in 25:44]). Again, Jesus here shows us that discipleship is not an optional component for salvation. Those who claim to follow Jesus will live a life of righteousness, and this is expressed as engaging in acts of mercy, compassion, and hospitality—especially for the vulnerable, poor, and marginalized. 11.5

Jesus's promises in the Beatitudes are fulfilled in the scene envisioned by this parable, as those who pursue peace, mercy, righteousness, poverty of spirit, meekness, and so forth in the name of Jesus (5:3–12) receive their eschatological inheritance. The one who has embodied mercy as the compassionate shepherd will, then, judge and evaluate people based on whether they too have demonstrated mercy and compassion in their care for fellow disciples (also 10:40–42). 11.6

SIDEBAR 11.5

Two Church Fathers on the Parable of the Sheep and the Goats

Epiphanius

"Does our Lord hunger and thirst? Is he who himself made everything in heaven and on earth, who feeds angels in heaven and every nation and race on earth, who needs nothing of an earthly character, as he is unfailing in his own nature, is this one naked? It is incredible to believe such a thing. Yet what must be confessed is easy to believe. For the Lord hungers not in his own nature but in his saints; the Lord thirsts not in his own nature but in his servants. . . . Our Lord, the one who can liberate every person, is not in prison in his own nature but in his saints. Therefore, you see, my most beloved, that the saints are not alone. They suffer all these things because of the Lord. In the same way, because of the saints the Lord suffers all these things with them" (*Interpretation of the Gospels* 38).[j]

John Chrysostom

"'For I was hungry, and you gave me no food.' For even though you should meet your enemy, is not his suffering enough to overcome and subdue your resistance to being merciful? And what about his hunger, cold, chains, nakedness and sickness? What about his homelessness? Are not these sufferings sufficient to overcome even your alienation? But you did not do these things for a friend, much less a foe. You could have at once befriended and done good. Even when you see a dog hungry you feel sympathy. But when you see the Lord hungry, you ignore it. You are without excuse" (*Homilies on the Gospel of Matthew* 79.2).[k]

SIDEBAR 11.6

Dorothy Day and the Catholic Workers Movement

There are many wonderful examples of individuals who have devoted their lives to peacemaking and acts of mercy. One worthy recent example is the Christian social activist Dorothy Day (1897–1980).[l] Though marked by doubts and loneliness, Day had a deep, enduring commitment to the Christian Scriptures and the teachings of Jesus. She was known, in part, along with Peter Maurin, for the development of "Houses of Hospitality"—individual local households living together communally and devoted to serving the poor and marginalized persons (typically in cities with impoverished communities).[m] Day's belief that both the material and the spiritual belonged together helps to explain why these Houses of Hospitality were devoted not only to the study of Scripture and theology but also to concrete acts of mercy such as the hospitable provision of shelter, food, and clothing.

Day's life in many ways embodies Jesus's exhortation in the parable of the sheep and the goats: the righteous perform acts of mercy *to Jesus when they do them for "the least of these."* Christ lived among the poor and called his disciples to be with the poor. Day believed that acts of mercy could not be divorced from voluntarily identifying with the poor, and this led her to embrace a life of material simplicity and direct contact with the marginalized.

Day was not a biblical exegete, but her life bears eloquent testimony to how one individual (and movement) sought to live out Jesus's call for compassion, mercy, peace, and love of neighbor. Note the echoes of Jesus's ministry and teaching in a couple of her famous quotes.

> We cannot love God unless we love each other, and to love we must know each other. We know Him in the breaking of bread, and we know each other in the breaking of bread, and we are not alone any more. Heaven is a banquet and life is a banquet, too, even with a crust, where there is companionship.[n]

God's love requires and is manifested through our shared love for one another, and this common life takes the form of hospitable sharing of one's provisions. And again, Day states,

> What we would like to do is change the world—make it a little simpler for people to feed, clothe, and shelter themselves as God intended them to do. . . . We repeat, there is nothing that we can do but love, and dear God—please enlarge our hearts to love each other, to love our neighbor, to love our enemy as well as our friend.[o]

Disciples of Jesus Share in His Mission to Make Disciples and Worshipers of All the Nations

Matthew's Gospel portrays Jesus as both starting and commissioning a church to carry on his ministry (Matt. 16:17–20; 18:15–18; 28:16–20). The church is called, then, to continue Jesus's ministry. As Jesus proclaimed the gospel and kingdom (4:17, 23; 9:35), so do his disciples (24:14). As Jesus forgives sins and shows mercy, so the members of the church are to extend mercy to and forgive one another (5:38–48; 6:12; 18:15–35). As Jesus lived a life of righteousness (3:15; 5:17–20), so his disciples devote themselves to righteousness through doing the will of God (5:6; 7:21–24; 12:46–50). As Jesus suffered faithfully even to death on the cross (20:28; chaps. 26–27), so his disciples can expect suffering as they engage in cross-bearing (10:16–23; 16:24–28). Matthew's Gospel demonstrates that "the mission of the church is . . . a continuation of what God has begun to accomplish in the mission of Jesus on the earth."[8]

One of the best-known scenes in Matthew's Gospel is its ending, where the risen Jesus gives what is known as the Great Commission to disciples

Figure 11.1. Kelly Latimore, *Dorothy Day and the Holy Family of the Streets*

on the mountain (28:16–20).[9] Here Jesus commissions the disciples, and by implication the church, to continue his task of making disciples *from all the nations*. Jesus promises his ongoing authority and presence to his people in their fulfillment of the task. When the disciples see the risen Jesus, Matthew notes that, although there were some who doubted, "they worshiped him" (28:17). This draws attention to an important theme in Matthew that I have barely mentioned: Jesus declares that no one should worship anyone but God alone (4:10), but he approvingly receives worship from the magi (2:11), someone with a skin disease (8:2), a synagogue leader (9:18), the disciples in the boat with Jesus (14:33), a Syrophoenician woman (15:25), the mother of the sons of Zebedee (20:20), and the two women disciples who encounter the empty tomb and the risen Jesus (28:8–9). The inescapable conclusion for the reader is that God is powerfully present and at work in the person of Jesus. One of the goals of the Great Commission is to draw all people to worship Jesus and to proclaim his salvation and teachings to the nations.

In the Great Commission, the risen Jesus uses the language of Daniel 7:13–14 as he declares, "All authority on heaven and earth has been given to me" (Matt. 28:18). Jesus rejected the offer of power and authority from the devil (4:8–10), but now, through his righteousness and faithful obedience to the Father, Jesus has received the promise that he will be the enthroned king over the nations (so also Ps. 2:7–8). Resurrected and enthroned, the Son of Man is now the royal judge over the nations, and his disciples have as their work the task to "go and make disciples of all the nations" (28:19a). We have seen that Jesus's ministry centered on the "lost sheep of the house of Israel" (10:6; 15:24; cf. 9:35–36; 26:31). But Matthew has repeatedly hinted and foreshadowed that the gentile nations would be brought to worship the Messiah and would "place their hope in his name" (12:21; cf. 2:1–12; 4:15–16; 8:5–13; 15:20–28).[10] We remember that Matthew began his Gospel with a genealogy that identified Jesus not only as "the son of David" but also as the "son of Abraham" (1:1)—Abraham being the one to whom it was promised that he would be the father of *many nations* (Gen. 12:1–4; 17:1–22; 22:15–18). The task of discipleship involves *teaching everything that Jesus commanded them* (28:20). And this must be seen, not only for them but also for us, as an explicit call to continue Jesus's mission by passing on Jesus's teachings as found in the Gospel of Matthew. Immediately preceding his exhortations in the Sermon on the Mount, Jesus declares that his followers are tasked to be "the salt of the earth" (5:13) and "the light of the world" (5:14), whose embodiment of Jesus's teachings would put God's truth on display before all people.

Jesus promised Peter, based on his confession that Jesus is the Messiah, that he would be the "rock" on which Christ would build the church. In other words, Jesus anticipated that his people be a temple-like community, built on the rejected and vindicated *cornerstone* of Christ (21:42; cf. Ps. 118:22). As such, Jesus promises the disciples that his risen presence as Emmanuel will be with them until the end of the age to empower them for their mission (28:20b; also 1:23; 18:20). Jesus's promise to give Peter the "keys of the kingdom of heaven" (16:19 [alluding to "the key of the house of David" in Isa. 22:21–22]) characterizes the disciples as the Messiah's priests, who, through their teaching, judging, and dispensing of Jesus's mercy and forgiveness, continue the mission of the Messiah.[11] The risen Jesus's powerful presence is at work in the church to gather all nations to Jesus.

Summary of Main Points on the Gospel of Matthew

1. Despite Mark's Gospel having pride of place as the first written Gospel, it was Matthew's Gospel that attained the honor of the most popular Gospel within the early church. The portrait of Jesus as a

wise teacher, the catechetical nature of Jesus's sayings, and the book's usefulness for understanding the relationship between "Christ" and his Jewish heritage all offer significant insight as to the overwhelming popularity of Matthew's Gospel within the early church.

2. Readings of Matthew's Gospel have often tragically perpetuated anti-Jewish sentiments through stereotyped and negative portraits of all Jewish people. Matthew portrays Jesus firmly within his Jewish heritage, as one who believes and practices the teachings of the Torah and as one who has come for his people *Israel*. The Gospel certainly contains difficult statements, but interpreters should be ethically accountable for their readings of these challenging texts and aware of some of the negative aspects of the history of Christian biblical interpretation.
3. Matthew's Gospel used Mark as its most important source, with somewhere around 90 percent of Markan material appearing in Matthew. In addition, we've noted the unique "M" material, which makes up some of the most memorable aspects of Matthew's Gospel, including the infancy narrative, Jesus's teachings in the Sermon on the Mount, and Jesus's parables about the final judgment.
4. Church tradition is unanimous that the author of the Gospel is Matthew the tax collector (9:9; 10:3). Given Matthew's low profile, it's hard to imagine why the early church would invent this. But, again, it's likely that the Gospel represents a blend of eyewitness material and the earliest church's collective memory of sayings and stories about Jesus.
5. Antioch is the most popular guess for the provenance of Matthew, and given Mark's likely dating to sometime around 66–73 CE, most have hypothesized a date for Matthew in the 70s CE.
6. The Gospel contains key elements regarding structure. Matthew uses biblical typology, temporal markers (4:17; 16:21), and alternation between blocks of narrative and discourse as a means of providing coherence to his Gospel.
7. Matthew uses key words to communicate his message. Each Gospel writer utilizes a particular vocabulary to tell his story and highlight some of its most important themes. I mentioned four of these in Matthew: righteousness, hypocrisy, kingdom of heaven/God, and mercy.
8. Narrative threads run through the entirety of the Gospel and give it its sense of literary unity and coherence. I noted four narrative threads that center on the identity and activity of Jesus Christ:
   a. Jesus is born as the son of Abraham and Davidic Messiah who will save his people Israel from their sins. Jesus's entire life,

culminating in his sacrificial death on the cross, pays the debt for his people's sins.

b. Jesus is the singularly wise teacher who rightly interprets God's will and law. While all of the Gospels show us a Jesus who is a wise and powerful teacher, Matthew in particular emphasizes how his teaching is full of wisdom and mercy, leading to a life of flourishing and holiness before God. Jesus interprets the Old Testament laws in a way that is congruent with their God-given merciful intention for humanity.

c. Jesus is the merciful shepherd-king. Only in Matthew do we hear of Israel described as a lost flock (10:5–6; 15:24). And dotting the landscape of Matthew's Gospel are individuals and groups who fail to shepherd God's people with mercy and justice. In contrast, Jesus is the compassionate shepherd-king whose teachings and actions dispense God's mercy and justice for his people.

9. The disciples of Jesus practice righteousness without hypocrisy, are committed to peace and nonviolence, seek mercy and forgiveness, and make disciples of all the nations.

Mark and History

Mark's Place in the History of Early Christianity

On occasion one will hear Mark's Gospel referred to as the earliest and thereby the most important and essential Gospel. This view rests squarely on the claim that what is earliest is the most important. But this goes entirely against the grain of almost eighteen hundred years of church history in that Mark's Gospel has been consistently overshadowed by the other three canonical Gospels, especially Matthew. When one gathers up the citations of each of the Gospels from patristic authors, Mark is by far the least frequently cited of the four.[1] As Luke Timothy Johnson notes, "Mark's Gospel was little read and less studied."[2]

This is not to say that Mark wasn't read, used, or valued in the early church. We certainly can find plenty of instances where the early church fathers speak of Mark as a known written Gospel and reproduce sayings of Jesus found only in Mark. But in almost every major patristic author the number of citations of Mark's Gospel are vastly lower than any of the other three. The manuscript evidence for Mark is unimpressive, as only one important third-century papyrus (𝔓⁴⁶) and two fourth-century codices (Sinaiticus and Vaticanus) provide witness to the Gospel.[3] There are no full-fledged commentaries on Mark by early church authors before the sixth century CE.[4]

In the early second century, Papias of Hierapolis even tries to defend the Gospel by quoting "the Elder" as saying that "Mark did nothing wrong in writing down some things as he remembered them, for he made it his one concern not to omit anything which he heard or to make any false statement in them" (Papias, *Fragments* 3.15).[5] On the one hand, Papias finds the Gospel of Mark to be inferior to the others in terms of its arrangement and order; but on the other hand, he explicitly defends Mark because Mark was simply acting as "Peter's interpreter." Augustine, too, in his *On the Harmony of the Gospels*, diminishes Mark's importance by referring to him as Matthew's "foot-slave and abbreviator" (1.2.4).[6]

Not until the early nineteenth century, when Gospel scholars begin to make strong arguments for Markan priority, does the Gospel of Mark start to gain some ascendancy, but even here Mark is largely valued as an important "source" in the puzzle of the Synoptic problem and, therefore, as the earliest text for engaging in the historical reconstruction of Jesus of Nazareth. Quests for the historical Jesus, especially from the mid-nineteenth century onward, almost invariably value Mark as a source that can get them as close as possible to the historical Jesus.

The great enigma here, however, is that despite the early church's preference for Matthew (and Luke) over Mark, Mark's Gospel not only was preserved but also was the clear source for both Matthew's and Luke's Gospels. One cannot escape the conclusion that both Matthew and Luke held Mark's Gospel in high regard, given their conservative editorial use of it as a source. Now, to be clear, both Matthew and Luke find it necessary to *write their own version*, but they do so both by preserving the majority of Mark's content and by often following Mark's order and arrangement of material. This, of course, provokes two questions: Why was Mark's Gospel preserved? And where did Mark's Gospel come from? 12.1

The Composition of Mark's Gospel

Who wrote Mark's Gospel? As we saw in an earlier chapter, Mark (like the other Gospel authors) does not actually provide us with his name, though

SIDEBAR 12.1

The Gospel of Mark and Quests for the Historical Jesus

The quests for the historical Jesus account, in part, for the Gospel of Mark receiving renewed attention and increased popularity beginning early in the nineteenth century. Most Christians through the centuries have read all four canonical Gospels together as offering a reliable and trustworthy account of the life and teachings of Jesus Christ. Beginning in the eighteenth century, however, some scholars began to use the contemporary and critical tools of historiography to distinguish between "the Jesus of history" and "the Christ of faith." The four Gospel evangelists often were viewed by these scholars as presenting a theological and dogmatic portrait of belief in Christ rather than a historically credible and accurate depiction of Jesus of Nazareth.

Scholars sought to carry out the task of historical investigation of Jesus free from the biases of faith and theology, which meant that they gave more focused attention to source criticism. What sources are the earliest? Which ones are likely to be most accurate and free of theological biases? The Gospels were used here not so much as important theological narratives in their own right but rather as windows into a history *behind the text*. The historical quests for Jesus of Nazareth were intertwined, then, with the research devoted to source criticism, especially as it pertained to understanding the relationships between the Synoptic Gospels. Almost all of these studies presumed that the Gospel of John was too obviously dogmatic to function as a reliable source. And almost equally scholars decided in favor of Mark's Gospel, that it was both the earliest and most nearly free of prejudicial dogmatic biases.

the superscriptions ("The Gospel according to X") are very early and unanimously indicate it as the Gospel according to *Mark*.

Wikimedia Commons

Figure 12.1. Emmanuel Tzanes, *Icon of St. Mark the Evangelist*

One can make an argument that the author is John Mark, the man who provided aid to the missionary efforts led by Paul and Barnabas (Acts 12:24–25; 13:5) and then, after a break with Paul, with Barnabas alone (Acts 15:36–41). According to Paul's testimony, John Mark was involved with Paul's missionary work (Col. 4:10; Philem. 24; 2 Tim. 4:11). There is also a possible connection between Mark and Peter as well. The author of 1 Peter sends his greetings along with "Mark my son" (1 Pet. 5:13), and Acts also depicts Peter as present in Mark's home in Jerusalem (Acts 12:11–17). Early church tradition is unanimous in its claim that Mark's Gospel was written by this John Mark. One can pile up the reference from Irenaeus, Tertullian, Clement of Alexandria, Origen, Eusebius, and others who all indicate that the Gospel was penned by John Mark.[7] Given John Mark's fairly insignificant profile and the fact that there are no other opinions in the early church as to the author, it's hard to imagine why anyone would creatively "invent" Mark as the authorized agent behind the Gospel.

Some have discounted the early church consensus, given that it likely derives from one source, again, the writings of Papias of Hierapolis. Papias mentions someone he refers to as "the Elder," from whom he derives his information regarding the origins of the Gospels. 12.2

Much ink has been spilled over Papias's statements. The identity of "the Elder" is not clear, and this makes evaluation of Papias's testimony all the more difficult. But for our purposes, I can make a few simple comments taking the statement at face value. First, it bears repeating once more that this provides very early evidence that the Gospel of Mark was an important, early, and valued source for the life of Jesus. Second, Papias indicates that "the Elder" already (125 CE or so) knew that our first two Gospels were being circulated *with the names of Matthew and Mark*. Third, the

SIDEBAR 12.2

Papias on the Gospel of Mark

"And the Elder used to say this: 'Mark, having become Peter's interpreter, wrote down accurately everything he remembered, though not in order, of the things either said or done by Christ. For he neither heard the Lord nor followed him, but afterward, as I said, followed Peter, who adapted his teachings as needed but had no intention of giving an ordered account of the Lord's sayings. Consequently Mark did nothing wrong in writing down some things as he remembered them, for he made it his one concern not to omit anything which he heard or to make any false statement in them'" (Papias, *Fragments* 3.15).[a]

quotation may also indicate that while Mark was valued as an important source, it was sometimes deemed inferior to the other Gospels due to its strange order and arrangement. Fourth, Papias defends Mark by noting that Mark wasn't an eyewitness to the events but functioned instead as the one tasked with recording "accurately and without omission the gospel story preached by Peter."[8] Some scholars remain suspicious of Papias's testimony because they see his remarks as being so obviously apologetic—he's working too hard to defend the origins of the Gospels. And it is true that Papias demonstrates a concern to defend Mark's Gospel both by rooting it in Peter's eyewitness testimony and by explaining why its order and arrangement are somewhat unusual. But given that the New Testament's testimony connects John Mark with Peter (see above), others find Papias's remarks highly plausible.

Based on this connection between Mark and Peter, some have searched through the Gospel to see if it indeed has a Petrine perspective. Richard Bauckham takes Papias's testimony seriously, and in his study of Mark he argues that the author "has deliberately designed the Gospel in such a way that it incorporates and conveys this Petrine perspective."[9] Martin Hengel further notes that Mark begins (1:16) and ends (16:7) with references to (Simon) Peter as a named disciple, and he sees this as a "deliberate rhetorical *inclusio*" meant to emphasize that the Gospel is based on Peter's tradition and authority.[10] Peter is also clearly the most prominent disciple in the Gospel, and there are actually more references to Peter in Mark (despite it being the shortest of the four) than in the other Gospels.[11] Peter speaks or functions as a representative of the other disciples at many of the key events, such as the confession of Jesus as the Messiah in Caesarea Philippi (8:27–33), Jesus's transfiguration (9:2–8), the Last Supper (14:22–31), Jesus's sufferings in the garden (14:32–42), and Jesus's trial (14:54–72). 12.3

I do not find any of the internal features of Mark's Gospel, however, to provide any obvious indication that it represents Peter's memories. Peter is the representative disciple in all three Synoptic Gospels, and Matthew actually seems to heighten his significance more than what one finds in Mark (e.g., Matt. 16:13–23; 18:21–22). Mark's Gospel actually presents Peter much more negatively than do the others. The supposed parallel between Mark's Gospel and Peter's speech in Acts 10 is quite general (see sidebar 12.3), and there's nothing specific about his speech that would set it apart as uniquely Markan (i.e., Peter's speech works equally as well as an outline for Matthew and Luke). Peter's prominence as the representative of the disciples is certainly evident, but this also holds true for Matthew and Luke.

Skepticism toward the view that Mark represents an obvious "Petrine perspective" does not mean that one needs to deny the traditional view of Mark as the author of the Gospel. And it is by no means impossible that Mark's Gospel does indeed stem, in part at least, from some of the remembrances of Peter as a firsthand eyewitness to Jesus's life and teachings. We have noted the potential connection between John Mark and Peter (from 1 Pet. 5:13). Although we should note that the Gospel is also likely a written account of many remembered oral traditions circulating in the earliest churches. The unanimous testimony of the early church that the Second Gospel was written and/or authorized by John Mark also need not be discounted even if one is skeptical of a Petrine viewpoint in Mark. As I have noted in earlier chapters, the connection between Mark's Gospel and Peter can further aid us in our quest to understand where the stories and sayings of Jesus might have come from. The connection with Peter can also aid us in our understanding of why Mark survived and was valued even if it was the least popular of the four Gospels. But we should not expect an emphasis on Peter (or a "Petrine perspective") to be one of the keys that will unlock the meaning of Mark's Gospel.

SIDEBAR 12.3

The Gospel of Mark in Outline in Peter's Speech in Acts 10:36–43

Some have argued that there are parallels between the outline of Mark's Gospel and Peter's speech in Acts 10:36–43. Peter's speech gives a condensed summary of the gospel and the story of Jesus's ministry, suffering, death, and resurrection.

> You know the message God sent to the people of Israel, announcing the good news of peace through Jesus Christ, who is Lord of all. You know what has happened throughout the province of Judea, beginning in Galilee after the baptism that John preached—how God anointed Jesus of Nazareth with the Holy Spirit and power, and how he went around doing good and healing all who were under the power of the devil, because God was with him. We are witnesses of everything he did in the country of the Jews and in Jerusalem. They killed him by hanging him on a cross, but God raised him from the dead on the third day and caused him to be seen. He was not seen by all the people, but by witnesses whom God had already chosen—by us who ate and drank with him after he rose from the dead. He commanded us to preach to the people and to testify that he is the one whom God appointed as judge of the living and the dead. All the prophets testify about him that everyone who believes in him receives forgiveness of sins through his name. (NIV)

Further complicating matters is that from time to time scholars have noted particular resonances between Paul and Mark's Gospel.[12] These scholars have tried to demonstrate that there is a significant amount of continuity between Paul and Mark and also that both take *minority positions* within early Christianity.[13] As a result, they propose that Mark may be Pauline theology in narrative form and that this might also account for Mark's survival as a Gospel writing. 12.4

As a result of these connections (and others), some have suggested that the Gospel of Mark may have arisen as an attempt to anchor Paul's theology in Jesus traditions.[14] There are indeed some interesting similarities between Mark's Gospel and Paul's Letters, but this view both requires a dismissal of early church tradition that connects Mark's Gospel to Peter and also must reckon with the fact that there is simply no ancient attestation for a connection between Mark's Gospel and Paul.[15] And many of the supposed connections between Mark and Paul can be just as well explained by theological themes, teachings, and traditions that were common to multiple early Christian communities.

In my view, there is not enough evidence to say with confidence that Mark's Gospel stems from Peter or that it stems from Paul. That said, I do not think it at all implausible, based on the evidence we've reviewed in this chapter and in previous ones, to see Mark as one who due to his ministry associations was privy to memories and traditions about Jesus that were passed on from both Peter and Paul and from other early Christian communities. John Mark, as an early Christian missionary, would have had contact not only with Peter and Paul but also with a variety of local Christian churches. Whether one can then find a uniquely "Petrine perspective" on Jesus or a distinct "Pauline theology" in narrative form may be pushing the evidence in a more specific direction than it can go.

The Location, Date, and Audience of Mark's Gospel

Mark's Gospel does not provide any clear and direct evidence as to the geographical location of its origins. Some have posited a Galilean provenance,

SIDEBAR 12.4

Pauline Theology in Mark's Gospel?

Some of the main arguments for the belief that Mark's Gospel is based on Paul's theology are the following.

First, both Mark and Paul share the term "gospel" and use it to speak of an oral proclamation that centers on Jesus's messianic identity (Mark 1:1, 14; Rom. 1:1–4; 1 Thess. 1:5).

Second, both Paul and Mark portray Jesus's crucifixion as an apocalyptic event, an event that paradoxically reveals God's saving act and his cosmic judgment, the significance of which is hidden from the world and revealed only to the unexpected. Paul describes his whole gospel as "the word of the cross" (1 Cor. 1:18) and his preaching as the "Messiah crucified" (1:23; cf. 2:2). The death of Jesus is, for Paul and Mark, the climax of an apocalyptic battle. In 1 Corinthians 2:8, Paul attributes the death of Jesus to the demons—"the rulers of this age . . . who crucified the Lord of glory" (see also Eph. 1:21; Col. 2:14–15). Mark's narrative portrays this apocalyptic battle even more vividly. Jesus is "the strongest man" (1:7) who through his exorcisms (1:24; 3:11; 5:7) binds "the strong man" (3:27) and plunders his possessions.[b] Through the temptation narrative (1:12–13) and the exorcisms, Mark portrays all opposition to Jesus as stemming from the demonic realm.

Third, Mark's unflattering and negative depiction of Jesus's family (3:21–35) and Peter (8:27–33) may reflect Paul's own conflict with the leaders of the Jerusalem church (see Gal. 2:1–14).

Fourth, some argue that both Paul and Mark agree in opposing obedience to the ritual commands of the Torah (at least for gentiles). Mark agrees with Paul's theology, so the argument goes, as he alone has Jesus opposing the food laws, concluding one episode with his own editorial comment that Jesus "declared all things clean" (7:19). Compare this with Paul's own statements on Jewish food laws in Romans 14:20, "All things are clean," and again, in Romans 14:14a, "I know and am persuaded *in the Lord Jesus* that nothing is unclean in itself." Matthew reproduces Jesus's teachings in Matthew 15:1–20 but noticeably does not include the editorial comment about Jesus cleansing all things.

noting the prominence of rural Galilee as a geographical location in the Gospel.[16] Only in Mark, for example, does Jesus promise a restoration with his disciples in Galilee after he has been raised from the dead (Mark 14:28; 16:7). Others have speculated that Syria might be the location of the Gospel's origins, given the prominence of gentile Christians in the region (Acts 11:27–30; 13:1–13; 15:23; Gal. 1:21) and Jesus's use of agricultural/rural images for his teachings (Mark 4:3–9, 26–29).[17]

The most popular suggestion, however, has been Rome.[18] There are usually three main pieces of evidence that support this. The first plank is the Gospel's traditional association with Peter, who was active, so the argument goes, in Rome during this time. The author of 1 Peter claims to be writing from Rome (referred to metaphorically as "Babylon"), and we have already noted that 1 Peter 5:13 makes a connection between the author of the epistle and someone referred to as "Mark my son." There is also broad and widespread support from the early church fathers for the association between Mark's Gospel and Rome. Second, Mark's Gospel is also unique for its abundant Latinisms, which may reflect its intended use for Roman readers. Mark uses many Latin terms and assumes that his audience will understand, whereas he usually translates or defines Aramaic words.[19] Some have pointed to, for example, how Mark translates Jesus's saying about the widow donating her "two copper coins" into the Roman monetary equivalent (12:42).[20] It's possible that this may reflect a general orientation to a non-Jewish audience, and this could also explain why so many Jewish customs are explained by the narrator, such as the Pharisees washing their hands before they eat (7:3–4). Third, many have rightly discerned the text's emphasis on the suffering and persecution that the early followers of Jesus will face from outsiders and have tried to connect this to Nero's persecution of Christians sometime around 70 CE. While the presence of the Latinisms, the patristic testimony, and the possible association of Mark and Peter make a Roman provenance more likely than the other options, most readings of the Gospel, including mine, are not dramatically affected by this decision.

There are also a variety of possibilities for dating Mark's Gospel, ranging anywhere from 40 to 70 CE.[21] Decisions almost invariably depend on using narrative details from the text as windows into the contemporary social and political situation. Mark 13, in particular, seems to offer details that might reflect the volatile situation of 66–70 CE, such as the impending destruction of the Jerusalem temple (vv. 14–27), the rise of many false prophets during the Jewish War (vv. 21–23), and Nero's persecution of the followers of Jesus (vv. 11–13).[22] Nero's persecution of Christians in Rome makes good historical sense of Jesus's frequent teachings in Mark to follow him and take up one's cross even in the midst of suffering (e.g., 8:31–38). Others look at Mark 13:14 as reflecting the events of the Jewish revolt against Rome as well. Here Jesus says, "When you see the abomination of desolation standing where it should not be ('Let the reader understand!'), then let those dwelling in Judea flee to the mountains." The "abomination of desolation" is taken as a reference to the pagan Roman desecration of Jerusalem and the temple, and the narrator's note to the reader warns those in Judea of impending persecution.

For whom was Mark's Gospel intended? At one level, Mark's Gospel is intended for *all followers of Jesus*.[23] In fact, the difficulties of pinpointing the date, location, and provenance of Mark likely arise in strong part because the Gospel was intended as an authoritative account of the memories and sayings of Jesus for all Christians. Again, Mark's purpose for writing is to proclaim the gospel of Jesus Christ (1:1, 14), to make known the way of life required for Jesus's disciples (8:22–10:52), and to give an authoritative narrative of Jesus's teachings and acts.[24] One may, in fact, argue that the presence of Latinisms, the explanation of particular Jewish customs, and the positive interactions between Jesus and non-Jewish characters (e.g., 7:24–30; 8:1–9) make the larger point that the gospel of Jesus Christ is to be proclaimed and made known *to all people*. It's hard to make the case that any particular aspect of Mark's Gospel is *for only one specific audience*. If Mark's Gospel is seen as concerned with warning against the possibility of false teachers (13:21–23), strengthening weak faith in the midst of suffering (8:34–38; 14:32–42), and offering warnings against apostasy (4:1–20; 13:9–13), then one has to admit that these experiences and teachings are by no means unique within early Christianity.

Mark and Narrative (1)

Key Structural Features and Plot

Although we are following the canonical ordering of the four Gospels, we should pause to recognize that Mark, as the first written Gospel known to us, was the first one to take the step of collecting, organizing, arranging, and editing the church's oral (and *perhaps* written) testimonies about Jesus of Nazareth into one coherent writing.[1] We have seen that stories and sayings of Jesus were circulating orally among the early Christians for somewhere around thirty years before Mark penned his narrative; and it certainly is possible, though by no means certain, that Mark's work reflects the prior ordering and arrangement of his preformed written and/or oral sources. For example, there are good reasons for supposing that Mark may have had access to the following sources in the writing of his Gospel: the controversy dialogues (2:1–3:6), the Olivet Discourse (chap. 13), and the passion narrative (14:1–16:8).

We have seen Papias's testimony that Mark functioned as something of a mouthpiece for Peter's memories and that his Gospel therefore lacks the careful literary order and arrangement of the other Gospels. Mark's frequent usage of "and" (*kai*) and "immediately" (*euthys*) strikes many as demonstrating an unsophisticated writing style and less polished narrative. But this view does not sit easily with the recent recognition of Mark's careful literary artistry, and in fact Mark's Gospel is a never-ending treasure trove of theological meaning for careful readers. Indeed, Mark's Gospel has become something of a textual playground for biblical interpreters attuned to the narrative and literary devices used by ancient writers.[2] In fact, the Gospel of Mark likely preserves many of the features of an oral composition, designed in such a way as to be remembered and even memorized by those who hear it.[3] Literary devices such as chiasm, repetition (doublets in stories), flashback, *inclusio*, intercalation/sandwiching, groupings of three, and summary statements present the material in a way that make it easier to remember and even memorize.[4] But these literary devices are by no means unique to oral narratives and are found in many good ancient literary compositions. While the author likely expected the Gospel to be read out loud, the devices are characteristic of, as Helen Bond argues, "an author who knew how to tell a good story."[5] As one interpreter notes, the best way to read Mark's story and discern its structure "is to follow it through as it was designed to be followed—indeed, to *listen* to it as it was designed to be heard—and so to experience it as it does its work."[6] One of the best ways to do this is by examining some of the key literary devices Mark uses to tell his story. As we account for Mark's literary devices, we can better learn how to recognize them when we see them, enjoy their contribution to the story Mark tells, and use them as aids for understanding the theological message Mark conveys to his audience.[7]

Questions. Mark frequently uses questions from both Jesus and characters in the story to heighten the dramatic quality of a scene and to emphasize the salient questions he wants his audience to answer as well. One of the best examples of this is the scene in Caesarea Philippi, right in the middle of the Gospel, where Jesus asks his disciples, "Who do people say that I am?" (8:27). After hearing the disciples share some of the popular responses regarding his identity, Jesus asks, "But who do you say that I am?" (8:29). The question of Jesus's identity dominates Mark's Gospel, and at the midway point the reader both witnesses Peter's response to the question and is forced to wrestle with Jesus's question and whether Peter's answer is accurate. 13.1

Duality or two-step progressions. Mark often includes two-step repetitions that serve to force the reader (or characters in the story) to take a second look as the *second and repeated* element adds further information or a clarification. Sometimes Mark does this on a small and fairly insignificant level: "When evening had come, and the sun had gone down" (1:32). One might chalk this up to needless repetition were it not for the fact that Mark so frequently uses the repetitive pattern for more important ends. For example, Mark's "travel section" has Jesus

SIDEBAR 13.1

Questions in the Gospel of Mark

In Mark's Gospel, the use of questions—whether by Jesus or by other characters—typically functions to invite the reader to consider and reflect on Jesus's identity.

- A crowd witnessing Jesus's exorcisms: "The people were all so amazed that they asked one another, 'What is this? A new teaching, and one with authority! He even gives orders to evil spirits and they obey him!'" (1:27).
- Some teachers of the law hearing Jesus declare the paralytic man's sins to be forgiven: "Why is this one speaking like this? He's blaspheming! Who is able to forgive sins except God alone?" (2:7).
- In response to the disciples' fear that they will perish in the storm: "Why are you cowards? Do you have no faith?" (4:40).
- In response to the disciples' failure to understand the miracle of the loaves: "Do you still not understand?" (8:21).
- On the disciples' inability to cast out a demon: "You unbelieving generation, how long shall I be with you, and how long shall I put up with you?" (9:19).

journeying to Jerusalem (8:27–10:45), but bracketing this section are two healing narratives that closely resemble each other (8:22–26 and 10:46–52). The disciples, wrestling with how Jesus's messianic identity could coexist with suffering and death, are like the blind man who is healed in two stages and, at first, can see things only in a hazy and unfocused manner (8:22–26). The disciples too may confess that Jesus is the Christ (8:27–31), but they need to take a second look and learn from Jesus on the way that Christ and cross will go together. Another example of Mark's use of the two-stage progression technique is the way in which characters refer to Jesus as the Messiah and Jesus responds by referring to himself as the Son of Man (e.g., 8:29–31).[8]

Threefold occurrences. Mark also includes numerous instances of a series of three episodes. For example, Jesus preaches three parables about seed (4:3–20, 26–29, 30–32). On three occasions Jesus predicts his rejection and death (8:31; 9:31; 10:33–34). Jesus prays three times in the garden (14:32–42). Peter denies Jesus three times (14:66–72).

Foreshadowing. Mark also creates suspense by hinting at climactic events through foreshadowing. After Jesus's authority and popularity have been established, Mark sets forth a handful of controversy stories (2:1–3:6) that conclude with the Pharisees and Herodians making common cause with one another to destroy Jesus (3:6). In another episode, Mark follows up Jesus's commission of his disciples to proclaim the gospel (6:7–13) with a grizzly story of Herod Antipas's murder of John the Baptist that functions to preview the persecution that Jesus and his followers will receive in their own missionary work (6:14–29).

Framing or inclusio. This refers to Mark's penchant for placing similar-sounding motifs and themes at both the beginning and the end of a section. So, for example, Mark's prologue begins with "the beginning of *the gospel* of Jesus Christ" (1:1) and concludes with a reference to Jesus proclaiming "*the gospel* of God" (1:14). A powerful example of this technique is seen in Mark's presentation of Jesus's baptism (1:9–11) and the death of Jesus on the cross (15:36–39). At the baptism, the heavens are "ripped open" (1:10), Jesus receives the Spirit from heaven (1:10), and God's voice declares that Jesus is his beloved Son (1:11). At Jesus's death, the temple curtain is "ripped into two" (15:38), Jesus breathes forth his spirit (15:37), and the Roman centurion identifies Jesus as God's Son (15:39).

Sandwiches or intercalation. One of Mark's most famous literary techniques is the way he sandwiches one episode into the middle of another story. The structure is that of A-B-A. The two stories are brought into an illuminating relationship with each other, and it is the interrupting episode (B) that often provides the theological key to the Markan sandwich.[9]

SIDEBAR 13.2

Study a Markan Sandwich for Yourself

Discerning the meaning and function of Mark's sandwiches requires the active engagement of the reader/hearer. I invite you to do this for yourself or, even better, in a group. Follow these steps in order.

First, choose one of the three sandwiches: Mark 5:21–43; 6:7–30; 14:17–31.

Second, read through the story and identify the A-B-A pattern (or the two outside pieces of bread and the turkey or peanut butter and jelly).

Third, spend some time identifying similarities and differences between the episodes. List as many of these (especially similarities) as you can.

Fourth, now comes the payoff: How do the episodes mutually illuminate each other? How does the middle story help us understand the meaning of the interrupted story?

For example, in Mark 3:20–35 we see the following structure: (A) Jesus's family tries to restrain him (vv. 20–21); (B) Jesus tells a parable of the plundering of Satan in response to the scribes' claim that he casts out demons by the power of demons (vv. 23–30); (A) Jesus teaches that his true family are those who listen to and do the will of God (vv. 31–35). How does the middle episode illuminate Jesus's response to his family members? It shows the reader that any attempt to restrain Jesus or deter him from his mission, even if it comes from his family, is blasphemous and may even represent the purposes of Satan (as also with Peter in 8:31–33). 13.2

Mark's Gospel resists attempts to find a clear and obvious structure, and this is due, at least in part, to how Mark's literary devices work to create something of a tapestry or mosaic that enables readers to see multiple interconnections between discrete Markan episodes.[10] As a result, if one examines how different commentators on Mark structure the Gospel, one will find many different proposals. Nevertheless, we can discern three major sections in the Gospel, and this structure is both accurate and malleable enough to be fleshed out with much more complexity as we continue to read and note more interconnections. The three sections are bracketed with a prologue and a conclusion (1:1–15; 16:1–8).[11] Mark's three major literary movements work together to create the grandest of Markan sandwiches and function to emphasize the major theme of Mark's Gospel: *Jesus is the powerful messianic Son of God who inaugurates God's kingdom and defeats the powers of Satan through voluntarily suffering death on a Roman cross.*

(A) Jesus powerfully enacts and proclaims the kingdom of God (1:16–8:21).

(B) Jesus teaches his disciples about the cross on the way to Jerusalem (8:22–10:52).

(A) Jesus is rejected by the temple leaders in Jerusalem, and this results in his death on the cross (11:1–15:47).

(Prologue) Mark 1:1–15: Jesus Is the Messianic Son of God Who Proclaims God's Gospel

The narrator provides the reader with an introduction to the major themes, characters, and historical and geographical context to make sense of the entire Gospel. Both Mark's story and Jesus's proclamation are "the gospel," which centers on the life of Jesus the messianic Son of God (1:1, 14–15). His mission fulfills the prophetic promises of Isaiah, who anticipated a day when God would come to restore and be with his people in a powerful way (1:2–3). In light of this, Mark introduces the prophetic figure of John the Baptist, whose ministry of a baptism of repentance calls God's people to prepare themselves for the Messiah's coming. Mark prepares the reader for Jesus's ministry, however, to be one of conflict. As the Spirit-anointed Son of God (1:7–11), Jesus will do battle with Satan and his powers as he establishes the kingdom of God (1:12–15).

(A) Mark 1:16–8:21: Jesus Powerfully Enacts and Proclaims the Kingdom of God

After the prologue, Mark immediately peppers his Gospel with vignettes in which Jesus's powerful authority displays the kingdom of God. Jesus is an astonishing miracle worker, healer, and teacher (1:16–45). But as Jesus forgives sins, eats with sinners and tax collectors, and heals on the Sabbath, he also provokes an angry opposition who want to kill him (2:1–3:6). But, alternatively, while some continue to oppose Jesus and reject his message of God's kingdom (3:20–35), there are others who follow him as his disciples (3:7–19). Jesus's powerful authority is also revealed in his teaching as he explains why some accept the good news of the gospel and others reject it (4:1–41). Jesus's powerful manifestation of the kingdom continues to provoke awe, acceptance, and intense opposition as he proclaims the kingdom even among many gentiles (5:1–8:21). Foreshadowing the impending crucifixion of Jesus is the gruesome and violent death of John the Baptist by Herod Antipas (6:17–29). Running through this section, however, is an increasing emphasis on the inability of Jesus's disciples to understand his identity and the meaning of his mission (e.g., 8:14–21).

(B) Mark 8:22–10:52: Jesus Teaches His Disciples about the Cross on the Way to Jerusalem

In this section, Jesus and the disciples are repeatedly spoken of as on "the way" to Jerusalem. Bracketing the journey are two very similar episodes in which Jesus heals a blind man. The first healing takes place in two stages, and its oddity thereby draws attention to *partial sight* and the need for those following Jesus on the way to take a second look at Jesus's teaching about his messianic identity (compare 8:22–26 with 8:17–18). The goal is that, by the end of the journey, the follower of Jesus will be able to see that his powerful enactment of God's kingdom will find its climax in his suffering and death. Thus, while there are still displays of Jesus's glory and power on his journey to Jerusalem (e.g., the transfiguration [9:2–8]; the healing of a young boy [9:14–27]), the section is marked by Jesus's three responses that he must be rejected, suffer, and be crucified (8:31–32; 9:31; 10:33–34) and three instances of the disciples' failure to understand Jesus's teaching (8:33; 9:32; 10:35–45).

(A) Mark 11:1–15:47: Jesus Is Rejected by the Temple Leaders in Jerusalem, and This Results in His Death on the Cross

Upon his entrance to Jerusalem, Jesus is praised as the one who will establish the Davidic kingdom, but conspicuously absent are the priests and temple leaders (11:1–11). Jesus's cleansing of the temple and cursing of the fig tree portend God's judgment on Israel's leadership and temple (11:12–25). Jesus's authority as the designated and authorized teacher of God's will is established as he bests the Jerusalem leaders and teachers through a variety of parables and riddles (11:27–12:44). Jesus's lengthy teaching (the Olivet Discourse) anticipates God's judgment on the temple and prophesies how the disciples will carry out God's mission to the nations until the Son of Man returns (13:1–37). In chapters 14–15, Mark presents the extended story of Jesus's unjust trial, his abandonment by his disciples, his betrayal by Judas and Peter, his sufferings, and his death on the cross. Upon his death, there is a ripping of the temple curtain and a Roman centurion who confesses Jesus to be the Son of God.

(Conclusion) Mark 16:1–8: Jesus Is Raised from the Dead

Mark's Gospel ends on a strange and open-ended note. The women come to the tomb and find that Jesus is not in the grave; rather, an angel says that the crucified one has been raised from the dead. The women are to report the news to Peter and wait for Jesus's appearance in Galilee. But the women run away from the tomb and say nothing because they are terrified.

Key Words and Phrases

Let's look at three key words/phrases that highlight significant Markan themes: "the way," "fear *and* faith," and "Son of God."

The way. In narratives, the term "settings" is used to speak of depictions of "space and time," "culture and society," "geographical locations," and "humanly constructed spaces."[12] One of the most important settings in the Gospel of Mark is "the way," which, based on its first usages in Mark 1:2–3, is often shorthand for "the way of the Lord." After a short title in Mark 1:1, the Gospel begins with a blend of three scriptural citations, each of which speaks of someone *preparing the way of the Lord* (Exod. 23:20; Mal. 3:1; Isa. 40:3). Mark writes, "Behold, I am sending my messenger before your face. He will prepare *your way*. He is the voice of one crying in the wilderness, 'Prepare *the way of the Lord*, make his paths straight'" (1:2–3). The Exodus citation speaks of God sending an angel before Moses and God's people in order to protect them on their way to the promised land (Exod. 23:20). Malachi foretells of God's prophetic messenger, a latter-day Elijah figure, who will prepare a way for the Lord before he comes to the temple (Mal. 3:1–2; also 4:5–6). And Isaiah uses the language of "the way of the Lord" to speak of the "good news" (*euangelion*) that one day God will enact a new exodus whereby he will come back to be with his people and will lead them on a pilgrimage ("the way") through the wilderness that will climax in their worship of God at the temple on Mount Zion (Isa. 40:1–11; 52:7–12).

Mark identifies John the Baptist as the prophetic messenger (the Elijah figure) who prepares the way of the Lord through his ministry of baptism and repentance for the forgiveness of sins (1:4–8). John's ministry is continued by Jesus, who will also proclaim the gospel, call people to repent, and proclaim forgiveness of sins (1:14–15; 2:5–7).[13] Thus, it is quite obvious that for Mark, John the Baptist goes before the person of Jesus, and so "the way of the Lord" is equated with the appearance of Jesus the Messiah.[14] By identifying John the Baptist and Jesus as the characters who play these scriptural roles—the prophetic messenger who makes preparations and the divine Lord—Mark is informing his readers to see Jesus's coming as initiating the climactic fulfillment of God's scriptural and gospel promises: God's coming to be with his people, to defeat their enemies, to rescue and heal them, and to transform Jerusalem and the temple into a place that is hospitable for God's dwelling.

The phrase "the way" does not occur much in the Gospel *until* Jesus begins his journey with his disciples to Jerusalem. The reader, then, has the prior scriptural knowledge about "the way of the Lord" (from 1:2–3) that this journey to Jerusalem is filled with deep significance because it is actually the divine Lord making his climactic return to Zion. But "the way" becomes a place where Jesus must teach his disciples that the kingdom of God will come by means of the cross and that power will be revealed in weakness and humility (see 8:27; 9:33–34; 10:17, 32, where the Greek text has *hodos*, "way"). The Messiah will be rejected by his own people, suffer at the hands of the Romans, and die on a Roman cross (8:31; 9:31; 10:33–34). The *way of the Lord* is, in other words, the Lord's journey to the cross. When Jesus makes his way to the Jerusalem temple on the donkey, Mark says that there are many who are laying down their garment "on the way" (11:8), but while some hail him as the blessed one "who comes in the name *of the Lord*" (11:9), the temple leaders, priests, and Jerusalem authorities do not welcome him as such.

Fear and *faith*. At the center of Mark's Gospel, and indeed all of the four Gospels, is the question of how people will respond to Jesus and his proclamation of the kingdom of God. And Mark's prologue immediately shows us that one of the primary and good responses to Jesus's proclamation is to believe in the gospel of God (1:15). We are accustomed to hearing many soft and weak definitions of "believe" and "belief," as if it's just adding an extra piece of information to what we already know, or as if it's a weak assent to a proposition: 5 + 5 =10. Some have argued, in fact, that the Greek word for "belief/faith" (*pistis*) often should be translated with a stronger and more active sense, such as "trust, allegiance, fidelity, loyalty."[15] In Mark's Gospel, faith is no simple or easy matter, for ultimately it is a humble posture of confidence and trust that Jesus is the Son of God—even as this is revealed through suffering, sacrifice, humility, and, ultimately, the cross. Alternatively, characters in Mark's story often respond with fear when they are amazed by, but do not fully grasp or submit to, the authority of Jesus (e.g., 5:15; 6:50; 16:8). Fear calls attention to Jesus's surprising authority and displays of power, but the observer of these must move from fear to faith. When we are told that the disciples, for example, are afraid but refuse to seek answers from Jesus that might move them to faith, this is a negative portrayal of discipleship (e.g., 9:32; cf. 9:22–24; 12:34).

We see the dynamic of "fear to faith" at work, for example, in Mark 4:35–41 when Jesus reveals his divine power by miraculously calming the storm. Jesus expects that his disciples should, by now, understand his ability to rescue them, and so he admonishes them: "Why are you being so cowardly? Do you have *no faith*?" (v. 40). But the disciples are not portrayed here as learning their lesson, for Mark tells us that they were "exceedingly filled with fear" and wondered "Who is this that even the wind and sea obey him?" (v. 41). Faith and fear as responses to Jesus's identity play an important role in the Markan sandwich in Mark 5:21–43. In the first episode ([A] vv. 21–24), we hear of Jairus, a synagogue leader whose daughter is deathly ill. Jairus comes to Jesus and begs him to come and touch her so that she "will be saved and will live" (v. 23). As Jesus is on the way to Jairus's house, the story is interrupted by a woman with a flow of blood ([B] vv. 25–34). She is telling herself that if she can just "touch"

Jesus (v. 28), she will be "saved" (v. 28). The woman is full of "fear and trembling" (v. 33), and yet she overcomes her fear and confesses to Jesus that she has touched him. Jesus responds, "Daughter, your *faith* has saved you" (v. 34). The woman's faith functions almost like an object lesson for Jairus as we now return to the final stage of the Markan sandwich ([A] vv. 35–43). As he and Jesus continue on their way, they are met by people from Jairus's house who tell them that his daughter has died, to which Jesus responds, "Do not fear, only have faith" (v. 36). Jesus enters the house, takes Jairus's daughter by the hand and tells her to get up, and she is healed (vv.41–43).

Son of God. Mark's opening title begins, "The beginning of the gospel of Jesus Christ, the Son of God" (1:1).[16] The Gospel finds a fitting ending, right before the epilogue of the women at the tomb (16:1–8), when the Roman centurion looks on the crucified Jesus and declares, "Truly this man was the Son of God" (15:39). If Mark is using the literary feature of *inclusio* or framing here, then this invites the reader to explore the entire Gospel as an account of Jesus's identity as God's beloved Son. Furthermore, God the Father speaks only twice in Mark's Gospel, at Jesus's baptism and at his transfiguration, and on both occasions the voice declares that Jesus is his beloved Son (1:11; 9:7). Jesus also speaks of himself as the beloved Son and refers to God as his Abba Father (12:6; 14:36). And when the high priest asks, "Are you the Christ, the Son of the Blessed One?" Jesus answers affirmatively, "I am" (14:61–62). So the reader knows without a doubt, from Mark's vantage point, that Jesus is indeed the beloved Son of God.

But what does the title "Son of God" actually mean? The title "Son of God" has a rich history in the Old Testament, often used as a title to

SIDEBAR 13.3

The Roman Emperor as a Son of God

The title "Son of God" often was used to speak of Augustus and, later, other Roman emperors as the divine Son of God.[a] Octavian, the biological nephew of Julius Caesar, was adopted by Caesar and thereby became a "Son of God." While the primary context for "Son of God" language in Mark's Gospel is Jewish Davidic messianic texts, it is likely that the term had imperial connotations for those in the Roman world. As we will see, Jesus does function like something of an alternative emperor, or counter-emperor, who proclaims God's kingdom and rules on his behalf. When Jesus is baptized and God declares, "You are my Son, whom I love," a dove descends on him. Instead of a Roman eagle, the symbol of military power, the descent of the dove demonstrates that "this counter-emperor will not rule in the spirit of the bellicose eagle, but in the spirit of the pure, gentle, peaceful, and even sacrificial dove."[b]

Till Nierman / CC BY-SA 3.0 / Wikimedia Commons

Figure 13.1. Statue of Augustus of Prima Porta discovered in the Villa of Livia

describe the relationship between God and his anointed Davidic king. So, for example, in 2 Samuel 7:12–14, God promises David that he will establish the kingdom of one of David's sons and says, "I will be a father to him, and he will be a son to me" (v. 14a). So also, Psalm 2 is an expansion of 2 Samuel 7:12–14, and here God declares to the Davidic king, "You are my son. Today I have begotten you" (Ps. 2:7). The response is that the rulers and kings are exhorted to recognize the reign of God and his anointed son and cease their opposition to his kingdom (Ps. 2:10–12) 13.3

For Mark, Jesus is clearly the Son of God. He is the messianic Son who is anointed by God to proclaim the gospel and inaugurate the kingdom of God. And he is manifestly no ordinary figure, given his authority to cast out demons, heal, and teach. But central to the Gospel of Mark is the paradox or tension between Mark's understanding of the meaning of Jesus's identity as the Son of God and its possible connotations of a conquering military war hero. Jesus's task as the Son of God consists in his vocation of sacrificial service culminating in his humiliating crucifixion on a Roman cross. Jesus is the Son of God not in spite of *but because of* his sacrificial leadership, faithful suffering, and appalling crucifixion. Mark's Gospel intends to teach its readers that one can truly understand Jesus's identity as the Messiah and Son of God only if one is able to join the Roman centurion in confessing the rejected, suffering, and crucified one as God's beloved Son.

Mark and Narrative (2)

Key Narrative Threads

The Apocalyptic Battle between the Son of God and Satan

Mark's Gospel has often been described as apocalyptic in orientation, meaning that the narrative invokes a world marked by a dualistic and cosmic conflict between God and Satan.[1] The present world is a place where Satan's rule is on display through demonic powers, debilitating illnesses, and wicked tyrants. Humans are desperately in need of a cosmic act of God to invade and reclaim the world, thereby making salvation possible. But Satan does not go down without a fight as he seeks to prevent and confuse human knowledge of God's work and tempts and tests those who follow Jesus. Let's look at how this theme works in more detail.

First, notice how Mark 1:9–11 describes Jesus's baptism as resulting in God's cosmic activity to establish God's kingdom through the messianic Son of God. Three divine events are narrated: (1) the heavens are "ripped open"; (2) God's Spirit descends as a dove on Jesus; (3) a voice from heaven declares, "You are my beloved Son; I am well pleased in you." The reader knows, then, that Messiah Jesus is God's beloved Son, the agent of the Spirit, the one who reveals God's will and purposes. And John the Baptist has also provided his testimony that Jesus is "the stronger one" who will act in the power of the Spirit (1:7–8). The baptism scene echoes language from the messianic Psalm 2, where God enthrones his messianic son to reign in power and calls all of his enemies and rebel kings to submit to him and his son.[2] So it is no surprise that immediately after Jesus's anointing by the Spirit we see Satan attacking and tempting him in the wilderness (1:12–13). Jesus successfully withstands the opposition from the realm of the demonic, however, and comes forth proclaiming God's gospel and kingdom and calling people to turn away from Satan's rule (1:14–15). Throughout

Mark, Jesus's teaching is dominated by proclaiming and teaching about "the kingdom of God." While it is very difficult to give a precise definition of "the kingdom of God," it pertains to God's dynamic rule over his people and the world. Throughout the Old Testament, God had repeatedly made declarations that he was the true king over his people and even over all of creation (e.g., Exod. 15:18; Pss. 10:16; 47:6–9; 103:15–19), and he had promised that one day he would establish his rule through a Davidic king (2 Sam. 7:12–14; 1 Chron. 17; Pss. 2; 89; 132). Now that the Son of God has come onto the scene, God's rule is something that can be seen in Jesus the very Son of God *even now*, is a reign that people are called to receive and enter, and is also something for which people still await a final future fulfillment (Mark 4:26–27; 9:1, 47; 10:14–15; 14:25).[3] Soon we will see that the kingdom of God is established not only through Jesus's powerful miracles but also through his sacrificial death on the cross.

Second, while the prologue tells the reader that Jesus is the mighty and triumphant Son of God, immediately thereafter Mark shows the reader how Jesus's power and authority reveal what the kingdom of God is. So, Jesus calls disciples to follow him, and they *immediately* leave behind their former ways of life (1:16–20; 2:13–14) and are appointed to "be with him" (3:7–19). Jesus has the authority to forgive sins (2:1–12). He can heal the sick (1:29–34, 40–45). And his ability to teach so far surpasses that of others that listeners often are amazed or baffled (1:21–22; 3:20–35; 12:13–17). But the primary way in which we see Jesus engage in conflict against Satan is through his exorcisms of people possessed by demons. As God's anointed messianic Son, Jesus has the power to establish God's kingdom by making demons flee from his presence and from those they afflict. And the demons are some of the *very few* who know who Jesus is. 14.1

What do Jesus's exorcisms mean? Jesus's first parable provides the critical lens here.[4] Some of the scribes in Jerusalem slander Jesus by speculating that he receives his power not from God but from "Beelzebub, the ruler of the demons" (3:22). But this is absurd, for why would the ruler of a kingdom make war against his own kingdom (3:23–26)? Instead, Jesus declares that he is "the stronger man" who, through his exorcisms, is making war against Satan's kingdom and thereby liberating people from his evil dominion (3:27–28).

SIDEBAR 14.1

The Demons' Knowledge of Jesus's Identity

When Jesus sees a man with an unclean spirit, the demon cries out, "What do you want with us, Jesus of Nazareth? Have you come to destroy us? I know who you are—the Holy One of God!" (Mark 1:24 NIV). The demon's reference to Jesus as "the Holy One of God" indicates the knowledge that Jesus is God's sacred, anointed ruler. Thus, the unclean spirit recognizes that Jesus is "the strong one" (1:7) who has God's Holy Spirit (1:11–12) and thereby has authority over the demons. On another occasion, Jesus is among a crowd, and he is healing the sick and casting out demons (3:10). Mark notes, "Whenever the unclean spirits saw him, they fell down before him and cried out, 'You are the Son of God.' But he gave them strict orders not to tell who he was" (3:11–12). When Jesus encounters a demon-possessed man in the region of the Gerasenes, the man falls down in front of Jesus and shouts, "What do you want with me, Jesus, Son of the Most High God? Swear by God that you won't torture me!" (5:7). Jesus then casts many demons out of the man and sends them into a herd of pigs (5:9–13).

Third, the opposition between God's kingdom and Satan's results in a situation where understanding Jesus's true identity and its meaning is remarkably difficult for almost every human character. In fact, this is the central tension in Mark's Gospel: Jesus is the messianic Son of God, the Spirit-anointed agent of God's kingdom, and yet Satan is consistently at work attempting to thwart true knowledge of Jesus's identity and also the way in which his mission is necessarily oriented to the cross. This tension is largely due to the incredible difficulty that people have in affirming both that Jesus is the powerful, triumphant Son of God and that the full revelation of his identity takes place in sacrifice, love, and suffering a shameful death on the cross. Let's look at a few aspects of this theme. Note, for example, that at the turning point of the Gospel at Caesarea Philippi, in the critical middle section that transitions to Jesus's journey to the cross, Peter confesses that Jesus is the Messiah (8:29). But, surprisingly, Jesus orders Peter and the other disciples not to tell anyone about him (8:30). Yet immediately after this, Peter rebukes Jesus for declaring that the Messiah will be rejected and killed in Jerusalem (8:31–32). Jesus, in turn, rebukes Peter and declares, "Get behind me Satan, for you are not thinking the thoughts of God but rather the thoughts of humans" (8:33). Jesus's statement makes it clear that it is possible to declare that Jesus is the Christ and yet be embodying the will of Satan if one does not follow and accept Jesus's teaching about sacrifice, service, and the cross. In fact, Jesus's first interpreted parable, the parable of the sower (4:1–20), explains why, if the messianic king of the kingdom has really come, there are so many different types of responses to Jesus's proclamation of the kingdom. Jesus teaches his disciples that while there are many who will rightly respond to the good news of the gospel (v. 20), Satan is at work to make sure that many people reject Jesus's teaching, and that others, even if they initially accept it, will later fall away (vv. 13–19). In fact, Jesus says that many will look but not truly see and will listen but not truly hear (v. 12). 14.2

SIDEBAR 14.2

The Messianic Secret

In Mark, those who truly know Jesus's identity include God (1:11; 9:7), demons (1:24, 34; 5:7), and those to whom God reveals "the secret of the kingdom of God" (4:11). As such, one of the very strange, even mysterious, elements of Mark's Gospel is that Jesus frequently demands that people keep silent about his identity. Jesus asks many of those whom he heals to keep it a secret (1:43–44; 5:43; 7:36). Almost all of the demons who yell out his identity as God's Holy One or Son of God are silenced by Jesus as well (1:23–35; 3:11–12). On important occasions such as Peter's confession of Jesus as the Christ and witnessing his transfiguration, Jesus likewise commands his disciples to keep their information to themselves (8:30; 9:9). Sometimes this literary dynamic is referred to as the "messianic secret," and there have been multiple attempts to explain why there is so much secrecy and silence demanded by Jesus in Mark's Gospel. But, at minimum, we can say that this theme makes it clear that true knowledge of Jesus's identity is not a matter that comes easily to persons whose thinking is patterned after a world under Satan's dominion. Jesus's identity as the powerful yet suffering messianic Son of God requires God's gracious revelation and a willingness to submit to Jesus's teaching. As such, one of the primary aspects of discipleship is found when Jesus calls his disciples to "come follow behind me" (1:17) and appoints them to "be with him" (3:14). These are short phrases, but they highlight the necessary role of the disciple as one who is in close proximity to Jesus and thereby listens to him, asks questions of him, and submits their own understanding to his authority and wisdom.

Proximity to Jesus is a primary mark of discipleship in the Gospel of Mark. We see this dynamic played out in a surprising way when Jesus's mother and siblings try to use force in order to prevent him from his teaching, saying, "He is out of his mind" (3:21). Notice the spatial imagery here. While Jesus is teaching, the narrator tells us, his family arrives and is standing "outside" (3:31) while a great crowd was sitting "around him" (3:32a). The crowd tells Jesus that his family is "outside" and looking for him (3:32b). Jesus responds, "'Who are my mother and my brothers?' And then, *looking around at those who were seated around him*, he said, 'Behold my mother and my brothers. For whoever does the will of God is my brother, my sister, and my mother'" (3:33–35).

Disciples are not necessarily those who model perfect insight or faith, but they are those who continue to listen to Jesus and seek to understand who he is based on his teachings rather than their own. Even in Jesus's parable of the soils, the disciples do not understand Jesus's teaching, and so "those *around* him along with the twelve disciples" ask Jesus what the parable means (4:10). Mark's description of this group as being "around" Jesus reminds us of the true family "around" Jesus who listen to him (3:31–35). As such, Jesus's response to their failure to understand the parable but willingness to stay with him and ask questions is exactly the point of his response: "To you the secret of the kingdom of God has been given" (4:11). Insofar as they *stay with Jesus* and continue to ask and listen, they are indeed the recipients of the secret of the kingdom. Jesus's disciples ask questions of him as part of their growth and learning (7:17; 9:11, 28; 10:10, 26). But when fear prevents them from asking Jesus questions about his teaching, this represents a serious lack of wisdom in their discipleship (9:32).[5]

In fact, many have noted that the twelve apostles are portrayed as remarkably obtuse and very rarely able to understand Jesus's teachings. Already we have noted Jesus's rebuke of Peter and reference to him as Satan (8:31–33) and how fear gets in the way of the disciples' spiritual perception and faith (4:40–41; 9:32). The disciples often represent an incredible dullness when they hear Jesus's teaching (8:14–21). Many readers will likely cringe as they hear the bold question posed to Jesus, as he is on his journey to the cross, by James and John, who ask him to do whatever they ask him to—specifically, to reserve special seats of honor for them in the kingdom (10:35–40). And, of course, readers likely know that the disciples fail Jesus in his greatest moment of need as they sleep while he labors in anguished prayer (14:32–42), the disciple Judas betrays him (14:43–47), all of the other disciples abandon Jesus as he's arrested (14:48–50), and three times Peter denies even knowing Jesus (14:66–72). 14.3

The Characterization of Jesus and Markan Christology

We have seen that the tension in Mark's Gospel arises from a portrait of Jesus that shows him to be both the powerful and triumphant Son of God and one whose way of life is marked by service, humility, and faithful submission to the will of God even as it leads him to the cross. Thus, the literary technique of characterization is at the heart of Mark's Christology.[6] Again, characterization simply refers to what the narrator tells us and shows about the main players in the story. Mark's characterization of Jesus is, of course, incredibly important because what Jesus says and does reveal God and God's kingdom and also because so frequently Jesus's values are at odds with the ways of the world (see 8:33).[7] As the entire Gospel is, in some ways, an unpacking of this theme, let's look at three strategies whereby Mark's characterization of Jesus functions to teach us about the surprising identity of the Son of God.

First, Mark portrays Jesus as a powerful ruler who uses his power to serve, sacrifice, and provide for others. One of the primary ways that ancient rulers fulfilled their royal task was through gifts to their people, and this often included the provisions of food, banquets, and protection (see sidebar 14.4).[8] Mark shows us the way that the kingdom of God and the kingdom of Satan operate by giving us two stories of very different kings who provide food and banquets for their guests. In Mark 6:14–44, we find the seemingly unrelated stories of Herod Antipas's execution of John the Baptist (vv. 14–29)—a decision made by the tetrarch during a banquet—and Jesus's compassionate provision of food for the hungry crowd of people in the wilderness (vv. 30–44). The banquets and gifts of these two royal figures display the way in which Jesus is set forth by Mark as embodying "a different kind of kingship over a different kind of kingdom."[9] 14.4

Mark's literary placement of Herod's decision to kill John the Baptist is striking because it represents a flashback to the narrative time from Mark 1:14 and also seems to interrupt Mark's account of the sending out of the Twelve (6:7–13) and their return (6:30).[10] Despite Herod Antipas's official title as "tetrarch" (Matt. 14:1; Luke 3:19; 9:7; Acts 13:1), Mark goes out of his way to refer to Herod as "king" (four times in a span of six verses: 6:22, 25, 26, 27). Dining together with the king at his banquet are "the great ones, commanders, and the first ones of Galilee" (6:21; cf. 10:42, 44). Given Jesus's

SIDEBAR 14.3

The Faith of "Minor Characters" in Mark

In contrast to the disciples, Mark often presents "minor characters" who respond positively to Jesus and his proclamation of the kingdom of God.[a] A woman with the flow of blood demonstrates great faith and is healed (5:25–34), the clever response and faith of a Syrophoenician woman result in Jesus's exorcism of a demon from her daughter (7:24–30), and another woman lavishly anoints Jesus with perfume for his burial (14:3–9). The contrast, then, between the twelve apostles and these minor characters continues to press home the point that understanding Jesus's identity is difficult and requires ongoing submission of oneself to Jesus and his teaching.

later teaching on "greatness" and "first-ness" (see 10:41–45), we are primed here to view this scene as an ironic and wrongheaded use of royal power. Mark characterizes Herod with the traits of a foolish tyrant. Herod is superstitious and emotionally unstable as his hearing of the reports of the miraculous healings and exorcisms by Jesus and the Twelve causes him to cry out, "John, the one I beheaded, has been raised!" (6:16). Herod is unstable, divided in his own mind, and unable to control his will as he puts John to death despite his desire to protect him (6:20). The king is tricked and manipulated by two women into putting John to death (6:24–28), ultimately as a result of his inability to control his sexual passions when the young girl dances in the company of his friends (6:22). The king foolishly offers the girl whatever she wants, even up to "half of my kingdom" (6:23). And despite being "greatly distressed" (6:26a), he follows through on her request lest he—the king!—lose face in front of his banqueting guests (6:26b). The banquet scene comes to an end with Herod's command to kill John and bring his head to the girl on a dinner platter (6:28). The feast is grotesque, as the serving platter with the head is passed from the executioner, to the young girl, and then to the mother (6:28). Herod's characteristics of instability of emotions, enslavement to sexual passions, arbitrary and grotesque use of violence against the innocent, manipulation by women, and superstition function to portray the so-called king as a foolish tyrant, as one who "merely *appears* to rule (cf. 10:42), whereas actually his strings are pulled by others."[11]

The contrast between King Herod's banquet and Jesus's provision of food for the hungry could not be greater (6:30–44). The setting for Jesus's banquet is the desolate wilderness, not the royal palace; the characters are "the many" who are pressing in on Jesus and his disciples, instead of "great" and "first" ones of Galilee; and the situation is one of hunger as they had scarcely had any time to eat (6:31). Upon seeing that the crowd was "like sheep without a shepherd," Jesus is characterized as having *compassion* on the crowd (6:34). Jesus involves his disciples in the feeding of the crowd by commanding them, "You give them something to eat" (6:37), and in his ordering of them to have the crowd sit in small banqueting groups (6:39). The disciples do

SIDEBAR 14.4

Augustus the Benefactor: The *Res Gestae*

The *Res Gestae* presents Augustus's own recounting of his superior benefactions. These benefactions are interconnected with his authority to supreme rule over the Roman people. In many ways, the following excerpts help us see how Jesus is something of a counterimperial figure as he refrains from the type of bold and hubristic claims of Augustus and ultimately reveals his kingship through weakness, suffering, and love.[b]

"Four times I supported the treasury with my money" (17.1).

"I built the senate house . . . and the temple of Apollo on the Palatine with its porticoes, the temple of the god Iulius, the shrine of Pan" (19.1).

"Three times I gave gladiatorial shows in my name and five times in the names of my sons or grandsons" (22.1).

"I enlarged the boundaries of all provinces of the Roman people" (26.1).

"Both the senate and the equestrian order and the people of Rome all together hailed me as father of the fatherland" (35.1).

participate in distributing the food to the great crowd, but only after they have received the provision of food from Jesus. The result is that all of the people eat and are satisfied at the messianic feast (6:42–44). Mark is drawing on Numbers 27:16–17 in his depiction of Jesus as a Moses-like shepherd of the people who both teaches and feeds the people (6:34b, 40–44). Readers are led to also see this as a fulfillment of God's promise to raise up a good shepherd from the house of David who will lead, nourish, feed, and save the lost sheep who had been scattered and exploited by Israel's corrupt leaders (Ezek. 34).[12] Two types of kings are on display here in Mark 6, but only one king uses his authority and power in a way that befits *God's* kingdom.

Second, Jesus's kingship is on display as he uses his unparalleled power in order to aid the afflicted, poor, and needy. Perhaps most memorable are Jesus's frequent exorcisms of demons from persons who formerly were precluded from health and inclusion within broader society (e.g., 1:23–29; 5:1–20). He liberates people from both their sins and their physical ailment (2:1–12; 5:21–43; 8:22–26; 10:46–52). He shares his presence and teaching about the kingdom with sinners and outcasts such as tax collectors (2:15–17). Jesus frequently attends to women and heals them or their loved ones (1:29–31; 5:25–34; 7:24–30). Jesus's "compassion for the crowd" (8:1–2) provides him with the needed motivation to share bread with the hungry (8:1–9; cf. 6:32–44). Likewise, he heals a man with skin disease because he feels compassion for him (1:39–45). And his compassion elicits his healing power for a child plagued by seizures (9:14–27).

Third, Jesus is often characterized as one who deflects honor and attention away from himself *and toward God*.[13] Many are familiar with the apostle Paul's description of Jesus as one who, despite "being in the form of God," humbled and lowered himself even to the point of death on a Roman cross (Phil. 2:6–8). But Mark also shows us a Jesus with incredible power who, nevertheless, surprisingly rejects using this power to achieve a high worldly status or privilege; rather, he consistently submits himself to God. When Jesus displays his divine power through healing or exorcisms, rather than drawing further attention to himself, he often demands secrecy about what the people have witnessed (1:43–44; 5:43; 7:36; 8:26) and, on other occasions, reveals that God is the source of his power (5:19–20). Similarly, right in the middle of Jesus's teachings and displays of power, Mark often tells us that Jesus abandons the crowds and withdraws to a quiet place where he prays to God (1:35; 3:9–12; 6:45–46). Jesus's teaching is also squarely centered on God. In fact, Jesus's statement to Peter, "You are not setting your thoughts on the things of God, but on the things of humans" (8:33b), is programmatic for the content of Jesus's teachings. Jesus proclaims "the gospel of God" (1:14), "the kingdom of God" (1:15; 4:11, 26, 30; 9:1, 47; 10:14–15), and "the commands of God" (7:8–9, 13). Jesus exhorts his disciples to do "the will of God" (3:35) and to "have faith in God" (11:22). When Jesus is tested with a variety of difficult questions from the religious leaders, his consistent claim is that those asking the question do not truly understand the ways of God (12:14, 24, 26). The greatest commandment is, of course, found in Deuteronomy 6:5: "Love the Lord your God with your whole heart, your whole soul, your whole mind, and your whole strength" (Mark 12:30). Jesus's final days also reveal a posture that trusts and obeys God even as it leads to his own suffering and death. He prays in the garden that God would spare his life but declares, "Not what I will, but what you will" (14:36). Jesus's life and teaching are paradoxical as they pertain to conventional understandings of "deity" or "power," for Jesus is truly the powerful Son of God who teaches, casts out demons, forgives sins, calms storms, and heals the sick; but in every aspect of his life, Jesus embodies a way of life oriented toward God.

Fourth, Mark shows us a Jesus who teaches his disciples that his kingdom is enacted through humility, service, and suffering. The literary structure of Mark's "way" section (8:22–10:52) is an excellent exemplification of this point.[14] We have seen that the section begins with a strange healing narrative in which Jesus heals a man in *two stages* (8:22–26). After the first stage, the man is only able to see people walking around like trees. He needs divine assistance in order to be able to see clearly. The story is a parable for the disciples who are following Jesus, listening to him, and confess him to be the Messiah—just as Peter will do in the next scene (8:27–30). But the disciples clearly do not understand that the powerful Messiah will enact God's kingdom through service, sacrifice, and a humiliating death on a cross (see sidebar 14.5). They need a "second look" at the meaning of Jesus's messiahship, and Jesus attempts to lead his disciples precisely to a knowledge that cross and kingdom are not antithetical but that, in fact, the kingdom comes *through* the cross.[15] If the disciples or any readers are able to embrace Jesus's teachings, they will be like the blind man Bartimaeus, who is healed by Jesus and able to see that Jesus is the Son of David, and will follow Jesus on the way (10:46–52).[16] Three times Jesus predicts that he will experience shame, rejection, suffering, and death as a result of his obedience to the Father. And three times the disciples respond with complete incomprehension. In one instance, Peter rebukes Jesus for this teaching (8:32); in another, the disciples are afraid to ask Jesus about the meaning of his words and instead have a dispute about which one of them is the greatest disciple (9:32–34); and in the third, James and John request privileged seats next to Jesus in the kingdom (10:35–41). 14.5

The disciples struggle to understand how God's rule could come through any means other than worldly power—and perhaps even through violent force. But Jesus explicitly contrasts his kingdom and power with the rule of the Roman and gentile rulers (10:42–45). In response to John and James's request for a special place in Jesus's messianic kingdom, Jesus asks them, "Are you able to drink the cup that I drink and be baptized with the baptism with which I am baptized?" (10:38). John and James have rightly understood Jesus's teaching that the kingdom of God is present in the ministry of the Messiah, but they have gone wrong in their failure to understand that sharing in Jesus's glory entails suffering, sacrifice, self-denial, and taking up one's cross as a disciple of Jesus (see 8:34–38). Drinking Jesus's "cup" and sharing in his "baptism" are metaphors pointing forward to Jesus's baptism unto death whereby he will inaugurate the new covenant (see 14:23–24). Jesus's teaching clarifies for his disciples one final time the true nature of discipleship: "You know that those who seem to rule among the nations lord it over them, and that the great ones act as tyrants over them" (10:42). Most rulers, including the Roman emperor, wield their power over their subjects in a tyrannical way that stands in contrast to the Son of Man, who came to die for his people.[17] Jesus's power and "greatness" are manifested through sacrificial service to others: "Whoever wants to be great among you will be your servant, and whoever wants to be first must be a slave to everyone" (10:43–44). Jesus's claim that greatness and good leadership are embodied in the humiliated identity of a slave transforms, or so it should, the disciples' understanding of power, authority, and messianic rule. And this form of greatness, leadership, and rule is such because it follows the pattern of the messianic Son of Man, who "did not come to be served but to serve and to give his life as a ransom for many people" (10:45). If John and James want to share in Jesus's messianic rule, they must recognize that this kingdom will be inaugurated by means of his suffering for the world on a Roman cross (also 14:22–25).

SIDEBAR 14.5

Cross, Misunderstanding, and Discipleship in Mark's Gospel

Jesus's prediction of passion and death	The disciples' misunderstanding	Jesus's correction with discipleship teaching
8:31	8:32–33	8:34–9:1
9:31	9:32–34	9:35–40
10:32–34	10:35–41	10:42–45

The Davidic Messiah and the Fate of the Jerusalem Temple

As Jesus's journey on "the way" draws to a conclusion, readers can discern that the Messiah's relationship to the Jerusalem temple is of utmost significance for the plot of the Gospel. The temple is both the dominant setting and an important topic of conversation throughout most of Mark 11–15. The Scriptures of Israel mark out the temple as the locus for God's name and glorious presence and look forward to a day when Mount Zion is lifted high and the nations stream to Jerusalem to worship God under his rule. What role does the Jerusalem temple play now that God's kingdom has come in the person of Jesus the Messiah? We can explore this question by examining three things: (1) Jesus's so-called triumphal entry into Jerusalem (11:1–11); (2) Jesus's disruptive act in the temple and his parable of the fig tree (11:12–25); (3) Jesus's eschatological teachings in the Olivet Discourse (chap. 13). 14.6

THE TRIUMPHAL ENTRY

As Jesus makes his way into Jerusalem, eschatological expectations that Jesus is God's long-awaited messianic king and that the fulfillment of God's promises are about to come to fruition are intense (11:1–11). People are asking, along with the blind man Bartimaeus, whether Jesus is the merciful Son of David (10:47–48). The symbolic act of Jesus seated on a colt riding into Jerusalem and receiving praise and acclamations before he makes his way to the temple evokes the enthronement of Solomon to a position of rule over God's people. More specifically, when Solomon takes his seat on the throne of David, he rides on King David's mule and is anointed by the priest Zadok as king, and all the people declare, "Long live King Solomon!" and "all the people went up following him, playing on pipes and rejoicing with great joy, so that the earth quaked at their noise" (1 Kings 1:38–40 NRSVue). But the scene also evokes later biblical prophecies such as Zechariah 9:9: "Rejoice greatly, Daughter Zion! Shout, Daughter Jeru-

SIDEBAR 14.6

What Is the Connection between Temple and Messianic King?

The Jerusalem temple is the place marked out by the God of Israel for his people to worship him through the sacrificial system under the leadership of the priesthood (Deut. 12:1–14). Understanding Mark's Gospel requires that we be familiar with how the Scriptures of Israel frequently speak of Davidic-messianic figures as connected with the building and proper functioning of the temple. David himself, for example, wanted to build a temple for God in Zion (2 Sam. 5:1–7:3). God tells David that it will not be David who builds a temple; rather, "I will raise up your seed after you, who will come forth from your body, and I will establish his kingdom; he will build a house for my name, and I will establish the throne of his kingdom forever" (2 Sam. 7:12–13). And we find, in 1 Kings, that God commissioned David's son Solomon to build a glorious temple for God's name and glorious presence to dwell in (chap. 8). We even see that gentiles and foreigners come to recognize God's glorious presence in the Jerusalem temple (King Hiram of Tyre [9:10–14]; the queen of Sheba [10:1–10]). Thus, "all the peoples of the earth" may know that the God of Israel who dwells in the temple is glorious and worthy of worship (8:41–43, 58–61). But God makes it clear that if the king and people do not walk in his ways, his presence will not always abide in the temple (8:56–61; 9:1–9). Sadly, the kings of Israel do not follow in the ways of David, and as a result the Jerusalem temple is destroyed by the Babylonians (in 587 BCE) and then later rebuilt by Zerubbabel after the exile. But the Old Testament writings witness to a hope that one day God will raise up a truly righteous Davidic messianic figure who will restore or rebuild the temple and usher in God's glorious kingdom. To give just one example, the prophet Zechariah expects a Davidic king whose name is "Branch," who "will branch out in his place, and he will build the temple of the Lord. It is he who will build the temple of the Lord; he will bear royal honor, and will sit upon his throne and rule" (Zech. 6:12–13a; cf. 3:8–10).

salem! See, your king comes to you, righteous and victorious, lowly and riding on a donkey, on a colt, the foal of a donkey" (NIV). 14.7

Mark wants us to see this scene as the enactment of "the Lord" coming to Zion and, therefore, as the fulfillment of the prophets' promises that God's people would together worship God under the reign of their messianic king (e.g., Isa. 40:1–11; 52:7–12). The association between Messiah and temple helps us understand why the crowds are crying out, "Hosanna! Blessed is he who comes in the name of the Lord! Blessed is the coming kingdom of our father David! Hosanna in the highest!" (11:9b–10). The crowds, like John and James in their request to sit on Jesus's left and right in his kingdom (10:35), are expectant that Jesus is the Davidic king who will inaugurate his kingdom in Jerusalem. The messianic king is indeed coming to his temple, but we may ask, Do the crowds really know *what kind of king* Jesus is and how the kingdom will come? There is an anticlimactic, even ominous, note struck at the end of the scene. Jesus is not enthroned as the messianic king in Jerusalem. There are no priests or religious leaders to greet him. And Jesus, after taking a look around the temple, retreats to Bethany with his disciples (11:11).[18]

SIDEBAR 14.7

Scripture and the Triumphal Entry

In order to get the full meaning of Mark's depiction of Jesus's triumphal entry, the reader must activate a variety of images and figures from the Old Testament Scriptures.

1 Kings 1:32–35, 39–40

King David said, "Call in Zadok the priest, Nathan the prophet and Benaiah son of Jehoiada." When they came before the king, he said to them: "Take your lord's servant with you and have Solomon my son mount my own mule and take him down to Gihon. There have Zadok the priest and Nathan the prophet anoint him king over Israel. Blow the trumpet and shout, 'Long live King Solomon!' Then you are to go up with him, and he is to come and sit on my throne and reign in my place. I have appointed him ruler over Israel and Judah."

. . . Zadok the priest took the horn of oil from the sacred tent and anointed Solomon. Then they sounded the trumpet and all the people shouted, "Long live King Solomon!" And all the people went up after him, playing pipes and rejoicing greatly, so that the ground shook with the sound. (NIV)

Psalm 118:19–22, 25–26

Open for me the gates of righteousness;
  I will enter and give thanks to the Lord.
This is the gate of the Lord
  through which the righteous may enter.
I will give you thanks, for you answered me;
  you have become my salvation.
The stone the builders rejected
  has become the cornerstone. . . .
Lord, save us!
  Lord, grant us success!
Blessed is he who comes in the name of the Lord.
  From the house of the Lord we bless you. (NIV)

Zechariah 9:9, 10b

Rejoice greatly, Daughter Zion!
  Shout, Daughter Jerusalem!
See, your king comes to you,
  righteous and victorious,
lowly and riding on a donkey,
  on a colt, the foal of a donkey. . . .
He will proclaim peace to the nations.
  His rule will extend from sea to sea
  and from the River to the ends of the earth. (NIV)

Aniely / CC BY 3.0 / Wikimedia Commons

Figure 14.1. Reconstructed model of the second temple

JESUS'S PROPHETIC JUDGMENT ON THE TEMPLE

The next scenes in the Gospel present the reader with an obvious example of a Markan sandwich: (A) Jesus curses the fig tree (11:12–14); (B) Jesus makes a prophetic judgment on the temple (11:15–19); (A) Jesus interprets the cursing of the fig tree (11:20–25). Given that the middle episode is often the key to making sense of the "outer pieces" of the sandwich, here I will make a few observations about Jesus's surprising action in the temple in verses 15–19. First, Jesus's action makes good sense as a prophetic enactment of God's judgment against the temple. The Old Testament contains stories in which God commands his prophets to engage in a surprising symbolic act that portends his future judgment (e.g., Isa. 20:1–3; Ezek. 4:4–8). Similarly, Jesus's action in the temple is rife with symbolic significance. Jesus's actions of casting out of the temple those who were buying and selling animals and of overturning the tables of the money changers make sacrifice within the temple an impossibility (11:15). On the one hand, the sacrifice of animals at the temple and the institution of the priesthood were ordained by God himself. Those selling animals for sacrifice as well as those exchanging money were providing a necessary service so that sacrifices could take place. Jesus's actions are aimed at stopping the sacrifices in the temple, even if only for a very short time.[19] Again, the narrator's note that Jesus "would not allow anyone to carry vessels through the temple" (11:16) draws attention to Jesus's act of prohibiting the tools necessary for blood sacrifice.[20]

But why would Jesus engage in a prophetic act of judgment against the temple? In Mark 11:17, Jesus's quotation of two Old Testament texts helps us interpret his actions: "Has it not been written: 'My house shall be called a house of prayer for all the nations' [Isa. 56:7]? But you have made it a den of thieves [Jer. 7:11]." Isaiah 56 is a prophetic oracle that anticipates how God's eschatological salvation for his people will result in a period where foreigners, eunuchs, outcasts, and all those who do justice will joyfully gather at God's temple to offer prayers and sacrifices (vv. 1–8). In this way, when God's kingdom comes, the temple must be "a house of prayer for all the peoples" (v. 7b). As we have seen, God's kingdom has indeed come. Jesus has proclaimed the gospel of God and the kingdom (Mark 1:14–15). His teaching, exorcisms, and healings have demonstrated that God has come back to be with his people. And yet the temple establishment has not embraced the true "Lord" as he has come to Jerusalem (11:3). Jesus has extended God's salvation and presence to all peoples in his ministry (see especially 5:1–20; 7:24–30; 10:46–52), but the temple is not functioning as a joyful house of prayer for all peoples. Implied within Jesus's quotation of Isaiah 56 is the critique that despite God's kingdom having come in the person of Jesus, the temple is operating according to the old age, the age of Satan, since it is not functioning as a place of prayer for *all peoples*.

Jesus contrasts Isaiah's eschatological hope for the temple with the prophetic judgment oracle of Jeremiah 7, saying that the temple has been turned into "a den of thieves." In Jeremiah 7, the prophet excoriates God's people for presuming that they have access to God's presence through the temple despite their immorality, injustice, and evil ways. A portion of the oracle helps us see this dynamic clearly: "Here you are, trusting in deceptive words to no avail. Will you steal, murder, commit adultery, swear falsely, make offerings to Baal, and go after other gods that you have not known and then come and stand before me in this house, which is called by my name, and say, 'We are safe!'—only to go on doing all these abominations? Has this house, which is called by my name, become a den of robbers in your sight?" (Jer. 7:8–11 NRSVue). The quotation presumes that the trade going on inside the temple is corrupt and demonstrates the lack of justice among the temple leaders (see also Zech. 14:20–21).[21] Jesus's action, then, portends the eschatological destruction of the temple. Jesus's action looks forward to a time when the temple, sadly, will no longer carry out sacrifices in service to God. We have seen that in the Old Testament and

SIDEBAR 14.8

Fruitful Abundance in the Eschatological Age

Making sense of Jesus's strange symbolic action and teaching regarding the fig tree requires some awareness of how the Old Testament speaks of the messianic age being a time of abundant fruitfulness and periods of judgment being times of lack.

Jeremiah 8:13

> "I will take away their harvest," declares the Lord. "There will be no grapes on the vine. There will be no figs on the tree, and their leaves will wither. What I have given them will be taken from them." (NIV)

Ezekiel 47:7, 12

> When I arrived there, I saw a great number of trees on each side of the river. . . . Fruit trees of all kinds will grow on both banks of the river. Their leaves will not wither, nor will their fruit fail. Every month they will bear fruit, because the water from the sanctuary flows to them. Their fruit will serve for food and their leaves for healing. (NIV)

Jewish traditions the Messiah and the temple are supposed to exist together in peace, but Israel's rejection of the Messiah leads to a sad state of affairs: the Messiah's prophetic demonstration and anticipation of the temple's destruction.[22]

So how does this story help us interpret the strange incident where Jesus curses the fig tree? Notice the strange detail that Jesus is looking for fruit from the fig tree, and when he finds no fruit, Mark declares that "it was not the time [*kairos*] for figs" (11:13b). Here the story obviously is functioning to make a symbolic point, and here it's crucial to recognize that fruit was frequently spoken of by the prophets as a sign of God's blessing in the eschatological age. When God inaugurated his kingdom and sent his Messiah, it would be a period of fruitful abundance.[23] 14.8

Here's the point: Although it is not the normal "season" for fruit on the fig tree, given that the gospel and the kingdom of God *are here in the person of the Messiah*, Jesus is nevertheless examining the tree and looking for fruitful abundance. Finding no fruit, Jesus curses the fig tree as a sign of God's impending judgment on the temple and its leadership. The lack of fruit signifies that the temple is not functioning as a place of real prayer and true faith.[24] So when Peter sees that the fig tree has withered, he rightly connects its destruction to Jesus's curse (11:20–21). Jesus's response to Peter must be interpreted in light of the expectation that God's temple will be destroyed because it is not fulfilling its function in the eschatological age:

> Jesus answered, "Have faith in God. Truly I say to you that whoever says to this mountain, 'Be lifted up and cast into the sea,' and does not doubt in their heart but believes that what is spoken will take place, so it shall be for that one. For this reason, I say to you, whatever you pray for and request, believe that you have received it and it shall be done for you. And whenever you stand praying, if you are holding anything against someone, forgive them so that even your heavenly Father may forgive you your transgressions." (11:22–25)

Jesus's words must be interpreted within the literary context and, as such, as providing more interpretation of his temple action and cursing of the fig tree. Jesus has indicted the temple and its leaders for failing to fulfill their divine purpose, and so now Jesus *calls his disciples to embody faith, prayer, and forgiveness*. The old temple is out, cursed, and under God's judgment. Jesus is calling his disciples "to be the fulfillment of the temple's purpose of being a house of prayer for all people, in the wake of Jesus's judgment and condemnation of it. They will be the place, also, where forgiveness is found."[25] 14.9

See sidebar 14.9, and note how this connects with Jesus's parable of the vineyard and the tenants in Mark 12:1–12. Here Jesus tells a story about an owner of a vineyard who hires tenants to do the work, but when the owner sends one messenger after another to collect *the fruit* (12:2), the tenants shame, mistreat, and kill the owner's servants. The audience of this parable would know that the owner of the vineyard is God, who is sending his prophets (i.e., the messengers) to call God's people and especially Israel's leaders to bear the fruit of repentance. In the parable, Jesus notes that the owner decides one last time to collect fruit and devises a plan whereby he will send his "one beloved son," and he says, "They will honor my son" (12:6). But instead of offering fruit, the tenants function as usurpers who hope to take ownership of the vineyard, and they kill the son and cast him out of the vineyard. Jesus concludes the parable by quoting Psalm 118:22: "The stone that the builders rejected—this has become the head cornerstone. This has come about from the Lord, and it is marvelous in our eyes" (Mark 12:10–11). This is the same psalm from which the crowd chanted at Jesus's triumphal entry when they acclaimed, "Hosanna! Blessed is the one who comes in the name of the Lord" (Mark 11:9; cf. Ps. 118:25–26). But now we see that Jesus reads the psalm as predicting the messianic king's *rejection, suffering, and ensuing vindication*. The old temple and the leadership will be destroyed for failing to bear fruit, but Jesus declares that he is the rejected but vindicated *cornerstone of the new temple*.

THE DESTRUCTION OF THE OLD TEMPLE AND THE CREATION OF THE NEW TEMPLE

The only charge brought against Jesus in his trial before the Sanhedrin was the testimony that he said, "I will destroy this temple made with human hands and in three days I will build another one not made with human hands" (14:58). As Jesus was hanging from the cross, we hear of some passing by and mocking Jesus, saying, "Ha! You who would destroy the temple and rebuild it in three days, save yourself and come

SIDEBAR 14.9

Israel as God's Beloved Yet Estranged Vineyard

The Old Testament often speaks of Israel as the vineyard that God has planted and tended with great care. But when he looks for grapes, he is disappointed to see the vineyard is producing wild grapes. Read the following texts to make sure you are familiar with how Jesus uses this image in Mark's Gospel: Psalm 80:8–18; Isaiah 5:1–7; 27:2–6; Jeremiah 2:21; 12:10.

down from the cross" (15:29–30). Although Mark presents the aforementioned testimony as false (14:57), we have seen Jesus's prophetic enactment of judgment in the temple (11:15–19), his teaching on the fig tree (11:12–14, 20–25), and his reference to himself and his disciples as taking on the role of the eschatological temple (11:22–25; 12:1–11). Thus, although Jesus does not destroy the temple, we do see him predict its demise. Most clearly, we see this in Mark 13, where Jesus uses an abundance of prophetic images drawn from Israel's Scriptures to speak both of the impending destruction of the temple and of how the role and function of the temple will be fulfilled by the crucified and resurrected Jesus and his followers. Many have noticed, in fact, how Mark 13 is framed by stories of two women. One woman makes an offering to the temple treasury (12:41–44), whereas the other woman anoints Jesus for his impending death (14:1–9). As Timothy Gombis notes, "These two temples—Jesus and the Jerusalem temple—are both headed for destruction, but Jesus will be raised from the dead as God's true temple."[26]

Jesus warns his disciples that the temple will indeed be destroyed but that the signs that accompany its demise do not indicate the final coming of the Son of Man. The disciples again prove themselves to have failed to understand Jesus's teaching when, in plain view of the temple, one of them declares, "Teacher, behold what marvelous stones and buildings!" (13:1). Jesus must make as plain as possible the meaning of his prior teachings and acts regarding the impending destruction of the temple, and so he declares, "Do you see these beautiful structures? Not one stone will be left on another stone; all of them will be thrown down" (13:2). Peter asks Jesus directly about the signs that will accompany the temple's destruction. And we should emphasize that Jesus's teaching is squarely centered on preparing his disciples for God's impending judgment on the temple, an event that took place around 66–73 CE and is narrated in Josephus's *Jewish War*. The period will be marked by wars and rumor of wars, the appearance of false messiahs, violence, and the desecration of the temple's sacred precincts. Most shocking will be when the disciples see "the desolating sacrilege standing where it should not" (13:14). The strange phrase "desolating sacrilege" comes from the book of Daniel and describes the pollution of the temple and the cessation of sacrifices (Dan. 9:27; 11:31; 12:11). But even still, Jesus prepares his disciples by telling them that although these are signs of the temple's destruction, *this is not yet the end!*

In fact, one of the primary purposes of Jesus's teaching is to warn his disciples against engaging in eschatological obsessions with any timetables for his return or for the end of history. So, Jesus issues warnings about being deceived (13:5–6, 21–23) and reminds them that "the end is still to come" (13:7b; cf. 13:8c, 10). Rather, these events function as signs that portend the imminent destruction of the Jerusalem temple. We have seen Jesus quote Jeremiah's oracle of judgment (Jer. 7:11 in Mark 11:17) that warns of God's people presuming that they are safe, secure, and invulnerable because they think that the temple indicates God is always on their side. Jesus also warns his disciples that when they see the signs, they should flee Jerusalem to avoid the effects of God's judgment against it (13:14–20). There will be trials, persecutions, and false messiahs attempting to deceive, but Jesus's pastoral teaching is summed up in his exhortation, "But you are to pay attention! I have told you everything ahead of time" (13:23). Despite Jesus's inauguration of the kingdom of God, Jesus's disciples will continue to experience trials and tribulations as they participate in the mission of taking the gospel to the nations (13:9–13, 24a). In other words, the sufferings and tribulations are not the signs of the end. In fact, no one—not even the Son of Man himself!—knows when the Son of Man will return (13:32). As they await his return, disciples of Jesus should focus on faithfulness and mission rather than on any eschatological speculations or predictions.

Jesus's claim to be the new "chief cornerstone" (12:10–11) and his teaching that the disciples embody functions of the temple such as prayer, faith, and forgiveness in their own community (11:20–25) enable us to see how Jesus and the church take on the role and functions of the temple in the kingdom of God. First, whereas Isaiah anticipated a day when *all the nations* would stream to Zion, to the temple in Jerusalem, to join Israel in the worship of the true God (Isa. 56:6–7; 66:18–20), now the disciples are the ones who will proclaim the gospel to all the nations (Mark 13:10). Jesus himself had quoted Isaiah 56:7 to make the connection between the temple and salvation for the nations (Mark 11:17). When Jesus is exalted in heaven as the powerful and glorious Son of Man, this will result in him sending messengers to the four corners of the earth to gather his people (13:26–27). "In other words, the disciples are to fulfill the divinely intended purpose of the temple by becoming the means by which the Gentiles come to worship God."[27] This helps explain the significance of both the veil of the temple being torn in two and a Roman centurion confessing that Jesus is God's Son when Jesus dies (15:38–39). The centurion represents the gentile nations who will now come to share in the kingdom of God through the crucified Jesus.

Second, Jesus institutes a new sacrifice in the eschatological temple. Mark makes it clear that the setting for Jesus's meal with his disciples is the celebration of the Passover (14:1, 12). Jesus and his disciples celebrate the Passover meal together, during which Jesus identifies his broken body and shed blood as the new and final sacrifice that will set God's people free and will inaugurate God's kingdom. Jesus's interpretation of his shed blood as "my blood of the covenant poured out for the sake of all" (14:24) echoes Old Testament texts that ratified God's covenants through the sacrifice of animals. The clearest Old Testament parallel is the account where God commands Moses to ratify the Sinai covenant. After the animals have been sacrificed, the book of Exodus says, "Moses then took the blood, sprinkled it on the people and said, 'This is the blood of the covenant that the LORD has made with you in accordance with all these words'" (Exod. 24:8 NIV). Jesus's language of his blood being "poured out" as a sacrifice is clearly similar to Moses's act of sprinkling the sacrificial blood on the altar. And both Moses's sacrificial offering and Jesus's anticipation of his sacrificial death take place within the context of a meal (Exod. 24:8–11).[28] Jesus is explicit that his death, symbolized through this new meal, is a substitutionary death whereby his life is given for the salvation of others (so Mark 10:42–45). But instead of the blood of a sacrificed animal, Jesus offers his own human blood to save his people and to make a new covenant (cf. Isa. 53:6, 12).[29] Jesus, whose life is embodied in the broken body and shed blood, is the new and saving sacrifice for God's people.

The Crucifixion and Resurrection of the Messianic Son of God

Mark's Gospel climaxes in the Messiah's suffering and crucifixion. Although Jesus's death is, of course, the climax of all four Gospels, Mark's narration of Jesus's death is unrelentingly dark and tragic as it emphasizes the surprising reality that God's kingdom and gospel come by way of the cross of Christ.[30] Mark's so-called *theologia crucis*, "theology of the cross," presents to us in narrative form the truth that God's wisdom and power are foolishness to the world but are salvation to those who have the Spirit and the eyes of faith (1 Cor. 1:18–25; 2:6–16). Let's look at four ways Mark drives this point home through his account of Jesus's suffering and death in Mark 14–15.

First, Mark emphasizes that (almost) everyone rejects and turns against Jesus.[31] Jesus is the object of hostility and an unjust trial, of course, by the chief priests and the scribes, who use treachery and deception to put Jesus to death (e.g., 14:1–2, 55, 63–64). Anonymous individuals give false testimony against Jesus and cry out demanding his crucifixion (14:56–59; 15:13–14). Mark emphasizes that it is all of the Jewish leaders who hand Jesus over to Pilate—the priests, the elders, the scribes, and the entire Sanhedrin (15:1). Pilate, despite knowing the trial and accusations against Jesus are a sham, willingly puts Jesus to death, his execution carried out by Roman soldiers (15:15–25). Mark tells us nothing positive about the criminals crucified on Jesus's left and right, only that they too were reviling Jesus

Figure 14.2. Garden of Gethsemane

(15:27, 32). But, most tragically, even the disciples abandon Jesus. Judas Iscariot defects from his discipleship and plans to hand over Jesus for the sake of money (14:10–11). The disciples' abandonment of Jesus is emphasized by the Markan sandwich whereby, bracketing the Last Supper, which emphasizes Jesus's covenant faithfulness for his people (14:22–26), one scene shows Jesus predicting his betrayal by a disciple (14:17–21) and another scene shows him predicting both Peter's and the rest of the disciples' abandonment of Jesus in his time of need (14:27–31). While Jesus is in agony and deep pain as he prays to the Father in the garden of Gethsemane, Peter, James, and John are repeatedly found sleeping (14:32–42). Peter, of course, three times denies even knowing Jesus (14:66–72). And even Jesus's cry from the cross, "My God, my God, why have you abandoned me?" (15:34, quoting Ps. 22:2), expresses the depths of his pain as he experiences God's hiddenness during his time of need. All of the world rejects the Son of God, and Jesus truly tastes death for his people (see Heb. 2:9–10).

But, surprisingly, Mark 14–15 portrays a woman anointing Jesus for his burial (14:3–9) and three named women at the cross (15:40), and even reports that there were many of his female followers from Galilee who were watching (15:41). And it is the three named women (Mary Magdalene, Mary the mother of James, and Salome) who visit the tomb to anoint Jesus's dead body (16:1–2). What does Mark intend for us to make of the dynamic of everyone rejecting and abandoning Jesus except these women? I suggest that this conforms to Mark's theology of the cross, whereby the world is accountable and culpable for its condemnation and rejection of Jesus, and yet there are women—most of whom are unnamed—who have the eyes of faith to see that indeed the crucified Jesus is truly the Son of God. As Dorothy Lee notes on women in Mark's Gospel, "Women are not mentioned as frequently as men, and their role is less visible than the Twelve. Yet in many ways, their ministry exceeds that of the apostles, and their role goes far beyond their cultural context. This portrait of women reflects the ministry of Jesus and his extraordinary openness to women as disciples."[32]

Second, Mark's Gospel draws on Davidic psalms of lament and suffering to emphasize the point that Jesus's kingship, kingdom, and power come by way of humble suffering and faithfulness to God. When Jesus is sharing his final meal with his disciples, he says that "the one who eats with me will betray me" (14:18). The phrase refers to Psalm 41, a Davidic psalm in which the king laments, "Even my close friend in whom I trusted, who ate of my bread, has lifted the heel against me" (Ps. 41:9 NRSVue). In the garden of Gethsemane, Jesus declares, "My soul is deeply troubled, even to the point of death" (14:34). This is an obvious citation from Psalms 42 and 43, where, three times, the psalmist laments, "My soul is cast down / distressed within me" (Pss. 42:6, 11; 43:5). Those who mock and crucify Jesus also play the role of the enemies of the Davidic king when they offer him sour wine and cast lots for his garments (compare Pss. 22:18; 69:21 with Mark 15:23–24). The theme comes to a climax when Jesus speaks the lament from Psalm 22:1, "'Eloi, Eloi, lema sabachthani?' which means, 'My God, my God, why have you forsaken me?'" (Mark 15:34). Jesus is indeed the messianic king, but a very different type of king, one who tastes the depths of human suffering even to the point of death.[33]

Third, Jesus's death is portrayed by Mark as a parody of a kingly coronation. Six times Mark shows those who engage in ironic mockery of Jesus using the term "king" as he is tried and then crucified (15:2, 9, 12, 18, 26, 32).[34] The soldiers clothe Jesus in purple, put on him a crown of thorns, make mocking gestures of obeisance to "the King of the Jews" (15:17–20), and engage in a mock ritual of a king's accession to his throne.[35] Jesus is placed on the cross with an inscription that reads, "The King of the Jews" (15:26). While hanging on the cross, Jesus is mocked for his messianic pretentions, such as his supposed plan to build another temple "in three days" (15:29) and the belief that he is Israel's savior, "the Messiah, the King of Israel" (15:31b–32a). The irony should be obvious as the mockery of Jesus's enemies speaks the deepest truth about Jesus's identity, for he is the saving messianic king precisely as he inaugurates God's kingdom through his sacrificial death on the cross.[36] Jesus *is* the Messiah, the Son of David. Jesus *is* the King of Israel. But the revelation of this identity forces us to reckon with a Messiah who reveals his saving kingship through renunciation of rights, through suffering, and ultimately through a crucified love. When the Roman centurion sees how Jesus dies and then declares, "Truly this man was the Son of God" (15:39), the statement is indeed highly ironic but nevertheless expresses the deepest truth of Mark's Gospel. Jesus's sonship and kingship are revealed through suffering and the cross. And now, the reader can see that Jesus's anointing as God's Son (1:9–11) and the vision of his glorious splendor at the transfiguration (9:2–9) were pointing toward the cross as Jesus's display of his royalty and sonship.

But, fourth, God's power to save and liberate a people for himself takes place through the cross, where Jesus assumes humanity's sin. We might view Mark's Gospel as a narrative depiction of Paul's propositional claims regarding the saving death of Jesus. Paul says that the cross is foolishness to the world but is "God's power to those of us who are being saved" (1 Cor. 1:18). God sends his own sinless Son to assume the sin of humanity and to condemn it on the cross (Rom. 8:3; 2 Cor. 5:21). Numerous aspects of Mark's Gospel indicate that Jesus takes the judgment and penalty of sin on himself so that he might rescue his people. For example, Jesus predicts (and Mark narrates) that he will be "handed over" into the hands of sinful men / human hands (9:30–31; 10:33; cf. 14:41), and this language recalls the suffering servant in the book of Isaiah, who is handed over "for the sake of our sins" (Isa. 53:6, 12).[37] Similarly, three times Jesus refers to his impending death using the language of "drinking the cup" (10:38–39; 14:23–24, 36). Drinking or draining a cup of its wine or liquid is often used in reference to undergoing God's judgment (Ps. 11:6; Isa. 51:17–21; Ezek. 23:31–34). Thus, Jesus interprets his death on the cross as entering into God's judgment.[38] When, echoing Psalm 22:1, Jesus cries out from the cross asking the Father, "My God, my God, why have you abandoned me?" Mark portrays Jesus as fully identifying with humanity's sin and taking sin's penalty and judgment on himself *for our sake* (15:34). Jesus "cries out like this because he has entered into our situation in the first place. . . . He has identified, in a real way, with us."[39] And, most obviously, Jesus explicitly interprets his death as a "ransom for many" (10:45; cf. Isa. 53:10–12) and his shed blood as "poured out for the sake of many" (14:24). Mark's Gospel is a powerful articulation of God's love for his people, for the Gospel proclaims a Father who sends his beloved Son to take the penalty and judgment for sin, a judgment that rightly belongs to all of humanity, on himself so that we might know God's love and salvation.

Finally, we should not ignore Jesus's promise that after his crucifixion God will vindicate him by raising him from the dead (8:31; 9:1, 31; 10:32–34). God's resurrection of Jesus functions not least to publicly reveal to the world that Jesus is truly the faithful and obedient Son of God (14:36). God's resurrection of the Son of Man is the means whereby Jesus receives power, dominion, and authority so that the nations should worship him (cf. Dan. 7:14–27). But given that Mark's original ending (the short ending [see sidebar 14.10]) is at Mark 16:8, the resurrection remains a surprising and even confusing event within Mark's narrative. Jesus has promised his disciples that although they would scatter and abandon him in his time of suffering and need, after his resurrection he would appear to them again and restore them in Galilee (14:28; 16:7). But Mark leaves the fulfillment of Jesus's promise *unnarrated*.

The Gospel concludes with eight verses that depict the women going to Jesus's tomb to anoint the body with incense (16:1–3), finding that the tomb is empty and hearing an angel declare that Jesus has been raised from the dead (16:4–6), and, out of their fear, failing to obey the angel's command, "Go and tell his disciples and Peter that he is going before you into Galilee; there you will see him just as he said" (16:7). The fact that the women are coming to anoint Jesus's dead body indicates that they have not yet understood or believed his teaching that he would be raised from

SIDEBAR 14.10

The Ending of Mark

Most English Bibles alert the reader to the fact that there are some serious difficulties for how we understand Mark's original ending. Remember that we do not have the original autographs of our earliest Christian texts; we have only multiple copies of these texts. With respect to Mark's Gospel, the manuscripts testify to at least three endings:[c]

1. The short ending: 16:1–8
2. The long ending: 16:1–8 and 16:9–20.
3. The intermediate ending: Some manuscripts contain this additional note after verse 8: "And all that had been commanded them they told briefly to those around Peter. And afterward Jesus himself sent out through them, from east to west, the sacred and imperishable proclamation of eternal salvation." One manuscript concludes with this note, but most continue on to include verses 9–20.

What do we make of these different endings? Most (not all!) scholars argue that the short ending is Mark's conclusion to the Gospel. While the long ending has the great majority of textual support from the manuscripts, two significant old manuscripts do not have these verses (Codex Sinaiticus and Codex Vaticanus). Furthermore, it's difficult to explain why a scribe copying the Gospel of Mark would delete or fail to copy verses 9–20. But one can easily explain why copyists would add the longer ending. A Gospel that concludes with the women being afraid and failing to tell the disciples what the angel had commanded them, along with the narrative's expectations that the resurrected Jesus was going to appear to his disciples (14:28; 16:7), could easily result in scribes resolving the ending a bit more neatly with a resurrection and commission of the disciples. Furthermore, the vocabulary and style of verses 9–20 are at odds with Mark's typical way of writing and telling his story. In addition, there are some oddities that do not fit neatly with the rest of Mark's Gospel, such as speaking in tongues and promised divine protection from vipers and poison. While the shorter ending is abrupt and strange, as I have noted already, it fits Mark's "overall tenor of mystery and awe that surrounds Jesus's person in Mark's gospel."[d]

Mark's Gospel constantly poses the question "Who is Jesus?" as well as "Will you follow a crucified Messiah?" And now, the readers hear—along with the women—the incredible claim that Jesus has been raised from the dead! How will the women, and how will we who read Mark's Gospel, respond?

the dead. While the women disciples here join the male disciples in fear and failure, the very existence of the Gospel of Mark primes the reader to understand that Jesus *will restore* the faith of his disciples. The hints are there: the sunlight is shining brightly (16:2), the stone at the entrance of the tomb has been rolled away (16:3–4), the angel announces Jesus's resurrection (16:5–6), and the report of the angel reminds the women of Jesus's teaching that he would appear to them after his death (16:7). Obviously, the reader is expecting a resurrection appearance! But Mark leaves the Gospel open-ended and allusive, with no account of Jesus's resurrection appearance. One scholar has commented on Mark's strange ending, "This is the end of Mark's story, because it is the beginning of discipleship."[40] In other words, Mark both invites readers to answer the question "Who is Jesus of Nazareth?" and poses the question as to whether they will follow him in discipleship as the crucified and resurrected Messiah. 14.10

Mark and Discipleship

Disciples of Jesus Are Called to *Be with Him*

Mark's Gospel is dominated by the christological themes of the kingdom of God, the gospel, and Jesus's messiahship. And yet these themes are consistently interconnected with Jesus's call to discipleship—that is, the frequent exhortations to follow Jesus's teachings and example (Mark 1:19–20; 8:34). Jesus's disciples not only confess that he is the messianic Son of God (1:11; 9:7; 15:39); they also participate in Jesus's mission to proclaim and live out the kingdom of God.[1] But if we have learned anything from our study of Mark's Gospel, it is that Jesus is by no means easy to understand—let alone to follow! Notice what Mark tells us about the role of the disciples when Jesus, after praying on a mountain, commissions the twelve apostles: "And he appointed the twelve *in order that they would be with him* and that he might send them to preach and to have authority over the demons" (3:14–15). Yes, disciples of Jesus proclaim the gospel of God and the kingdom of God (1:14–15 with 1:16–20; 6:12). And disciples of Jesus even share in Jesus's ministry to heal and rescue people from the powers of darkness (also 6:13). But these activities are predicated on them *being with Jesus* (3:14b). In one of the very next scenes, we see that while Jesus is teaching, Jesus's biological family is standing *outside*, but there is a group of listeners who are gathered *with and around Jesus* who listen to and "do the will of God" (3:21, 31–35). Proximity to Jesus means that one's life orientation is continuously directed by him and his teaching. 15.1

One commentator explains it this way: "[Being with Jesus] means . . . that their agendas must be ordered by his kingdom agenda. Being with Jesus in Mark means doing what Jesus says, following his lead, recognizing the manner in which he is the Messiah and the true nature of the kingdom, and letting that shape how they inhabit the kingdom of God."[2] The call to *be with Jesus* indicates the relational orientation of Christian discipleship. While, of course, Jesus wants his disciples to grow in true knowledge of his identity as well as cross-shaped character, discipleship involves the posture of humility, question asking, and continual listening and learning.

SIDEBAR 15.1

Excerpt from Wendell Berry, "A Gracious Sabbath Stood Here While They Stood"

For we are fallen like the trees, our peace
Broken, and so we must
Love where we cannot trust,
Trust where we cannot know,
And must await the wayward-coming grace
That joins living and dead,
Taking us where we would not go—
Into the boundless dark.
When what was made has been unmade
The Maker comes to His work.[a]

Notice, for example, that after Jesus shares the parable of the soils with the large crowd, a smaller group of listeners, including the Twelve, gather "around him" to ask Jesus about the meaning of the parable (4:10). Jesus makes an amazing declaration to this group when he says, "The mystery of the kingdom of God has been given to you" (4:11). But the disciples have just indicated that they do not fully understand Jesus's teaching! Jesus is declaring that the knowledge of God's kingdom is given to those who stay with Jesus to ask him questions and to learn from him as disciples. And so Jesus proceeds to explain the parable's meaning to those who stay with him and learn. Jesus's parable, in fact, explains the very situation the disciples are experiencing. Many will hear Jesus's teaching. Some will even respond in ways that look, at least initially, to be very positive and fruitful. But "the cares of the age, the deception of riches, and the desire for many other things" will often result in would-be disciples abandoning Jesus (4:19). In fact, the disciples are portrayed positively as they repeatedly ask Jesus questions when they don't fully understand his teachings or their circumstances (7:17; 9:11, 28; 10:10, 26). Asking questions of Jesus assumes a posture of submission to him and willingness to *stay with him* as the authoritative teacher of the will of God. Asking Jesus questions demonstrates both humility and a recognition that Jesus is exactly the one to whom they should take their questions. When we see the disciples failing to understand Jesus's teaching about his impending sufferings and crucifixion but being too afraid to ask him about their meaning, we can see that this represents a sad failure of discipleship on their part (9:32). It shouldn't surprise us that in the next scene, after the disciples refuse to ask Jesus about the meaning of his teaching, we find the disciples arguing about which one of them is the greatest (9:33–37). In other words, they demonstrate that, in this moment, they have not fully learned the lesson of humility and submission to Jesus as their teacher.

Mark's Gospel does not present Jesus as a person who is easy to understand or to follow. We've already seen how the Gospel demonstrates an

Museo del Prado / Wikimedia Commons

Figure 15.1. Diego Velázquez, *Christ Crucified*, ca. 1632

apocalyptic contrast, and even battle, between the kingdom of God and the kingdom of Satan (again, 1:9–13). Understanding the things of God requires divine revelation, and it requires that we retrain our minds—something that comes only through discipleship with Jesus. There is, then, a seemingly constant conflict between Jesus and the disciples especially as it pertains to power, glory, and greatness. Embracing the message of a crucified messianic king as the one who inaugurates the very reign of God is given to those who humbly submit their minds and wills to Jesus's teaching. The frequent failures and obtuseness of the disciples actually highlights how strange and how difficult this Messiah truly is—something we've seen in our examination of Mark's characterization of Jesus.[3]

Disciples of Jesus continue to receive the call to *be with Jesus* as they face the challenges of living out his kingdom agenda in a world that is not yet redeemed. While I certainly do not think that we should valorize doubts or make a virtue out of lacking settled convictions, Mark's Gospel is good news for those who have doubts, who struggle to find God's presence in a world marked by pain and suffering, and who find humble submission to Jesus's kingdom ways to be a constant challenge. We, too, can join the cry of the man in Mark 9:24—"I believe! Help my unbelief!" Some Christians are blessed with absolute certainty in their convictions, and rarely do doubts or difficult questions unsettle them. But there are some followers of Jesus who do wrestle with doubts, some who deeply feel the pain and suffering of the world and, not unlike Jesus on the cross, feel as though God is absent and wonder where he is (15:34). Mark's Gospel is good news for those who feel God's absence, who experience the challenge of aligning their life plans with Jesus's call to take up one's cross (8:34), and who love Jesus and yet have times of doubt and confusion. Mark's Gospel is good news because it repeatedly encourages these readers, "Even if you don't fully understand, even if it feels like God is absent, even if you are frustrated by your own inability to 'take up your cross,' stay with Jesus. Ask him questions and pray for understanding."

Disciples of Jesus Are Called to a Lifestyle of Service

Jesus's call to his disciples to "deny themselves and to take up their cross and follow me" (8:34b) is an exhortation to embrace Jesus's way of life, whereby power is used in service for the good of others and one's desires are often sacrificed or used in order to serve others. Given that discipleship flows from Christology, built into the very fabric of our lifestyle are the traits of humility, service, and sacrifice. Just as Jesus's sonship is marked by obedience and submission to God the Father (14:36), so Jesus's disciples are called to the same pattern of cruciform obedience and service.

But all too often our own lives show us that the normal human inclination is to gain power so that it can be used to exalt oneself or to maximize one's ability to implement one's personal preferences. Mark has shown us two different styles of leadership and power as he puts the story of Herod's kingship and kingdom right next to the story of Jesus's use of power (compare 6:14–29 and 6:31–44). Herod's power, as we have seen, is self-serving and even uses violence in order to get his way, whereas Jesus uses his messianic power to feed and nourish those in need. All throughout we see both that Jesus is indeed a person endowed with mighty power and that this power is consistently used to serve others and to lead them to health, flourishing, and salvation. Jesus himself models his own teaching that the one who wants to be "first" must become a "slave" (10:44) and the one who wants to be greatest must become a "servant" (9:34–35). We might think of the Gospel of Mark's portrait of Jesus as a narrative representation of Paul's paradoxical claim that the message of the cross is "the power and wisdom of God" (1 Cor. 1:24).[4] Tim Gombis describes Jesus's leadership as "an unrelenting commitment to the delivery of the love and grace of God into the lives of others and the taking of initiative to see to it that this happens."[5] Jesus's power heals the sick, releases persons from the power of the demonic, interprets God's gracious wisdom for how to live well, and ultimately rescues people from the grip of sin. The message is one of power and leadership for the sake of service, *even if* that service results in humiliation and suffering.

Familiar as we are with Jesus's character, when we read about Jesus's journey to Jerusalem, we are tempted to deride or maybe even mock the obtuseness of James and John, who approach Jesus, asking him for positions of power and honor when he enters into his kingdom (10:32–41). But Jesus clearly shows them—and us—that his way of life embodies a very different kind of leadership: "You know that those who seem to rule over the nations exert their lordship over them, and their great officials exercise authority over them. But not so with you. Instead, whoever wants to become great among you must be your servant, and whoever wants to be first must be slave of all. For the Son of Man did not come to be served, but to serve, and to give his life as a ransom for many" (10:42–45).

The pattern of the Messiah is the same pattern for the character and discipleship of all Jesus's followers. Jesus's leadership and exercise of power mark a major contrast with the normal activities of leaders who so often lead through force. Jesus does not use violence or force to implement his agenda. Jesus does not do the things, in fact, that would necessarily result in a "larger platform." In fact, there's some humor in watching Jesus do exactly the opposite of what most leaders would do! At the height of his popularity, Jesus often will leave the crowds and find a quiet and hidden place to pray. When Jesus performs a great act of power, he often either commands people to tell no one about what he has done or redirects attention away from himself and toward God.

Jesus's life and so-called leadership style should cause us to reflect on the kind of power we aspire to as well as the kind of leaders we admire. Honest reflection on our lives, and even the lives of many Christian ministers, should reveal to us how frequently we wrongly desire greater fame or status and how we often want more power in order to increase our influence or

SIDEBAR 15.2

Resisting Celebrity Culture in the Church

Christian leaders should be the very best examples of those who model Christ's humble way of life centered on serving others. And yet the human temptation to use "spiritual matters" in order to elevate one's platform and increase one's status exerts its pull on many of us—even pastors and seminary professors. Scot McKnight and Laura Barringer have written an immensely helpful book that takes seriously how too many churches in our day allow, enable, and hide the abuses of power often perpetuated by Christian leaders against the most vulnerable. This, of course, should not be so! So why does it happen? At least one reason is that some churches with powerful and gifted pastors and leaders have fallen prey to "the celebrity syndrome" and have created a "celebrity culture."[b] A leader may want fame or recognition because of their gift, and all too often the church is complicit in giving excessive adoration, and this can work to create a narcissistic celebrity culture oriented toward popularity, excitement, and competition. Not unlike in the ancient world where a client benefited from the heightened popularity of his patron or benefactor, so churches can think that the increased fame of their pastor will benefit the congregation such that they become a "celebrity church." I quote McKnight and Barringer here at length:

> When a pastor and a church become celebrities, when visibility, fame, reputation, and branding get the upper hand, the church will no longer be people-first (if it ever was), empathy no longer shapes the culture, grace is subverted, truth is no longer instinctive, and doing what is right can be subverted by works that seek to enhance the church's glory. Such a culture becomes toxic and potentially abusive—especially for those who cross paths or cross wires with the narcissistic pastor at the helm. . . .[c]
>
> It goes without saying that a culture that is focused on celebrity, fame, envy, and competition is entirely antithetical to both Jesus's "leadership style" and to his teaching about true discipleship.
>
> Celebrities want glory and fame. Jesus wants followers who deny glory and fame to pursue a life of service. Pastors are not celebrities, and churches are not celebrity churches. Pastors, leaders, and churches are to be known for what their Lord and Savior is known for: sacrifice for the sake of others. Service. Servanthood.[d]

Christians worship and follow a king who did not pursue celebrity and status, whose kingship was revealed in humility, service, and sacrifice. Our churches, then, should be places where the life of Jesus is on display for the world to see, and this happens only when we turn away from our temptation for greatness and replace it with a commitment to serve and give of ourselves.

platform. Disciples of Jesus are not called to build a platform. They are, rather, called to use their time, gifts, and resources to serve others. One book describes the church's life of service in this way: "A life in service to others is not heroic. Rather, it is ordinary people helping ordinary people who happen to be in their path as they travel through life."[6] Disciples of Jesus are called to cultivate a life of humility and service that, as Paul so often says, looks to the needs and interests of others (e.g., Phil. 2:1–4). This may take the form of such ordinary acts of service as volunteering in ministries that receive few or no accolades, praying for one another, encouraging others who lead and serve, and sharing one's resources with those in need. The possibilities are, of course, endless and dependent on particular life circumstances. 15.2

Disciples of Jesus Are Called to Be God's Holy Temple

Despite it being a commonplace assertion, it is nevertheless true that our Western society is remarkably individualistic. There are strong forces at work that tempt us to think that the pursuit of our own individual desires, longings, and dreams is the greatest good. Right now, the common phrase "You do you" encapsulates the belief that what makes each person special is simply their ability to "be themselves"—that is, the personal freedom to choose how to express themselves. Our families, our ecclesial denomination, and our local communities do not provide the primary orientation for most contemporary Western Christians. While there are certainly some good things that come from an emphasis on the individual, we should reckon with the fact that the ideology of individualism often goes hand in hand with a consumer mentality, and this can have seriously negative consequences for following Jesus's teachings. In other words, we often wrongly think of discipleship as involving just "God and me," when, in reality, God has called an entire group of people to himself and tasked them with a collective mission. Likewise, when relationships are difficult or fellow disciples of Christ seem odd or too different for our tastes, we can easily treat them as if they are expendable. And when we run into conflict or frustration with our local churches, it is all too easy to leave and try to find another one that better suits our tastes and preferences. When the Disney-movie narrative of "pursuing your own dreams" and "following your heart" and "being true to yourself" is one's highest good, the foundation for friendship and deep forms of belonging are weak and vulnerable.[7] In this way, friendships, civic engagement, and community commitment are often largely instrumental and subservient to one's personal self-fulfillment.[8] It is, therefore, not surprising that numerous studies argue that humans in North America suffer today more than ever due to isolation, loneliness, lack of friendship, narcissism, and meaninglessness. Humans are inherently social creatures in need of meaningful social connection.

But the Gospel of Mark shows us that disciples of Jesus are not simply a bunch of isolated individuals who are responsible for creating their own identity; rather, they are called as one sacred community and with a common mission. And, in fact, while Matthew is the only one of the four Gospels that uses the Greek word *ekklēsia*, which we translate as "church" (Matt. 16:18; 18:17), Mark's Gospel envisions the gathered assembly of Jesus followers as a holy temple. The rest of the New Testament frequently speaks of the church as God's holy temple. For example, Paul tells the church, "So then, you are no longer strangers and aliens, but you are fellow citizens with the saints and also members of the household of God, built upon the foundation of the apostles and prophets, with Christ Jesus himself as the cornerstone; in him the whole structure is joined together and grows into a holy temple in the Lord, in whom you are also built together spiritually into a dwelling place for God" (Eph. 2:19–22 NRSVue).[9] Likewise, Peter says, "Come to him, a living stone, though rejected by mortals yet chosen and precious in God's sight, and like living stones let yourselves be built into a spiritual house, to be a holy priesthood, to offer spiritual sacrifices acceptable to God through Jesus Christ" (1 Pet. 2:4–5 NRSVue).

The Letter to the Hebrews declares that Jesus Christ is our great high priest, who entered into the heavenly tabernacle and offered his own life and blood as a saving sacrifice and now intercedes for his people (e.g., Heb. 7–10). As a result, the author exhorts the church, "Through him, then, let us continually offer a sacrifice of praise to God, that is, the fruit of lips that confess his name. Do not neglect to do good and to share what you have, for such sacrifices are pleasing to God" (Heb. 13:15–16 NRSVue).

In these texts we see that the temple is not a structure made out of physical materials but is, rather, composed of living persons—"living stones," as Peter says. The temple is a community of people related to the resurrected and enthroned-in-heaven Jesus Christ—the chief cornerstone of the temple. And the task of these persons who now make up this temple is to offer sacrifices, to devote themselves to praising God, doing good to one another, and living a holy lifestyle.

Paul, Peter, and the author of Hebrews did not make up this idea but rather are developing the teachings of Jesus that we have seen in the Gospel of Mark. As the crucified and resurrected Messiah, Jesus is both the saving sacrifice and the foundational cornerstone of God's new temple. The crucified Jesus is the sacrificial atonement that provides the ransom for humanity's sin (Mark 10:45). Jesus offers his broken body, symbolized through the consumption of the bread, as the new sacrificial meal (14:22). And his shed blood "poured out for many" atones for the sins of his people (14:24). The Letter to the Hebrews is a faithful interpretation of Mark, then, in that it emphasizes the finality and effectiveness of Jesus's sacrifice: "It is by God's will that we have been sanctified through the offering of the body of Jesus Christ once for all" (10:10 NRSVue). And again, "For by a single offering he has perfected for all time those who are sanctified" (10:14 NRSVue). God's gift of salvation through the atoning death of Jesus provides the singular and necessary sacrifice for *all of Jesus's disciples*. We are bound to one another precisely because this sacrifice is the ground of our identity and salvation. In other words, as disciples of Jesus, we are not expected to "invent" or "create" our personal identity; rather, Jesus gives us (plural) one shared identity as the people of God, and this is based on the saving sacrifice of Jesus on the cross.

This means that the community of disciples gathered together forms the very place where God's presence dwells! Sadly, God's judgment has come on the Jerusalem temple and the leaders of Israel, given their rejection and crucifixion of the Son of God (Mark 11:12–16; 15:36–39). But the resurrected Jesus is the cornerstone of God's eschatological temple, and so disciples of Jesus have the privilege of access to God's very presence. But this privilege comes with a responsibility and mission for disciples of Jesus! God's new temple, as we have seen, is now to be the place where prayer, forgiveness, and justice are present (11:17–25). Internally, this new community is to embody the traits and characteristics that marked Jesus's life. One commentator puts it this way: "Mark emphasizes Jesus as the temple in order to stress the absolute necessity of the church being a community of ongoing justice for the needy, hospitality for the marginalized, and service to the vulnerable."[10] Unlike those in Jesus's day, God's people must not claim the privilege of being God's holy temple apart from a commitment to practice prayer, reconciliation, justice, and a commitment to share God's good news with all people. God's people do not "own" God's presence by right or privilege and must take care to honor God's holy presence with a lifestyle committed to truth, justice, and holiness.

But externally, the new temple is now a place for all people. Whereas Jesus criticized the old temple (due to the temple leaders) for its failure to function as a "house of prayer for all the nations" (Mark 11:17, quoting Isa. 56:7), now disciples of Jesus take on the task of the temple by engaging in active mission to the world. Jesus does not envision all the nations of the earth streaming to Jerusalem in order to find God (see Isa. 56; 66; Zech. 6); rather, the disciples of Jesus are the ones who will take God's gospel and proclaim it "to all the nations" (Mark 13:10). Some have even said that Mark 13:9–13 is a compact summary of the message of the Acts of the Apostles, meaning that Jesus commissions his disciples as the ambassadors of God to proclaim the name of Jesus even in the midst of great adversity so that *all the nations* will hear the gospel of God.

Summary of Main Points on the Gospel of Mark

1. Mark's Gospel was the least popular of the canonical Gospels at least up until the early nineteenth century, when source critics began to convince others that Mark was the first written Gospel. Nevertheless, Mark's Gospel was known, studied, and named as an authentic Gospel in the early church. And its value is obvious in that it was used as the primary source for both Matthew and Luke.
2. Mark's Gospel is technically anonymous, as the superscription "The Gospel according to Mark" was added at a later date. Many have recently suggested that the Gospel stems from a Pauline influence and have noted particular convergences between Mark and Paul as it pertains to their view of the gospel, the death of Jesus, the law, and other matters. Others have remained agnostic as to the possibility of locating the actual (or historical) author. But the majority view has been the traditional one that identifies Mark as receiving his information from the apostle Peter. While I remain skeptical that one can discern a "Petrine bias" simply by reading the Gospel, the church's testimony that Peter stands behind the Gospel is not without some merit. If John Mark is the author of the Gospel, then his missionary work among multiple early Christian communities would have enabled him to receive multiple stories, traditions, and sayings about Jesus of Nazareth.
3. Various locations have been offered for the provenance of Mark's Gospel. Galilee could account for some of the rural flavor of Jesus's teachings as well as his promise to meet the disciples in Galilee after his resurrection (14:28; 16:7). Syria could also account for some of the rural flavor and emphasis on positive portraits of gentiles. But Rome is still the most likely because it makes good sense of the Latinisms, the positive portrait of gentiles, and the connection between Mark and Peter.
4. It is difficult to offer a definitive date for the writing. Almost every scholar argues for a date between 40 and 80 CE, and most find the

events prophesied in Mark 13—persecution, fleeing to the hills of Judea, the rise of false prophets—to suggest a date sometime immediately prior to the Jewish revolt against Rome (ca. 66–73 CE).

5. With respect to the audience, I think Mark's Gospel was likely intended to reach as wide an audience as possible. This is not to say that the text doesn't contain local details that reflect its location, but the openness to the gentiles, the explanation of Jewish customs, and the Latinisms, along with the emphasis that the gospel of Jesus Christ is *for all people*, suggest that Mark hoped that his Gospel would receive the widest possible circulation among the earliest followers of Jesus.
6. Mark's Gospel uses a variety of literary devices that may stem from oral storytelling. The author makes the story even more memorable through narrative devices such as frequent use of questions, two-step progression, *inclusio*, and sandwiching. Attending to these literary devices not only makes the story more engaging but also often provokes the reader to wrestle with Jesus's identity.
7. There are many key words and phrases in Mark's Gospel, but some of the most crucial are "the way," "fear *and* faith," and "Son of God."
8. Some of the main narrative threads of Mark's narrative center on
    a. Jesus's proclamation and enactment of the kingdom of God and the ensuing apocalyptic battle with the dominion of Satan and the demons;
    b. the strange and mysterious characterization of Jesus as the Son of God who is authoritative and powerful along with his depiction as one who embraces weakness, suffers, and is crucified;
    c. how the Jerusalem temple and leadership enter into God's judgment as Jesus is not embraced as the Messiah, and how Jesus's body and blood become an atoning sacrifice for believers;
    d. Mark's "theology of the cross," whereby God's wisdom and power are foolishness to the world but salvation to those who have the eyes of faith.
9. Disciples of Jesus in Mark are called to be "with Jesus," are called to a lifestyle of service, and are God's holy temple.

Luke and History

Luke's Place in the History of Early Christianity

While impossible to verify empirically, it may well be that, at least in North America, the Gospel of Luke is the most beloved of our four canonical Gospels. Luke's stories of Jesus's birth, his famous parables such as those of the good Samaritan and the prodigal son, Zacchaeus's encounter with Jesus, the repentant thief on the cross, and the account of the resurrected Jesus's mysterious appearance to the disciples on the Emmaus Road—these stories and more are near and dear to the heart of most Christians today. Given that within the earliest period of Christianity the clear preference was for the Gospels of Matthew and John, we find that Luke was the subject of sustained exposition (in term of homilies and commentaries) only in the writings of Origen, Ambrose, Cyril of Alexandria, and the Venerable Bede.[1] In earlier chapters we saw comments from Papias of Hierapolis on the origins of Matthew and Mark, but we have no such comments from Papias on Luke.

Luke's Gospel composition is technically anonymous, despite the external evidence of early church tradition identifying its author as "the beloved physician" known as Luke (Col. 4:14; Philem. 24; 2 Tim. 4:10–11). Church tradition identifies the author with Paul's traveling companion and the author of the Acts of the Apostles (note in particular the sections of Acts known as the "we" passages: 16:10–17; 20:5–15; 21:1–18; 27:1–28:16; in these passages the author appears to include himself as a traveling companion of the apostle Paul). So, in his defense of the Fourfold Gospel, Irenaeus of Lyons, at around 180 CE, is the first, so far as we know, to explicitly refer to the Gospel of Luke by name: "Luke also, the companion of Paul, recorded in a book the Gospel preached by him" (*Against Heresies* 3.1.1). Irenaeus also reports that the famous arch-heretic Marcion used and "mutilated" the Gospel of Luke to support his own false teaching: "[Marcion] mutilates the Gospel which is according to Luke, removing all that is written respecting the generation of the Lord, and setting aside a great deal of the teaching of the Lord, in which the Lord is recorded as most dearly confessing that the Maker of the universe is his Father" (*Against Heresies* 1.27.2). Marcion's "Gospel" likely bore a strong resemblance to the canonical Gospel of Luke in terms of material and structure, but it almost certainly lacked stories emphasizing the Jewishness of Jesus and the positive appropriation of Old Testament texts.[2] The canon list known as the Muratorian Fragment, also likely a late-second-century composition, states this about the Gospel of Luke:

> The third book of the Gospel is that according to Luke. Luke, the well-known physician, after the ascension of Christ, when Paul had taken him with him as one zealous for the law, composed it in his own name, according to [the general] belief. Yet he himself had not seen the Lord in the flesh; and therefore, as he was able to ascertain events, so indeed he begins to tell the story from the birth of John.[3]

As is the case with all four canonical Gospels, there are no known versions of Luke's Gospel that circulated without a superscription such as "according to Luke."[4] The earliest Greek manuscript of the third canonical Gospel (𝔓[75]) is titled "The Gospel According to Luke" and stems from around 200 CE. Thus, at some point toward the end of the second century CE, it appears that the association between "Luke" and the third canonical Gospel is largely taken for granted.

Many have rightly recognized that our author's vocabulary and knowledge of the ancient world are the richest of the four Gospel writers. As a result, some have noted his description of Jesus's healings and claimed that Luke's detailed medical knowledge suggests that he was a physician. Others have recognized his deep familiarity with the Jewish Scriptures and exegetical practices and so have claimed that Luke was likely a Jew or, at least, a God-fearer—that is, a gentile who honored certain Jewish practices and traditions without fully converting to Judaism. And still others have been impressed with Luke's awareness of ancient philosophy and Greco-Roman poetry and so have claimed that the author was an educated gentile. But moving from the author's knowledge and writing competence to his ethnic identity or profession goes beyond our evidence. Mark Allan Powell's summary is helpful: "In sum, the author of Luke's Gospel was a well-educated second-generation Christian, either a Hellenistic Jew or a gentile with deep knowledge of Jewish Scripture. . . . Beyond this is only speculation."[5]

The Composition of Luke's Gospel

Luke's Gospel begins with a lengthy and semitechnical preface that gives the readers some very important clues for how the author conceptualizes his task of writing the Gospel.

> Since many have undertaken to compile a narrative about the events that have been fulfilled among us, just as they were handed on to us by those who from the beginning were eyewitnesses and servants of the word, I, too, decided, as one having a grasp of everything from the start, to write a well-ordered account for you, most excellent Theophilus, so that you may have a firm grasp of the words in which you have been instructed. (Luke 1:1–4 NRSVue)

Luke's claim that he has investigated his sources carefully so that he can write an orderly and accurate account of recent events indicates that he is writing a work of (biographical) history.[6] Luke does have some interest in situating the story he tells within larger historical events. So, immediately after his preface he situates the birth of John the Baptist within the historical context of Herod the Great's reign over Judea (1:5). Similarly, he relates that Jesus's birth took place during the time of Caesar Augustus's census, when Quirinius was governor of Syria (2:1–2).

We need to note right away that the author acknowledges the existence of "many" others who have written Gospels but that, at minimum, these other Gospels are incomplete and can be improved on. Whether this is with respect to the style, order, exclusion, or lack of access to important traditions about Jesus of the "many" predecessors, Luke's Gospel makes the bold claim that it will improve on the Gospel writings that preceded it. As we have seen in earlier chapters, the church made the bold claim that all four of our now-canonical Gospels were sacred Scripture and rendered a truthful account of Jesus of Nazareth, but each of these Gospels has its own unique way of telling the story of Jesus. While it is impossible to know with certainty what exactly makes up the "many," Luke's use of Mark's Gospel and *perhaps* Matthew's Gospel (and/or the hypothetical sayings source often referred to as "Q") as sources for his own Gospel both indicates his respect for these texts as he uses them to "hand on" the traditions about Jesus and shows how he conceives of his own work as an attempt to improve on them—the improvement consisting largely in the inclusion of additional sources and the rhetorical arrangement and narrative sequencing.[7] More specifically, though, what does Luke's preface tell us about the types of improvements he hopes to make in his Gospel?

First, Luke conceptualizes his task as providing both the proper beginning and the proper ending. Luke claims to have investigated all of these events starting from "the very beginning" (1:3), and this accounts for his inclusion of the stories surrounding Jesus's and John's births and childhood stories about Jesus (chaps. 1–2). This makes Luke different from Mark (and Q), which passes over the beginnings of Jesus's birth and earliest years. Similarly, Luke improves on Mark by including something that Mark alludes to but leaves out: Jesus's resurrection appearances to his disciples. In Mark's Gospel, Jesus predicts that the disciples will abandon him during his arrest and crucifixion but that later the resurrected Jesus will visit them in Galilee (Mark 14:27–28; 16:7). But, somewhat oddly, Mark shares only a short story about the empty tomb and never narrates the risen Jesus's appearance to the disciples (16:1–8). Luke "improves" on Mark here by including the stories of Jesus's resurrection appearances, commission to the disciples, and ascension to heaven (Luke 24:1–53).

Second, Luke argues that the sources for his Gospel stem from those who were "eyewitnesses and servants of the word" (1:2). Luke is making a claim here to the historiographical practice of *autopsia*—that is, basing his own writing on those who were personally present and involved in the events he recounts.[8] Luke's claim that they were eyewitnesses "from the beginning" (Luke 1:2) and then later, in the book of Acts, the note that the apostolic replacement for Judas must be someone who accompanied Jesus "beginning from the baptism of John" until Jesus's resurrection (Acts 1:21–22) suggest that Luke wants us to understand that his Gospel writing stems from carefully preserved eyewitness testimony that he himself has "investigated carefully" (Luke 1:3). In fact, the English word translated as "investigated" might even be better translated as "having a thoroughly informed acquaintance" that comes from personal involvement in the events recounted.[9] As Richard Bauckham states, "Luke can tell the story 'from the beginning' because he is familiar with the traditions of those who were eyewitnesses 'from the beginning.'"[10] Who, then, exactly were Luke's sources? As a good historian, Luke reworks his sources in such a way that it is difficult (if perhaps even impossible) to always identify his sources (at least outside of Mark's Gospel and potentially Q). It is likely that much of Luke's material originated from the disciples who followed Jesus, foremost of whom were the Twelve, but also likely the group of women who followed Jesus (see 8:1–3).

Luke's claim to have investigated the matters more carefully likely also accounts for his inclusion of additional teachings of Jesus and stories about Jesus that do not appear in the work of his predecessors. This would include, for example, Jesus's reading of Isaiah in the Nazareth synagogue

Figure 16.1. The restored interior of the fourth- to fifth-century-CE synagogue in Capernaum. The remains of what many believe to be the first-century-CE synagogue lie beneath.

(4:16–30), the disciples' miraculous catching of fish (5:1–11), Jesus's cleansing of those with skin disease (17:11–19), and numerous parables (e.g., 10:25–37; 15:1–32; 16:19–31; 18:15–17). Scholars often refer to this uniquely Lukan material as "L" tradition and as possibly stemming from a source (whether oral or written) that Mark and Matthew did not have access to. In fact, most estimates put the uniquely Lukan material as accounting for approximately half of this Gospel.

Third, one of the areas where Luke expects his Gospel writing to improve on his predecessors' is with respect to the narrative's ordering, arrangement, and sequence. Here there are many ways where Luke improves—or at least changes—the narrative sequence. We can look at only a few of the most important.

1. Luke differs from Matthew's use of Mark's Gospel as a source in his omission of two sections of Mark: 6:45–8:26 and 9:41–10:12. Sometimes these are referred to as Luke's "great omission" and "little omission."[11] It's impossible to know exactly why Luke would omit these sections. What can we say? Luke does not include the so-called Markan doublets. For example, whereas Mark includes two stories of Jesus's miraculous feeding of the multitudes (Mark 6:32–44; 8:1–9), Luke includes only one (Luke 9:11–17). Whereas Mark passes on

two very similar stories of Jesus healing a blind man (Mark 8:22–26; 10:46–52), Luke includes only one (Luke 18:35–43). Luke may also pass over the Markan Jesus's time in gentile territory (many of the scenes in the "great omission"), believing that the mission to the gentiles is contingent on Israel's restoration and, therefore, an undertaking for the early church (see Acts 10:1–11:18).

2. Luke also includes a lengthy section that contains material not found in Mark (Luke 6:20–8:3), and this includes Jesus's Sermon on the Plain (6:20–49), Jesus's encounter with the disciples of John the Baptist (7:18–34), and narrative depictions of Jesus's merciful acts of healing and forgiveness to those in need (7:1–17, 36–50). Some of Jesus's teaching here overlaps with the Matthean Sermon on the Mount (Matt. 5–7), but there are notable differences, such as the Lukan Jesus's pronouncement of woes on the rich and comfortable (Luke 6:24–26).
3. Luke takes Mark's story of Jesus's preaching and rejection in his hometown of Nazareth (Mark 6:1–6) and moves it to the very beginning of Jesus's public ministry (Luke 4:16–30). Luke also expands the story to include the content of what Jesus teaches (i.e., Jesus interprets his mission in terms of Isa. 58 and 61) and offers precedents from Israel's Scriptures that explain Nazareth's rejection of his prophetic ministry (4:24–30).
4. Luke also expands the Markan Jesus's trip to Jerusalem (Mark 10:32–11:18) into a lengthy journey narrative to Jerusalem comprising approximately ten chapters of his Gospel (Luke 9:51–19:44). Luke's journey narrative provides him with the opportunity to emphasize Jesus's teaching, to focus on the importance of Jesus's resolve to make his way to Jerusalem (e.g., 9:51–56; 13:22; 17:11), to depict Jesus as a traveler who is dependent on the hospitality of others (13:22, 31–33; 14:25; 18:31, 35–36; 19:11, 28), and to color Jesus's ministry with shades of Israel's journey during the exodus. I will spend more time unpacking these themes in the next chapter.

Fourth, Luke likely views his Gospel as improving the style of his predecessors. For example, Luke does not find it necessary to include Mark's Aramaic expressions such as Jesus's reference to God as "Abba" (Mark 14:36) or Jesus's cry from the cross, "Eloi, Eloi, lema sabachthani?" (Mark 15:34). Luke reserves the language of "sea" for the Mediterranean Sea and so changes Mark's references to the "sea" of Galilee to the more appropriate "lake" (e.g., compare Mark 4:39–41 with Luke 8:22). Luke changes

Mark's reference to "King Herod" (Mark 6:14, 22) to the more accurate "Herod the tetrarch" (Luke 9:7). Luke also deletes many of the unnecessary and repetitious uses of "and" and "immediately" from Mark. Luke abbreviates and deletes aspects of Mark that are superfluous for his story, including the episode of the naked youth who flees in the garden (compare Mark 14:43–52 with Luke 22:47–53) and the editorial note denigrating the competence of physicians to help the woman with the flow of blood (compare Mark 5:25–26 with Luke 8:43).

Fifth, Luke sometimes softens or even deletes some of the harsher or offensive portrayals of Jesus. Like Mark, Luke tells the story of Jesus's family coming to find him while he is teaching, but Luke deletes the Markan note that his family was trying "to seize him" because some were saying, "He is out of his mind" (compare Mark 3:19b–21 with Luke 8:19–21). Some of the potentially negative emotions of the Markan Jesus are deleted or minimized by Luke, such as Jesus's anger (Mark 3:5; 10:14), deep distress (3:5), and amazement (6:6). Conversely, Luke does include frequent references to characters expressing the emotion of joy (e.g., Luke 1:14; 2:10; 15:7, 10; 24:41). Luke does not pass along the strange Markan story where Jesus angrily curses a fig tree for failing to bear fruit when it is not even harvest season (Mark 11:12–14, 20–25). And Luke does not repeat the Markan note that Jesus "was unable to do any miracle there" (Mark 6:5a).

Sixth, while calling this an "improvement" will simply be a matter of one's taste, Luke does not depict Jesus as a preacher of lengthy sermons in the same way as does Matthew's Gospel, which, we remember, alternates between story and discourse in large blocks. Rather, the Lukan Jesus is portrayed as more of a storyteller and a wisdom teacher who communicates through proverbs and aphorisms.

Seventh, perhaps the biggest Lukan improvement consists in the author's commitment to write a comprehensive narrative of "the events that have been fulfilled among us" (Luke 1:1), and this involves his authorship of a second volume as a sequel to the Gospel, as indicated by the preface for the Acts of the Apostles: "In the first book, Theophilus, I wrote about all that Jesus began to do and teach until the day when he was taken to heaven, after giving instructions through the Holy Spirit to the apostles whom he had chosen" (Acts 1:1–2 NRSVue). We know nothing of certainty about Theophilus, the addressee of these two volumes, except that he has already had some "instruction" (Luke 1:4) in the Christian faith. Luke's decision to write two volumes—a Gospel and a second writing on the apostles and the growth of the church—shows how Luke sets forth key themes and expectations that are fulfilled only in the book of Acts. For example, John the Baptist prophesies about a coming one who will baptize with "the Holy

Spirit and fire" (Luke 3:16), and the literary fulfillment of this takes place only at Pentecost, when the Spirit is poured out on the church with flames of fire (Acts 2:1–4). Or, Simeon's (Luke 2:25–32) and John the Baptist's (Luke 3:1–6) promises that all people will see God's salvation are recounted as beginning to be fulfilled only upon Peter's encounter with Cornelius in Acts 10, an event that initiates the mission to all the nations. How does this contribute to Theophilus and other Christians increasing in "the certainty of the things about which you have been instructed" (Luke 1:4)? Luke wants his readers to see that the story of Jesus finds its meaning and conclusion in the story of the church, and that this demonstrates God's faithfulness to the scriptural promises he has made to his people. 16.1

SIDEBAR 16.1

Luke Timothy Johnson on God's Faithfulness to Israel

"By showing the story of Jesus to be rooted in that of Israel and by demonstrating how God's promises were realized in a restored Israel, Luke assures gentile Christians that they can trust the 'good news' that has reached them."[a]

The Date and Audience of Luke's Gospel

Dating Luke's Gospel is an already difficult task complicated even further by its relationship to its sequel, the Acts of the Apostles. If the scholarly consensus is right that Mark is the first Gospel—one of the "many" predecessors to which Luke refers (Luke 1:1)—and if Mark was written just prior to the Jewish war (ca. mid-60s CE), then Luke's Gospel obviously needs to be dated sometime later. With respect to Luke's relationship to Acts, it seems likely that the Gospel was penned before its sequel. And here we should note that the final episode depicts Paul's imprisonment in Rome sometime around 62 CE (Acts 28:30–31). It seems unlikely that Luke would have penned this as his final (enigmatic!) episode if he had more detailed knowledge of the events surrounding Paul's death, and so perhaps this would also suggest a date for Luke and Acts sometime in the mid-60s. Some have pointed to the Lukan Jesus's prediction of the destruction of the temple and the war with Rome in Jerusalem as providing evidence that the Gospel was written after the war (see especially Luke 19:41–44; 20:20–24).

Some have compared the Lukan account of Jerusalem's destruction with the Matthean and Markan versions and have suggested that Luke's specificity indicates that he writes with detailed knowledge of the actual historical events. But this argument is not a strong one. Luke does refer to Jerusalem being surrounded by armies and being trampled on by gentiles, but these are not very specific or detailed descriptions. And much of Jesus's language is, in fact, rooted in scriptural language from Israel's prophets.[12]

In conclusion, it is difficult to be overly dogmatic about the dating of Luke's Gospel, but there are good reasons for seeing it as stemming from the mid-60s or thereabouts.

With respect to Luke's implied audience, we can at least make the following observations. First, given that the Gospel's addressee, Theophilus, is one who already has some familiarity with and instruction in the contents of the Christian faith (1:3–4), it is likely that Luke expects his broader audience to also be Christian converts or, at a minimum, those who have sympathy for and knowledge of the Christian movement. Second, Luke expects a high level of knowledge and appreciation for the Jewish people, their history, customs, and Scriptures. We have seen that Luke begins his Gospel with a preface comparable to Hellenistic historiography (1:1–4), but he immediately transitions into a way of telling his story that is remarkably biblical, involving the stories of a barren womb, Jewish priests in the temple, angels, hymns that use scriptural language, a circumcision on the eighth day—all of these draw the reader into the world of Israel's Scriptures (chaps. 1–2). In fact, the Gospel of Luke is not a story different from that told in the Old Testament but is, rather, the continuation and climax of God's promises to Israel. But, third, Luke also writes his story in such a way that indicates that his audience is familiar with the urban environment of the Roman Empire. For example, many of Luke's stories draw on cultural scripts, customs, and values that stem from a Greco-Roman environment. This includes stories of Jesus participating in symposium-like meals and table talk (e.g., 5:27–32; 14:1–24; 22:24–27), details about the Herodian court (13:31–35; 23:1–12), and Jesus's resurrection appearance taking the form of a deity's divine visitation (24:13–35). Most would also agree that Luke's "cultivated language indicates that the author's roots are in one of the higher strata of society, and that the author had a good education encompassing Greek rhetoric as well as Jewish methods of exegesis."[13]

CHAPTER SEVENTEEN

Luke and Narrative (1)

Key Structural Features and Plot

The organization and structure of the Gospel of Luke are probably the least complicated of the Synoptic Gospels and reflect the author's desire to craft an "orderly account" for his audience (Luke 1:3). 17.1

Journeying to Jerusalem

Luke's literary artistry is of such high quality that it takes no great skill for the reader to discern Luke's transitions from one scene of the story to the next. Luke uses geography and journeying as basic structural devices. Luke consistently emphasizes Jesus's relationship and movement toward the city of Jerusalem. The story begins, for example, with Zechariah the priest performing his priestly duties in the Jerusalem temple (1:5–20). Anna the prophetess sees Jesus and prophesies about the child to "all those who were waiting for the restoration of Jerusalem" (2:38). Luke alone includes two stories of Jesus visiting Jerusalem: one as an infant (2:22–40) and one as a twelve-year-old (2:41–52).

The setting for Jesus's early ministry is Galilee (4:14–9:50), but even here, at Jesus's transfiguration, Jesus is depicted as conversing with Moses and Elijah about "his exodus, which he was about to fulfill in Jerusalem" (9:31). The commencement of Jesus's lengthy journey to Jerusalem is marked by the Lukan declaration, "And it came about that when the days drew near for him to be taken up, he set his face to journey to Jerusalem" (9:51). The next ten chapters depict Jesus as an itinerant journeyer (9:51–19:44).

SIDEBAR 17.1

The Basic Structure of Luke's Gospel

- 1:1–4: The preface to the Gospel
- 1:5–2:52: John the Baptist's and Jesus's births and childhoods
- 3:1–4:13: John's preaching of repentance and Jesus's Spirit-baptism and testing in the wilderness
- 4:14–9:50: Jesus's ministry in Galilee
- 9:51–19:44: Jesus's journey to Jerusalem
- 19:45–24:53: Jesus in Jerusalem: teaching, crucifixion, resurrection, and ascension

But Luke shows no interest in offering a geographical itinerary of where Jesus journeyed; rather, his unrelenting focus is on Jesus's destination: Jerusalem (see 9:53; 13:22; 17:11; 18:31; 19:11, 28). When Jesus arrives in Jerusalem and makes his way to the temple, only a group of his disciples acclaim him as the messianic king (19:37–39). The Pharisees seek to silence the disciples, and there are no Jerusalem priests present (19:39–40). Jesus interprets this as a sign of his impending rejection as he weeps over the impending fate of the city (19:41–44). While Jesus is rejected and crucified in Jerusalem, Luke further emphasizes the importance of the city by narrating all of Jesus's resurrection appearances in (and around the vicinity of) Jerusalem (24:1–43). Included in Jesus's parting exhortations is the command to his disciples to stay in Jerusalem until they receive the gift of the Holy Spirit (24:47–49; also Acts 1:4), and indeed, after Jesus's ascension his disciples return to the Jerusalem temple with great joy (24:52–53).

Later in this chapter we will see that Luke's emphasis on Jerusalem is of one piece with his concern to show how Jesus brings salvation and glory to the people of Israel even as he is initially rejected by his people. Luke's second volume, the Acts of the Apostles, makes this clear. God has been faithful to his people Israel despite appearances to the contrary. Jesus of Nazareth is the agent of salvation and peace for his fellow Jews. And it is precisely through Jerusalem's rejection and crucifixion of Jesus that God will, surprisingly, bring messianic blessings to Israel by raising Jesus from the dead, exalting him to God's very right hand, and pouring forth the Holy Spirit upon those who turn to God. 17.2

Parallelism

A second literary feature that Luke uses to great effect is the drawing of parallels or repetitive patterns between characters in his story. One can see this right away in Luke's infancy narrative, where the births of John

SIDEBAR 17.2

Peter Proclaims God's Saving Faithfulness through the Crucified Messiah

Acts 2:22–24

Fellow Israelites, listen to this: Jesus of Nazareth was a man accredited by God to you by miracles, wonders and signs, which God did among you through him, as you yourselves know. This man was handed over to you by God's deliberate plan and foreknowledge; and you, with the help of wicked men, put him to death by nailing him to the cross. But God raised him from the dead, freeing him from the agony of death, because it was impossible for death to keep its hold on him. (NIV)

Acts 3:17–21

Now, fellow Israelites, I know that you acted in ignorance, as did your leaders. But this is how God fulfilled what he had foretold through all the prophets, saying that his Messiah would suffer. Repent, then, and turn to God, so that your sins may be wiped out, that times of refreshing may come from the Lord, and that he may send the Messiah, who has been appointed for you—even Jesus. Heaven must receive him until the time comes for God to restore everything, as he promised long ago through his holy prophets. (NIV)

The York Project / Wikimedia Commons

Figure 17.1. Diego Velázquez, *Christ in the House of Martha and Mary*, ca. 1618

the Baptist and Jesus are told in such a way so as to "emphasize the unity of their task. They share roles in a single design of God which is working itself out in a consistent way."[1] One can also see a parallel between Mary's hymn (1:46–55 [the Magnificat]) and Zechariah's hymn (1:67–79 [the Benedictus]). The parallels function to indicate that God is using both John and Jesus as a means to accomplish the restoration of Israel and the salvation of all persons (2:25–38). But the parallels, while drawing John and Jesus tightly together, also work to show Jesus's superiority to John. John will be called "a prophet of the Most High" and "will go before the Lord to make his paths ready" (1:76), but Jesus is the messianic Lord and the Savior who will enact God's saving purposes for his people (2:10–11). 17.3

The astute reader will also recognize that Luke loves to pair parallel stories about women and men. We have already seen one example where both Mary and Zechariah respond with prophetic hymns that interpret and foretell God's saving work in John and Jesus (1:46–55; 1:67–79). Also within the infancy narrative, Luke pairs the stories of the prophets Simeon (2:25–35) and Anna (2:36–38). See sidebar 17.4, where the list of parallels is not exhaustive but should give the reader a good sense of how Luke frequently pairs women and men together in his stories. 17.4

SIDEBAR 17.3

Parallels between the Births of John and Jesus in Luke's Gospel

- An angelic announcement of impending birth is made to the parents (1:8–23 // 1:28–38).
- The mothers respond with confession and praise to God (1:24–25 // 1:39–56).
- The children are born, named, and circumcised (1:57–66 // 2:1–24).
- The Spirit inspires prophetic words about the children (1:67–79 // 2:25–38).
- The children grow strong in the Spirit and in wisdom (1:80 // 2:40, 52).

These parallel stories highlight Luke's heightened emphasis on women when compared with the other Gospels. One of the themes that we will explore later in this chapter is Luke's emphasis on Jesus providing salvation for *all people* (e.g., 2:30–32; 3:1–6). Here we can see how Luke is concerned to show that Jesus is the Savior of both women and men. As Justo González notes, "One can safely say that among all the Evangelists it is Luke who pays the most attention to women and their place in the story he is telling."[2] Luke's parallel stories make this point with clarity. So, in the infancy narrative, it is not Zechariah or Joseph who is the hero; rather, it is Mary who is the model disciple (1:38, 45). Amy Peeler states the parallel and contrast between Zechariah and Mary memorably: "Zechariah had been given the privilege of entering the holy of holies; but now the presence in the holy of holies is poised to enter Mary herself."[3] Women are also praised for responding to Jesus with hospitality and love (4:39; 7:46–50). Luke alone lists and names Jesus's female disciples (8:1–3). Women are characterized as Spirit-filled prophets who proclaim God's mighty deeds (see Acts 2:17–18; 21:8–9).

When an unnamed woman in a crowd declares to Jesus, "Blessed is the womb that gave birth to you and the breasts that nursed you," he turns the focus from motherhood to discipleship: "Blessed, rather, are those who hear the word of God and keep it" (11:27–28). When Martha is preoccupied with domestic responsibilities and Mary is seated at the feet of Jesus listening to his teaching, Mary's desire to listen and learn as a disciple is praised by Jesus (10:38–42). At minimum, we can say that Luke goes out of his way to depict women as faithful disciples of Jesus.

Characterization: Responding to Divine Activity

Luke uses a variety of ways to characterize the persons in his story. For example, Luke's antagonists are often portrayed as greedy or handling their possessions incorrectly (e.g., 16:14–15), whereas his protagonists are generous and humble (e.g., 10:30–37; 18:9–14). But the third literary feature of Luke's Gospel I want to explore here consists in his depiction of a number

SIDEBAR 17.4

Male/Female Parallels in Luke's Gospel

Jesus rebukes the demon from the possessed man (4:33–37)	//	Jesus rebukes fever of Peter's mother-in-law (4:38–39)
Jesus forgives a man in great need (5:17–26)	//	Jesus forgives a woman in great need (7:36–50)
Luke lists Jesus's male disciples (6:12–16)	//	Luke lists Jesus's female disciples (8:1–3)
Jesus heals the nearly dead slave of a centurion (7:1–10)	//	Jesus restores life to the dead son of a widow (7:11–17)
Jesus heals a woman on the Sabbath (13:10–17)	//	Jesus heals a man on the Sabbath (14:1–6)
The parable of the man who loses a sheep (15:4–7)	//	The parable of the woman who loses a coin (15:8–10)

of characters who see and hear divine activity at work in Jesus and then appropriately respond by rejoicing in God and giving God praise and glory. There are many places where Luke makes an addition to his Markan source by adding a note that a character responds to Jesus with praise or rejoicing (e.g., compare Luke 5:25 with Mark 2:12; Luke 18:43 with Mark 10:52). The infancy narrative establishes this theme immediately as, in response to Elizabeth's blessing on Mary for believing "the things spoken to her by the Lord" (1:45), Mary responds by singing a hymn praising God for his mighty deeds (1:46–55). Even though Zechariah is initially silenced by the angel for his failure to believe and so praise God, upon receiving back his speech he "speaks to bless God" (1:64) and then gives glory to God for visiting his people (1:68–79). The shepherds "give glory and praise to God" for what they see and hear (2:20). And Simeon "blesses God" and proclaims, "My eyes have seen your salvation" when he sees the child Jesus (2:28, 30).

Figure 17.2. Rembrandt van Rijn, *Simeon's Song of Praise*, 1631

This literary feature enables the reader to assess positively all those characters who see Jesus's mighty deeds and then respond with praise and glory to God. This includes the paralytic who, when he is healed and forgiven of his sins, "gives glory to God" (5:25) as well as the crowds who exclaim, "We have seen incredible things today" (5:26). Readers should positively assess the reaction of the crowd who witnesses Jesus bring a dead child back to life and "gives glory to God, saying, 'A great prophet has been raised up for us and God has visited his people'" (7:16). When a woman with a bent back is healed, she gives glory to God (13:13), and this results in "the entire crowd rejoicing over all the glorious things Jesus was doing" (13:17b). We could add more examples, but the point should be sufficient from the preceding ones that the appropriate response to Jesus's mighty deeds is the verbal expression of worship and praise of God (see also 17:18; 18:41–43; 19:37; 23:47).

Luke's literary pattern whereby characters move from recognizing God's activity to giving praise and glory to God works to form readers who recognize God's activity in the work of the crucified, resurrected Jesus and to respond by giving praise to God for what God is doing. Luke works to lead his readers to adopt a liturgical response of rejoicing in, giving glory to, and praising God for what God has done.

Reading the Gospel of Luke and the Acts of the Apostles as One Story in Two Parts

While our focus in this book is on the Gospels, the reader should be aware that the Gospel of Luke and the Acts of the Apostles mutually illuminate each other, given that they are two parts of one story. Luke begins Acts, his second volume, by referring to his Gospel, where he "wrote about all that Jesus began to do and to teach" until his ascension (Acts 1:1). The implication is that Acts is the continuation of Jesus's activities. There are a number of features that indicate that Acts continues the story of Jesus from the Gospel of Luke. For example, the apostles in Acts are characterized according to the pattern of Jesus whereby they share the same Spirit, perform signs and wonders, proclaim the word with authority, and are rejected by the people. On occasion, Acts will narrate the fulfillment of an event predicted in the Gospel of Luke. So, for example, John the Baptist prophesies in Luke 3:16 that a coming one will baptize "with the Holy Spirit and fire" (see also 24:47–49), and Acts narrates the fulfillment of this prophecy when the Spirit is poured out on the disciples with fiery flames (Acts 2:1–4). Many more examples could be added, but these should suffice to demonstrate that readers will benefit by examining how Acts continues the story of Jesus from Luke's Gospel.

Key Words and Phrases

Let's look at four key words/phrases that also highlight significant Lukan themes: "salvation, Savior, save," "repentance," "it is necessary, it must happen," and "Lord."

Salvation, Savior, save. One of Luke's most important but basic claims is that Jesus is the agent of God's salvation. In fact, both God (i.e., the God of Israel) and Jesus are identified with the title "Savior" (see 1:47; 2:11). Zechariah's hymn declares three times that the birth of Jesus will result in salvation, identified as protection from one's enemies and as forgiveness of sins (1:69, 71, 77). And John the Baptist, whose primary task is to prepare God's people for the coming of Jesus, declares, "All people will see God's salvation" (3:6). Salvation, for Luke, involves a liberating encounter with Jesus, and so Luke highlights Jesus's proclamation of God's word, his healings and exorcisms, and his fellowship with sinners as the means whereby he enacts God's salvation (e.g., 7:48–50; 8:36, 48, 58; 17:19). While Luke's Jesus by no means denies the future aspect to salvation, he often speaks of salvation as a present reality. We can connect this insight to another key Lukan word, "today," which emphasizes how Jesus brings salvation to people *now*. Thus, the angel declares to the shepherds, "Today a savior who is Christ the Lord has been born in the city of David" (2:11). To the thief on the cross Jesus promises, "Today you will be with me in Paradise" (23:43). To Zacchaeus he declares, "Today I must stay in your house" (19:5), and then, "Today salvation has come to this house" (19:9). This salvation, further, is especially for those on the margins, since Jesus has come "to seek and to save the lost" (19:10).

Repentance. The language of repentance is used in Luke (and Acts) to speak of both turning away from one's sinful lifestyle and turning toward God. Although in our present time language of repentance often has negative and fearful connotations ("Repent, or face God's judgment!"), Luke portrays repentance as embracing God's merciful, compassionate forgiveness and as turning toward true life, as opposed to contenting oneself with false good such as the greedy acquisition of possessions or pridefully exalting oneself over others. Those who turn to God are promised forgiveness and salvation (e.g., 7:48–50; 15:8–10, 32; 19:9). Perhaps surprisingly, it is often those sinners who are on the margins who experience God's gracious presence in Jesus and who, as a result of their encounters and fellowship with Jesus, repent from their former way of life (see 5:27–32; 7:36–50; and exemplified in the parables in 15:1–10). This is stated poignantly by Jesus: "I have not come to call the righteous but rather sinners to repentance" (5:32). Those who repent demonstrate their turn to God by means of what John the Baptist refers to as producing "fruit worthy of repentance" (3:8). When Levi repents, he divests himself of his possessions to follow Jesus and hosts a banquet for Jesus and other tax collectors and sinners (5:27–32). When Zacchaeus the tax collector has a saving encounter with Jesus, he demonstrates his repentance by generously making things right with those he has defrauded (19:8).

It is necessary, it must happen. Luke uses a variety of terms, the foremost being the Greek word *dei*, to refer to the necessity of certain events taking place due to having been ordained by God. Luke wants his readers to see that God's plan is coming to fruition just as it has been divinely ordained in the events surrounding the life and ministry of Jesus, and also he wants to

SIDEBAR 17.5

"Must" in Luke's Gospel

- Jesus "must" be in his Father's house (2:49).
- Jesus "must" proclaim the good news of the kingdom of God (4:43).
- Jesus "must" suffer and be rejected by the scribes, priests, and elders and then be raised from the dead on the third day (9:22; 17:25; 24:7, 26).
- Jesus "must" heal and liberate the oppressed (13:14–16).
- Jesus "must" share hospitality with Zacchaeus (19:5).
- The Scriptures about Jesus "must" be fulfilled (22:37; 24:44).

invite his readers to embrace God's redemptive purposes. Luke repeatedly uses the language of necessity, "must," to refer to how everything that Jesus does in his ministry—even the most surprising events—takes place according to God's plan. 17.5

Luke puts this theme to great use also in the Acts of the Apostles, where he shows that God's plan was accomplished in a surprising way through humanity's rejection of Jesus and God's resurrection of him from the dead (e.g., Acts 3:18; 4:27–28). Luke's Gospel and Acts demonstrate that God is faithful to his scriptural promises and that he is sovereign over world history (see Acts 17:26–31). And, despite how things may appear—Jesus's rejection by his own people, Jesus's death on a Roman cross, Judas's apostasy and betrayal—God is accomplishing his purposes exactly as he has planned.

Lord. Luke uses a variety of christological titles and images to describe Jesus, such as Messiah, prophet like Moses, Isaianic servant, and Savior. But perhaps the most distinctive title he uses is that of Lord. While the word "Lord" (*kyrios*) might be taken in some instances as simply a polite and deferential descriptor, similar to that of "Master" (e.g., Luke 5:5; 8:24; 9:33), in other instances it seems to connote a remarkably high view of Jesus that would associate him with the God of Israel.[4] In the Greek translation of the Scriptures of Israel, the term *kyrios* often was employed to render the sacred name of the God of Israel, "Yahweh." And in Luke's Gospel, one finds that Luke uses the term "Lord" to make an intentional overlap between the God of Israel as Lord and Jesus as Lord. For example, when Mary refers to herself as "the servant of the Lord" (1:38), it is clear by the context that she is referring here to the God of Israel (see also 1:46). But when Elizabeth refers to Mary as "the mother of my Lord" (1:43), the reference clearly is to Jesus. When the angel announces to the shepherds the birth of a Savior "who is Christ the Lord" (2:11), we can see that Luke leads the reader to view Jesus's messianic lordship as implementing and embodying the saving reign of the God of Israel. Thus, when Luke frequently refers to Jesus as "Lord" simply in passing (e.g., "the Lord said" [12:42]; "the Lord responded" [13:15]), he seeks to draw a close correlation between the God of Israel and Jesus's life and ministry.

Luke and Narrative (2)

Key Narrative Threads

Jesus Is the Climax of Israel's Prophets

On the Emmaus Road, two disciples encounter the resurrected Jesus and, thinking they are talking to a stranger, give the following report about Jesus: "He was a powerful prophet in both word and deed before God and all the people" (Luke 24:19). God's resurrection of Jesus from the dead will transform their understanding of Jesus's identity, but both Luke's Gospel and the book of Acts characterize Jesus as the climax of Israel's prophetic heritage.[1] 18.1

National Gallery, London / Wikimedia Commons

Figure 18.1. Caravaggio, *Supper at Emmaus*, 1601

Luke's infancy narrative indicates that Jesus is born into a prophetic people—a family whose speech and lives are under the control of the Spirit of God. Mary, Elizabeth, Zechariah, Simeon, and Anna are filled with the Spirit and make prophetic declarations about God's redemptive work through Jesus. 18.2

But the greatest prophet of all (except for Jesus) is John the Baptist. Later in the narrative Jesus refers to John as a "prophet" and even "more than a prophet" (7:26). He too is filled by the Spirit of God even from his mother's womb (1:15). He is commissioned with the prophetic task of calling Israel to repentance and will go before the Lord "in the Spirit and power of Elijah" (1:16–17; see also 1:76). We are not surprised, then, to find "the word of God" coming to John while he is in the wilderness and resulting in John's proclamation of "a baptism of repentance for the forgiveness of sins" (3:2–3). Luke reports that in the proclamation made by John the prophet the prophetic promises of Isaiah (specifically Isa. 40) are in the process of being fulfilled: "The voice of one crying in the wilderness: 'Prepare the way of the Lord, make his paths straight. Every valley shall be filled, and every mountain and hill shall be made low, and the crooked shall be made straight, and the rough ways made smooth, and all flesh shall see the salvation of God'" (Luke 3:4b–6 NRSVue).

John's proclamation of Isaiah 40 is of central significance, as this chapter marks a turning point in Isaiah. After prophetic messages of judgment, Isaiah announces that God is going to do a work to save his people, that God will come back to be present with his people in a powerful way, that the time of Israel's punishment for sin is over (see Isa. 40:1–11). John the Baptist's task, then, is to prepare Israel to embrace the message of the coming one. John's prophetic message is one that calls people to repentance, to "fruit worthy of repentance" (3:8), in light of God's coming eschatological judgment. People cannot presume upon their status, ethnic identity, vocation, or anything else but repentance as providing an opportunity to escape. Herod's locking up John in prison due to his preaching

SIDEBAR 18.1

What Does It Mean to Be a Prophet?

In brief, we can say that Israel's prophets were commissioned and sent by God, called through the Spirit to speak God's Word, preachers of repentance, enactors of God's message through their bodies, and frequently opposed and rejected by those in power. Many of these themes are evident in the prophetic calls in the Old Testament, such as that of the prophet Jeremiah.

> The word of the Lord came to me [Jeremiah], saying,
>
> "Before I formed you in the womb I knew you,
> before you were born I set you apart;
> I appointed you as a prophet to the nations."
>
> "Alas, Sovereign Lord," I said, "I do not know how to speak; I am only a child."
>
> But the Lord said to me, "Do not say, 'I am only a child.' You must go to everyone I send you to and say whatever I command you. Do not be afraid of them, for I am with you and will rescue you," declares the Lord.
>
> Then the Lord reached out his hand and touched my mouth and said to me, "Now, I have put my words in your mouth. See, today I appoint you over nations and kingdoms to uproot and tear down, to destroy and overthrow, to build and to plant." (Jer. 1:4–10 NIV)

of repentance also highlights the Lukan theme of the rejection of God's prophets (3:19–20).

Let's look at four aspects of Jesus's prophetic identity and how Luke portrays him as the climax of Israel's prophetic heritage. First, Luke makes it clear that everything Jesus does is under the direction of God's Spirit. Jesus's baptism functions like a prophetic commission whereby the Spirit of God descends on Jesus and empowers him for his messianic task (3:21–22). Jesus is "full of the Holy Spirit" (4:1a), is "led into the wilderness by the Spirit" (4:1b), and returns from the wilderness "in the power of the Spirit" (4:14). After Jesus successfully resists the devil's temptations, he enters into a synagogue in his hometown of Nazareth and reads from the scroll of Isaiah: "The Spirit of the Lord is upon me, because he has anointed me to proclaim good news to the poor. He has sent me to preach release for the captives and to open the eyes of the blind, to give release to the oppressed, and to proclaim the year of the Lord's welcome" (4:18–19; cf. Isa. 61:1; see also 58:6). We will return to this text later, but for now we can note that Jesus proclaims that God's Spirit has uniquely anointed him to be the agent who will fulfill God's promises from the prophet Isaiah. 18.3

The second aspect of Jesus's prophetic identity consists in his task to proclaim God's word and call God's people to repentance. The importance of Jesus's prophetic task to teach and proclaim God's word is highlighted in Luke's transfiguration account (9:28–36). Here we see that the luminous Jesus is conversing with two of Israel's greatest prophets: Moses and Elijah (9:30). The episode is reminiscent of Moses on Sinai (see sidebar 18.3). Jesus "goes up on a mountain" (9:28; cf. Exod. 19:20). Jesus is speaking with Moses and Elijah about his "departure" or "exodus" (9:31). A great cloud overshadows everyone, and the disciples are afraid (9:34; cf. Exod. 19:9; 20:18). The divine voice from the cloud states, "This is my chosen Son. Listen to him" (9:35b). God's exhortation "Listen to him" is reminiscent of the prophet greater than Moses spoken of in Deuteronomy 18. Moses promises God's people,

SIDEBAR 18.2

The Prophetic Spirit in Luke's Infancy Narrative

Mary

The angel [Gabriel] answered [Mary], "The Holy Spirit will come upon you, and the power of the Most High will overshadow you. So the holy one to be born will be called the Son of God." (1:35 NIV)

Elizabeth

When Elizabeth heard Mary's greeting, the baby leaped in her womb, and Elizabeth was filled with the Holy Spirit. In a loud voice she exclaimed . . . (1:41 NIV)

Zechariah

His father Zechariah was filled with the Holy Spirit and prophesied . . . (1:67)

Simeon

Moved by the Spirit, Simeon went into the temple courts. . . . Simeon took the child Jesus in his arms and praised God, saying . . . (2:27a, 28)

Anna

She never left the temple but worshiped night and day, fasting and praying. Coming up to them at that very moment, she gave thanks to God and spoke about the child to all who were looking forward to the redemption of Jerusalem. (2:37–38 NIV)

"The Lord your God will raise up for you a prophet like me from among you, from your fellow Israelites. You must listen to him. . . . I will raise up for them a prophet like you from among their fellow Israelites, and I will put my words in his mouth. He will tell them everything I command him" (Deut. 18:15, 18 NIV). Jesus is this prophet greater than Moses who is the uniquely authoritative interpreter and teacher of God's word (see also Acts 3:22–23; 7:35–37). Jesus is the one who proclaims "the word of God" (Luke 8:11) and who is looking for people who hear "the word with an honest and good heart, hold on to it, and by enduring produce fruit" (8:15).

One of the frequent messages of the ancient prophets was that God would be pleased with Israel's worship only when the people demonstrated true repentance by caring for all of their neighbors, by refraining from economic exploitation of the vulnerable, and by sharing their possessions. Isaiah 58:6–7 offers a good example: "Isn't this the fast I choose: To break the chains of wickedness, to untie the ropes of the yoke, to set the oppressed free, and to tear off every yoke? Is it not to share your bread with the hungry, to bring the poor and homeless into your house, to clothe the naked when you see him, and not to ignore your own flesh and blood?" (CSB).

Jesus's message is steeped in the teaching of Israel's prophets, calling God's people to a way of life that cares for the poor and marginalized. When Jesus proclaims, "Blessed are you who are poor, for yours is the kingdom of God" (Luke 6:20), this draws us back to his earlier and programmatic declaration that God's Spirit had anointed him "to proclaim good news to the poor" (4:18). Jesus's Sermon on the Plain, in Luke 6:20–49, begins with programmatic blessings on the poor and vulnerable and words of judgment on the rich, selfishly contented, and those of high status or repute (vv. 20–26). Jesus calls God's people to a lifestyle that rejects violence, pursues peace and forgiveness even with one's enemies, and gives generously to those in need (vv. 27–49). Jesus calls disciples to model their lives on God's merciful goodness to all people. Since God is gracious to the ungrateful and evil, God's people are to love their enemies and be merciful to all people (vv. 27, 35–36). 18.4

SIDEBAR 18.3

Parallels between Jesus's Transfiguration and Moses at Sinai

Jesus is on a mountain (Luke 9:28)	//	Moses is on a mountain (Exod. 24:12)
Jesus's face radiates with glory (Luke 9:29)	//	Moses's face radiates with divine glory (Exod. 34:29–30)
Jesus and the disciples are enveloped by a cloud (Luke 9:34)	//	A cloud covers the mountain (Exod. 24:15–18)
A voice from the cloud calls Jesus "my Son" (Luke 9:35)	//	God speaks to Moses from the cloud (Exod. 24:16)[a]

SIDEBAR 18.4

New Testament Exhortations on Economic Justice

Jesus is not alone in calling his disciples to enact economic justice. In fact, it is likely that many of the New Testament authors directly carry forth Jesus's vision on economic justice.

- James: "Look here, you rich people: Weep and groan with anguish because of all the terrible troubles ahead of you. Your wealth is rotting away, and your fine clothes are moth-eaten rags. Your gold and silver are corroded. The very wealth you were counting on will eat away your flesh like fire. This corroded treasure you have hoarded will testify against you on the day of judgment. For listen! Hear the cries of the field workers whom you have cheated of their pay. The cries of those who harvest your fields have reached the ears of the LORD of Heaven's Armies" (James 5:1–4 NLT).
- Paul: Paul declares that he was deeply committed to helping the poor (Gal. 2:10), and this is exemplified in his financial collection for the churches struggling with famine in Judea (Rom. 15:25–33; 2 Cor. 8–9), his frequent exhortations to show hospitality and bear one another's burdens (Rom. 12:13; Gal. 6:2, 9–10; 1 Thess. 5:14–15), and his exhortation to care for the needs of widows (1 Tim. 5:3–16).
- John of Patmos: In Revelation 18 John celebrates the downfall of Rome's imperial economic system because it has devoted itself to extravagant luxury and consumption (vv. 3, 9–14), benefited the elite at the expense of the majority (vv. 15–19), exploited human lives through slavery (v. 13), and killed the righteous (vv. 20–24).

Third, Jesus's prophetic identity is revealed in his ability to perform signs and wonders. Just like Israel's greatest prophets—Moses, Elijah, and Elisha—Jesus's divine power is displayed in his liberative exorcisms and healings. We will look at these healings and exorcisms in more detail in the next section, but for now it is important to note that the goal of the signs and wonders is to bring freedom, release, and liberation for the oppressed and vulnerable. In other words, Jesus embodies God's power for the good of those in need. So before narrating Jesus's healing of the paralytic, Luke notes that "the power of the Lord to heal was in him" (5:17). Crowds are trying to touch him because "power was coming out from him and he was healing all of them" (6:19). Jesus's defeat of Satan is evident in his ability to drive out demons "by the finger of God" (11:20). Luke describes Jesus's restoration of life to a widow's dead son in a way that evokes the prophet Elijah's similar miracle (Luke 7:11–17; 1 Kings 17:17–24). When the crowd sees the dead child come to life, they "give glory to God, saying, 'A great prophet has been raised up for us and God has visited his people'" (Luke 7:16). 18.5

Fourth, like Israel's ancient prophets, Jesus is a rejected prophet. After his initial announcement of his mission, Jesus provokes those in the Nazareth synagogue and declares, "No doubt you will quote this proverb to me: 'Physician, heal yourself.' And you will tell me, 'Do here also in your hometown the things that we've heard you did in Capernaum.'" He then adds, "I say to you that no prophet is welcome in his hometown" (4:23–24). God's gifts cannot be selfishly demanded or hoarded, but rather will be freely bestowed on whomever Jesus desires to do so. Jesus goes on to declare that although in the days of the ancient prophets there were

SIDEBAR 18.5

Examine Jesus's Prophetic Characterization for Yourself: 1 Kings 17:17–24 // Luke 7:11–17

Readers of Luke's Gospel have long noted the similarities between Jesus and Israel's prophets Elijah and Elisha. Read through the story of Jesus's raising of the widow's son at Nain in Luke 7:11–17. Then read through Elijah's interactions with the widow at Zarephath in 1 Kings 17:7–24. How many parallels can you find between these two stories? What might Luke be trying to communicate about Jesus's identity and work by way of the similarities to Elijah?

many hungry widows, Elijah was sent only to the widow in Sidon; and there were many with skin diseases in need of healing, but Elijah cleansed only Naaman the Syrian (4:25–27). Jesus's prophecy is fulfilled as his audience is filled with rage and unsuccessfully attempts to kill him (4:28–30). As we have seen, those who are rich, satisfied, happy, and of high status will so often be precisely those people who will reject Jesus's teaching (6:24–26). They are those who "are not open to the good news announced by God through the prophet. They profit from the present dispositions and arrangements and therefore resist the change that the prophet Jesus demands."[2] Rather than the Pharisees and experts in the law, it is the ordinary people, even the tax collectors, who have heeded John the Baptist's call for repentance and who embrace Jesus's prophetic teaching (see 7:18–30). 18.6

The motif of Jesus as the climax of Israel's rejected prophets comes into focus as he journeys to Jerusalem and the opposition to his prophetic teaching increases. As Jesus hears the report of Herod's desire to kill him from the Pharisees, he laments, "It is not possible for a prophet to perish outside of Jerusalem! Jerusalem, Jerusalem, who kills the prophets and stones those who are sent to you, how often I wanted to gather your children together, as a hen gathers her chicks under her wings, but you were not willing!" (13:33b–34). Jesus weeps for Jerusalem's failure to recognize his message of peace and the ensuing destruction that will come as a result (19:41–44). When Jesus declares that the Jerusalem temple has been turned into a "den of thieves" (19:46), he not only quotes from Jeremiah (Jer. 7:11; but see the entire speech in 7:1–11) but also takes on the role of Jeremiah, who warned God's people from within the temple that only true repentance and a faithful heeding of the prophet's message could protect them from God's judgment.

Jesus is *the* rejected prophet who is arrested and put to death, but the Acts of the Apostles makes it clear that this is not the end of the story. In Peter's speech to those in the Jerusalem temple, he connects God's promise to "raise up for you a prophet" like Moses (Deut. 18:15–19) with God's act of raising Jesus from the dead (see Acts 3:22, 26). Despite the people's rejection of Jesus's prophetic word, God has raised Jesus from the dead and is visiting his people again, providing them with another chance to turn to the Lord (see Acts 3:22–26).

Jesus Shares God's Liberating Hospitality with Sinners and Strangers

We can draw on what we have learned about the Gospels as narratives to see how Luke presents Jesus's preaching in his hometown synagogue in Nazareth as a programmatic depiction of Jesus's ministry (4:16–21). Notice how Luke's description is slow-paced, detailed, and almost laborious: "He came to Nazareth, where he had been raised, and he entered in as was his custom on the Sabbath day. He stood up to read. And the scroll of the prophet Isaiah was given to him, and he unrolled the scroll and found the place where it was written: . . . He then rolled up the scroll, gave it back to the attendant, and sat down. And the eyes of everyone in the synagogue were fixed on him" (4:16–17, 20). One can see that narrative time slows down to encourage the reader likewise to slow down and pay close attention to what happens. When Jesus declares, "Today this Scripture has been fulfilled in your hearing" (4:21), the reader knows that this episode is of supreme importance for understanding Jesus's vocation and identity.

You may also remember from an earlier chapter how Luke has taken this episode from Mark's Gospel (Mark 6:1–6) and has both fronted it so that it occurs much earlier in Luke's Gospel (than in Mark's) and expanded it significantly.

The reader will also note that this scene is the first of Jesus's public acts. Jesus's Spirit-anointed identity has not yet been described in any detail, nor has he engaged in any teaching or performed any mighty deeds. Jesus's proclamation in the Nazareth synagogue, in fact, stands as a concrete depiction of the preceding Lukan summary: "And Jesus returned in the power of the Spirit to Galilee. And news about him spread throughout the entire countryside. And he was teaching in their synagogues, being glorified by everyone" (4:14–15). Throughout the Gospel, Luke will refer to Jesus conducting his ministry in synagogues, but this is the only detailed account of what Jesus says and

SIDEBAR 18.6

Israel's Rejection of the Prophets

Jesus assumes that his audience is familiar with the scriptural motif of Israel's rejection of God's prophets.

Isaiah 6:8–10

Then I heard the voice of the Lord saying, "Whom shall I send? And who will go for us?"
And I said, "Here am I. Send me!"
He said, "Go and tell this people:

'Be ever hearing, but never understanding;
be ever seeinzg, but never perceiving.'
Make the heart of this people calloused;
make their ears dull
and close their eyes.
Otherwise they might see with their eyes,
hear with their ears,
understand with their hearts,
and turn and be healed." (NIV)

Jeremiah 7:24–27

But they did not listen or pay attention; instead, they followed the stubborn inclinations of their evil hearts. They went backward and not forward. From the time your ancestors left Egypt until now, day after day, again and again I sent you my servants the prophets. But they did not listen to me or pay attention. They were stiff-necked and did more evil than their ancestors. When you tell them all this, they will not listen to you; when you call to them, they will not answer. (NIV)

SIDEBAR 18.7

God Banqueting with His People

The Old Testament uses the image of a banquet between God and his people in order to symbolize the joy and festivity of God and his people dwelling together in peaceful unity (e.g., Isa. 55:1–2; Ezek. 34:23–24). One of the most powerful of these texts is Isaiah 25:6–9:

> On this mountain the LORD of hosts will make for all peoples
> a feast of rich food, a feast of well-aged wines,
> of rich food filled with marrow, of well-aged wines strained clear.
> And he will destroy on this mountain
> the shroud that is cast over all peoples,
> the covering that is spread over all nations;
> he will swallow up death forever.
> Then the Lord GOD will wipe away the tears from all faces,
> and the disgrace of his people he will take away from all the earth,
> for the LORD has spoken.
> It will be said on that day,
> "See, this is our God; we have waited for him, so that he might save us.
> This is the LORD for whom we have waited;
> let us be glad and rejoice in his salvation." (NRSVue)

does in the synagogue (cf. 4:31–37, 44; 6:6; 13:10–17).

But the most significant and obvious reason as to why this scene is programmatic is the way in which Jesus's proclamation of Isaiah functions as his vocational mission throughout the entire Gospel. Once again, Jesus proclaims, "The Spirit of the Lord is upon me, because he has anointed me to preach good news to the poor. He has sent me to proclaim release to the captives and sight for the blind, to give release to the oppressed, and to proclaim the year of the Lord's welcome" (4:18–19).[3]

In the Old Testament, God is spoken of as Israel's host who nourishes his people in the wilderness (Exod. 16:4, 15; Num. 11:1–19; Ps. 78:24–38), spreads a table of peace for the psalmist (Ps. 23:5), and grants Israel the gift of living on his good land as guests (Lev. 25:23). But God also promises that one day he will come back to save his people and to reveal his presence by means of a banquet feast with his people. 18.7

This is the context for Luke's depiction of Jesus as the agent of God's hospitality, the one who shares God's presence with his people through table fellowship. Let's look at Luke 4:18–19 in a bit more detail.

First, Jesus's preaching indicates that his ministry will enact *God's* hospitality. Note that Jesus has declared that "the Spirit of *the Lord* is upon me" (4:18) and that his ministry is "to proclaim the year of *the Lord's* welcome" (4:19). Jesus is more than a great teacher or wonderful miracle worker. Jesus's ministry is the very embodiment of God's hospitality toward the stranger. Second, many English translations speak of Jesus as proclaiming the "year of the Lord's *favor*" rather than "the year of the Lord's *welcome*." But given that Luke uses the same Greek word (*dektos*) in 4:24 to refer to a prophet's *lack of welcome* and frequently uses the same Greek root for hospitality (e.g., 9:5, 48, 53; 10:8–10), and especially the fact that recipients of the Lord's welcome are stereotypical outsiders in need of welcome, it makes good sense to understand 4:19 as Jesus's programmatic proclamation that he has come to enact divine welcome and hospitality to the stranger and the outcast. The programmatic function of Jesus's sermon invites us to pay attention to the way in which the entirety of Jesus's ministry, especially his meals with strangers, enacts divine hospitality to the poor, the captives, the blind, and the oppressed. Third, the phrase "to give release to the oppressed" (4:18b) comes from Isaiah 58:6, and it is worth quoting the prophetic oracle in more detail: "Isn't this the fast I choose: to break the chains of wickedness, to loose the ropes of the yoke, to give release to the oppressed, and to tear off every yoke? Is it not to share your bread with the hungry, to bring the poor and homeless into your house, to clothe the naked when you see him and not to ignore your own flesh and blood?" (Isa. 58:6–7).

Both Isaiah 61:1–2 and 58:6–7, the texts quoted by Jesus in Luke 4:18–19, share the words "release" and "welcome" and indicate that Jesus's ministry will provide the social justice, release, forgiveness of debts, and hospitality that Israel's prophets had demanded of Israel. Thus, the entire ministry of Jesus is appropriately captured in the phrase "divine hospitality to the stranger and sinner."[4]

Let's look at three ways in which Jesus extends the Lord's hospitality to strangers and sinners. First, one of the primary ways Jesus enacts the year of the Lord's welcome is through eating meals with outsiders that creates the hospitable space where outsiders can experience the saving presence of God and are thereby transformed from strangers to friends of God. For example, Jesus interprets the "great feast" (5:29) hosted by Levi the tax collector as signifying Jesus's healing of Levi's ruptured relationships (5:31–32). Jesus's meal with Simon the Pharisee ironically provides the hospitable space for the so-called sinful woman to encounter the saving presence of Jesus, a presence that enables her to experience divine forgiveness, peace, and incorporation into the kingdom of God (7:36–50). Zacchaeus's quest to see Jesus is more than fulfilled when Jesus demands hospitality from the tax collector: "I must receive hospitality in your house today" (19:5). After their shared hospitality, Jesus makes a similar declaration: "Salvation has come to this house today" (19:9). The shared hospitality between Jesus and Zacchaeus has provided the context for Jesus to share his presence with the outcast and incorporate him into God's family as a "son of Abraham" (19:9).

In the ancient world it was common practice to share meals with one's family, friends, and clients. As a result, there is much philosophical instruction and advice given as to the kinds of people with whom one should and should not share meals. 18.8

One of the major marks of Jesus's table practices is his indiscriminate and noncalculating offer of hospitality to all people. Jesus eats with tax collectors (5:27–32; 19:1–10), a sinful woman (7:36–50), two women

(10:38–42), and with the Pharisees (7:39; 11:37–54; 14:1–6). It is no surprise, then, that Israel's religious leaders are said to have taken offense and complain about the guests to whom Jesus extends hospitality (5:30–32; 15:1–2; 19:6–7). Jesus is tangibly extending God's friendship to those who, in the eyes of others, are not righteous, have a low status, and are unworthy of friendship with God. Jesus shares some of the most beloved and famous parables precisely to counter this view. Jesus tells the parables of the lost sheep (15:3–7), the lost coin (15:8–10), and the lost son (15:11–32) in response to the Pharisees and scribes who were complaining about his extension of hospitality to the wrong people: "And all the tax collectors and sinners were coming near to listen to him. And the Pharisees and scribes were grumbling, saying, 'This one extends hospitality to sinners and he eats with them!'" (15:1–2). It should not escape us here that the charge brought against Jesus (extending hospitality to sinners and tax collectors) is exactly what Jesus himself had described as the purpose of his mission ("to proclaim the year of the Lord's welcome" [4:19]). Jesus's three parables, then, are commentary on the meaning of his extension of welcome through shared meals with sinners and tax collectors. When Jesus shares table fellowship, this is a symbolic enactment of the divine shepherd's recovery of the lost sheep of Israel (15:3–7). Jesus's extension of hospitality to sinners is the expression of the father's welcome of "my son who was dead and is alive again, who was lost and now is found" (15:24, 32). The father's response to the recovery of his lost son is significant because, like Jesus's meals with sinners and outcasts, his response is one of joyous and celebratory feasting (15:27, 30). Thus, in these three parables Jesus links his hospitality to sinners with divine joy (15:7, 10, 24–32). The joy that occurs when sinners are restored to friendship with God through Jesus's extension of hospitality corresponds to the joy shared between Jesus and sinners over these shared meals. 18.9

Second, Jesus enacts the year of the Lord's welcome through liberating healings and exorcisms. Jesus inaugurates God's kingdom as he wages war against Satan and the demonic as he heals the sick and diseased and proclaims the good news of God's kingdom. Jesus's healings exemplify God's release and liberation from the satanic oppression and into the peace, freedom, and life that God intends. In fact, when John the Baptist's disciples ask Jesus whether he is truly the expected coming one, Jesus responds with blended quotations of Isaiah to set

SIDEBAR 18.8

Advice from Sirach on Choosing One's Guests Wisely

Sirach 9:16

Take the righteous for your table companions;
and let your glory be in the fear of God.

Sirach 11:29, 34

Not everyone should be brought into your house,
for many are the snares of the crafty. . . .
Admit strangers into your home, and they will stir up trouble
and make you a stranger to your own family.

forth the claim that his ministry is enacting God's release, peace, and welcome: "Go, report to John what you have seen and heard: the blind see, the lame walk, those with skin disease are cleansed and the mute hear, the dead are raised, and the poor have the good news proclaimed to them" (7:22 [see Isa. 29:18; 35:5–6; 42:18; 26:19; 61:1]).

The sheer number of healings that pepper Luke's Gospel is remarkable, and it is further striking how many different types of people experience healing. Jesus's mission to the poor, blind, captive, and oppressed (4:18–19) and his blessings on the poor, hungry, and excluded (6:20–23) are being worked out among those he heals. 18.10

Jesus's healings reflect his *compassionate concern* for holistic peace and restoration of humans to full-capacity health, well-being, and social functioning. Jesus's cleansing of a man with a skin disease overturns and reverses his place in society (5:12–14). The healing restores him from a place of banishment on the margins of society, unable to participate in the religious, communal life of Israel (see Lev. 13:44–46) and into a place of full communion within the people of God, which is why Jesus orders him to show himself to the priests and make an offering as a testimony to them (5:14). Similarly, note how when Jesus sees the widow and her dead son, he "feels compassion for her" (7:13) as one who is likely economically vulnerable. His restoration of life to the dead son essentially secures her ability to have the life and subsistence that her son can provide.

Notice how in the story of the Gerasene demoniac (8:26–39) the man is initially described as "one who had demons" (v. 27) and then later is spoken of as "the man from whom the demons had gone" (vv. 35, 36, 38). The man is an example of one who is in bondage and oppression (cf. 4:18–19). The portrait is of an individual who is totally dehumanized, as he has been driven out of his house and city and now forced to live among the dead (v. 27). He is literally "shackled in chains and bonds" (v. 29). Jesus's exorcism and healing result in a point-by-point overturning of the man's prior condition: (1) many demons possessed him (v. 27) // the demons have left him (v. 35); (2) he had worn no clothes (v. 27) // he is clothed (v. 35); (3) he lived not in a house but among tombs (v. 27) // he returns to his own home (v. 39);

SIDEBAR 18.9

George Herbert, "Love (III)"

George Herbert's poem "Love (III)" can be read as a powerful reflection on Jesus's (i.e., "Love's") willingness not only to bestow but even to receive hospitality from sinners.[b]

Love bade me welcome, yet my soul drew back,
  Guilty of dust and sin.
But quick-eyed Love, observing me grow slack
  From my first entrance in,
Drew nearer to me, sweetly questioning
  If I lacked any thing.
"A guest," I answered, "worthy to be here."
  Love said, "You shall be he."
"I, the unkind, ungrateful? Ah, my dear,
  I cannot look on thee."
Love took my hand, and smiling did reply,
  "Who made the eyes but I?"
"Truth Lord, but I have marred them; let my shame
  Go where it doth deserve."
"And you know not," says Love, "who bore the blame?"
  "My dear, then I will serve."
"You must sit down," says Love, "and taste my meat."
  So I did sit and eat.

SIDEBAR 18.10

Jesus's Healings and Exorcisms in Luke's Gospel

- A demon-possessed man (4:33–37)
- Simon's mother-in-law (4:38–39)
- A crowd of people with various diseases and possessed by demons (4:40–41)
- A man covered with skin disease (5:12–16)
- A man with paralysis (5:17–26)
- A man with a shriveled hand (6:6–11)
- Summary report of healing and exorcisms of a large crowd (6:18–19)
- The deathly ill servant of a centurion (7:1–10)
- A widow's son raised from death (7:11–17)
- Summary report of healings and exorcisms (7:21–23)
- A Gerasene man possessed by demons (8:26–39)
- A dying twelve-year-old girl and a woman with chronic hemorrhages (8:40–56)
- A young boy possessed by an unclean spirit (9:37–43)
- A man possessed by a mute demon (11:14)
- A woman with a bent back (13:10–17)
- Ten Samaritans with a skin disease (17:11–19)
- A blind man who was begging (18:35–43)

(4) he was out of control (v. 29) // he is in his right mind (v. 35).

Likewise, the story of the healing of a woman with a bent back (13:10–17) shows us that Jesus's healings are signs of the kingdom of God's liberating release from Satan's power. This is why the story is filled with the language of "binding and loosing" ("You have been set free" [v. 12]; "Each of you frees your cow or donkey" [v. 15]; the woman is set free from Satan's bonds [v. 16]). Her malady is due to her being possessed by a crippling "spirit" (v. 11). So, Jesus asks, "Ought not this daughter of Abraham, whom Satan has oppressed for eighteen years, be set free from this bondage on the Sabbath?" (v. 16). Her healing, then, is a form of release that signifies wholeness and freedom from diabolic oppression. The Messiah's healings are a form of release and welcome that liberate humans from bondage and oppression, restore them to proper physical and social engagement, and flow from Jesus's compassion for human suffering. 18.11

The third way Jesus enacts God's welcome and release for all people is through the proclamation of the forgiveness of sins. For Jesus, release from sins is not simply "wiping the slate clean." Rather, it is liberation and freedom from the domineering, dehumanizing, humanity-distorting effects of sin and an unreconciled relationship with God. Let's look at two representative narratives where Jesus enacts divine forgiveness for sinners. In Luke 5:17–26 it is fascinating that when the paralytic and his friends come to Jesus, Luke tells us, "The power of the Lord was with him *to heal*" (5:17). So, it is initially surprising when Jesus does not immediately address the physical malady but rather treats the spiritual illness: *sin*. Humanity is created for a peaceful relationship with a loving God, but sin is a fracture of this relationship. Sin is the disease of alienation from this loving God. Sin is the foolish turning away from the joy and peace that come from fellowship with the Father to the worthlessness of pursuing one's own selfish desire (see 15:11–32). Thus, Jesus makes two transformative pronouncements: "Your sins are forgiven you" (5:20b) and "Get up, take your mat, and go to your home" (5:24).

In Luke 7:36–50, Simon the Pharisee and the sinful woman provide two contrasting responses to Jesus's vision of the kingdom of God. Simon has invited Jesus to dine with him. But surprisingly, there is present an unnamed woman who stands "alongside [Jesus's] feet," bathes and dries "his feet" with her own tears, and kisses and anoints "his feet" with her ointment. Instead of water for washing, the woman uses her tears; instead of a towel for drying, the woman uses her hair; instead of anointing his head, the woman kisses and anoints his feet. The contrast to Simon's inhospitality is obvious. The repeated posture and action of the woman as caring for the feet of Jesus is a symbolic depiction of her wholehearted recognition of his authority, a favorable response to Jesus that indicates a state of obedience and love (see also 10:39).

Simon the Pharisee balks at Jesus's willingness to receive this loving display of hospitality from the woman, saying to himself, "If this one was a prophet, he would have known who and what type of woman this is touching him—that she is a sinner" (7:39b). In response, Jesus tells Simon a short story. There was once a moneylender who had two debtors. One owed five hundred denarii, while the other owed fifty. But neither could repay the debt, so the lender "freely forgave" both debtors (7:42). We know that Jesus is playing the role of the one who "freely forgives" debtors and "brings release" to the captives (cf. 4:18–19). So, Jesus asks Simon, "Which one of them will love him more?" (7:42b). Simon gives the obvious answer: "I suppose the one for whom he freely forgave the greater debt" (7:43). Jesus is attempting to lead Simon to a reevaluation of the woman's hospitality as an expression of deep love to the one who is able to bestow divine forgiveness on her. The woman functions like an object lesson for Simon as Jesus "turns to the woman" but "speaks to Simon" (7:44a). Despite her

SIDEBAR 18.11

The Church as a Healing Community

We have seen that Jesus's healings are a form of release and welcome that liberate humans from bondage and oppression, restore them to proper physical and social engagement, and flow from Jesus's compassion for human suffering and vulnerability. Jan-Olav Henriksen and Karl Olav Sandnes state the importance of Jesus's healing ministry well: "As healer, Jesus reveals a God of love and compassion, who does not turn away from the suffering of creation but instead makes possible concrete hope for redemption and fulfillment by acting in, with, and under creaturely conditions in order to reveal the kingdom. . . . [Jesus] engages the powers of creation in his graceful approach to humanity in order to alleviate the suffering of the sick and destitute."[c]

Jesus's healing ministry functions as a reminder that Jesus cared deeply about human flourishing and stands opposed to death and that which inflicts harm and evil on humanity. In fact, the church's care for the sick in the early centuries of the church's existence was rooted in Jesus's healing ministry. Amanda Porterfield states this well: "Care for the sick was a distinctive and remarkable characteristic of early Christian missionary outreach. Early Christians nursed the sick to emulate the healing ministry of Jesus, to express their faith in the ongoing healing power of Christ, and to distinguish Christian heroism in the face of sickness and death from pagan fear."[d] The church's indiscriminate concern for the poor was one of the major factors that led to the creation of institutions such as "poorhouses" that supported widows, the sick, and the poor, as well as hospitals, which were, Gary Ferngren notes, "in origin and conception, a distinctively Christian institution, rooted in Christian concepts of charity and philanthropy."[e]

many sins, Jesus declares that she has been forgiven because of her deep love for Jesus (7:47). Her hospitality to Jesus signifies her recognition of her sin and that Jesus is the singular agent who offers divine forgiveness. And so, Jesus turns to the woman and makes two pronouncements: "Your sins have been forgiven" (7:48) and "Your faith has saved you; go in peace" (7:50).

In conclusion, we should emphasize that Jesus's ministry of release and welcome has been extended to those who were regarded in the ancient world as deserving of little attention and worth on the scale of social prestige. In other words, Jesus enacts his ministry of release and welcome through the social form of fellowship and inclusion of the poor and the outcasts.

Women: Luke shows Jesus reversing ancient conventional gender standards through his consistent act of inviting women into fellowship (e.g., Elizabeth, Mary, Anna, Peter's mother-in-law, the sinful woman).

Children: In ancient society, children were thought of as weak, needy, and ignorant. And yet Jesus ministers to children: He raises the woman's dead son (7:11–16). Jesus responds to the father's plea, "Teacher, I beg you, look at my son; he is my only child" (9:38), by "healing the boy and returning him to his father" (9:42). He responds to the plea of Jairus, whose daughter was dying at twelve years old (8:41–42), by going to his house and touching her and calling to her, "Child, rise!" (8:54). On two occasions he uses children as the measure whereby to understand the kingdom of God (9:48; 18:15–17).

People of all ethnicities: Jesus's extension of welcome and release is given to all types of people as he welcomes non-Jews into the people of God and bestows the benefits of the kingdom on them—for example, the Roman centurion (7:2–10), the Gerasene demoniac (8:26–39), and Samaritans (17:11–17).

Sinners and tax collectors: But what is most surprising and most angers those with alternative views of God and his kingdom is his embrace and inclusion of sinners into his family. Notice how the Pharisees and experts of the law characterize Jesus: "The Son of Man has come eating and drinking, and you say, 'Behold, a glutton and drunkard, a friend of tax collectors and sinners'" (7:34). This is the narrative frame for Jesus's meal with Simon the Pharisee and the sinful woman, and Jesus does not deny the charge. He *has* come eating and drinking with sinners and tax collectors, for his divine mission consists in welcoming and liberating the poor and the outcasts (5:27–32; 19:1–10).

Living Out Jesus's Kingdom Teachings

In the Gospel of Luke, as with all four Gospels, Jesus calls forth a group to follow him in order to listen to *and live out* his teachings. So, immediately before Jesus's Sermon on the Plain, where he sets forth his fundamental teachings, Luke tells us that Jesus spends the night on a mountain in prayer and then calls twelve disciples (6:12–16). Jesus's disciples are called to a particular way of life that flows from his teaching about and enactment of the kingdom of God. It is a way of life that brings liberative justice, divine hospitality, and flourishing *for all people*. And, as we will see, it is a way of life that is controversial as it upends many of the presumed social norms taught by Jesus's contemporaries. Let's look at three aspects of this way of life.

GUARD AGAINST GREED BY GENEROUSLY SHARING POSSESSIONS

A remarkable number of passages in Luke's Gospel address the theme of wealth and possessions, setting up an almost simple way of evaluating Luke's characters: protagonists share possessions, while antagonists do not share possessions. 18.12

Many of Jesus's most essential points about wealth and possessions are exemplified in Luke 12:13–34. The economy of Roman Palestine during the time of Jesus was oriented primarily around subsistence agriculture. Wealth was tied up in the very few landowners. The cities were places

SIDEBAR 18.12

Possessions in the Gospel of Luke

- John the Baptist exhorts hearers to repent by sharing their possessions (3:10–14).
- Jesus declares that his mission is to bring good news to the poor (4:18–19).
- Disciples leave their possessions in order to follow Jesus (5:1–11).
- Levi leaves his possessions and uses them to provide a hospitality feast for outcasts with Jesus (5:27–32).
- Jesus pronounces a blessing on the poor and woes on the rich (6:20–26).
- Jesus exhorts followers to share and give even to their enemies (6:27–36).
- Jesus upholds as a model the Samaritan who uses his resources to help the beaten man (10:25–37).
- Jesus declares that almsgiving leads to purity (11:37–41).
- Jesus teaches the parable of the rich man who loses his possessions by foolishly hoarding them (12:13–21).
- Jesus teaches disciples not to be anxious about possessions but to give alms for heavenly treasures (12:22–35).
- Jesus teaches parables centering on sharing possessions with the poor, crippled, lame, and blind (14:7–24).
- Jesus teaches parables focused on the rejection of greed (16:1–31).
- The wealthy leader does not want to give up his possessions in order to inherit eternal life (18:18–30).
- Zacchaeus repents by showing hospitality and making restitution to those he's cheated (19:1–10).
- The poor widow is blessed for giving to the temple all that she has to live on (21:1–4).

of consumption and extraction (rather than production). In this ancient economy, a man from the crowd comes to Jesus and shouts out, "Teacher, tell my brother to divide the inheritance with me" (v. 13). Jesus, surprisingly, refuses to enter into the brother's economic concerns and asks, "Who appointed me as a judge or arbiter over you?" (v. 14). Jesus discerns that underlying the brother's concern for land, for his inheritance, for what most of us would say justly belongs to him is the disease of greed: "Watch out and be on guard against all greed because one's life does not consist in the abundance of one's possessions" (v. 15). Jesus criticizes the brother's greedy desire for more possessions by making an antithesis between "life" and "possessions" (v. 15b).

Jesus exemplifies his teaching through the parable of the foolish rich landowner in Luke 12:16–21. When the man's land has an extraordinarily productive harvest, he supposes that he can make his life safe and secure by hoarding his possessions. Readers should note both the man's self-reference to his soul (i.e., life), "I will say to my soul, 'Soul'" (v. 19), and his making of plans without reference to God or other humans: he says to *himself*, "What should *I* do, since *I* don't have anywhere to store *my* crops? *I* will do this: *I* will tear down *my* barns and build bigger ones and store all *my* grain and *my* goods there. Then *I* will say to *my* soul . . .'" In an economy where most live at subsistence level, the man's decision to store up his excess crops for himself demonstrates an obvious lack of concern for the needs of others around him. The man is, for Jesus, a symbol of the wealthy, extractive, consuming, exploitative landowner who greedily profits off of his land. He makes his plans not only with no regard for the needs of others but also without respect to God: he is a man who "stores up treasures for himself but is not rich toward God" (v. 21).

Jesus sets forth an alternative way of life that takes God as the ultimate starting point for how one uses wealth and possessions (12:22–34). Instead of greedily hoarding possessions to make one's life safe and secure, disciples of Jesus trust God as the one who generously provides for his people and even all of creation (12:24–31). Instead of the constant anxiousness that comes from focusing on food, drink, and clothing, disciples of Jesus fixate on God's kingdom and thereby find a gracious Father who generously provides them with life's necessities (12:30–31). Instead of greedily hoarding possessions, Jesus insists, his disciples must divest themselves of their wealth by sharing with those in need: "Sell your possessions and give alms. Make money bags for yourselves that will never grow old, an inexhaustible treasure in heaven, where no thief comes near and no moth destroys" (12:33). Notice that those who give alms, who share their wealth and possessions, will find that God will pay them back with eternal life.

The rich man's folly consists in storing up his fortune for his own use instead of sharing it with the poor and thereby securing for himself an eternal treasure that will never depreciate in value.

Jesus's command to give alms as an antidote to greed also occurs in a passage where he criticizes the Pharisees for focusing on their rules for ritual washings but who are filled with "greed and wickedness" (11:37–39). Jesus tells them that rather than focusing on washing the "outside" of dishes and cups, they must focus on what is inside of them. How do they do this? Jesus says, "Give alms with respect to the things inside, and see, all will be made clean for you" (11:41). Acts of mercy exemplified through the generous sharing of their possessions can atone for and even transform the greed of the Pharisees such that they will no longer be susceptible to Jesus's accusation that they have ignored "justice and love for God" (11:42).

OBEY THE CALL OF THE TORAH AND THE PROPHETS FOR MERCY AND LOVE

Luke presents both Jesus and the Pharisees and scribes as holding to the importance and authority of the Torah and the prophets, but Jesus claims that their interpretation of the Scriptures is wrongheaded. In fact, Jesus claims that their insistence on human traditions results in their exclusion of the vast majority of the people of Israel from full fellowship in the people of God (cf. Matt. 15:1–9; Mark 7:1–13). As a result, Jesus says that they are the ones who have exalted themselves as "keepers of the law" but who ignore its weightier commands (see especially 11:37–54; 14:2–6). Jesus declares that all of the Torah remains in force and should be obeyed but that its fundamental features and primary starting point are divine justice and love: "But woe to you Pharisees! You give a tenth of mint, rue, and every kind of herb, and you bypass justice and love for God. These things you should have done without neglecting the others!" (11:42). Jesus offers a lengthy and vitriolic set of "woes" against the Pharisees and scribes, most of which center on how their interpretation of the law functions simultaneously to exalt themselves and to exclude or harm those they teach (see 11:43–54).

Jesus's teachings are surprising and controversial for most, and yet Jesus consistently claims that his calls for radical mercy, generosity, forgiveness, hospitality, and love for both neighbor and enemy are rooted in the true meaning of Israel's Scriptures.

With respect to Israel's prophets, we have seen how Jesus's ministry embodies and brings to fulfillment Isaiah's announcement of good news for the poor, oppressed, and captive (Isa. 58:6–7 and 61:1–2 in Luke

SIDEBAR 18.13

Dominique DuBois Gilliard on True Repentance

"Zacchaeus understood that repentance required more than words. His repentant heart inspired him not only to give half of his possessions to the poor but also to calculate the cumulative effect his oppression had on families and the community and then commit himself to paying reparations accordingly."[f]

4:18–19). We can see how Jesus's interpretation of the Torah and the prophets plays an important role in the parable of Lazarus and the rich man in Luke 16:19–31. The rich man feasts in luxury every day, all the while completely ignoring the desperate plight of the poor and hungry Lazarus (vv. 19–21). Both die on the same day, with Lazarus safely in Abraham's bosom and the rich man in agonizing torment (vv. 22–24). The rich man begs Abraham to send Lazarus back to warn his brothers so they won't come to the same place of torment. Abraham responds, "They have Moses and the prophets. They should listen to them" (v. 29). Why would Abraham respond in this way, by claiming that the unrepentant brothers should pay attention to Moses and the prophets? It's because, as Jesus interprets them, Moses and the prophets reveal the authoritative will of God, which calls God's people to a life of hospitality, neighbor love, and generous sharing of one's possessions: "Is not this the fast that I choose: to loose the bonds of injustice, . . . to share your bread with the hungry, and bring the homeless poor into your house; when you see the naked, to cover them, and not to hide yourself from your own kin?" (Isa. 58:6–7 NRSVue). If the brothers know that Moses and the prophets teach these things but they refuse to follow them, then, as Jesus declares, "They will not be persuaded even if someone rises from the dead" (Luke 16:31). 18.13

Now let's take a look at how Jesus understands the teachings of the Torah. Jesus's fundamental teachings in the Sermon on the Plain in Luke 6:27–36 are, in fact, an interpretation of Leviticus 19, a text that many saw as a summary of the Torah. Let's looks at four examples.

1. Neighbor love and enemy love:

   "Love your neighbor as yourself. . . . You are to love the stranger (sojourner) as yourself, for you were strangers in the land of Egypt" (Lev. 19:18b, 34b).

   "Love your enemies, and do good to those who hate you" (Luke 6:27).
2. Imitation of God as the basis of ethical behavior:

   "Be holy because I, the Lord your God, am holy" (Lev. 19:2b).

   "Be merciful, just as your Father is merciful" (Luke 6:36).
3. Prohibition of revenge:

   "Do not harbor hatred against your neighbor. Rebuke your neighbor directly, and you will not incur guilt because of him. Do not take revenge or bear a grudge against members of your community" (Lev. 19:17–18b).

"If anyone hits you on one cheek, offer the other also. And if anyone takes away your coat, do not hold back your shirt. Give to everyone who asks you, and if someone takes your things, do not ask for them back. Just as you want others to do for you, do the same to them" (Luke 6:29–31).

4. Just and generous judgments:

"Do not act unjustly when deciding a case. Do not be partial to the poor or give preference to the rich; judge your neighbor fairly" (Lev. 19:15).

"Do not judge, and you will not be judged. Do not condemn, and you will not be condemned. Forgive, and you will be forgiven. Give, and it will be given to you; a good measure, pressed down, shaken together, and running over, will be poured into your lap. For with the measure you measure, so shall it be measured back to you" (Luke 6:37–38).

Jesus's interpretation of Leviticus 19 can give us deeper insight into the parable of the good Samaritan in Luke 10:25–37.[5] Notice how the parable is given in the context of how to correctly interpret the law. An expert in the law asks Jesus, "What is written in the law? How do you read it?" (v. 26). When the law expert (rightly) responds by affirming the centrality of the two greatest commandments (love God [Deut. 6:5]; love your neighbor [Lev. 19:18]), Jesus tells him that he has answered correctly (v. 28a). But the man then asks Jesus, "Who is my neighbor?" (v. 29). The man likely expects that Jesus will vindicate him by offering a definition of "neighbor" that fits his categories. His question further exploits the ambiguity of the meaning of "neighbor" from Leviticus 19:18. Jesus responds with the well-known parable of the good Samaritan to answer the man's question. Jesus's parable sets mercy above (not against!) the Torah's purity regulations. Notice that both the priest and the Levite who see the half-dead man (v. 30) are in a hermeneutical quandary. Either they risk defilement by showing mercy to the man (Lev. 21:1–11) or they refuse mercy to the man but maintain ritual purity (Lev. 19:18, 33–34; Hosea 6:6). Notice that the Samaritan is a narrative exemplar of Jesus's call to his disciples to be people who show mercy (vv. 36–37a; cf. 6:35–36) and "do" what is good (vv. 25, 28, 37b; cf. 6:27, 31, 32, 33) precisely to those who have no ability to pay them back. Furthermore, one should understand the Samaritan and the half-dead traveler as religious and ethnic enemies of one another. The Samaritan, then, is surprisingly lifted up as an exemplar of one who *loves his neighbor as himself*

(Lev. 19:18b). Jesus's parable insists that we see the merciful Samaritan as doing what the Torah really demands. Jesus thus expands the command to love neighbor (Lev. 19:18b) to include the command to love strangers (Lev. 19:33–34), for the latter text demands that Israel "love the stranger as yourself."

EXTEND HOSPITALITY AND KINDNESS TO THE MARGINALIZED, THE POOR, THE OPPRESSED

It is not difficult to see that if Jesus embodies divine welcome and hospitality to those on the margins, then he also expects his disciples to do the same. One of the ways Jesus does this throughout Luke's Gospel is, as we have seen, through sharing table fellowship with sinners and outcasts (5:27–32; 7:36–50; 19:1–10). In fact, one of the main criticisms of Jesus recorded in the Gospel of Luke is that he eats and spends time with the wrong people. "The Son of Man has come eating and drinking, and you say, 'Behold, a glutton and drunkard, a friend of tax collectors and sinners'" (7:34). Why is this such a big deal? In the ancient Mediterranean world meals often were social events. Table fellowship with others expressed intimacy, solidarity, and acceptance; it was, in other words, a way of expressing who were your family and friends.

Jesus calls his disciples to share generously with the poor in imitation of the divine welcome that they have received. In one meal scene, for example, one of the guests interrupts Jesus's teaching and exclaims, "Blessed is the one who eats bread in the kingdom of God" (14:15b). In response, Jesus tells a parable in Luke 14:16–24 that clarifies who exactly will enjoy divine hospitality at "the resurrection of the righteous." In the parable, a host invites many people to a feast, but surprisingly and tragically the guests refuse to come because they are preoccupied with wealth, possessions, and personal matters—fields, oxen, marriage (vv. 18–20). They are offered hospitality but refuse to embrace it. So the master now invites guests who have no status and possessions, ordering his servant to "bring in the poor, the crippled, the blind, and the lame" (v. 21b). We can see quite clearly that this guest list evokes the audience of Jesus's ministry from Luke 4:18–19, and it functions as a call to join Jesus's ministry in extending divine hospitality to the poor. Jesus's parable functions as a call to recognize and treat *all of God's people* as friends and family. Only those who can see that they are all recipients of divine welcome will—to return to the guest's initial statement about eating bread in the kingdom of God—feast at the messianic banquet. And so, a second time the host issues an invitation, ordering his servant to "go into the streets and the lanes" to find more guests and "compel them to come in so that my house may be filled" (v. 23b). Jesus's audience, then, must both receive his invitation and imitate him in extending hospitality and welcome to the poor and the outcast. Those who refuse to do so will not join in his messianic banquet (v. 24).

The Rejected (by Humans) but Resurrected (by God) Messiah

Luke's Gospel depicts the world as corrupt and wicked, but with Jesus alone as the singularly righteous messianic king.[6] Jesus alone is obedient and faithful, a true and righteous Son of God who submits himself wholly to his Father. This theme is previewed at the beginning of the Gospel when Satan tempts Jesus in Luke 4:1–13. Three times Satan tempts Jesus to use his messianic power to serve himself: to satisfy his hunger through a miraculous provision of bread, to take rule over the kingdoms of the world, and to demonstrate his wonder-working abilities by jumping off the pinnacle of the temple. All of these temptations center on what type of Messiah or Son of God Jesus will be ("If you are the Son of God . . ." [vv. 3, 9]). Will he live like the kings of this world or will he follow his Father's vision of using his power to love and serve God and others? Jesus's response previews what the entirety of his life will look like as he rejects Satan's tests, quoting God's revelatory word in each instance (Deut. 8:3 in v. 4; Deut. 6:13 in v. 8; Deut. 6:16 in v. 12), and demonstrating that he will remain obedient to his Father and will use his power and authority only for the purpose of his messianic commission.

Luke returns to the theme of Jesus as the righteous and faithful Messiah toward the end of the Gospel as Jesus makes his way to the cross. Luke shows the reader that the threefold denial from Peter (22:54–60), the betrayal by Judas (22:47–52), and the attacks against Jesus from the scribes and priests are the result of Satan's attack on God's righteous one. As Jesus declares to those who arrest him, "This is your time and the dominion of darkness" (22:53). Luke depicts Jesus's final days as a conflict between the satanic kingdom of darkness and the singular, faithful, and obedient messianic king. But even as hostility against him increases, Jesus does not turn away from his mission but instead goes to the cross giving his own body as the Passover offering (22:14–20), praying for Peter's faithfulness under trial (22:31–32), and enduring in faithful prayer (22:39–46).

In Luke's account of Jesus's crucifixion, we see Jesus's opponents mocking him as they presume that his sufferings disqualify him from being the Messiah. They say, "Let him save himself if he is the Messiah, the chosen one of God" (23:35b), "Save yourself, if you are the King of the Jews" (23:37), and "Are you not the Messiah? Save yourself and us!" (23:39b).

Pilate engages in mockery by placing an epitaph on a placard that reads, "This one is the King of the Jews" (23:38b). But ironically, it is the Messiah's sufferings and death that are the very means whereby Jesus enters into his messianic coronation. To those who have been discipled in Israel's Scriptures, this depiction of a righteous Messiah who suffers at the hands of the wicked will make sense. Israel's psalms, as we have already noted, portray the Davidic messianic king as suffering but remaining righteous, steadfast, and obedient to God. So, within Luke's account of Jesus's crucifixion, we see an abundance of quotations from the Davidic psalms. Let's look at three examples.

Psalm 69: When the soldiers mock Jesus as the messiah, they offer him sour wine even as King David had experienced: "They gave me gall for my food, and for my thirst they gave me vinegar to drink" (Ps. 69:21 in Luke 23:36).

Psalm 31: Jesus's final breath speaks the very words of David: "Into your hands I commit my spirit" (Ps. 31:5 in Luke 23:46).

Psalm 38: Luke says that after Jesus's final breath, his friends and companions were far from him, and this resonates with Psalm 38, where the king laments, "My companions stood at a distance" (Ps. 38:11 in Luke 23:49a).

When the reader reaches the Roman centurion's statement, "Truly this man was righteous" (23:47b), it becomes obvious that Luke is showing us that Jesus is the righteous, suffering Messiah spoken of in the psalms.

Luke shows that Jesus alone is righteous and that his condemnation is an absolute miscarriage of justice. Pilate knows and declares that there are no reasonable grounds for making a charge against Jesus (23:4). When Pilate sends Jesus to Herod Antipas, Herod demonstrates only a hope that Jesus might perform a spectacle rather than any concern for justice. The criminal Barabbas—one who actually is guilty of murder and revolt—is released from prison, whereas Jesus is handed over to crucifixion (23:13–25). When Jesus is crucified between two criminals, one of them rightly states with respect to Jesus, "This man has done nothing wrong" (23:41b). Again, the point is simple enough: Jesus is the innocent, righteous one, and his death is an absolute travesty of justice.

God's response, however, is to demonstrate that humanity is in the wrong and Jesus is in the right by means of resurrecting Jesus from the dead. Many have noted, in fact, that Luke gives more emphasis to the resurrection than do the other Gospels. This theme—encapsulated in Jesus's quotation of Psalm 118:22: "The stone that the builders rejected has become the head cornerstone" (Luke 20:17b)—is reflected throughout Luke's Gospel. In a prominent example, when Jesus tells the parable of the vineyard in Luke 20:9–18, he makes it clear that the temple leaders are playing the role of Psalm 118's builders as they reject God's beloved Son (v. 13), the now rejected stone, who will be vindicated by God and made to be the chief cornerstone of God's temple and kingdom (v. 17). Thus, when Jesus is raised from the dead, he declares that the disciples should have understood that Israel's Scriptures prophetically speak of a Messiah who must suffer so that he can be raised from the dead (24:25–27, 44–49). And indeed, Luke's Gospel concludes with the resurrected Jesus offering a blessing to his disciples and then ascending into heaven (24:50–53).

Luke and Discipleship

Disciples of Jesus Are Committed Both to Spiritual Formation and to Liberative Justice

Many Christians, at least in North America, are familiar with a dichotomy between two versions of Christianity: one focused on spiritual formation, and one centered on social justice. Should disciples of Jesus focus their energies on prayer and the reading of Scripture, or should their efforts be oriented toward justice and compassion for the poor and oppressed? Of course, Luke's answer to this question is, "Yes." Disciples of Jesus who take the witness of Luke's Gospel seriously recognize that any bifurcation between spiritual formation and social justice leads to a deficient form of discipleship. This should not surprise us, given that Jesus was not only influenced by but also the climax of Israel's prophetic heritage. As Daniel Carroll has argued, Israel's prophets will allow no dichotomy between worship or piety and social justice.[1]

In fact, if you have read the preceding chapter, then you know that according to Luke's Gospel, faithful disciples recognize that following Jesus demands sharing one's possessions with those in need (3:10–14; 12:15–34; 16:19–31; 18:18–30; 19:1–10), practicing mercy and compassion even for one's enemies (6:27–36; 10:25–37), giving alms for the poor (11:41), and treating the marginalized and oppressed as friends and family (14:7–14).

You also know that Jesus pronounces blessings on the poor and hungry and woes on the rich and satisfied (6:20–26). You have seen him declare that the target of his ministry is the poor, the captive, the blind, and the oppressed (4:18–19; 14:21). You know that those who embrace Jesus are women, children, tax collectors, and the poor.

We can see here again how Jesus is the climax of Israel's prophetic heritage in that he holds together both piety and justice. Esau McCaulley states it well as he comments on Jesus's quotation of the prophet Isaiah:

For Isaiah, piety must bear fruit in justice. Jesus knew that inasmuch as his message of justice impinged on the lives of the powerful, he was liable to rejection and death. Jesus not only embraced this prophetic tradition, he declared himself the climax of it by claiming that the acceptable day of the Lord (Is 61:1–2) had arrived in him (Lk 4:14–21). . . . Jesus saw his ministry as a part of a tradition of Israel's prophets who told the truth about unfaithfulness to God that manifested itself in the oppression of the disinherited. Jesus drew on the prophets as he spoke truth to power.[2]

But, in addition to Jesus's expectation that his disciples will share his liberative and generous hospitality with others, we should also note the Lukan Jesus's emphasis on prayer and receptivity to God's word. Jesus is a model of devoted prayer to God. Only Luke indicates that during Jesus's baptism, the Holy Spirit descends on Jesus *while he is praying* (3:21–22). Luke notes that Jesus's regular habit was to frequently withdraw from the crowds to a quiet place where he could pray (5:16; 9:18; 11:1). Before Jesus calls the twelve disciples to follow him, "he went out to the mountain to pray and spent all night in prayer to God" (6:12). Preceding Jesus's transfiguration, Luke notes that "he took along Peter, John, and James and went upon the mountain to pray" (9:28). Jesus declares that he has prayed for Peter that his faith might not fail during the time of his testing (22:31–32). And, of course, Jesus prays for endurance for his mission during his final moments in the garden of Gethsemane (22:39–45).

What does Jesus pray for? Jesus teaches his disciples how to pray in the so-called Lord's Prayer: "Father, let your name be sanctified. Let your kingdom come. Give us today our daily bread. Forgive us of our sins even as we forgive everyone indebted to us. And do not bring us into temptation" (11:2–4). We can simply note here that Jesus's prayer is oriented toward God's kingdom and toward disciples being agents of forgiveness and mercy and for empowerment to endure in God's mission. As Catherine Wright states, "Prayer is essentially about aligning oneself with God's will, getting on board with the kingdom work that God is doing, and asking for grace and help in participating in that

SIDEBAR 19.1

The Witness of the "Brown Church" according to Robert Chao Romero

Robert Chao Romero has written a helpful guide to how Latino/a followers of Jesus have lived out the teachings of Jesus, often in a context of oppression and exploitation. His description of the Brown Church's most important values includes both "commitment to social justice in discipleship" and devotion to "God's Word."[a] Scholars and practitioners such as René Padilla and Samuel Escobar, among many others, founded the Fraternidad Teológica Latinoamericana (FTL) and have advocated a theology of *misión integral* ("integral mission"). FTL members argue that faithful discipleship involves "both proclamation and demonstration of the good news of the Reign of God through Christian teaching, presence, and social engagement for transformation."[b] Central to their work is the conviction that one cannot divorce proclamation of the gospel, spiritual formation, and piety from the embodiment of the gospel in a life of service, social justice, and care of the poor and the marginalized. René Padilla, commenting on Jesus's manifesto on mission presented in the Nazareth synagogue (Luke 4:18–19), notes, "The blessings of the kingdom ushered in by Jesus relate to the totality of human existence. . . . [Jesus's] proclamation is good news because it means the end of poverty through the establishment of a new order characterized by justice and love."[c]

mission."[3] We can already see here that prayer and Jesus's ministry of liberative justice are not at odds with each other; in fact, it is precisely the opposite, as prayer fuels Jesus's commitment to God's kingdom work. 19.1

We can look at Mary as an example of one who simultaneously humbly submits to God's word and expresses the conviction that God's kingdom results in divine generosity for the poor and marginalized. When Mary hears God's message from the angel, she responds with submission and trust: "I am the Lord's servant. May this be done to me according to your word" (1:38). And Elizabeth rightly pronounces a blessing on Mary for her trust in the Lord's word despite the seemingly impossible news that both of them will give birth miraculously: "Blessed is she who has believed that the Lord would fulfill what he has spoken to her" (1:45). When Mary hears the shepherds' testimony (which they receive from the Lord's angel) that Jesus is Israel's Savior and Messiah (2:8–14), Mary is said to be "treasuring up all these things in her heart and meditating on them" (2:19). Furthermore, Mary responds to God's announcement with praise and worship as she sings a hymn to God for his mighty deeds (1:46–55). So, Mary is an ideal disciple in that she listens to God's word and responds with humility, faith, meditation, and praise. But notice how Mary's ability to listen to God's word enables her to praise God for his promises to show surprising kindness to the poor and humble and to judge the wicked and the proud. Look at Luke 1:51–54 and note for whom Mary's song is good news and for whom it is bad news: "God has done a mighty deed with his arm; he has scattered *the proud* because of the thoughts of their hearts; he has toppled *the mighty* from their *thrones* and exalted *the lowly*. He has satisfied *the hungry* with good things and sent *the rich* away empty. He has helped his servant Israel, remembering his mercy" (CSB). Good news for whom? The lowly and the hungry. Bad news for whom? The proud, the mighty, those sitting on thrones, and the rich. Mary's song shouldn't be all that surprising if we've been paying attention to Luke's story. After all, Mary gets it; the priest Zechariah doesn't (at least, not at first). God bypasses political rulers like the Herods, religious leaders like the priests at the temple, and the rich. God instead communicates with the barren and elderly Elizabeth, the poor like Mary, the shepherds in the field, the tax collectors—the nobodies.

Mary is a model disciple who prays and sings and who humbly listens and responds with faith to God's word, but she is also a model disciple in

SIDEBAR 19.2

Esau McCaulley on Mary's Song and the Hope of Black Christians

Commenting on Mary's song, Esau McCaulley writes, "Is not this the hope of every Black Christian, that God might hear and save? That he might look upon those who deny us loans for houses or charge exorbitant interest rates in order to cordon us off into little pockets of poverty and say to them your oppression has been met with the advent of God? This is Mary's claim, that God reveals himself in glory by turning his attention towards those that the world deems unworthy and lifting them up to a place of honor. . . . The testimony of Mary is that even in the shadow of the empire there is a space for hope and that sometimes in that space, God calls us from the shadows to join him in his great work of salvation and liberation."[d]

that she recognizes how God's kingdom purposes will bring divine generosity, liberation, and justice for the poor, the hungry, and the humble. 19.2 19.3

Disciples of Jesus Continue His Ministry of Hospitality for All People

We have seen that Jesus shares God's generous welcome with sinners, outcasts, and the poor, often through the sharing of hospitality or table fellowship. Jesus's meals created space for sinners to encounter God's kingdom and to turn their lives to him. Jesus's hospitality meals are often marked by joy, inclusivity, and a sense of divine presence as outsiders move to being friends and family of God. The defining marker of God's people is that they are recipients of God's hospitality. But not only that. As God's friends and family, we are invited, even commanded, to be a people of hospitality to one another, ever seeking ways to extend God's welcome and friendship to all people.

Notice how Jesus commissions his disciples to continue his ministry of sharing God's hospitality with others. After Jesus's institution of the meal that will continually celebrate his sacrificial death, Luke shows how the risen presence of Jesus will continue even after his heavenly ascent. Jesus confers upon the disciples his kingdom: "You are those who have remained with me in my trials, so I confer upon you [the kingdom] just as my Father has conferred the kingdom upon me" (22:28–29). The kingdom of God has been present in Jesus's ministry, and, Jesus declares, it will continue within the ministry of the apostles. But how? Notice what Jesus says next. The disciples will rule over God's people through table fellowship: "so that you may eat and drink at my table in my kingdom, and you will sit on thrones judging the twelve tribes of Israel" (22:30). The apostles manifest their rule over the people of God through stewarding "the Lord's table." Jesus's kingdom has been manifested through table fellowship and hospitality, and now the apostles are commissioned to continue his ministry through the stewardship of food. This is

SIDEBAR 19.3

Excerpts from Marjorie Maddox, "Her Stations of the Cross"

I.
Here mothers move more than others
into Mary's mourning, each chorus
a soul full of crosses, weighted
with her child dying
continuously in the contemplation
of our contrition.

II.
That once-upon-a-time angel's voice
stretching anew her middle-aged womb,
she who once sang Magnify, O Magnify,
when all she screams for now
is mercy in her urgent rebirth
of sorrow.

....

IV.
Besides the tree, he carries
the tears of the one who carried him
beneath her Eve ribs, lifted him
into a world he breathed as good,
gone now into this God-crucified-
as-her-son-catastrophe
for salvation's sake.

....

XIV.
The hewn tomb seals her grief.
She remembers his first words,
his final prayer. All else rots
within her. They swaddle him,
implant him quickly behind stone.[e]

why Jesus provides the disciples with a reminder that his meals have been marked by humility, service, and inclusion rather than being an opportunity to advertise one's power, social status, and hierarchy. Proper stewardship of the Lord's table requires that they reject the pursuit of status that pervades benefaction (22:25). Presiding as leaders over the table is not an opportunity for "greatness" (22:24) or for acting like kings, lords, and benefactors. Standard hospitality and meal practices were opportunities for these things, but Jesus declares, "Not so for you!" (22:26). Rather, Jesus asks, "Who is greater? The one who reclines at the table or waits on the table? . . . I have been among you as one who waits on tables" (22:27). Jesus's statement recalls the meal he has served where he has given his sacrificial body and blood for their food and drink (22:14–20). Jesus has shown his "greatness" through table service. Given that the meal is to be repeated "in remembrance" of Jesus (22:19b), one can be certain that the apostles' stewardship over the food discloses the Lord to those who participate in this table.

The point is driven home through Luke's conclusion where he narrates how the risen Jesus was made known to two disciples who traveled together with him on the Emmaus Road. The two disciples see and recognize the risen Jesus *only after* they welcome the stranger into their home and the guest is transformed into the host. Just as he did both during the feeding of the five thousand and at the Last Supper, Jesus "takes" bread, "blesses" and "breaks" the bread, and "gives" it to the disciples to feed the crowd. The point is that the Emmaus meal symbolizes the active, experiential, ongoing presence of the risen Jesus, who enacts God's hospitality and welcome to his people. The presence of Jesus the divine host, then, finally initiates the disciples' recognition of the stranger's identity, moving them from a state of blindness (24:16) to one of insight and recognition: "and their eyes were opened and they recognized him" (24:31a). Shared hospitality between Jesus and the two disciples functions as the catalyst for moving the disciples from blindness to sight.

When we come to Acts 1–6, we see that the church has implemented Jesus's actions and his commission with respect to food and hospitality. The church is described as being all together "breaking bread" (2:42), "selling their property and possessions and distributing them to anyone in need" (2:45), and "breaking bread from house to house and receiving food with joy and sincerity of heart" (2:46). The indiscriminate sharing of food and the rejection of pursuing power and status, seen, for example, in Barnabas's selling of his field for the church, implement Jesus's commands to share one's wealth and extend welcome to all people (4:36–37). The book of Acts, in fact, frequently draws attention to the church's following the way of Jesus through hospitality, sharing possessions, and table fellowship (see also 4:32–35; 6:1–7; 10:1–48; 16:11–15; 28:1–10).

As Eric Barreto has noted, Luke and "Acts can help us imagine that our differences are gifts from God, not problems to overcome or obstacles on the way to becoming God's church."[4] There are many practical implications that followers of Jesus might draw from this. First, if Jesus commissioned his disciples to continue his ministry of hospitality, and if the risen Jesus continues to share his saving presence through table fellowship, then disciples of Jesus should look for ways to practice his ministry of hospitality for all people. As I have argued elsewhere, this may simply take the form of looking for opportunities to institute shared meals or potlucks as part of the church's communal life where Jesus's own table practices are remembered.[5]

Second, disciples of Jesus can extend Jesus-like hospitality only if they reject fear of strangers and the perpetuation of harmful stereotypes. One of the greatest barriers today standing in the way of the "communal power" of hospitality is fear. Henri Nouwen observes, "Our society seems to be increasingly full of fearful, defensive, aggressive people anxiously clinging to their property and inclined to look at their surrounding world with suspicion, always expecting an enemy to suddenly appear, intrude and do harm."[6] This fearful posture does not correspond to Jesus's way of life. Jesus grants divine hospitality to "the other" without distinction, and this is exemplified in his welcome to sinners and the religious, men and women, rich and poor, Jew and gentile. These were the binaries of Jesus's day; perhaps in our day it would mean that Jesus extends divine hospitality to white, Black, Asian, and Latino/a; to evangelical, pentecostal, Catholic, Orthodox, and mainline; to the typically and the differently abled; to city dwellers, suburbanites, and country folk. These meals are marked by joy, generosity, inclusivity, the rejection of status and hierarchy, and, most importantly, the experiential and saving presence of the Messiah among his people. Jesus shows no apprehension or fear of associating with the stigmatized among society. And, further, he is markedly unimpressed by appeals to ethnicity, formal religious observance, and gender as means of social worth. Thus, divine welcome does not correspond to some type of merit or preexisting social worth, for Jesus's extension of divine hospitality appears as indiscriminate—precisely the feature of his ministry that annoys so many of Israel's religious leaders.

So how is it that divine hospitality enables us to provide a witness to our culture of fear? Perhaps the following exhortations and encouragements may help stimulate our imaginations. First, we have seen that Jesus calls his disciples to be a people defined by love of both neighbor and enemy, as well as a community committed to habits and practices of peacemaking. But in order to do this, we need to have the honesty to come together to name our fears. If we truly want to confront our fears, then part of this process should involve real relationships and firsthand knowledge of other cultures, ethnicities, religions, and experiences.

Second, disciples of Jesus and churches should scrutinize their usually unstated commitments to safety and exclusive boundaries that are privileged over the consistent witness that the church is a community that embraces stigma. Most of us are too quick to take culturally constructed categories for others as the basis for our lack of interactions with those we deem to be unsafe, uncomfortable, contagious, or too sinful. The consistent witness of the Scriptures, especially Luke-Acts, is that those stigmatized and negatively stereotyped by the broader society are precisely those who are the recipients of divine hospitality. Heather Vacek, author of *Madness: American Protestant Responses to Mental Illness*, states that if the church is to embrace its identity as the recipient of divine hospitality, it will have to "resist social norms contrary to Christian belief and practice, to eat with outcasts and tax collectors, with sinners, and with those who fail, and to remember that Christian identity is defined by baptism into the body of Christ, not by adherence (or lack of adherence) to social norms. . . . Being damned by association should be an expected part of Christian witness, but it is a reality difficult to embrace in a society, like modern America, where a safer, more sanitized Christian belief and practice are deemed normative."[7]

The church's mission is stunted when it is overwhelmed by its acceptance of certain societal stereotypes of individuals labeled as dangerous, risky, or worthless. It is similarly stunted when the church fails to listen to the experiences of others, when we do nothing about structural racism and the perpetuation of dehumanizing stereotypes and violence against persons of color, to name just two examples. The church shares in Jesus's hospitality when we are known as fellow friends and allies of the mentally ill, current and former prisoners, refugees and immigrants, and all who are oppressed and marginalized.

Third, disciples of Jesus have a vocation to both speak and act against those forces in our society that peddle and market fear toward deadly ends. I believe that churches continue to provide a witness to Jesus's hospitality when they are awakened to the injustice and continued racism of our current penal system, when they rise up to seek more just alternatives for crime and punishment in our society, when they speak out against exploitative legislation, and when they actively seek ways to reintegrate prisoners into society. In efforts to assist prisoners, churches can partner with organizations that hold Bible studies, lead educational seminars and classes, and, most importantly, build friendships through regular visits and written letters. One should not underestimate the importance of simple but consistent face-to-face visits with those who are incarcerated, as a form of Christian hospitality. Organizationally, with respect to immigration, it is encouraging that many Christian organizations repudiate popular xenophobic rhetoric by debunking many of the myths about immigrants that produce fear and suspicion, actively resettling refugees, providing tangible care for immigrants, and advocating for immigration reform. Many of these organizations have done so precisely because they have rediscovered the importance of the biblical tradition of hospitality toward the stranger. There are also very practical steps that ordinary followers of Jesus can take to enact hospitality to the immigrant. Christians should evaluate political rhetoric and candidates running for public office within the framework of what the Scriptures say about the immigrant rather than being guided by personal economic, national, and racial ideologies. The ethnic and cultural stereotyping as well as scapegoating techniques that blame society's ills on migrants should be rejected and called out as non-Christian fear-mongering. Christians should educate themselves about migration—its causes, legislation, and personal stories of immigrants—so that they can advocate for just and equitable legislation regarding national immigration policies. Christians must also reckon with globalization and the recent transformations in the global economy and take seriously the very real consequences that the policies of their own country have had on would-be migrants. It takes work and education to realize how in our globalized economy our own lifestyle and consumer choices as well as our nation's public policy (past and present) can create the necessary conditions for those seeking to migrate to the United States. And churches can engage in meaningful relationships with immigrants and refugees by volunteering with programs such as World Relief, Church World Service, Catholic Legal Immigration Network, and more. All kinds of ministry opportunities are available to those who would take the risk of welcoming the immigrant into one's church, family, and home.

Disciples of Jesus Are Humble Because They Live out of God's Mercy Rather Than Human Status and Achievement

One temptation that is nearly universally endemic to human existence is the desire to suppose that one's identity is achieved rather than given. Today people often pursue personal worth and value through putting themselves in a position to consume and obtain luxury goods and services, sculpting and engineering their body for maximum beauty and health, projecting their own personal style or brand through their clothing, and advertising—often through social media—that they are always insiders and active participants who are "in the know." Or, perhaps if they are a bit more "religious," they find their identity and value in their particular and zealously performed spiritual practices or their theological insights and traditions. Jesus's teachings in the Gospel of Luke are a powerful rebuke of thinking that our personal value and worth are something we achieve or work for. Humility requires an understanding that God is not impressed with humanity's attempts to climb the social ladder, outperform others in terms of religious zeal, or procure wealth. Jesus directly rejects humanity's preoccupation with procuring status and honor in the eyes of others. To the Pharisees, he declares, "You are those who justify yourself before humans, but God knows your hearts; that which is highly exalted among humans is an abomination before God" (Luke 16:15). To those who seek places of high honor and status, Jesus teaches, "Those who exalt themselves will be humbled, and those who humble themselves will be exalted" (14:11).

Jesus affirms that human value and worth are something graciously gifted to us by God. We have already seen that Jesus consistently extends God's generosity and hospitable welcome to all people regardless of status or identity markers—rich or poor, male or female, adult or child, religious insiders or tax collectors and sinners, and so forth.

This is why an essential character trait of Jesus's disciples is humility. Humility here is to be thought of not as a self-deprecating or self-demeaning posture but rather as a grateful recognition that God's love in the person of Jesus is the sole basis of one's identity. Humility requires that one also undergo the painful process (at least for many) of competitively trying to outperform others. Catherine Wright states this dynamic well: "In Luke's Gospel, the religious leaders' negative depiction is linked . . . to the tenacity with which they cling to their false selves and to their blindness concerning their own spiritual state. . . . When we live out of a false self, we are reduced to a life of petty competitiveness and anxious attempts to bolster our own honor and importance in society and even with God. Luke's ideal of humility centers around a true sense of self in relationship to God."[8]

This dynamic is depicted clearly in two Lukan parables. In the parable of the Pharisee and the tax collector (18:9–14), we are told that Jesus directs the parable to "some who trusted in themselves that they were righteous and despised everyone else" (18:9). The parable depicts a Pharisee who is standing while praying and criticizing the praying tax collector. His gratitude is for his own religious observances: "I thank you, God, that I am not like other people—greedy, unrighteous, adulterers—or even like this tax collector. I fast twice a week, and I give a tenth of everything I get" (vv. 10–11). He is the embodiment of pride, but he is also foolish as he supposes that his identity and acceptance before God are predicated on being better than other people. The tax collector, however, embodies humility. He prays at a distance, humbly recognizes his need for grace and forgiveness, and appeals to God, "God, have mercy on me, a sinner" (v. 13). The parable concludes with Jesus claiming, "Everyone who exalts themselves will be humbled, but everyone who humbles themselves will be exalted" (v. 14b). 19.4

With respect to the parable of the prodigal son (15:11–32), we remember that the Pharisees and scribes are grumbling because Jesus is extending hospitality to the wrong people—tax collectors and sinners (15:1–2). This "grumbling" is a frequent Lukan motif that shows up when the religious leaders are angry at Jesus for associating with the nonreligious (5:30; 7:34; 19:7). And this is the stance taken by the elder son, who will not rejoice that his younger brother has encountered his father's mercy and welcome. Whereas the younger son is indeed humble ("Father, I have sinned against heaven in your eyes. I'm no longer worthy to be called your son" [15:18b–19a, 21]), the elder son essentially rebukes his father for being unfair in extending his lavish love and welcome to his repentant son. The elder son is angry and refuses to join in the celebration (15:28). His response to his father is latent with obvious implications for the Pharisees and scribes: "Look, I have been slaving many years for you, and I have never disobeyed your orders, yet you never gave me a goat so that I could celebrate with my friends" (15:29). The statement is the antithesis of humility, for the elder brother believes that his "slaving" for his father and his obedience to the commands should result in some special favor that exalts him over his younger brother. The older brother, if he is to truly experience his father's love, will need the humility to recognize that it is not his honor, status, or religious observance that are the basis of his identity. Disciples of Jesus embrace humility because it is the requisite posture for those who recognize that they are mere recipients of God's merciful kindness and acceptance.

Disciples of Jesus Reject Greed and Share Their Resources with Others

Disciples of Jesus also humbly live out of God's merciful provisions by rejecting greed and hoarding. Stated positively, this means that disciples of Jesus recognize that what they have is a gift from God, and therefore they are both grateful to God for his gifts and freed to share his resources with those in need. Jesus's depiction of God is of one who is generously abundant in his sharing of gifts with his people. In fact, Jesus says that God is even "gracious to the ungrateful and the evil" (Luke 6:35b). If God provides for ravens, then his disciples can trust that

SIDEBAR 19.4

Denise Levertov, "The Avowal"

"The Avowal" is a beautiful poem that reflects on the gracious Creator God's care and sustenance. The speaker imagines a swimmer peacefully resting in a back float on the water. She prays that so she too might rest in the arms of the Spirit, "knowing no effort earns / that all-surrounding grace."[f]

God will provide for them (12:24–28). In fact, Jesus teaches his disciples to entrust their future needs to God when they pray: "Give us each day our daily bread" (11:3).

This type of humility rejects the common belief that resources are scarce and therefore must be hoarded in order for our lives to be safe and secure. The accumulation of money and possessions is often pursued out of the wrongheaded belief that they will make our lives secure. "If I can just get enough money to have a big-enough safety net for my family, we'll be secure. If I can just get enough money to make sure my children can afford an elite college education, our family will be in good shape." This type of thinking, however, clearly represents the thought process of the rich landowner with barns in Jesus's parable in Luke 12:16–21. But the fatal flaw in the landowner's reasoning is that no amount of money or possessions can protect him from death. Some of the most chilling words of the entire Bible occur when God says to the man whose life has been required of him, "So, all these things that you've worked for—now whose will they be?" (v. 21b). Wealth and possessions do not guard against death.

The life that God intends for his people does not consist in possessions (12:15). Greed tricks us into thinking that life or happiness is about food, drink, houses, cars, net worth and investments, education, and pedigree. Greed tricks us into thinking we will be happy when we finally have all the possessions we want. Then, finally, we'll be able to say to ourselves, "Let's rest, eat, drink, and enjoy life!" (12:19). Marketing tactics bank on the fact that we are not content, not satisfied with what we have. Our economy banks on the fact that you will not be satisfied with what you purchase. In fact, our economy banks on turning you into an addict—someone addicted to buying, discarding what you've bought, and buying again.[9] We call it "shopping." We buy and consume in order to discard and then buy and consume again—and we like it. But at the end of the day, we know that sooner or later we'll grow tired and bored of these things and that the happiness they promise is simply an illusion.

Greed is also deadly because it blinds us to the needs of others. After the rich landowner has had a bumper crop and doesn't know what to do with all of the produce, he says, "What should I do, since I don't have anywhere to store my crops?" (12:17). His question invites us to give a better answer than the one he gave. Let's look at a brief sketch of his societal context:

- Approximately 25–33 percent of the population was "absolutely poor"—that is, barely surviving, but only through dependence on others, often through begging—and suffering from severe malnutrition.

- Death by starvation was a very real prospect for a good percentage of the population.
- The upper class—those who didn't live at subsistence level and probably didn't need to worry about going hungry—made up only 2–3 percent.
- Most small farmers made enough of a profit only to pay their inordinate taxes to the empire and the priestly authority and then hope somehow to provide for themselves and their family.

For this landowner to then declare, in that society, "I know what I'll do. I will build more barns" might sound like good business sense, but for Jesus it actually demonstrates a remarkable inability to see or care about the very real needs of others. In other words, he could have said, "I have more than enough. I can use the surplus to share with others." But the man's posture is *entirely* oriented toward himself, his own needs, his own wants. When we are like this man, preoccupied with *ourselves*, preoccupied with acquiring more possessions, daydreaming about our vacations and cars and home renovations, working hard to make our lives more secure and protected from vulnerabilities, then the likelihood of us using our resources for sharing with others becomes slim; in fact, the likelihood of us even seeing and encountering those in need becomes almost zero. We have already seen in Luke's Gospel how Jesus teaches us that the antidote to greed and apathy is the sharing of our possessions with one another (e.g., 11:41; 14:12–14).

Summary of Main Points on the Gospel of Luke

1. While the Gospel of Luke is technically anonymous, both Irenaeus and the Muratorian Fragment identify the Gospel's author, along with its sequel the Acts of the Apostles, as Luke, the so-called beloved physician and traveling companion of Paul. In addition, all of our ancient manuscripts circulated with a superscription identifying the author as Luke.
2. Luke's preface to his Gospel (1:1–4) indicates his intention to write a historiographical narrative about Jesus that will improve on his predecessors'. While we do not know the exact predecessors or sources to which Luke refers, we can see how he respects but also transforms the Gospel of Mark (along with either Q or Matthew). For example, Luke has access to more testimonies about Jesus, including a vast

array of Jesus's vivid parables and stories. Luke also begins at what he sees as the proper starting point (i.e., Jesus's birth) and concludes at what he sees as the proper end point (i.e., Jesus's resurrection appearances and ascension). Luke also connects the story of Jesus with the story of the church by writing his sequel, the book of Acts. Luke also sees himself as improving on the style, narrative sequencing, and inaccuracies of his predecessors.

3. Dating any of our Gospels is difficult and speculative, but there are good reasons for dating Luke's Gospel shortly after Mark's Gospel but before the Jewish War (66–70 CE). This would suggest a date in the mid-60s.
4. Luke's implied audience likely consists of somewhat-educated urban folk who are both knowledgeable of Greco-Roman cultures and deeply sympathetic to the Jewish people and the Scriptures of Israel.
5. The structure of Luke's Gospel is straightforward and reflects his stated purpose to craft an orderly narrative (1:1–4). Luke depicts Jesus as an itinerant journeyer in the travel narrative (9:51–19:44) who is often dependent on the hospitality of others. One of his favorite techniques is the use of parallelism to make connections between different characters. While our focus is only on the Gospel, the text functions as the first part of a two-volume story, and the Acts of the Apostles can provide insights into Luke's agenda. Luke often aligns his audience with his point of view by showing his characters rejoicing, praising, and giving glory to God.
6. Four narrative themes were examined.
   a. Luke depicts Jesus as the climax of Israel's prophets, and this allows him to articulate Jesus's message and ministry as focused on repentance and calling God's people to practice mercy and love for one's neighbors as well as to explain why Jesus is rejected by his own people.
   b. Hospitality permeates the Gospel. Jesus functions as the divine host who extends God's hospitality to all people through his own meals, healings, and teachings. He thereby seeks to transform people's understanding such that they now see strangers as friends and family of one another and of God. Jesus is also depicted as a vulnerable guest who reveals his identity in the context of hospitality settings.
   c. Jesus's kingdom teachings are demanding and challenging as they call God's people to show the fruits of repentance by sharing their possessions with one another, by listening to the Torah and the

prophets and their call for mercy and love, and by caring especially for the vulnerable, marginalized, and poor.

   d. Jesus is rejected by humans and thereby condemned to death, but he is resurrected and thereby vindicated by God as the truly righteous one. Luke draws on the Davidic psalms to depict Jesus as the righteous, suffering Messiah.

7. Luke's Jesus calls his disciples to focus on prayer and social justice, extend hospitality to all types of people, embrace humility out of an awareness that their identity is a gift from God and not a personal achievement, and reject greed by sharing their possessions and resources with others.

John and History

John's Place in the History of Early Christianity

The influence of the Gospel of John's testimony to Jesus is "so simple and powerful that its influence on Christian consciousness is unsurpassed."[1] It has nourished countless Christians with simple but profound statements: "God so loved the world . . ." (John 3:16), "You must be born again" (3:7), "Let not your hearts be troubled . . ." (14:1); with memorable characters such as Nicodemus (3:1–15), the Samaritan woman (4:4–42), the healed blind man (chap. 9), and Lazarus, Mary, and Martha (11:1–44); and with philosophical claims like "In the beginning was the Word . . ." (1:1) and "No one has greater love than this, that he lay down his life for his friends" (15:13).

As we begin our study of John's Gospel, we should pause to reflect on how remarkable it is that our canonical Fourfold Gospel includes three different Gospels, the Synoptic Gospels, that clearly are related to one another, and also another Gospel, the Gospel of John, which tells a story about *the same Jesus of Nazareth* but with some remarkable differences. In other words, John's Gospel depicts Jesus as teaching, healing, entering into conflict with the temple authorities, claiming to have a unique relationship with God the Father, and so forth. Jesus's ministry is preceded by John the Baptist. Jesus is crucified, buried, and raised from the dead. He commissions his disciples to continue his ministry. There are, then, good reasons for affirming what church tradition and the Christian canon have maintained: the Jesus of the Synoptics and the Jesus of the Gospel of John are the same Jesus. And yet there are, of course, some remarkable differences. We will return to this in the next section in more detail, but for now we can simply note that John overlaps with the Synoptic Gospels only about 10 percent of the time. Most of the stories and speeches that we find in John's Gospel have no counterpart in the Synoptics.

Despite John's differences from the Synoptic Gospels, we find that John's Gospel was well known, frequently used, and read together with the Synoptics in the early church. In chapter 4, we examined how Irenaeus, at around 180 CE, provides our first clear articulation of Matthew, Mark, Luke, and John as the only apostolic, true, and authoritative Gospels for the church (*Against Heresies* 3.11.8). But the roots of John's inclusion here are likely much earlier. As one expert notes, "The practice of reading the four Gospels together as interdependent and mutually interpreting . . . began at an early time."[2] Early codices confirm that John was bound together with Luke ($\mathfrak{P}^{75}$ [late second century]) and bound with all three Synoptic Gospels ($\mathfrak{P}^{45}$ [third century]). Early church writers, in fact, use both Synoptic and Johannine language when they pass on Jesus's teachings and life events (e.g., Ignatius of Antioch). Both Theophilus of Antioch and Tatian produced Gospel harmonies based on the canonical Gospels. Justin Martyr (mid-second century) draws on John 3:3–5 to set forth his thoughts on baptism (*First Apology* 61.4), and Clement of Alexandria refers to John's Gospel as a "spiritual" Gospel (Eusebius, *Ecclesiastical History* 6.14.7). Our earliest canon list, the Muratorian Fragment, includes John's Gospel as the fourth Gospel. Origen claims that the four canonical Gospels are the firstfruits of the Christian Scriptures, but it is the Gospel of John that is "the first fruits of the Gospels" (*Commentary on the Gospel of John* 1.23).[3]

John's Gospel was an important resource for a variety of vastly differently inclined Christian groups.[4] Origen's commentary on the Gospel of John is, in part, a reaction against a prior Valentinian reading of John's Gospel by Heracleon. Many so-called orthodox theologians engaged John's Gospel (particularly 1:1–5, 14–18) at length and with great frequency in order to clarify christological and trinitarian debates. John Chrysostom, for example, left behind 88 sermons on John, while 124 of Augustine's sermons on John remain. Augustine draws on John's Gospel repeatedly to set forth some of his primary teachings, such as the Trinity, the role of love in the Christian life, and the renunciation of works in soteriology. Polycarp, Justin, and Athanasius are a few of the many so-called orthodox theologians who draw on John's *logos* Christology and his incarnational claims to develop the orthodox doctrine of Christ. Cyril of Alexandria penned a lengthy commentary on John's Gospel in the early fifth century CE and repeatedly argued against pagans, Jews, and other Christian groups that Jesus is the eternal Son of God by nature who has had fellowship with the Holy Spirit from eternity.[5]

The Composition of John's Gospel

A quick reading of John's Gospel reveals that there are indeed many similarities with the Synoptic Gospels. Jesus's ministry is preceded by that of

John the Baptist (John 1:19–34; 3:22–36). Jesus frequently engages in miraculous healings (e.g., 5:1–16; 11:1–44). He is a powerful teacher who captivates his audience, although his miracles and teachings often result in conflict with the religious authorities (e.g., 5:17–47; 9:1–41). Others speculate that Jesus is Israel's Messiah (1:25, 41; 7:41), the Son of God (1:34, 49), and the final prophet (1:21; 7:40). Jesus performs a controversial act of symbolic judgment in the temple (2:13–21). Jesus celebrates a final meal with his disciples on or near the Passover and prepares them for his impending departure (chaps. 13–17). The story climaxes with a passion narrative wherein Jesus is rejected by his people and handed over to Roman authorities, is crucified, is raised from the dead, and appears to his disciples (18:1–21:25). And there are multiple stories and sayings that do seem to have a Synoptic counterpart. For example, Jesus miraculously feeds a multitude (John 6:1–15; see Mark 6:32–44) and passes by his disciples while walking on the sea (John 6:16–21; see Mark 6:45–51). Some of Jesus's sayings in John are distinctly reminiscent of, and likely show some type of relationship with, sayings in the Synoptic Gospels (compare John 12:25 and 13:20 with Matt. 10:39–40).

And yet the differences are striking. In terms of apparent omissions, John's Jesus engages in no exorcisms, is not in dialogue with the Pharisees, is not transfigured on the mountain, does not undergo baptism by John, and is not tempted by the devil in the wilderness—to name only a few. There is no divine conception or birth narrative of the type we find in Matthew 1–2 and Luke 1–2. And, of course, many of John's most beloved stories are found only in his Gospel, such as Jesus's turning of water to wine (2:1–11), his encounter with Nicodemus (3:1–15), his encounter with the Samaritan woman (4:4–42), his raising of Lazarus from the dead (11:1–44), and his washing of the disciples' feet (13:1–20). Mark's "messianic secret," wherein Jesus often is depicted as deflecting public acclaim away from himself, seems to find no place in John's Gospel, where Jesus frequently makes public claims about his personal identity, saying, "I am . . ." (e.g., 6:35; 8:12; 10:7; 11:25). Jesus's ministry takes place over the span of three years in John's Gospel as he is depicted as celebrating three Passover festivals (2:13; 6:4; 11:55) and making multiple journeys between Judea and Galilee, whereas in the Synoptics Jesus makes only one visit to Jerusalem to celebrate the Passover.

Some have noticed that the surprising differences between John and the Synoptics indicate that John's Gospel is a "maverick Gospel" that was written in order to compete with and even upend the traditions of the Synoptic Gospels.[6] The claim that John's Gospel was written to compete with the Synoptic Gospels is often coupled with the recognition that many sectarian (nonmainstream) Christian groups (often associated with Gnostic tendencies) used John's Gospel.

So, the similarities and differences between John and the Synoptics do indeed raise some difficult questions. Did John write with knowledge of any of the Synoptic Gospels or did he write independently of them? If John did know of one (or more) of the Synoptic Gospels, did he intend his work as a supplement and complement to the Synoptic Gospels or perhaps, rather, as a replacement of them? And what can we say about the authorship of the Gospel? Answers to these questions are difficult and require a great deal of nuance. Here I can only offer a sketch of what I find most convincing.

I can offer an answer to the first two questions with the following statement: *John writes a theologically and spiritually engaged narrative of Jesus that stands on its own as a coherent account of the life of Jesus, but it also likely assumes an audience familiar with Synoptic-like traditions about Jesus and can, therefore, be read as a complementary supplement to the Synoptic Gospels.* While I will suggest the likelihood of this point based on internal evidence with the Gospel primarily, it also conforms to the claim of the second-century church father Clement of Alexandria, who states, "John, last of all, perceiving that what had reference to the body of the gospel of our Savior was sufficiently detailed, and being encouraged by his familiar friends, and urged by the spirit, wrote a spiritual gospel" (Eusebius, *Ecclesiastical History* 6.14.7).

I certainly do not mean to imply that the Synoptic Gospels are nontheological or nonspiritual, but most have recognized that John is especially intent to draw out the theological implications of Jesus's life and teachings—with a heavy dose of symbolism. Let me give just a handful of examples. First, rather than writing a traditional birth narrative, John situates Jesus within God's eternal and cosmic purposes from the beginning of time in his prologue (1:1–18). John makes it plain that Jesus is the true and ultimate revelation of the invisible God (1:14, 18; 10:30). Second, the presence of the incarnate Logos results in an eschatological urgency for individuals in John. Since the light has come into the world, the eschatological judgment is a *present* reality, and one's response to Jesus determines whether one experiences life and death even now (3:18–21; 5:19–30). The final resurrection of the dead is certainly affirmed, and yet Jesus himself is "the resurrection and the life" (11:25), and so those who trust in Jesus are able to have "eternal life" *now* (1:4–5; 3:16–21; 17:3). Third, as we will see in more detail in the next chapter, Jesus is not just a miracle worker but rather is one who performs signs that reveal the divine glory and are intended to draw people to a true faith (see 2:11–12, 23–25). Fourth, almost everything in John's Gospel has a symbolic function—light, water, wine, Jewish festivals, temple, bread—that reveals something about Jesus's identity and work. Fifth, John seems intent to develop the spiritual significance of the practices of the church. The wine of the new covenant (2:1–11) and the bread of life (6:26–71) are given deeper meaning as they are rooted in the ongoing presence of the crucified and risen Jesus. Many more examples could be offered, but the basic point should be clear enough: John's Gospel offers a spiritual and theologically substantive story of Jesus.

In fact, it may actually be the case that John is "transposing" some of the claims of the Synoptic Gospels into a new theological "key" (see sidebar 20.1).[7] That is, John is drawing out the spiritual and theological implications of Jesus's life and ministry as narrated by the Synoptic Gospels.[8] 20.1

While John's Gospel is fully capable of standing on its own literary integrity in its narrative account of Jesus, there are good reasons for thinking that John had *some* access to either Synoptic-like oral traditions about Jesus or (at least) one of the Synoptic Gospels and was crafted to supplement (not replace) them.

First, as mentioned earlier, John follows the basic plotline, ordering, and arrangement of events in the life of Jesus.[9] In both John and the Synoptic tradition, the story commences with John the Baptist's preparatory ministry; then Jesus comes into conflict with the authorities due to his controversial ministry of teaching and miraculous signs and wonders, calls and prepares a group of disciples to continue his ministry, is tried before the religious authorities, is crucified, and makes resurrection appearances to his disciples. More details could drive this point home with more force, but these should suffice to justify the claim that John very likely had access to some Synoptic Gospel traditions (whether in oral or textual form). There are also clearly overlapping traditions with respect to stories such as Jesus's

SIDEBAR 20.1

Transposing the Synoptics into a Johannine Key

Synoptic Gospels	John's Gospel
Kingdom of God	Eternal life
Lord's Supper (Matt. 26:26–29; Mark 14:22–25; Luke 22:15–20)	Eating Jesus's flesh and drinking his blood (John 6:53–58)
Last Supper (Matt. 26:17–35; Mark 14:12–31; Luke 22:7–34)	Farewell Discourse (John 13–17)
Jesus's transfiguration (Matt. 17:1–9; Mark 9:2–10; Luke 9:28–36)	Jesus's revelation of the Father's glory
Prediction of the temple's destruction	Death and resurrection of Jesus's body as the temple
Miracles	Signs
Cross as an instrument of shame	Cross as the revelation of glory and honor
Historical Jewish lawsuit	Cosmic lawsuit
Virgin birth of Jesus (Matt. 1:18–25; Luke 1:30–38)	Eternal preexistence of Jesus (John 1:1–18)
Exorcism of demons	Satan as constant chief antagonist of Jesus

cleansing of the temple, the feeding of the multitude, the triumphal entry, the woman's anointing of Jesus at Bethany, and Judas's betrayal of Jesus. And some of the Johannine Jesus's sayings show a clear relation with Synoptic counterparts (compare John 2:19 with Mark 14:58; and John 11:25 with Mark 8:34–35).

Second, notice how John's two concluding authorial claims about his Gospel-writing process openly acknowledge the legitimate possibility of prior Gospel writings (and even future Gospel narratives).

> So, then, Jesus performed many other signs in the presence of his disciples, which have not been written in this book. But these things have been written so that you might believe that the Messiah the Son of God is Jesus, and so that by believing you might have life in his name. (20:30–31)

> And Jesus performed many other things, which if every one of them had been written down, I suppose that not even the entire world could contain the books to be written. (21:25)

Notice here that the author notes something about his task of narrative selection and purpose. There are many traditions—stories and speeches—about Jesus that he might draw on or that another Gospel writer might have drawn on. But his narrative goal consists in selecting material that will fulfill his authorial goal of showing how Jesus's signs have as their purpose the identification of Jesus of Nazareth as the life-giving messianic Son of God. It may strike us as strange that the author would not pass on traditions such as Jesus's teaching in the Sermon on the Mount (Matt. 5–7), his temptation in the garden of Gethsemane (Mark 14:32–42), and his resurrection appearance on the Emmaus Road (Luke 24:13–35). But John likely is indicating to his readers that there are many important and famous stories about Jesus that he will not include precisely so that he can offer his unique take on Jesus and accomplish his specific purpose (20:30–31).[10] Thus, John's purpose statements may indicate that his account is intended for those who are familiar with the Synoptic Gospel traditions but that the author has drawn on different stories and sayings of Jesus in order to communicate his specific purposes.

Third, we should take note of places where there are apparent interlocking connections between John and the Synoptic Gospels.[11] Richard Bauckham has drawn attention to instances where John offers a parenthetical comment that would be pointless *apart* from its function to make an interlocking connection between John's Gospel and Mark's. So, for example, in John 3:24 John offers a parenthetical comment related to John the

Baptist's ministry of baptism: "John had not yet been thrown into prison." The point is so banal that most readers are likely to move right over it without even recognizing the apparent pointlessness of the statement. In other words, of course John the Baptist isn't in prison if he's baptizing people! But if John wrote for an audience that had some familiarity with the Synoptic traditions (whether in written or oral form), then John may be making "a point about the chronological relationship of Jesus' ministry to John's."[12] In other words, the statement in John 3:24 locates all that occurs in the Johannine Jesus's Judean ministry in John 1:19–4:43 as taking place before John's imprisonment, which is mentioned in Mark 1:14.[13]

We can also note how John can refer to Jesus's calling of the twelve disciples—an event that John's Gospel never actually narrates—as if it is something that his readers already know about. Stated differently, it is likely that John 6:67–71 presumes readers who know Mark 3:13–19. The quick and enthusiastic response of the disciples to Jesus in Mark 1:16–20 makes more sense in light of what is narrated in John 1:19–52, where the disciples would have had some prior interactions with Jesus. John's account of John the Baptist's testimony about seeing the Spirit descend on Jesus (John 1:31–34) likely presumes the reader's familiarity with the Synoptic account of Jesus's baptism. While the Markan Jesus is accused of making violent threats of judgment against the temple (Mark 14:58), it is only John's Gospel that provides an explanatory statement: "Destroy this temple, and in three days I will raise it up" (John 2:19). More examples could be added to make the point here, that there are significant interlocking connections between John and Synoptic traditions that thereby support the contention that John was written not to replace or compete with the Synoptic Gospels but rather as a complementary supplement to them—a supplement that, nevertheless, has its own literary integrity and stands on its own.

One of the most challenging questions regarding the composition of John's Gospel concerns the sources that John might have used and whether the Gospel underwent stages of editing. We have already noted that John's Gospel has its own coherent literary integrity, even if it knew and drew on some Synoptic traditions and sources. It certainly is possible that John used a "signs source" (composed of seven miracle stories, such as 2:1–12; 4:46–54; 5:1–9; see 20:30–31) or prior teaching source(s) (as the basis for chaps. 13–17), but if these sources did exist, John has very successfully rewritten them into his Gospel such that the final product can be read as a coherent piece of literature.[14] More advanced studies may also examine the difficult question of whether the Gospel underwent stages of editing. For example, the final chapter of John (chap. 21) reads like an epilogue that was added after the rest of the writing of the Gospel; the prologue (1:1–18) might reflect an earlier Christian hymn; and some other oddities might provide evidence that John's Gospel underwent editorial reworking in stages (e.g., after a long discourse at the Passover supper [chap. 14], Jesus says, "Rise up, let us go from here" [14:31b], but then he continues his discourse for three more chapters [chaps. 15–17] before arriving at the garden).[15]

Finally, we need to address the question of the authorship of John's Gospel. As is the case with the Synoptics, John's Gospel is technically anonymous. The superscriptions in the earliest manuscripts are unanimous in attributing the writing to John. The Gospel writing itself doesn't refer to a "John" as its author, but it does almost force the reader to speculate about its authorship. One of the opening episodes of the text is the story of unnamed disciples who are invited by Jesus to "come and see" where Jesus is staying (1:35–39). Later there is the mention of another unnamed disciple—one who is known to the high priest—who is with Simon Peter at Jesus's trial (18:15–18). The Gospel also speaks of "the disciple whom Jesus loved" (13:23; 19:26; 20:2; 21:7, 20)—the Beloved Disciple—someone who claims to have direct eyewitness testimony to the events described. The Gospel's conclusion contains this statement: "This is the disciple who testifies about these things and who wrote them, and we know that his testimony is true" (21:24).

At key points within the narrative the Beloved Disciple appears as one uniquely close to Jesus and important among the disciples (see 13:23), as one who is a witness to Jesus's crucifixion (19:25–27), and who, having outrun Peter, believes upon seeing the empty tomb (20:2–10). "The one who has seen these things has given testimony, and his testimony is true, and that one knows that what he says is true, in order that you may believe" (19:35). As such, the claims of the Beloved Disciple function to validate the story's unique testimony to the truth of the narrative as he articulates it.[16]

Many have attempted to identify the Beloved Disciple with a known historical figure (see sidebar 2.4). Perhaps the most frequently named guesses are those of Lazarus, Thomas, John the Elder, and the disciple John the son of Zebedee.[17] Others have suggested that the Beloved Disciple functions as a literary device that symbolizes the ideal readers of the Gospel. David Ford notes that the Beloved Disciple "is the model of discipleship, defined by being loved by Jesus, resting on the breast of Jesus as Jesus does on his Father's, and testifying to Jesus."[18] There is, however, little internal evidence to adjudicate the matter with any type of certainty. So, many have turned to church tradition, and here the majority of the texts assume that the Gospel was written by John the disciple (the son of Zebedee). In the second century, Irenaeus wrote, "Afterwards, John, *the disciple of the Lord, who also leaned upon his breast*, did himself publish a Gospel during his residence at

Ephesus in Asia" (*Against Heresies* 3.1.1).[19] The weight of early church tradition, among both "orthodox" and "sectarian" Christian groups, strongly supports the identification of the author with the disciple John. While it is difficult to determine with any high degree of certainty, many recent scholars have pointed out that it makes good sense that the author would be one of Jesus's select disciples (6:67–70), since he was reclining on Jesus's breast at the Last Supper (13:23) and claims to be present at important moments of Jesus's ministry. Whoever the author was, his knowledge of Judean customs, festivals, geography, and Hebrew indicates one well acquainted with first-century Israel (e.g., 1:41; 2:6; 4:2–5, 20–25; 6:4; 10:23; 12:20; 18:13).

The Location, Date, and Audience of John's Gospel

Since the discovery of Rylands Library papyrus $\mathfrak{P}^{52}$, a fragment that contains bits of several lines from John 18 and dates to about 100–150 CE, most scholars now date the Gospel of John to the late first century, still with the assumption that it likely postdates all three Synoptic Gospels. We have noted that the Gospel demonstrates accurate knowledge of Palestinian geography, topography, customs, and language; some have, as a result, concluded that the Gospel was written in Palestine. However, second century (and later) church tradition has postulated that the Gospel was written by (the apostle) John in Ephesus toward the end of his life (so Irenaeus, *Against Heresies* 3.1.1–2; 3.3.4). While this is impossible to prove with a strong degree of conviction, Ephesus did have a large Jewish population, and the evidence from the book of Revelation also depicts an internecine Jewish dispute over Jesus in the Ephesian church (Rev. 2:9; 3:9).

There is more textually grounded information for us when we come to the questions of why and for whom the Gospel was written. Throughout John's Gospel the author depicts Jesus as the one in whom Israel's Scriptures find their climax. Jesus is the Son of God, the final prophet, the Son of Man, and the messianic King of Israel. Jesus is the one who offers the wine of the new covenant (2:1–11); he is the true temple (2:13–22); he is the new manna (6:22–59); he is the resurrection from the dead (11:25–27). John the Baptist identifies Jesus as the Lamb of God, and a series of soon-to-be disciples confess him as the Messiah, the one spoken of by the law and the prophets, the Son of God, and the King of Israel (1:29–51). I will flesh this out in more detail in the next chapter, but here we can simply note that these themes fit well with John's purpose statement: "These things have been written so that you may believe that Jesus is the Messiah, the Son of God, and that by believing you may have life in his name" (20:30–31).

John's audience, then, would seem to be those who have already deeply identified with Israel's theological traditions and who have a strong understanding of the Jewish Scriptures.[20] John's Gospel does not depict Jesus positively engaging non-Jewish supplicants (cf. Matt. 15:21–28; Mark 7:24–30); nor does it show Jesus traveling to the Decapolis or to Caesarea Philippi (cf. Mark 6–8). Rather, Jesus's mission is focused on the Jewish people and the related Samaritans (John 4:1–42).[21] One of John's goals appears to have been evangelistic—that is, to invite his audience to consider Jesus as Israel's Messiah by creatively showing how his life, death, and glorification bring these traditions to their fulfillment.

We should also connect this theme to the text's depiction of serious social tension between Jewish believers in Jesus and the Jewish synagogue. For example, after Jesus heals a blind man, the man's parents will no longer answer the questions of the Pharisees and the Jews, and John adds this note: "For the Jews had already agreed that anyone who confessed Jesus to be the Messiah would be put out of the synagogue" (9:22). This is one of three instances where John speaks of the confession "Jesus is the Messiah" as resulting in expulsion from the Jewish synagogue (9:22; 12:42; 16:2). The Gospel frequently reflects an intense intramural hostility between Jewish believers and the synagogue over whether belief in and worship of Jesus are compatible with a Jewish way of life. John's Gospel, then, may simultaneously function as both an evangelistic text (i.e., calling others to embrace Jesus as Israel's Messiah) and an apologetic-edification writing for Jewish believers in Jesus struggling to understand the relationship between the Jewish Scriptures and their conviction that Jesus is Israel's Messiah.

John and Narrative (1)

Key Structural Features and Plot

Before we look at some of John's distinctive literary features, it will be helpful to know something about the Gospel's primary theme: divine revelation. The entirety of the Gospel has an unrelenting focus on this question: If God is a heavenly and transcendent being, how is it possible for humans to have knowledge of God? This is a matter of life or death for the Gospel author. Given that the triune God alone has life and the capacity to give life, the author's goal is to communicate knowledge of God to the audience and thereby draw them into the very life of God (see 1:4–5; 17:1–4). That question must be kept in mind as we explore three key literary features of John's Gospel: symbolism, dualism, and irony/misunderstanding.[1] A symbol is similar to a metaphor in that it takes an activity, an event, or a person beyond their literal reference. Dualism refers to a spatial contrast between two different orders of reality—for example, the heavenly and the earthly, the reality and the shadow. And irony refers to the way in which the surface level of a statement may be at odds with the actual truth of the matter. These literary features of the Gospel encourage the reader to adopt something like a sacramental vision of the world whereby heavenly and divine realities are communicated by means of the earthly.

In John's Gospel the symbolism functions to communicate a higher-order truth or heavenly reality. Jesus is the Word (1:1–2), the light (1:5, 9), the tabernacle (1:14), the Lamb of God (1:29, 36). John, for example, declares that Jesus ("the Word") is "the light of humanity, and the light was shining in the darkness, and the darkness did not comprehend it" (1:4b–5); and again, "He was the true light, who enlightens all people, who had come into the world" (1:9). The rest of the Gospel, then, will use the imagery of darkness or night to symbolize unbelief, sin, and rejection of Jesus (3:2,

19–21), while light symbolizes a believing response to Jesus's ministry and mission as the one who has been sent by God (8:12; 9:5; 11:9–10).

The use of symbolism is of one piece with John's Christology. Jesus is the heavenly Son of Man (1:51; 3:13), the divine Word who has been with God eternally (1:1–2), and the one who is in the bosom of the Father (1:18). In other words, John's Gospel has a stark *dualism* whereby God is from above and humans are from below. Jesus declares this in the starkest possible way: "You are from below; I am from above. You are from this world; I am not from this world" (8:23). No one, emphatically *no one*, according to this Gospel, has seen God or has ascended into heaven where God dwells—except for Jesus, the eternal Word of God. Jesus is the man from heaven who leaves his original habitat in order to share divine and heavenly knowledge with humanity. Jesus and the author of the Gospel frequently speak of him as the one who has come from and will return or ascend to God the Father (5:36–37; 6:44, 57; 8:16, 18, 42; 12:49; 13:1, 3; 14:24, 28; 16:10, 17, 28; 20:17, 21). Again, we need to remember that the primary question that drives the entirety of John's Gospel is this: How is knowledge of God possible? We can state the primary theme of John's Gospel in one phrase: *divine revelation*.

Jesus performs symbolic actions, often called "signs," to mediate divine knowledge (2:11, 18, 23; 3:2; 4:48, 54; 6:2, 14, 26, 30; 7:31; 9:16; 12:18, 37; 20:30). Jesus's transformation of water into wine at the wedding in Cana (2:1–11), his overturning of the money changers' tables in the temple (2:13–22), his feeding of the multitude with bread (6:22–58), his healing of the blind man (9:1–41), his washing of the feet of his disciples (13:1–20), and even his crucifixion (18:33–19:42) are, among other actions, symbolic in that they bear transcendent meaning. After Jesus's first sign, for example, in the story of Jesus at the wedding in Cana, the narrator makes a programmatic claim: "This was the first of his signs whereby Jesus revealed his glory; and his disciples believe in him" (2:11b). The reader, then, is invited to consider that Jesus is indeed a great miracle worker and, even more importantly, to reflect on how the wine that the Messiah gives at the wedding banquet symbolizes God's new-covenant presence with his people at the messianic banquet.

Jewish feasts and festivals play a symbolic role in John's Gospel. The Feast of Tabernacles (or Feast of Booths), for example, was a time for Israel's remembrance of their forty years in the wilderness. Worshipers gathered in the women's court of the temple and kept four large lamps burning throughout the night in remembrance of God giving them light to lead them by the pillar of fire at night (Exod. 12–13). Worshipers also engaged in a water ritual during the feast that commemorated God's provision of water for Israel in the wilderness.[2] It is during this Jewish feast that Jesus, in the temple, cries out that he is both the one who provides "streams of living water" (7:37–39) and is the "light of the world" (8:12).

With respect to the Jewish feast of Passover, which Jesus celebrates on three occasions (2:13; 6:4; 11:55), imagery of the sacrificial lamb (1:29, 36) as well as the bread (6:26–57) is ascribed to Jesus. Jesus's third time (as narrated by John) of celebrating the Passover looms over the second half of the Gospel as it foreshadows his impending death as the Passover lamb (11:55; 12:1, 12, 20; 13:1). On the cross, Jesus fulfills Scripture by drinking wine vinegar from a sponge attached to a branch of hyssop (19:29–30); hyssop was used to smear blood from the Passover lamb on a house's doorframe (Exod. 12:22). And John notes that, just like the Passover lamb, Jesus's legs are not broken (as would be customary for one crucified by the Romans): "Not one of his bones will be broken" (19:36; see Exod. 12:46; Num. 9:12). The point is that Jesus is the Passover lamb, the one who provides true freedom and liberation from sin and death (8:21–28).[3]

Characters in the Gospel often find themselves confused by Jesus when they fail to discern the way in which earthly speech and events communicate heavenly realities. Thus, John's Gospel is filled with human characters who misunderstand Jesus, at times in a way that is ironic and almost humorous. John depicts these characters with vividness but also in ways that highlight them as representative characters. For example, when Jesus tells Nicodemus, a male Pharisee and ruler of the Jews (3:1), that he must be born again, Nicodemus interprets this with utter perplexity, asking, "How is a person able to be born when he is old? He is not able to enter into the womb of his mother a second time and be born" (3:4). Jesus is confounded that Nicodemus is "the teacher of Israel" (3:10) and yet cannot rightly understand that Jesus is speaking about a birth of "water and spirit" (3:5). Jesus's dialogue with the Samaritan woman moves back and forth on two levels as Jesus is speaking about the gift of the "living water" of eternal life, while the woman presumes that he is speaking about actual physical wells, buckets,

SIDEBAR 21.1

Did Nicodemus Become a True Believer?

Nicodemus is a tantalizing figure, showing up in John's story on three occasions. In each instance he is interested in and concerned with Jesus, but it is difficult to tell whether he comes to true faith. First, he comes to Jesus "at night," curious about the signs that Jesus is performing (3:1–2). But Jesus's teaching makes it clear that Nicodemus does not understand the meaning of being born from God (3:3–10). Later, when hostility to Jesus has reached a boiling point during his teaching at the Feast of Tabernacles, Nicodemus opposes those Jewish leaders who want to kill him: "Does our law condemn a man without first hearing him to find out what he has been doing?" (7:51). And after Jesus is crucified, Nicodemus (along with Joseph of Arimathea) buries Jesus's body and anoints it with perfumes and spices (19:38–42). The Gospel doesn't make it entirely clear whether Nicodemus comes to a full saving faith in Jesus; at minimum, however, Nicodemus functions as a symbolic figure who embodies a continual searching for truth and its relationship to Jesus.

thirst, and water (4:10–15). The blind man who is healed by Jesus functions as a vivid parable for spiritual perceptivity as he confesses Jesus as Lord and then worships him (9:35–38), whereas the Pharisees who reject Jesus are symbolic of those who falsely claim to have spiritual perceptivity (9:39–41).[4] 21.1

When Jesus tells the disciples that he has his own food, they presume that he is talking about literal bread and water, thereby eliciting Jesus's plain statement: "My food is to do the will of him who sent me" (4:34). Jesus's declaration to his disciples that their friend Lazarus has "fallen asleep" and he is journeying to wake him up is met by the incredulous response whereby they inform Jesus, "If he has fallen asleep, he will recover" (11:11–12). When two disciples ask Jesus where he is "dwelling" and he responds by inviting them to "come and see" where he "dwells" (1:38–39), the language foreshadows the mutual indwelling that occurs between disciples and the triune God (of which Jesus teaches in 14:1–14; 15:1–11; 17:1–26).

When Jesus declares, on three occasions, that he must be "lifted up" (3:14; 8:28; 12:32–33), the reader knows that the language works on two levels: Jesus will be physically lifted up onto the cross, and this lifting up will be his spiritual glorification and enthronement. 21.2

SIDEBAR 21.2

Misunderstanding in John's Gospel

Often Jesus's heavenly origins as the one who has been sent by God result in misunderstanding. The reader knows the answer and is stimulated to accept the truth of Jesus's teaching, in part, by watching how characters misunderstand Jesus.

- When Jesus declares that he will give his body as the bread of life, Jesus's opponents ask, "Is not this Jesus, the son of Joseph, whose father and mother we know? How can he now say, 'I have come down from heaven'?" (6:42).
- When the Pharisees are questioning the (formerly) blind man, they declare, "We know that God has spoken to Moses, but as for this man [Jesus], we do not know where he comes from" (9:29).
- Jesus's heavenly origins result in conflicts and misunderstandings between Jesus and the authorities, climaxing in Pilate asking Jesus, "Where are you from?" (19:9).

Irony also results from the way in which the literary characters often speak better than they know; that is to say, the readers are capable of discerning deeper meaning in what is expressed by the characters. The most remarkable example of this comes when the high priest Caiaphas declares that they should put Jesus to death because "it is better for one man to die for the people than for the whole nation to perish" (11:50). And Pilate's question of Jesus, "What is truth?" (18:38a), is filled with irony and even some humor, given that John's Gospel has repeatedly depicted Jesus himself as the truth (e.g., 1:14; 14:6).

John's frequent use of this theme of misunderstanding and irony functions to stimulate the reader to a particular way of reading John's Gospel that is sensitive to the relationship between the earthly and the heavenly and how Jesus uses the former to communicate transcendent heavenly realities.

In regard to the overall structure and plot, we can divide John's Gospel into four sections of unequal length.

1. *The Prologue (1:1–18)*

Whereas Matthew and Luke narrate the birth of Jesus and situate him in relationship to Israel's historical ancestors, John uses philosophical and elevated prose to describe Jesus as the one who, in the very bosom of God the Father, is involved with God in the creation of the world. Jesus is not only Creator; he is also the divine Word incarnate as he takes on human flesh in order to reveal the glory of God.

2. *The Book of Signs (1:19–12:50)*

Jesus performs miracles or "signs" that are intended to move the audience to see divine glory in Jesus and his work and so thereby come to true faith. Jesus also engages in lengthy speeches, many of which interpret his signs and thereby center on his identity as the life-giving presence of God. The midway point of the Gospel comes in chapter 11, where Jesus, who himself is the resurrection and the life, raises Lazarus from the dead. This initiates the conflict whereby the religious authorities seek to put Jesus to death.

3. *The Book of Glory (13:1–20:31)*

There are three major movements here. First, Jesus prepares his disciples for his impending death as he washes their feet as an act of love that they are to emulate (chap. 13). Second, Jesus's final teachings center on the themes of consolation and commission as Jesus prepares and prays for his disciples for their mission after he returns to the Father (14:1–17:26). Throughout the Farewell Discourse (chaps. 14–17) and Jesus's trial, death, and resurrection, John leads the reader to see Jesus's crucifixion as his glorification whereby he will both save the world and return to the Father. Jesus promises his disciples that his return to the Father will initiate the sending of another helper, the Holy Spirit, who will empower the disciples in their mission to the world. Third, John includes an account of Jesus's arrest, trial before Pilate, crucifixion, and resurrection (18:1–20:31). John also declares his reason for writing the Gospel: he wants people to come to faith in Jesus as the Messiah and Son of God and thereby have life.

4. *The Epilogue (21:1–25)*

Another resurrection appearance of Jesus is narrated whereby Jesus restores Peter and commissions him to shepherd God's people. Jesus also addresses some controversy regarding the impending death of the Beloved Disciple.

Key Words and Phrases

As we did with each of the Synoptic Gospels, here we will look at some key words and phrases that highlight significant themes in John's Gospel: "Logos," "world," "life, eternal life," "I am," and "Son of Man."

Logos. The Gospel of John begins by speaking of a figure, "the Word" (Greek: *ho logos*), that is both distinct from and identified with God: "In the beginning was the Word, and the Word was *with* God, and the Word *was* God. This one was in the beginning with God" (1:1–2). This point must be reemphasized: the Logos is clearly described as both distinct from and identified with God! So, the Logos is involved with God in creation (1:3), is life and light (1:4–5), is the fullness of "grace and truth" (1:14), and is the only one who has seen God (1:18). Both ancient Greek philosophy and Jewish theology had rich concepts of a divine or divine-like mediator, often referred to as the Logos, that was somehow involved in the creation of the world. In the Old Testament there is the notion of "the word of the LORD," whereby God creates, saves, delivers, and judges. And, in Genesis 1, God is consistently depicted as creating the world by the spoken word: "God said . . ." (vv. 3, 6, 9, 11, 14, 20, 24, 26). Of course, the first words of John's Gospel, "In the beginning," are the first words of Genesis 1. So, John interprets the Genesis creation account in such a way that all things were created by God the Father with the Word. Jesus (later identified as such) as the Word of God is doing what only God himself can do: create. Perhaps even more shocking is the claim then offered in John 1:14 that the eternal and preexistent Word of God becomes incarnate and takes on human flesh: "The Word became flesh and tabernacled among us, and we have seen his glory, the glory of the one and only Son who came from the Father, full of grace and truth." John's reference to Jesus as the Logos allows him both to depict Jesus as his own unique person and to identify him with God. Throughout the Gospel we will see Jesus consistently do the things that only God can do: he gives life, he saves, he creates, he judges, and he receives worship. But the Logos also becomes a

SIDEBAR 21.3

The "Word"

Psalm 33:6

By the word of the LORD the heavens were made,
their starry host by the breath of his mouth. (NIV)

Isaiah 55:10–11

As the rain and the snow
come down from heaven,
and do not return to it
without watering the earth
and making it bud and flourish,
so that it yields seed for the sower and bread for the eater,
so is my word that goes out from my mouth:
It will not return to me empty,
but will accomplish what I desire
and achieve the purpose for which I sent it. (NIV)

Marcus Aurelius, *Meditations* 5.32

Why do unskilled and ignorant souls disturb him who has skill and knowledge? What soul then has skill and knowledge? That which knows beginning and end, and knows the *logos* which pervades all substance and through all time by fixed periods administers the universe.

human and is, therefore, spoken of as being sent by God, obeying, listening to, and loving God. 21.3 21.4

World. The prologue not only describes the Logos as involved in creation; it also refers to what he creates: the "world." God and the Logos have created the world and, as a result, love the world. And yet the world has gone astray and has rejected its Creator. This is stated compactly in John 1:10–11: "He [the Logos] was in the world, and the world came about through him, and the world did not know him. He came to his own and his own did not receive him." God's mission is for the world, and yet we see that the world's response to divine revelation will largely consist in misunderstanding, confusion, and, ultimately, rejection. The world, then, is created by God and is the object of God's love, and this provides the reason for the incarnation of the Son and his saving mission: "God loved the world in this way, such that he gave his one and only Son so that whoever believes in him may not perish but have eternal life. For God did not send his Son into the world so that he might judge the world, but so that he might save the world through him" (3:16–17). Created and loved by God, the world is, however, alienated from and hostile to Jesus and his followers (15:18–19). Jesus even speaks of the devil as "the ruler of this world" (12:31; 14:30; 16:11). Jesus calls his disciples to be "in" the world even though they are not "of" the world (see 17:14–19). The disciples are commissioned and sent by Jesus into the world to reveal God's love and truth to it (17:18–23; 20:19–21). 21.5

Life, eternal life. One of the main terms used to express salvation and the reason for which humanity was created is "life" or "eternal life." In fact, as we have already noted, the stated purpose of John's Gospel is that it will move people to faith in Jesus so that they might have eternal life in his name (20:30–31). God the Father and the Son have life in themselves, and they have created humanity to share in this life. So, in the prologue, John states, "In him [the Logos] was life, and the life was the light of humanity" (1:4). In Jesus's discourse on the good shepherd he states, "I have come so that they might have life, even abundant life" (10:10b). This life involves rescue, good pasture, care of injuries, justice, security and peace,

SIDEBAR 21.4

Marianne Meye Thompson on Jesus the Incarnate Word

"God entered the world as a fully embodied human being, living and dying as human beings do. . . . John does not separate the divine and human aspects of Jesus, predicating some actions of the divine Word and others of the human Jesus. All that Jesus says and does he does as the Word made flesh, a human being who suffered under Pontius Pilate, and was crucified, dead, and buried."[a]

SIDEBAR 21.5

Denise Levertov, "On the Mystery of the Incarnation"

Denise Levertov's poem draws together beautifully the inexplicable love of God made known in the incarnation of Christ for sinful humans. The poem begins by reflecting on the sheer capacity for humans to inflict all kinds of harm on one another, realizing that this sin is in the heart of all of us. But how incredible, Levertov writes, that it is to humans—not to an animal or to those innocent of sin—that God

. . . entrusts,
as guest, as brother,
the Word.[b]

satisfaction of hunger, freedom from fear and slavery, and a right relationship with God.[5] The relationship between life and divine revelation is seen also in Jesus's programmatic claim, "This is eternal life: that they know you, the only true God, and the one whom you have sent, Jesus Christ" (17:3). Knowing the triune God *is* eternal life; true life is a participatory and relational knowledge of the true God. One of the most remarkable features of this "eternal life" is that it is available to believers *now*. Many Jews expected an eschatological general resurrection from the dead (see Dan. 12:1–2). Jesus indeed affirms that there is a future resurrection from the dead that will take place on the last day (see John 6:39–44), and likewise Martha believes that her brother Lazarus, who has died, will receive life at the final resurrection (11:24). However, Jesus tells her that this life is also present, in some way, *now*: "I am the resurrection and the life. Those who believe in me will live even if they die. And everyone who lives and believes in me will never die" (11:25–26). Those who have rejected Jesus and his teaching have already entered into judgment, whereas those who have embraced Jesus have already entered into life (see 3:18–21; 5:23–29). 21.6

"I am." Jesus frequently makes self-referential claims that include the phrase "I am" (Greek: *egō eimi*). At times, there is a predicate or attribute that follows the "I am" statement, such as "I am the bread of life" (6:35).[6] All of these "I am" claims are connected to Jesus as the giver of true life. Jesus often draws on an Old Testament theme or metaphor, such as the manna in the wilderness (Exod. 16), God/Messiah as the good shepherd (Ezek. 34), and Israel as God's vine (Ps. 80). There are seven of these "I am" statements (see sidebar 21.7), and it is likely that

SIDEBAR 21.6

Craig Koester on Human Need for Divine Life

"People do not have life in themselves. They must receive life from an outside source. The idea that human beings are created in this way means that they have an inescapable need for the life that comes from God."[c]

SIDEBAR 21.7

Jesus's "I Am" Statements in John's Gospel

With Predicates

I am the bread of life / from heaven (6:35, 41, 48).
I am the light of the world (8:12).
I am the gate (for the sheep) (10:7, 9).
I am the good shepherd (10:11, 14).
I am the resurrection and the life (11:25).
I am the way, the truth, and the life (14:6).
I am the vine (15:1).

As Absolutes

To the Samaritan woman: "**I am** the one speaking to you" (4:26).
To the disciples in the boat: "**I am**. Don't be afraid" (6:20).
To the Jewish leaders: "If you do not believe that **I am**, you will indeed die in your sins" (8:24).
To the Jewish leaders: "When you have lifted up the Son of Man, then you will know that **I am**, and that I do nothing on my own but speak just what the Father has taught me" (8:28).
To the Jewish leaders: "I tell you the truth, before Abraham was born, **I am**" (8:58).
To the disciples: "I am telling you now before it happens, so that when it does happen you will believe that **I am**" (13:19).
During Jesus's arrest: "Jesus . . . asked them, 'Who is it you want?' 'Jesus of Nazareth,' they replied. '**I am**,' Jesus said. . . . When Jesus said, '**I am**,' they drew back and fell to the ground. Again, he asked them, 'Who is it you want?' They said, 'Jesus of Nazareth.' Jesus answered, 'I told you that **I am**'" (18:4b–8a).

they, along with the seven signs performed by Jesus, are intended to lead us to see Jesus as the agent of new creation.

And, on other occasions, an "I am" statement will stand alone and is often translated as something like "I am he," as in, for example, Jesus's response to the Samaritan woman's speculation about a coming Messiah: "I am he, the one speaking with you" (4:26). Often these absolute "I am" statements occur in theophanic contexts. As Jesus passes by his fearful disciples while walking on the water at night—something only God can do!—he declares to them, "I am. Do not be afraid" (6:20). And when the soldiers are looking to arrest Jesus, they fall to their knees when they hear him say, "I am" (18:5–6).

There are multiple reasons why these "I am" statements should be interpreted as Jesus making claims to be identified with the one God of Israel. For example, he is accused of blasphemy upon his declaration, "Truly, truly I say to you, before Abraham was, I am" (8:58). Furthermore, Jesus is almost certainly employing language from the Old Testament that was used to set forth the absolute and unique identity of the God of Israel. So, in the book of Exodus, God reveals his identity to Moses with this statement: "I am the one who is" (Exod. 3:14). And in Isaiah 40–55, the prophet frequently depicts God as making similar "I am" claims that emphasize that his actions reveal him to be the only true God (e.g., Isa. 43:10). It is important to see, then, that Jesus is not merely claiming to be a "second god" in addition to the God of Israel; rather, he is making the claim that he shares in the unique identity of the God of Israel. 21.7 21.8

Son of Man. One of the most important titles for Jesus in John's Gospel is "Son of Man." We should remember here the origins of this title in apocalyptic Jewish texts, most notably Daniel 7, which depicts "one like a son of man" (v. 13) who ascends to God's throne, receives worship, and is endowed with power and authority: "In my vision at night I looked, and there before me was one like a son of man, coming with the clouds of heaven. He approached the Ancient of Days and was led into his presence. He was given authority, glory and sovereign power; all nations and peoples of every language worshiped him. His dominion is an everlasting dominion that will not pass away, and his kingdom is one that will never be destroyed" (Dan. 7:13–14 NIV).

SIDEBAR 21.8

"I Am" Statements in the Old Testament

Exodus 3:14

> God said to Moses, "**I AM WHO I AM**. This is what you are to say to the Israelites: '**I AM** has sent me to you.'" (NIV)

Isaiah 43:10–12, 25

> "You are my witnesses," declares the LORD,
> "and my servant whom I have chosen,
> so that you may know and believe me
> and understand that **I am**.
> Before me no god was formed,
> nor will there be one after me.
> **I**, even **I**, **am** the LORD,
> and apart from me there is no savior.
> I have revealed and saved and proclaimed—
> I, and not some foreign god among you. . . .
> **I**, even **I**, **am** he who blots out
> your transgressions, for my own sake,
> and remembers your sins no more."

John's Jesus shares at least two major features with this Danielic son of man. First, when Jesus refers to himself as the Son of Man, he often stresses his singular ability to provide divine revelation because he is the only one who has descended from and ascended to heaven (1:51; 3:11–13). And, second, as the Son of Man, he alone can provide true judgment (5:25–27; 9:35–41). When Jesus receives the mock acclamation from Pilate during his trial, "Behold the man!" (19:5), the reader can see the irony at play: Jesus is indeed the true Son of Man, the one ultimately invested with authority and judgment.

John and Narrative (2)

Key Narrative Threads

The Prologue as a Guide to Understanding John's Gospel

Many of the key words and phrases examined in chapter 21 derive from John's prologue (1:1–18), but, even at the risk of being repetitive, it is crucial that we spend some time with the first eighteen verses of the Gospel to see how they frame and guide our reading of John's Gospel. More specifically, as stated by John scholar Christopher Skinner, "The Prologue lays a foundation for an informed reading of the story but also helps to create a tension that begs for resolution. In this way, the Gospel of John develops understanding in the reader with the promise that even greater understanding will come about at the conclusion of the story."[1] In other words, John's prologue performs at least two important functions for readers. First, it introduces some of the key themes, vocabulary, and ideas that will be critical for a robust reading of the entire story. Second, the prologue creates literary tension, given, for example, that we know that Jesus is the life-giving Word of God but the characters in the story do not. Many significant themes are introduced in the prologue, including Jesus's association with new creation, light, and life (1:1–5); disciples as those who are "sent" (1:6); the right response to Jesus as faith/belief (1:7, 12); Jesus's rejection by his people (1:10–11); and new birth (1:12–13). But, for now, let's just take an extended look at four themes.

CHRISTOLOGY AND REVELATION

The prologue alerts us to the fact that the primary theme of John's Gospel is that of divine revelation. How can people truly know God? Many Second Temple Jewish texts wrestled with this question as well. Some of them posited a personified Torah or Wisdom that was involved with God in creation and was capable of communicating true knowledge of God to God's people.[2] 22.1

Jesus as the Word of God, however, is neither something created by God nor simply a personification of God. For John, the Word was not created; as he says, "In the beginning *was* the Word" (John 1:1a). Jesus, as the Word of God, is the climactic revelation of God. Jesus is the divine Logos, the light that illuminates all things, the glory of God, and the unique Son in the bosom of the Father who makes God known. John is unrelenting in its emphasis on the way in which Jesus is the exclusive, singular revelation of God. Those like Abraham, Moses, and Isaiah who were thought to have seen God actually saw the glory of the preexistent Word, for Jesus is the only one who has descended from and ascended into heaven. 22.2

SIDEBAR 22.1

Wisdom in Jewish Texts

There are a variety of Jewish texts that speak of Wisdom either as another divine figure next to God or as a personification of the God of Israel. For example, in Proverbs 8, Wisdom is next to God before the creation of the world and is present with God when the world is created. Wisdom is even the helper craftsman next to God who rejoices in God's creative work (Prov. 8:22–31). In some Second Temple Jewish texts, Wisdom not only is the Creator with God but also is identified with the Torah and God's commandments (Sir. 24; Bar. 3:29–4:1).

SIDEBAR 22.2

The Preexistence of Jesus in John's Gospel

- Jesus declares that he has already been with the Father in heaven: "No one has ever gone into heaven except the one who came from heaven—the Son of Man" (3:13).
- Jesus declares, "Before Abraham was born, I am" (8:58).
- John declares that when the prophet Isaiah was called by God and saw God's glory in the temple, it was the glory of Jesus that he actually saw (12:41).

As the unique Son of God, Jesus is able to do what only God (according to the Old Testament Scriptures) can do: create, save, and judge. We have seen that Jesus is involved with the Father in creating all things (1:2–3). When asked why he chooses to heal on the Sabbath, Jesus grounds his right to work on the Father's continuing to work on the Sabbath: "My Father is working even now, so also I work" (5:17). Jesus's word is that which gives, and will give on the final day, resurrection life to those who hear and believe (5:24–30).

We are prepared, then, for Jesus's "I am" statements (see sidebar 21.7), his claims to preexistence (8:58), his declarations of his unity with the Father (10:30; 14:5–11), and his receiving of divine worship from the disciples (20:28). To see and know Jesus is to see and know God. Jesus is identified with God, and yet he is, as later Christians would say, a distinct person. Jesus's teachings speak of a relationship of mutuality between the Father and the Son. The Father and the Son love each other, the Son obeys and does the will of the Father, the Son glorifies the Father, the Son is sent by the Father.

> The Father loves the Son and shows him everything that he is doing. (5:20a)

> When you have lifted up the Son of Man, then you will know that I am he; and I do nothing from myself, but just as the Father has instructed me, so I teach these things. (8:28)

> So that the world may know that I love the Father, just as the Father has commanded me, so I also do. (14:31)

> Just as you [the Father] have sent me into the world, so also I send them into the world. (17:18)

Again, the very first verses of the prologue prepare us for both the identity between the Father and the Son as God ("the Word *was* God") and the distinction of persons between the Father and the Son ("the Word was *with* God"). 22.3

The key point for our reading of the entire Gospel, then, is this: everything that Jesus says and does carries the weight of divine authority and revelation. As one author notes, Jesus "acts and speaks as the incarnate expression of God's speech. As word gives body to thought, so does Jesus give visible expression in the world to the invisible power and presence of God."[3] 22.4

Jesus is, as we have seen, the very Word of God, but he is also fully human. John makes this claim when he declares that "the Word became flesh and tabernacled among us" (1:14). Perhaps surprisingly to some, it is John's Gospel that most emphatically stresses Jesus's humanity. So, for example, Jesus goes to the well for a drink because he is tired from his journey (4:6–7; see also 19:28); he weeps over the death of his friend Lazarus (11:33–35); he feels anxiety and sadness over his impending trial and death (12:27; 13:21); he loves his friends (13:1–20; 15:9–14); and, of course, he is crucified and put to death (19:25–30).

SIDEBAR 22.3

Richard Bauckham on the Deity of Jesus

"The opening verses of the Prologue, read in the light of the later statement that the Word became flesh and lived among us as Jesus Christ (1:14), include Jesus in the unique divine identity by identifying him with the Word that was with God in the beginning and that as God's agent created all things. It places Jesus unequivocally on the divine side of the absolute distinction between the one Creator and all things."[a]

SIDEBAR 22.4

Athanasius, *On the Incarnation*

Athanasius, a fourth-century-CE Alexandrian church father, wrote beautifully about the necessity of the incarnation. Humans were created by the Word and in the image of the Word. When humanity fell into sin and death, God became a man so that humans might be renewed in true knowledge of God and so thereby be able to share in the life of God:

> What, then, was God to do? What else could He possibly do, being God, but renew His image in mankind, so that through it men might once more come to know Him? And how could this be done save by the coming of the very Image Himself, our Savior Jesus Christ? Men could not have done it, for they are only made after the Image; nor could angels have done it, for they are not the images of God. The Word of God came in His own Person, because it was He alone, the Image of the Father, Who could recreate man made after the Image.[b]

TESTIMONY TO THE TRUTH

The prologue introduces its readers to the Gospel's unrelenting emphasis on Jesus as the supreme expression of truth and the role that the concept of testimony plays in inviting humans to embrace the truth (1:9, 14, 17). Jesus tells those who believe in him, "You will know the truth, and the truth will set you free" (8:32). Jesus is "the way, the truth, and the life" (14:6).

Truth is found in the person of Jesus. The Gospel's primary intent is to convince the reader of this claim, and one of the ways it does this is through giving testimony.

Some scholars have found the verses about John the Baptist in the prologue strange because they seemingly interrupt John's elevated prose and his elegant theological claims (see 1:6–8, 15). But these verses actually introduce one of the Gospel's key themes: the way in which the story operates as a contest over whether Jesus is to be identified with the truth and the critical role that testimony plays in pointing to Jesus as the embodiment of truth.[4] The prologue twice identifies Jesus with truth: "We have seen his glory, the glory of the one and only Son, who came from the Father, full of grace and truth" (1:14b); "grace and truth came about through Jesus Christ" (1:17b). The prologue uses the language of testimony/witness four times to describe John the Baptist's task: "He came for the purpose of *testimony*, so that he might *testify* about the light in order that all might believe through him. He was not the light, but had the purpose to *give testimony* about the light" (1:7–8); "John *testified* about him and cried out, saying, 'This was the one of whom I said, "He who comes after me is greater than me because he existed before me"'" (1:15a). John's testimony, then, consists in his rejection of human glory and praise and his truthful affirmation of Jesus's identity. As the story begins to unfold, John the Baptist testifies that he *is not* the Messiah (1:19–28) and that Jesus *is* the Lamb of God and the Spirit-anointed Son of God (1:29–34). The Baptist's words "[Jesus] must increase, and I must decrease" (3:30) encapsulate his role of refusing human glory and instead pointing to Jesus as the supreme and truthful revelation of God.

As the heavenly Son of Man, sent by God the Father, Jesus is the primary witness who testifies to the truth (3:11–12). Jesus is the one who has been sent by God with the commission to share the words that the Father has given to him (3:34; 7:28–29). Like the Baptist, Jesus refuses to accept glory from humans (5:41). Jesus claims that the signs and works that he performs testify that "the Father has sent him" (5:36). But Jesus not only shares or testifies to the truth; as the life-giving Word of God, he himself *is the truth*. When Philip asks Jesus to show the Father to Philip and the disciples, Jesus responds, "The one who has seen me has seen the Father. How can you say, 'Show the Father to us'? Do you not believe that I am in the Father and the Father is in me? The words that I speak to you I do not speak from myself; but the Father who abides in me is doing his works" (14:9b–10).

The high point of this theme comes in John's lengthy trial scene, which includes a dialogue between Jesus and Pilate over the nature of Jesus's origins,

SIDEBAR 22.5

Cyril of Alexandria on John 1:16–17

Cyril of Alexandria, drawing from the apostle Paul, helpfully sees how John is depicting both Moses (the old covenant) and Jesus (the new covenant) as God's gracious gift, but with the latter as surpassing the former: "Although the supremely wise Moses has such great superiority over the saints of old, the Evangelist shows the Only Begotten to be greater and more glorious in every way so that he may clearly have 'first place in all things,' as Paul says. Therefore, he says, 'And grace in place of grace, because the law was given through Moses, but grace and truth through Jesus Christ'" (*Commentary on John* 1:16–17).

kingship, and truth. Pilate asks whether Jesus is a king, to which Jesus responds, "You say *I am* a king" (18:37b). In my view, the italicized words indicate that this statement should be understood as one of Jesus's "I am" statements (e.g., 4:26; 8:24, 28).[5] However, Jesus's divine kingship is not in political power but rather is in his reign of truth and testimony to the Father. Jesus continues by telling Pilate, "The reason I was born and came into the world is that I might testify to the truth. Everyone who is from the truth hears my voice" (18:37b). Jesus's kingship is revealed, then, in that he is the Son of God sent by the Father, the one who is the true judge (3:19; 5:30; 9:39; 12:31).

JESUS'S RELATIONSHIP TO MOSES AND THE JEWISH SCRIPTURES

Corresponding to the prologue's depiction of Jesus as the full embodiment of divine revelation is the theme of Jesus as the one in whom all of the Jewish Scriptures—including individuals, institutions, the law, rituals, feasts and festivals—find their fulfillment. Notice this statement in the prologue: "From his fullness we have all received grace *anti* grace. For the law was given through Moses; grace and truth came about through Jesus Christ" (1:16–17). I have left the Greek preposition *anti* untranslated because there are important differences of opinion among Bible scholars as to what it communicates. While many translations opt for a rendering that reads the expression "grace *anti* grace" as referring simply to the manifold gracious blessings that come to the believer in Jesus, the context strongly favors a translation of "grace instead of grace." In other words, verse 17 explains what the expression means: *we have received the grace of Jesus Christ—that is, the grace of the new covenant—instead of the grace or gift of the law*. On this view, John refers to Moses and the Torah as a gracious gift, but one that finds its fulfillment or pinnacle in the "grace and truth that comes through Jesus Christ" (1:17b). 22.5

The law of Moses, and all that is contained therein, is a gracious gift of God, but it is a gift surpassed by Jesus Christ as the supreme revelation of God. We should not, however, use the language of replacement to describe this dynamic, for the gift of Moses foreshadows and anticipates the gift of Jesus Christ. The prologue itself shows this to the reader quite clearly in 1:14–18 by drawing parallels, especially using the language of Exodus 33–34, between God's two primary forms of revelation: "the law" and "the word."[6]

- As God's presence was made manifest among Israel in the tabernacle, so John describes the incarnate Word as "tabernacling among us" (1:14a). While some translations will understandably use the language of "dwelling," the verb that John uses (*skēnoō*) recalls the tabernacle or "tent of meeting," where God would speak to Moses (Exod. 25:8–9; 33:7–11).
- As Moses asked that he might see God's glory (Exod. 33:17–18), so "we have seen his [the Word's] glory, the glory of the unique one from the Father" (1:14b).
- God reveals himself to Moses as abounding in "compassion and truth" (Exod. 34:6), and Jesus is "full of grace and truth" (1:14c, 17b).
- Moses, hidden by God in the cleft of a rock, sees only the back of God's glory passing by after God removes his hand from blocking Moses's view (Exod. 33:17–23), but Jesus is the visible expression of God (1:18).

John's Gospel does not reject or criticize Moses and the law. The law is not spoken of in any way as leading to legalism, works righteousness, or a false, external piety. Moses foreshadows and points toward the greater grace and revelation of Jesus. Moses is, we might say, one of those who provide testimony and bear witness to Jesus as the full expression of God's truth. Jesus states this clearly when, in response to his opponents, he says, "Do not think that I will accuse you before the Father. Moses is your accuser, upon whom you have set your hope. For if you had believed Moses, you would have believed me. For he wrote about me" (5:45–46). 22.6

SIDEBAR 22.6

John's Gospel and Israel's Scriptures

John's Gospel reads Israel's Scriptures as a sourcebook whereby its events, institutions, and symbols prefigure Jesus as God's visible and revelatory presence in the world. On almost every page John uses the symbols, metaphors, and images of Israel's Scriptures to make claims about the identity and work of Jesus. Note the following as a few examples.

- *Jacob's ladder.* When Nathanael is surprised that Jesus knows who he is, Jesus responds, "You will see greater things than these. . . . Truly, truly I say to you, you will see heaven opened up and the angels of God ascending and descending upon the Son of Man" (1:50b–51). Jesus's statement draws on Genesis 28, where Jacob sees a ladder extending into an open heaven (vv. 10–17). Jesus is, then, the revelatory link between heaven and earth. He is the Son of Man who descends from heaven to reveal God in word and deed, and who will return to the Father in heaven.
- *The Passover lamb.* Jesus is the sacrificial Lamb of God who takes away the sins of the world (1:29, 36).
- *The tabernacle and the Jerusalem temple.* The flesh of the incarnate Jesus is the supreme locale for the presence of God (1:14; 2:17–22).
- *The serpent in the wilderness.* During Israel's wilderness wanderings, God commanded Moses to lift up a bronze snake in order to provide healing for those Israelites who had, as a result of God's judgment, been bitten by venomous snakes (Num. 21:4–9). Likewise, Jesus declares that he, as the Son of Man, "must be lifted up" and that he will give life to those who believe in him (3:13–15).
- *Manna in the wilderness.* Just as God gave the Israelites manna for sustenance and nourishment in the wilderness (Exod. 16), so Jesus gives his broken body as "the bread of life" to nourish his people (6:30–58).

JESUS AND "THE JEWS"

The symbolic relationship between Moses and Jesus also foreshadows the larger theme of Jesus's relationship to Judaism. This topic has been the subject of an incredible amount of research over the past few decades, given both its difficulty and its importance. Stated simply, the Gospel of John looks as if it might be, as one John scholar puts it, "Jewish and anti-Jewish at the same time."[7]

The Gospel of John is clearly Jewish in that, as we have just seen at length, it consistently draws on Jewish imagery, Scriptures, and symbols in a positive way as a means of expressing its claims about Jesus. Almost all of the major characters in John's story are Jewish. The christological titles that are used to express Jesus's identity—Messiah, Son of God, Son of Man, King of Israel, Lamb of God—derive from Israel's Scriptures. John's geography is focused on Judea and Galilee.[8] Jesus makes a remarkably Israel-centered statement in response to the Samaritan woman when he says, "You worship what you do not know. We worship what we do know, for salvation is from the Jews" (4:22). Even if Jesus is depicted as the pinnacle of God's revelation and the one who fully reveals the meaning of Moses, Torah, and the Jewish institutions, it is critical to note that John's Gospel does not depict a Jesus (or a "Christian" community) that critiques or rejects Judaism.[9] Jesus repeatedly affirms the goodness and revelatory nature of the Hebrew Scriptures, including, of course, the law of Moses (e.g., 1:16–17; 2:17; 5:41–44); Jesus does not criticize or reject the appropriate practices of circumcision, Sabbath observance, or food and purity regulations. Perhaps most notably, Jesus is portrayed as repeatedly celebrating the Jewish feasts and festivals such as Passover (2:13; 6:4; 11:55), the Feast of Tabernacles (7:2), and the Feast of Dedication (10:22). In chapters 5–10, Jesus consistently uses the Jewish feasts as the occasion to unpack the meaning of his identity: Sabbath (chap. 5); Passover (chap. 6); Tabernacles (chaps 7–8); Dedication (chap. 10).

But the Gospel makes some notoriously harsh and difficult statements not about just a sect or a group of Jews but about *hoi Ioudaioi*. The Greek phrase is the subject of differences of opinion on translation. Is John referring to all Jews, or to the religious authorities, or to Jews in the region of Judea, or is he making some other type of symbolic association? As a result of the ambiguity, some render the phrase as "the Jews," others "the Judeans," and others interpret it as "the Jewish leaders." This group functions as Jesus's opponents; they are angered by his doing works of healing on the Sabbath (5:1–15); they antagonize the blind man healed by Jesus (9:1–41); they do not understand Jesus's teachings and slander him as being demon-possessed (8:22, 48–52); they accuse him of blasphemy (10:30–33); they are even spoken of as violent and wanting to murder Jesus (7:19; 8:37, 40). Jesus refers to *hoi Ioudaioi* as "children of the devil" due to their desire to kill him (8:44), as threatening to expel believers in Jesus from the synagogue (9:22; 12:42; 16:2), and their chief priests as so full of rage against Jesus that they declare, "We have no king but Caesar" (19:15).

We will not be able to solve this challenge here, but I hope the following four claims will be helpful for students trying to navigate John's relationship to Judaism. First, Christians need to reckon with and be fully responsible for unethical, damaging, and violent uses of their Scriptures. In this case, Christians should lament and reject the way in which texts like John 8:44 (among others) have been used to vilify Jewish people throughout the centuries. The sad and tragic truth is that the Gospel of John and its negative statements about "the Jews" have been used for anti-Semitic purposes, even to the extent of Nazi propaganda and the horrific genocide of six million Jews during the Holocaust. When Christians read a text in which its major character, the one who is worshiped as the very eternal Word of God, denounces other characters as having the devil as their father (John 8:44), they must handle this text with utmost care such that it is not used to perpetuate violence or racism.

Second, Jesus does speak positively of many Jews or Israelites. He refers to Nathanael as "an Israelite in whom there is no guile" (1:47). All of his disciples are Jewish (4:9). He patiently explains his teaching to Nicodemus, "a ruler of the Jews" (3:1). According to the logic of John's Gospel, any negative stereotyping claims about Jews as a people group are clearly unacceptable.

Third, the Gospel of John needs to be understood, as do the Synoptic Gospels, as arising out of and reflecting intra-Jewish conflict over the identity of Jesus. In other words, the historical setting of the text is not one of "Christianity" versus "Judaism"; rather, the text reflects conflict over whether Jesus is or is not Israel's Messiah. The first occurrence of *hoi Ioudaioi* is in John 1, where "the Jews" are associated both with Jerusalem (v. 19) and then with the Pharisees (v. 24), thereby working to associate *hoi Ioudaioi* with Jesus's opponents.[10] We can see this conflict portrayed vividly when Jesus heals the blind man in John 9. John notes that the parents of the healed blind man stop engaging the Pharisees and "the Jews" because they are afraid of the social consequences: "The Jews had already agreed that anyone who confessed Jesus to be the Messiah would be put out of the synagogue" (9:22b). This is the first of three instances where John uses the language of "synagogue expulsion" to describe the social consequences for those who confess Jesus to be the Messiah (see also 12:42; 16:2). Whether this makes better sense as happening within Jesus's own lifetime or, as many scholars have argued recently, as stemming from a later first-century conflict, the texts clearly depict a situation of intrareligious conflict between *Jews who confess Jesus as the Messiah and Jews who reject Jesus as the Messiah*. Most of the occurrences of *hoi Ioudaioi* describe the religious authorities or opponents of Jesus who misunderstand and/or reject his teaching, persecute him, and seek to put him to death. The Gospel of John, in other words, depicts two "different *Jewish* ways of construing 'Israel.'"[11] And the Gospel of John uses invective, a common ancient rhetorical technique, to set apart the Johannine Jesus's vision of Israel from that of his opponents.

Fourth, John's Gospel does not reject Judaism or Jewish ethnicity—a point I hope is clear enough by now—but the Gospel does reject making salvation contingent on ethnicity or natural birth.[12] The prologue also foreshadows this theme: "To as many as received him, he gave them the right to become children of God, to those who believe in his name. They are those who are not born from blood, nor from a fleshly will, nor from a human will—but they are born from God" (1:12–13). Believers in Jesus are born from God by virtue of their belief in Jesus and not because of their ethnic descent. This is expanded on by Jesus in his speech to Nicodemus, himself "a Pharisee . . . a ruler of the Jews" (3:1b). Jesus declares that one can enter into the kingdom of God only through being born "from above" (3:3). Human birth and ethnic descent—"that which is born from flesh is flesh" (3:6a; note also 1:13: "not born from blood, nor from a fleshly will, nor from a human will")—are not prerequisites for salvation. Rather, salvation is a matter of "divine birth" and is something that takes place by means of "water and the Spirit" (3:5). Jesus affirms this in his discourse on the bread of life: "It is the Spirit that gives life; the flesh is useless" (6:63). As we see in Jesus's conversation with the Samaritan woman, he is a Jewish man, and salvation is from the Jews (4:9, 22). And yet, Jesus indicates that ethnic descent is not a prerequisite or condition for salvation: "An hour is coming and now is here, when true worshipers will worship the Father in Spirit and truth. For the Father desires such worshipers as these. God is Spirit,

SIDEBAR 22.7

Abraham's Hospitality

When *hoi Ioudaioi* declare that their father is Abraham, Jesus exhorts them to "do the works of Abraham" (John 8:39). In other words, for Jesus, the debate centers not on biological descent but on who acts like Abraham. It is highly likely that "the works of Abraham" refer to the patriarch's famed hospitality to the divine visitors (Gen. 18:1–14). *Hoi Ioudaioi* are appealing to their biological descent from Abraham (see John 8:33, 39), and yet they are persisting in inhospitality to Jesus and his teaching (8:37). They want to kill Jesus because his word does not remain in them (8:31, 37, 45–46); they have heard divine truth but are trying to kill him (8:40). In other words, salvation is a matter not of biological descent but, instead, of divine birth that comes through receptivity to Jesus's word. It is their attempts to kill Jesus that result in him telling them, "You are from your father, the devil" (8:44). Abraham's children are those who extend hospitality and receptivity to God and God's teaching; the attempt by Jesus's opponents to murder him is, of course, the exact opposite.[c] Jesus does not critique or contest their Abrahamic paternity or their Jewish ethnicity. As one scholar states, "The intent to kill is not inherently *Jewish*—it is inherently *diabolical*."[d]

and those who worship him must worship him in Spirit and truth" (4:23–24). Thus, a Samaritan woman can experience this new birth and true worship of God by virtue of her faith in Jesus as the Messiah (see 4:27–29, 39–42). Salvation originates from the Jewish people and is centered on a Jewish Messiah, and yet John insists that ethnic identity is not a sufficient condition for new birth. 22.7

The Signs of the Messiah

We remember that the stated goal of the Gospel of John is to lead people to believe that Jesus is the Messiah, the Son of God (20:30–31). The Gospel of John's depiction of Jesus's messiahship bears a surprising similarity to that of the Gospel of Mark. For both Gospels, Jesus is indeed the Messiah, the King of Israel. And yet the meaning of the confession "Jesus is the Messiah" is anything but straightforward and easy to understand. Rather, an accurate understanding of Jesus's messiahship requires that the reader embark on an active and difficult quest into the paradoxical and strange nature of Jesus's messianic rule.

This coheres with how John opens his narrative by relating a series of vignettes that depict people's initial encounter with the Messiah as a prelude to Jesus's revelatory signs (chaps. 2–12). These "quest stories" heighten the expectations for the reader that this Jesus might be the Messiah, the Son of God, the Lamb of God, the King of Israel, and the Son of Man.[13] These quest stories center on individuals asking about the identity of Jesus, and they help indicate that the very heart of John's Gospel will center on the question, Who is Jesus? Pervading the stories are questions, the language of finding (five times in 1:41–45), coming (1:29, 30, 39, 47), knowing and revealing (1:31, 33), testifying (1:19, 32, 34), seeing (1:36, 39, 48, 50), hearing (1:37), following (1:38, 40, 43), seeking (1:38), and staying/abiding (1:38–39). These active search terms function as metaphors for faith or belief as the characters are engaged in an active quest for the messianic identity of Jesus. And throughout these stories, Jesus is described as the coming one (1:27, 30), the Messiah (1:41), the Lamb of God (1:29, 36), the Spirit-anointed one (1:32–33), the Son of God (1:34, 49), the one prophesied by Moses and the prophets (1:45), the King of Israel (1:49), and the Son of Man (1:51). As the characters encounter Jesus and make their initial confessions about him, Jesus gives cryptic and indirect responses. He asks the disciples, "What are you seeking?" (1:38). When asked where he is staying, he says, "Come and see" (1:39). He heightens the expectations of Philip and Nathanael and exhorts them to come and follow him (1:43, 50). The climax of this theme comes toward the end of the Gospel where the crucified and resurrected Jesus reveals his identity to Mary and asks her, "Whom are you looking for?" (20:15).

In this way, the Gospel begins its story by inviting its readers, together with the first disciples of Jesus, to seek after Jesus in their quest to see, understand, and believe that Jesus is the Messiah. And this messianic speculation does not end with the quest stories in John 1; it pervades numerous episodes throughout John 2–12 as well. In fact, Jesus frequently uses the language of seeing (3:31–36; 4:29, 45, 48; 6:40; 11:40, 45), hearing (5:24–28; 8:38; 10:3), believing (5:24; 6:29–47; 11:25–27), and following (8:12; 10:4, 27) in metaphors for inviting his would-be disciples to believe his words, become a disciple, and share in his mission. 22.8

SIDEBAR 22.8

Messianic Speculation in the Gospel of John

- The Samaritan woman: "I know that Messiah is coming, the one who is called the Christ; when that one comes, he will declare all things to us" (4:25).
- The crowd seeing Jesus's multiplication of the loaves: "This must surely be the Prophet who comes into the world" (6:14).
- Some people from Jerusalem at the Feast of Tabernacles: "Do the rulers truly know that this is the Messiah? But we know from where this man has come. When the Messiah comes, no one will know where he is from" (7:26–27).
- Others: "When the Messiah comes, will he do more signs than what he has done?" (7:31); "This one is truly the Prophet" (7:40); "This one is the Messiah" (7:41a); "The Messiah cannot come from Galilee" (7:41b).
- The Jews: "How long will you keep us in suspense? If you are the Messiah, tell it to us plainly" (10:24).
- The crowd: "We have heard from the law that the Messiah will remain forever. How can you say that the Son of Man must be lifted up? Who is this Son of Man?" (12:34).
- Pilate to Jesus: "So, then, you are a king?" (18:37a).

One of the primary ways that John's story works to elicit appropriate faith in Jesus is through the use of signs. Most agree that there are seven signs that correspond to seven days of new creation, and this is why John 1:19–12:50 is often labeled as the "Book of Signs."[14] 22.9

SIDEBAR 22.9

Jesus's Signs in the Gospel of John

1. Changing water into wine at the wedding in Cana (2:1–11)
2. Healing the royal officer's son in Capernaum (4:46–54)
3. Healing the lame man in Jerusalem (5:1–15)
4. Feeding the multitude (6:1–15)
5. Walking on water (6:16–21)
6. Healing the blind man (9:1–41)
7. Raising Lazarus from death (11:1–44)

The signs are tangible, experiential, and symbolic acts that are intended to reveal the identity of Jesus, specifically his divine glory, and thereby elicit true faith. While the "signs" are things that Jesus does and can be seen (e.g., 2:11; 3:2; 4:54), in many instances his teaching will provide authoritative interpretation for how to understand the meaning of the signs. Let's spend some extended time with Jesus's first sign at the wedding in Cana.

First, John gives the readers privileged narrative information to help us understand the purpose of Jesus's signs with the concluding statement, "This was the first of Jesus's signs that he did in Cana of Galilee, and he revealed his glory, and his disciples believed in him" (2:11). We have already seen how the prologue identifies Jesus, the incarnate Word, with the very glory of God: "The Word became flesh and tabernacled among us, and we have seen his glory, the glory of the unique one

Figure 22.1. Veronese, *The Wedding at Cana*

from the Father, full of grace and truth" (1:14). In later chapters, John will repeatedly speak of Jesus's coming "glorification"—the time when Jesus will be exalted and lifted up on the cross as the surprising and paradoxical moment when the glory of God is ultimately and climactically revealed (e.g., 8:24, 28; 12:20–23, 28; 13:31–32). Jesus's enthronement on the cross is the means whereby God's kingdom is established (18:36; cf. 3:3, 5), Jesus's divine identity is revealed (8:28), and God's love is made known (12:32). As we encounter Jesus's signs, then, we should be alert to how Jesus manifests divine glory.

Second, the reader should be alert to potential symbolism from the start. Notice, for example, the potential symbolic valences of a wedding festival, water, pots for purification, wine, and Mary. Immediately after the confession that Jesus is "the Son of God" and "the King of Israel" (1:49), Jesus turns water into wine, and this likely symbolizes the wine of the new covenant—that is, the wine of the messianic age. The reader here needs to be attentive to the Old Testament symbolism at work. So, in Israel's prophets, an abundance of good wine was an important image that reflected the coming of the Messiah and messianic age (e.g., Isa. 25:6; Jer. 31:12; Joel 3:18; see also, in extrabiblical Jewish literature, 2 Baruch 29:5). Notice how the prophet Amos connects the restoration of the Davidic monarchy with fertility, peace, and wine:

"In that day

"I will restore David's fallen shelter—
I will repair its broken walls
and restore its ruins—
and will rebuild it as it used to be. . . ."

"The days are coming," declares the LORD,

"when the reaper will be overtaken by the plowman
and the planter by the one treading grapes.
New wine will drip from the mountains
and flow from all the hills,
and I will bring my people Israel back from exile.

"They will rebuild the ruined cities and live in them.
They will plant vineyards and drink their wine;
they will make gardens and eat their fruit." (Amos 9:11, 13–14 NIV)

John tells us that there were six stone water pots used for "the Jewish rites of purification" (2:6), and Jesus commands that these pots now be filled with water (2:7), which will be transformed into wine. So, when the amazed wedding host responds to the bridegroom by exclaiming, "You have saved the good wine until now!" (2:10b), the symbolism works in such a way so as to show us that the water used for purification has been surpassed by the Messiah's better wine of the new covenant. We should also note that later John the Baptist will identify Jesus as "the bridegroom" (3:29–30); likewise, in John 2:1–11, Jesus is the true bridegroom who supplies the new and better wine.

The sign also foreshadows, albeit in cryptic ways, the surprising manner whereby God's glory will be revealed at Jesus's crucifixion. The seven signs actually foreshadow a final and eighth sign: the time when Jesus brings to fulfillment and completion his new creation work at his cross and resurrection. For example, in contrast to the water pots used for purification (2:6), Jesus later will declare that *his word and his washing of the disciples' feet*—an act that foreshadows his saving and loving death on the cross—have provided the ultimate *cleansing and washing* of his disciples (13:10–11; 15:3). The odd exchange with Jesus's mother also foreshadows the cross. When Mary says to Jesus, "They have no wine," and Jesus responds, "My hour has not yet come" (2:4)—a phrase that foreshadows the "hour" of Jesus's death (see 7:30; 8:20; 16:32), where his mother will again make an appearance (19:25–27)—it is as if Jesus is responding to her question by saying, "The time for the ultimate revelation of divine glory at the cross, when I will provide the wine of the new covenant, is not yet here." As one author notes, "The presence of Jesus' mother at Cana and his cross reinforces the idea that the glory manifested in the wine and in Jesus' death must be understood together. . . . Jesus's messiahship would lead to Golgotha, and his glorification would be accomplished through crucifixion and resurrection. The divine favor revealed by his gift of wine was a prelude to the gift of his own life."[15]

Third, John shows us in John 2:11 that the purpose of Jesus's signs is to create faith or belief in Jesus. John's prologue (1:7, 12), the purpose statement for the Gospel (20:30–31), and famous texts like John 3:16—all these prepare us for faith as the appropriate human response to Jesus. Faith certainly involves cognitive content; that is, there are facts about Jesus that are to be affirmed and embraced: he is the Messiah, he is sent by God from heaven, and so forth. But faith is also relational in that "believers" are called to friendship with Jesus, a relationship of love, and a form of discipleship whereby they abide in Jesus.[16] The goal of Jesus's signs, then, is not the sign itself, not the sheer surprising miracle, but rather a deeper faith and understanding of who Jesus is—his relationship to the Father, the truth of his words, and the glory to be revealed at the cross.

However, the signs are often ambiguous and difficult for the human characters to understand. Positively, we find that the disciples believe at the wedding in Cana (2:11), the royal official believes when his son is healed (4:53), and many of "the Jews" believe after Jesus raises Lazarus (11:45). Negatively, the signs do not always work as they should. After his miracle of the loaves, the crowd asks Jesus for yet another sign (6:26, 30)! When Jesus raises Lazarus from the dead, this actually leads some to want to put Jesus to death (11:45–57). Sandwiched in between Jesus's first sign (2:1–11) and his encounter with Nicodemus—an individual who comes to Jesus because of the remarkable signs (3:2)—is John's key statement about the ambiguity of the signs: "Now while he was in Jerusalem at the Passover Feast, many people saw the miraculous signs he was doing and believed in his name. But Jesus would not entrust himself to them, for he knew all people. He did not need human testimony about humanity, for he knew what was in humans" (2:23–25).

John offers an anthropological diagnosis here: there is a faith in Jesus that is not quite right, a faith that sees the signs and recognizes something special about Jesus but does not move to a deeper and more accurate knowledge of who he truly is. John's statement that Jesus "knew what was in humans" makes the point that people are generally predisposed to fascination with the sign or the gift rather than the actual giver. And, so, even Jesus at times is somewhat ambivalent about the signs he performs! He declares in seeming exasperation, before his healing of the royal officer's son, "Unless you see signs and wonders, you won't believe!" (4:48). To those seeking him after his multiplication of the loaves, he says, "You seek me not because you saw the signs but because you ate from the bread and were satisfied" (6:26).

It is important to remember something we observed in the preceding chapter: John's twin emphasis on "dualism" and "misunderstanding." In other words, the crowd is following Jesus because of bread, not because of what the bread signifies: Jesus is the bread of life sent from heaven by God. Let's look at another example, in John 2:13–22. After Jesus performs his symbolic act of judgment in the Jerusalem temple whereby he clears out the money changers, "the Jews" ask him for a sign to prove his authority (v. 18). Jesus responds with something of a riddle: "Destroy this temple, and in three days I will raise it up" (v. 19). Notice that they think he is talking about "the below"—that is, the earthly Jerusalem temple that Herod built in forty-six years (v. 20). But John tells the reader that Jesus was "speaking about the temple of his body" (v. 21). After Jesus is raised from the dead, his disciples remember Jesus's teachings and are thereby rightly enabled to interpret his temple action (v. 22). Jesus's crucified and resurrected body is the place where God's presence dwells and is, then, the true eschatological temple. Jesus's signs require that the observer (and we as readers) be able to see the relationship between the physical/earthly and the true/heavenly.

Light signifies Jesus as "the light of the world" (8:12; also 1:4–5, 9).

Bread signifies Jesus as the one who gives his body as "the bread of life" (6:27–51).

Water signifies Jesus as the one who gives "the living water" (4:10–26; 7:37–39).

Physical birth signifies Jesus as the one who grants divine birth (1:12–13; 3:1–9).

John often depicts a right and believing response to Jesus by using sensory metaphors such as seeing, hearing, and even tasting.[17] Humans are invited to see and believe (6:40; 11:45; 14:8). In this regard, the healing of the blind man in John 9 works not only to communicate his physical blindness but also to show how he grows in spiritual insight as he moves from calling Jesus a rabbi (v. 2), to identifying him as a prophet (v. 17), and then finally to confessing his belief in Jesus as the Son of Man and offering him worship (9:35–38). John also associates true belief with hearing and unbelief with an inability to hear: "Truly, truly I tell you that the one *hearing my word* and believing the one who sent me has eternal life" (5:24; see also 6:60).

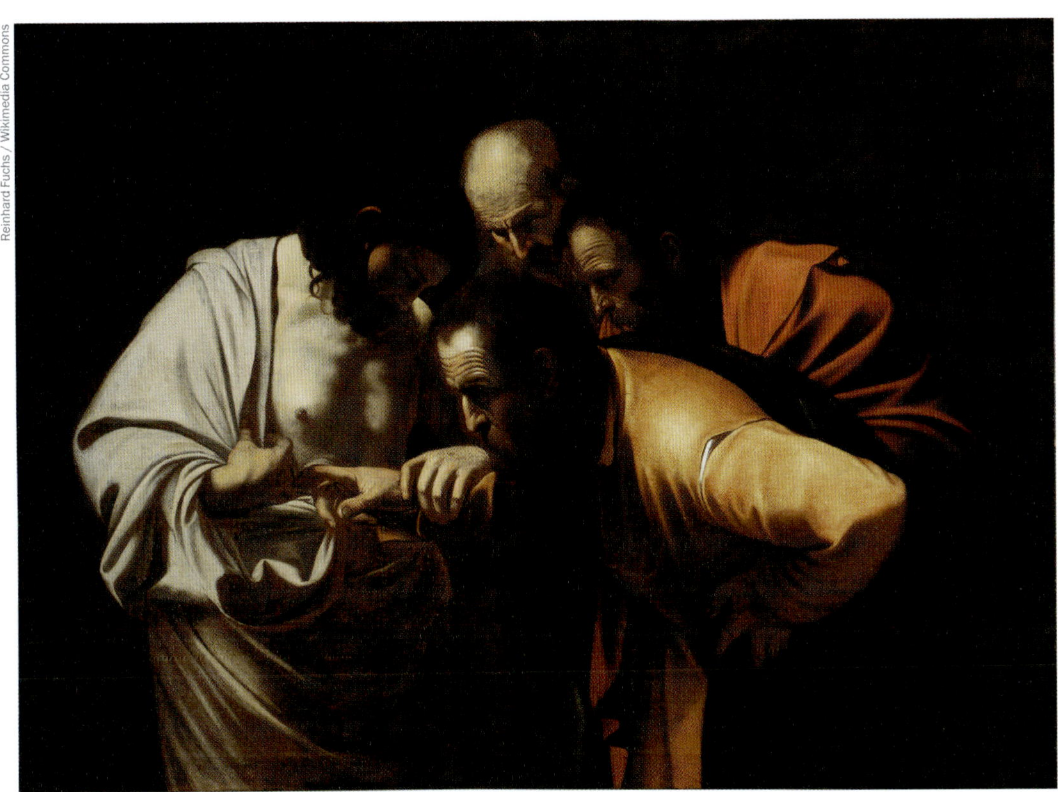

Figure 22.2. Caravaggio, *The Incredulity of Saint Thomas*, 1601

But, as Jesus often notes, humans consistently prefer their own glory over the glory of God (5:41, 44) and have dulled senses, unable to discern the work of God in the midst of the physical and earthly. Love for human glory results in an inability to see God's glory at work in Jesus and the signs he performs. And toward the conclusion of the Book of Signs, the narrator summarizes, "Even after Jesus performed all these signs in their presence, they still did not believe in him" (12:37). Three times here John notes that the signs did not produce true faith (12:37, 38, 39). The reason for the lack of faith, according to John's diagnosis, is the human preference for "the glory of humans rather than the glory of God" (12:43).

Jesus the Life-Giving and Loving Host

John's prologue also highlights the key Gospel theme of life when he declares, "In him [the Logos] was life, and the life was the light of humanity" (1:4).[18] Humanity was created for life, specifically to share in the very life of God. And yet John's Gospel presumes that humanity is alienated from the life of God and in need, as we have seen, of God to reveal himself and thereby bestow true life to humanity. John uses the major symbols of hospitality to depict Jesus as the divine host of humanity who shares the saving and revelatory presence of God through wine (2:1–11), water (4:4–42), bread (6:1–71), washing the disciples' feet (13:1–20), and providing an eternal home (14:1–6). All of the hospitality elements symbolize God's hospitality to humanity. Just as hospitality was a social custom whereby a stranger's identity could be safely and effectively revealed, so Jesus the Son of Man from heaven uses the symbols of hospitality to make his true identity known.

WATER

Jesus's encounter with the Samaritan woman in John 4:4–42 follows the pattern of Jesus the stranger transformed into the divine host. Jesus's hospitality encounter with the woman provides the occasion for the revelation of the fact that he is the Messiah (vv. 25–26) and the Savior of the world (v. 42). The story begins with Jesus and his disciples needing to go through Samaria, and Jesus, being tired from the journey, sitting down near Jacob's well (vv. 4–6). The story of a Jewish man encountering a woman near a well (Jacob's well!) calls to mind the betrothal stories of the patriarchs (e.g., Gen. 29). Jesus is depicted as a vulnerable stranger-guest as he asks the Samaritan woman for a drink (v. 7). But the Samaritan woman is surprised by this, given that he is a Jewish male, she is a Samaritan woman, and "Jews have no relations with Samaritans" (v. 9). But Jesus reverses their roles as he now begins to take on the guise of the host: "If you knew the gift of God, and who it is that is saying to you, 'Give me a drink,' you would have asked him and he would have given you living water" (v. 10). This living water that Jesus provides is a gift from God (v. 10), satisfies humanity's thirst forever (vv. 10, 14–15), and becomes "a spring of water gushing up to eternal life" from within those who drink it (v. 14).

When Jesus asks her to call her husband, the woman responds that she does not have a husband, and Jesus notes that she has had five husbands (vv. 16–18). The woman's marital history likely symbolizes how the Samaritans were viewed as having engaged in intermarriage with the Assyrians (2 Kings 17)—part of the reason for the ethnic divide between Jews and Samaritans. Ultimately, the Samaritan woman responds to Jesus's questioning of her marital status by making more advanced claims about his identity: from prophet (v. 19), to Messiah (vv. 25–26, 29), until finally, through her testimony, the people of her town recognize Jesus as the Savior of the world (v. 42). 22.10

Returning to the theme of water, we note that during the Feast of Tabernacles, in a dispute about Jesus's identity, Jesus invites the crowd to come to him to receive living water: "'If anyone thirsts, let him come to me and drink. For whoever believes in me, just as the Scriptures have said, rivers of living water will flow out of his belly.' And he said this about the Spirit, which those who believed in him were about to receive; for the Spirit had not yet been given, since Jesus had not yet been glorified" (7:37b–39).

Earlier we noted how Jesus's invitation to drink the living water works so as to portray Jesus as the fulfillment of the Feast of Tabernacles—a festival associated with God's provision of water for Israel in the wilderness (Exod. 17:1–6; Num. 20:2–13).[19] This living water presumes confession of the crucified and risen Jesus as the Messiah, given that the living water is identified with the Spirit.

Returning to John 4, we see that the conversation between the Samaritan woman and Jesus centers on his identity. Is he greater than "our father Jacob" (v. 12)? Is he a prophet (v. 19)? Is he related in some way to the coming Messiah (vv. 25–26)? The climax of the story comes when Jesus declares, responding to her speculations, "I am he, the one who is speaking to you" (v. 26). Jesus's words "I am" resonate, as we have seen, with the God of Israel's self-designation and reinforce Jesus's divine identity. God's gift of living water is the experiential knowledge that Jesus is the divine Messiah, the one who gives the living water. The Samaritan woman becomes one of the first evangelists. She leaves behind her earthly water jar and goes into the town to proclaim that Jesus is the Messiah (vv. 28–29). The result is that many Samaritans believe in Jesus "because of the woman's testimony" (v. 39).

SIDEBAR 22.10

The Samaritan Woman as a Preacher of the Messiah

Many scholars have rightly started to question some of the ways in which interpreters have overtly sexualized women in the Gospels, including the woman in Luke 7:36–50, Mary Magdalene, and especially the Samaritan woman in John 4:4–42. There is nothing, for example, in the story of the Samaritan woman to suggest that she is a prostitute or that she was a "loose woman" moving around from man to man. In fact, in a patriarchal society, where women typically were vulnerable, our imagination should be inclined to sympathize with her as one who had likely experienced the death of her husbands and/or divorce. Regardless, Jesus mentions nothing of her sin, and John presents her as having more insight into the true identity of Jesus than does the high-status male Nicodemus (John 3:1–10). She is the first one in John's Gospel to whom Jesus clearly and unambiguously states his messianic identity. And she is the first evangelist, through whom the Samaritan villages hear and believe the gospel. Caryn Reeder observes, "Instead of a sexualized sinner, the woman becomes an insightful theologian. Instead of a danger to the men around her, she becomes a teacher who helps others understand the truth."[e]

BREAD

After Jesus's miraculous multiplication of the loaves (6:1–15), Jesus presents a lengthy interpretation of the sign in John 6:25–59 whereby he makes a contrast between the manna during the days of Moses (vv. 31–32; see Exod. 16:1–21) and "the food that endures for eternal life" (v. 27). Jesus provides "the true bread that comes down from heaven" (v. 32b). The Israelites who experienced manna in the wilderness died (v. 49; see Exod. 16:4, 15; Num. 14:28–35), but "the bread of God is that which comes down from heaven and gives life to the world" (v. 33). Jesus is not only the *giver* of the bread of life; he also *is* the bread of life (vv. 35, 48). Jesus repeatedly declares that he is "the bread that came down from heaven" (v. 41; also vv. 33, 38, 42, 50, 51, 58). More specifically, it is Jesus's crucified body that is able to provide divine nourishment for those who eat. Those who eat this bread of life, Jesus promises, will receive resurrection life now and on the last day (vv. 44–48). Throughout this teaching, Jesus uses language of seeing and believing to describe how people consume the body of the crucified Jesus (vv. 26, 30, 35, 36, 40, 46, 47).

FOOTWASHING

Jesus's greatest and most surprising act of hospitality, the act that ensures that his people will have an eternal home (14:1–4), is his washing of his disciples' feet in John 13:1–20. Jesus's footwashing is situated within the context of his impending death, for the narrator begins, "Before the feast of Passover, Jesus knowing that his hour had come that he should journey from this world to the Father, having loved his own who were in the world, he loved them to the end" (13:1). Passover, Jesus's impending hour, returning to the Father, and loving his disciples to the end—all of these foreshadow the death of Jesus and thereby give his act profound significance. The note that Jesus had loved his disciples "to the end" is John's way of telling us that Jesus's manner of love is an unimaginably perfect love that he will reveal for his disciples at the cross, where he will declare, "It is finished" (19:30). During the meal, Jesus "takes off" his outer garment and "takes up" his towel and wraps it around himself (13:4). The language of "take off" and "take up" is reminiscent of how Jesus describes his death and resurrection when he depicts himself as the good shepherd: "For this reason the Father loves me, because I lay down [i.e., *take off*] my life in order to *take it up* again" (10:17; also 10:11, 15, 18).[20] Jesus embodies his role as the good shepherd, then, through his supreme act of love whereby he lays down his life for his people—an act foreshadowed by his assuming the role of servant-host and washing the feet of his disciples.

Jesus's act of footwashing is a symbolic one of redemptive hospitality that shows how the disciples are transformed into God's friends and family.[21] In the ancient world, the host often provided water for the washing of the feet of the guests, but the actual washing typically was done by a slave or servant of the host or by the guest (e.g., Gen. 18:4; 19:2; 24:32;

1 Sam. 25:41; Homer, *Odyssey* 19.308–19). But here Jesus assumes the form of a servant-host and washes the feet of his disciples (13:4–5). This is almost certainly why Peter cries out in astonishment, "Lord, you will never wash my feet!" (13:8a). But Jesus declares, "Unless I wash you, you have no share with me" (13:8b). Peter must accept Jesus's voluntarily enacting of the service of a slave if he will embrace the saving death of Jesus, who will die as a slave on the cross (cf. Phil. 2:6–8). Jesus's washing of his disciples' feet is the proleptic sign of God's hospitality that Jesus will enact at the cross and is necessary for the disciples, and the cross is the means whereby the disciples will be washed, cleansed, and purified (13:10–11).

SIDEBAR 22.11

God's Family and Home in John's Gospel

The disciples of Jesus become the family of God and the place where God dwells. Jesus's loving hospitality in the footwashing (13:1–20) enables his people to have the promise of entering into the household of God (14:1–4). In the meantime, Jesus promises that the Father, Son, and Spirit will dwell with, make their home with, the disciples (14:23–27; 15:1–8). As Mary Coloe states, "A community of believers becomes the dwelling place of God in becoming part of Jesus' 'family' at the cross and so being drawn into his Father's household" (19:25–30).[f]

Jesus also declares that even though the disciples do not understand what he is doing, later, at the cross, the disciples "will believe that I am" (13:19b). Jesus's divine identity will be revealed on the cross, where God's unimaginable love is revealed for his people—an act foreshadowed now as Jesus washes their feet. The Gospel of John, in fact, depicts the Father and the Son as friends, as joined together in a relationship of unity, love, and intimacy (5:20; 10:17; 14:31; 17:1–25). Love, trust, and sharing secret knowledge—all of this resonates with ancient notions of friendship. And John is clear that the Son's relationship with the Father is the foundation for Jesus's extension of friendship to the disciples.

Jesus's act of hospitality cleanses his disciples so that they can be welcomed into the Father's house (14:2). Jesus is the agent of the Father's gracious hospitality whose loving act of washing enables the disciples to follow in Jesus's trajectory. Jesus's journey back to his Father, in fact, is for the purpose of preparing dwelling places in the Father's mansion for his disciples (14:3). Jesus's act of footwashing is also the basis for his statement to his disciples, "You are my friends" (15:14). Jesus lays down his life for his friends. Jesus has shared all things with his disciples. He has made known the secret of the Father as he revealed God's identity to them in full: "I said you are friends, because everything that I have heard from the Father I have made known to you" (15:15b). 22.11

The Mission of God and the Mission of the Church

The final theme we will take a brief look at is the way in which John speaks of the disciples (and other believers) as sharing in God's mission.[22]

We have already had occasion to note quite frequently that John emphasizes Jesus's heavenly origins. One of the ways this theme is communicated is through the depiction of God (the Father) sending the Son and authorizing him for a specific task. Jesus has been sent by the Father and given a mission, a task that he must complete (4:34; 5:36). Everything that Jesus does and says is what the Father does and says precisely because the Father has sent the Son. Since Jesus is the sent one, all of his words originate from the will of the Father (3:34; 5:30; 8:26; 14:24). As the one sent by the Father, Jesus alone is able to share full knowledge of the Father and give life (5:24–29; 17:3). The Father shows Jesus everything that he does, so that Jesus may share this with his disciples (5:19–29; 7:29). Stated simply, the Father and the Son have a mutual loving relationship whereby the Father sends the Son and gives him the mission of providing saving revelation to humanity.

The Father sends the Son, and the Son commissions his disciples to share in his new-creation work (4:38; 15:16). Two texts in particular are striking for how they depict the disciples as sharing in the very mission of the Son. While Jesus is praying to the Father, he declares, "Just as you have sent me into the world, so I also send them into the world" (17:18). And, again, after he has been raised from the dead, Jesus commissions the disciples: "'Peace to you. Just as the Father has sent me, so I also send you.' And saying this, he breathed upon them and said, 'Receive the Holy Spirit'" (20:21–22). Jesus's breathing upon his disciples is an act of new creation rooted in the new birth from "the water and the Spirit" (3:5; see also 1:12–13).[23] Jesus commissions the disciples to be the Spirit-empowered means whereby God communicates his life-giving presence and salvation to the world. 22.12

SIDEBAR 22.12

Participating in the Life of God

Most of us are probably more familiar with Paul's teaching on "union with Christ" or "participation in Christ" than we are with this theme in John. Paul frequently refers to believers as being "in Christ" as well as to Christ dwelling within believers. Those who belong to Christ have been crucified with him, buried with him, and raised with him (e.g., Rom. 6:3–11). And Paul can even say that he no longer lives, but rather "Christ lives in [him]" (Gal. 2:20; cf. Rom. 8:9–11). But John's Gospel also offers a powerful vision of how Christians share in the life of God by virtue of their union with Christ. First, Jesus frequently claims that there is a mutual indwelling between the Father and Jesus the Son. Jesus often makes claims such as "I am in the Father and the Father is in me" (14:11; also 10:38; 14:20; 17:20–23). There is a relational intimacy between the Father and the Son. Second, as we have seen, Jesus is the incarnate and preexistent Logos who shares in human existence by taking on human flesh (1:14). The Father and the Son take the initiative to come dwell with, save, make their glory known to, and share their life with humanity (17:1–5). Third, Jesus uses a variety of metaphors to speak of how he enables humans to share in the life-giving presence of God. Jesus's disciples "abide" in him (6:56; 15:3–8), have a "share" in him (13:8), share in his and the Father's holiness (10:36; 17:17–19), and have seen the glory of God (1:14; 17:20–23).

Let's look at Jesus's teachings in John 13–17 in order to explain what it might mean to say that the church shares in the mission of the Father and the Son.

First, Jesus teaches his disciples that they are called to be a visible embodiment to the world of the love shared between the Father and the Son. That is to say, the church's love is grounded in the loving relationships of the triune God.

> A new commandment I give to you, that you love one another. *Just as* I have loved you, so you also must love one another. (13:34)
>
> *Just as* the Father has loved me, so I have loved you; abide in my love. If you keep my commandments, you will abide in my love, just as I have kept the commandments of my Father and I abide in his love. (15:9–10)
>
> This is my commandment, that you love one another *just as* I have loved you. Greater love has no one than this, that he lay down his life for the sake of his friends. You are my friends if you do the things I command you. (15:12–13)

Notice how the italicized "just as" statements ground the disciples' love in the love shared between Jesus and the Father, a love that has now been made known to them. Jesus's teachings here have been visibly communicated in his washing of the disciples' feet, as this action functions both to foreshadow Jesus's loving death and to call his people to imitate his example of love (13:1–20). I have already commented on the former—how Jesus's footwashing prefigures the climactic display of love at the cross ("Having loved his own who were in the world, he loved them until the end" [13:1])—but here we should note how Jesus also calls his disciples to share in this divine love and so mediate it to the world. Jesus tells his disciples that he has given them an example to follow. Look at how, once again, he uses "just as" language to express how their love shares in the divine love: "I have given to you an example, that *just as* I have done for you, so you also should do the same" (13:15). Furthermore, Jesus twice refers to his disciples as his emissaries, envoys of the one who has sent them, whose task is to communicate the cruciform love of the triune God to the world (13:16, 20). When the resurrected Jesus appears to Peter and three times commissions him to "tend my sheep" (21:15–17), we can see that Peter, and the church, are called to share in Jesus's mission as the good shepherd, a mission that, as John 10 and Ezekiel 34 indicate, involves practical love and service for God's people. 22.13

Second, Jesus's prayer shows us that the disciples are to share in Jesus's mission by also being a visible embodiment of the unity shared

SIDEBAR 22.13

Jesus the Priest

John's Gospel never refers to Jesus as a priest, but this hasn't prevented scholars from seeing Jesus depicted as one.[9] In fact, Jesus's prayer in John 17 is often referred to as his "high priestly" prayer, as he represents God to humanity and humanity to God. In this prayer, Jesus declares that he "sanctifies" (or "consecrates") himself in order that his disciples might also be sanctified for God (17:19). Jesus is the sacrificial Lamb who takes away the sins of the world (1:29, 36). John plays with the irony of one priestly good shepherd who lays down his life for the sheep (10:1–18), and another priestly figure, the high priest Caiaphas, a bad shepherd in the mold of Ezekiel 34, who wishes to see Jesus put to death (11:44–54). And when John notes that the Roman soldiers cast lots for Jesus's "seamless tunic" (19:23–25), this may recall the type of tunic worn by the high priest. Note how Josephus describes the tunic of the high priest as "composed of two pieces to be stitched at the shoulders and at the sides: it is one long, woven cloth with a slit for the neck, parted not crosswise but lengthwise from the breast to a point in the middle of the back" (*Jewish Antiquities* 3.161).

between the Father and the Son. This is one of the main themes of Jesus's "high priestly" prayer in John 17. Jesus prays to the Father that "they might be one *just as* we are one" (17:11b). And again: "I have given them the glory that you gave me, so that they may be one *just as* we are one. I in them and you in me, so that they may be perfected as one and so that the world may know that you sent me and have loved them *just as* you have loved me" (17:22–23). The shared unity between the Father and the Son is communicated by Jesus's glorification of the Father. The glory of the Father is revealed most climactically in Jesus's death, which is the completion and fulfillment of the work given to him by the Father. As such, the cross simultaneously glorifies the Father and the Son (12:23–28; 13:31–32; 17:1–5). Jesus's disciples are also to glorify the Father by "bearing much fruit" (15:8; also 15:16).

Third, the disciples of Jesus are called to "do" what Jesus has already "done." Disciples will be empowered to do Jesus's work by means of the Spirit. So, Jesus frequently speaks of the "work" that the Father has given him "to do" (e.g., 13:7, 12, 15, 17; 14:10, 12; 15:14–15; 17:4). But the disciples share in this trinitarian work only by means of the power of the Holy Spirit—that is, the Paraclete, whom they will receive when the Son returns to the Father. The Paraclete will, then, testify to the truth about the Son and the Father to the disciples, and will enable the disciples to give testimony about Jesus to the world (15:26–27). Jesus declares that the Spirit, upon the Son's ascension, will enable the church to do the works that the Son does and, in fact, "even greater works" (14:12). The Spirit will empower the church to give true testimony, convict the world of its sin and unrighteousness, and bestow forgiveness (16:8–11; 20:22–23).

John and Discipleship

Disciples of Jesus Confess Christ's Kingship as One of Love and Truth

When we come to the account of the crucifixion of Jesus, John uses a heavy dose of irony and reversal of expectations to force us to think very carefully about the relationship between appearance and truth. This is part of John's strategy to show us that in the cross of Christ, God is creating a new world, a new creation, and it will require new minds that can see and understand this surprising cross-shaped world. 23.1

At the start of Jesus's trial, in John 18:33–38, Pilate questions Jesus as to whether he indeed is a king. Jesus is accused of fomenting rebellion against Rome; he is a popular charismatic teacher with a group of followers; he has made a prophetic demonstration in the temple declaring his unique authority; he has given royal benefactions of bread to the hungry; he has spoken of himself openly as the Son of God. So Pilate wants to know, "Are you indeed the King of the Jews?" (v. 33). To which Jesus twice replies, "My kingdom is not from this world" (v. 36). Well, Pilate reasons, Jesus doesn't deny it, so he says, "You really are a king, then!" (v. 37a). Jesus cannot give a straightforward answer to Pilate's question because Pilate will not understand the difference between truth, that Jesus is a king, and appearance, that Jesus is a subject of Roman imperial authority. So Jesus declares, "You say that I am a king. And for this I

SIDEBAR 23.1

Reality and Appearance in the Gospel of John and Shakespeare's *Macbeth*

"Fair is foul, foul is fair." One of the most well-known lines of any of Shakespeare's plays, the phrase "fair is foul, foul is fair" from *Macbeth* lets the audience know that they are watching a drama where what looks good may be bad and what looks bad may be good. In other words, almost as soon as you think you understand something, there's a complete reversal of expectation—fair is foul, foul is fair. You see it often enough that you begin to question or think more critically about the relationship between appearance—what you see at first—and reality. The relationship between appearance and truth, in other words, is not so straightforward, and it provokes us to look very carefully, recognizing that discerning truth, or reality, may require some hard work. The same dynamics are at work in the Gospel of John's depiction of Jesus's trial and his encounter with the Roman Pilate.

was born and for this I have come into the world, that I might testify to the truth. Everyone who is born from truth hears my voice" (v. 37b). To which Pilate responds, "What is truth?" (v. 38), thereby indicating his complete obliviousness to and disinterest in the truth. These verses function as our hermeneutical "in" for making sense of what follows: Jesus's kingship and kingdom versus Pilate and the kingdom of this world. And so the rest of the crucifixion scene operates with an abundance of irony and reversal—many of them tragic ironies—forcing this question on the readers: Do you identify with Pilate's perspective (i.e., this is the suffering and death of an insignificant Jewish criminal, handed over out of jealousy by the Jewish leaders) or with John's perspective (i.e., Jesus's death on the cross is his inauguration of God's kingdom)? Notice the abundance of irony that follows in Jesus's trial and crucifixion.

- Pilate, knowing that Jesus is innocent, offers to release him (18:38b–39). The decision by the Jewish leaders to choose Barabbas rather than Jesus demonstrates that the trial is a travesty of justice (18:40).
- Jesus, referred to twelve times in John 18:33–19:25 as "king," is given a mock royal coronation: a crown of thorns; a purple robe; mock acclamations of "Hail, king of the Jews," "Behold the man," "Behold your king"; a placard that reads "king of the Jews" (19:1–5, 13–14, 19–22).
- The Jewish leaders accuse Jesus of blasphemy for making himself out to be the Son of God (19:7), but the audience knows that he really *is* the Son of God.
- Pilate is the representative of imperial Rome and the acting judge over the trial. And yet Jesus repeatedly puts Pilate on trial, leading him to ask in exasperation, "I'm not a Jew, am I?" "What is truth?" "Do you refuse to answer me?" "Don't you understand the authority I have?" (18:35, 38; 19:10).
- The Jewish leaders make themselves out to be more loyal to Caesar than Pilate is! In putting Jesus to death, the Jewish leaders declare that they, not Pilate, are the true friends of Caesar and that they have no king but Caesar (19:12–15).
- The mocking declarations made by Jesus's opponents of him as "the Son of God," "the man," and "the king" are meant to ridicule him, but in fact he *is* precisely all of these things. He is indeed the Son of God come down from heaven to reveal God to a lost world; he is indeed the true man who took on human flesh to reveal the glory of the Father to us; and, of course, he is the messianic King of Israel.

What do we learn about Jesus's kingdom of truth when we put together all of these ironic reversals? The ironies, the reversals, the struggle to relate appearance to truth—all these are part of what John is trying to tell us about God's surprising kingdom. There are at least three aspects of this kingdom that John wants us to understand.

First, Jesus's kingship is enacted through the cross. In many New Testament texts, Jesus's kingship is most closely connected with his resurrection and exaltation to the right hand of God. But John wants us to see that the cross is, in reality, the throne of the Messiah. It's not cross and then enthronement; rather, the cross *is* Jesus's royal enthronement. The messianic king inaugurates God's kingdom in voluntarily laying down his life. In the preceding chapter, we saw how John three times shows Jesus declaring that he will be *lifted up*—a double entendre by which Jesus means he will be lifted up on the cross *and* will be exalted (3:14; 8:28; 12:32). Christ's cross *is* his throne. The cross *is* his glorification, his exaltation. So when Pilate, the Roman soldiers, and the Jewish leaders mock Jesus with a crown, a purple robe, royal acclamations, and a placard that ridicules the crucified one as king of the Jews, they are ironically participating in the revelation of Jesus's kingship. Disciples of Jesus know that the cross reveals who the triune God is. The Father, Son, and Spirit—the love and communion that they share with one another and that they reveal and pour out in their accomplishment of humanity's salvation at the cross—are the revelation of God. Disciples of Jesus know the power, wisdom, and salvation of God only when their eyes are opened to see Christ's glory in his sacrificial and loving giving up of himself for us at the cross.

Second, Jesus's kingship operates through love. In the ancient world, good kings were committed to justice, were good military strategists or warriors, exercised self-control, protected their territory, gave gifts, built temples and theaters, and so forth—in other words, they were heroic men. But while Jesus's kingship shares many of these characteristics of "the good king," the nature of Jesus's kingship is quite different! The Father sends the Son out of their mutual love for one another and for humanity. As such, Jesus's kingship is one not of violence or coercive power but of love. The pouring out of the fullness of God's love takes place when Jesus is revealed as king on the cross. The power of Jesus's kingship is revealed not in force or coercion but in its ability to draw all people to this loving triune God. Jesus said, "When I am *lifted up* from the earth, I will draw all people to myself" (12:32). When Jesus is lifted up on the cross, all people will see the depth of the love of a Father who would send his own Son to reveal, save, and reconcile. People will see *the* king, who is humble and gentle enough to call his disciples his friends. People will see divine love in a way that they never had before and will be drawn to the triune God.

Third, Jesus's kingship creates a people who know the difference between his kingdom and the kingdoms of the world. The values and priorities of Jesus's kingdom are not the values and the priorities of Pilate. We have seen this throughout our study of the Gospels in the way each of them carries out an ongoing comparison between Jesus's kingship and the flawed, oppressive, and violent rule enacted by human rulers. Herod, Pilate, and other imperial authorities are exposed as fraudulent counterfeits of Jesus, who embodies true kingship (e.g., Matt. 2:1–15; Mark 6:14–29; 10:44–45). We see all this in the sham nature of Jesus's trial before Pilate. Pilate knows that Jesus is innocent, but he doesn't care. He knows that this is all a sham, and yet he hands Jesus over to be crucified anyway. Pilate, empires, and kingdoms of this world aren't interested in truth or justice. Jesus's kingship and glory are manifested in his obedience to the Father and display of love in his sacrificial death on the cross. Jesus's kingship is revealed in his establishment of a reign of truth that has revealed the Father and the divine love that is capable of drawing all people to God rather than the violence and force of imperial Rome. John's Gospel applies the common ruling imagery of shepherding to Jesus to show that he is the good and just king. He does not exploit or profit off of God's flock but instead voluntarily lays down his life for his people (10:9–18). In this way, Jesus's kingship is of a completely different kind than that of the customary kings and kingdoms of the world, as Jesus made clear in his refusal to let the crowds force him to be a king (6:14–15) and in his response to Pilate, "My kingdom is not of this world. If my kingdom were of this world, my servants would fight so that I would not be handed over to the Jews. But now my kingdom is not of this place" (18:36).

Disciples of Jesus Are Made to Receive and Share True Life

There is perhaps no bigger question than, What is the meaning of life? As powerful as any ancient or contemporary text, the Gospel of John consistently raises questions of human existence, desire, and the meaning of life. In the preceding chapter, we saw that John's Gospel is focused on the theme of divine revelation. The Gospel consistently raises this question: How is it that humans who are alienated from the God of life come to know God and thereby have life? John's Gospel is in agreement with Paul's well-known statements on the relationship between sin and death: "All have sinned and fallen short of the glory of God" and "The wages of sin is death" (Rom. 3:23; 6:23). Since Jesus alone has true life within himself and is capable of illuminating humans so that they come to the truth (John 1:4–5), he declares that the negative side of this is that people will die in their sins if they do not receive his teaching (8:21–24). Just as those who trust in Jesus have a true taste of life right now, so those who refuse his teaching are spiritually dead now even as their bodies live (3:18–21; 5:24–29). Those who see the light of Jesus shining but reject it and remain in their unbelief are those, Jesus teaches, who remain in the darkness due to their sin (9:39–41). Only the truth that Jesus offers can set humans free from enslavement to sin (8:31–34). Jesus's defeat of Satan, which takes place at the cross—the moment of the revelation of truth—is what enables Jesus to draw all people to himself (12:31–33).

The characters in John's Gospel are frequently depicted as hungry, thirsty, confused (in the dark), and in desperate need of life. As one scholar notes, "The Gospel uses these images to show that people have an inherent need for God, yet it also discloses that the need may take people away from God and prompt them to seek life in other ways."[1] Jesus intentionally enters into a variety of encounters—as a guest at a wedding (2:1–11), as a Jewish stranger holding conversation with a Samaritan woman (4:4–26), as the host who feeds a multitude with bread (6:1–15), and as the healer of a blind man (9:1–41)—in order to share God's life-giving presence with hungry and thirsty humans who are in need of life.

Zombies fascinate so many people because they literally are walking dead people—no relationships, no meaningful activity or real enjoyment, no food and drink. Augustine says that before Christ gave him life, his was "a deathly life" and a "living death."[2] He was entirely unsettled with his identity. He tried romantic sexual relationships with many women; he tried ambition and status in academic performance and achievement; he tried the wisdom of philosophy. But all he found was "living death." The job of the devil, Jesus tells his disciples, is to steal, kill, and destroy (John 10:10a). The stench of death is everywhere around us and can take many forms—addictions, loneliness, apathy, relational brokenness, false pursuits of happiness, depression and

SIDEBAR 23.2

Frances Ellen Watkins Harper, "I Thirst"

First Voice

I thirst, but earth cannot allay
The fever coursing through my veins,
The healing stream is far away—
It flows through Salem's lovely plains.

The murmurs of its crystal flow
Break ever o'er this world of strife;
My heart is weary, let me go,
To bathe it in the stream of life;

For many worn and weary hearts
Have bathed in this pure healing stream,
And felt their griefs and cares depart,
E'en like some sad forgotten dream.

Second Voice

"The Word is nigh thee, even in thy heart."

Say not, within thy weary heart,
Who shall ascend above,
To bring unto thy fever'd lips
The fount of joy and love.

Nor do thou seek to vainly delve
Where death's pale angels tread,
To hear the murmur of its flow
Around the silent dead.

Within, in thee is one living fount,
Fed from the springs above;
There quench thy thirst till thou shalt bathe
In God's own sea of love.[a]

anxiety, loss of loved ones, and so much more. To be fully dead means that you cannot by your own effort resurrect yourself to new life—no amount of money, possessions, distractions, or relationships, however good and admirable or evil and deplorable, will ever be enough to rescue one from death to life. 23.2

Perhaps this is why John tells the story of Lazarus right at the center point of his Gospel (11:1–44). The story is long, but the main points are very clear. Lazarus was truly dead. Lazarus was deeply loved by Jesus. And Jesus resurrected him from the dead. The point of the story is also clear as Jesus declares to Martha, "I am the resurrection and the life. The one who believes in me will live even if they die. And everyone who lives and believes in me will never die. Do you believe this?" (11:25–26). Yes, there is a coming final resurrection of the dead. But since Jesus himself *is* life and resurrection, those who trust in him share in true life even now (5:24–29). Jesus came to provide abundant life for his people *even now* (10:10b).

Disciples of Jesus Are Friends with God and with One Another

God created humans to be social and relational beings. We are inherently social creatures in desperate need of meaningful friendship and social interaction. The philosopher Aristotle says that even the wealthiest, most powerful, most self-sufficient virtuous person would be entirely unhappy without friends. No friendship equals no happiness (*Nicomachean Ethics* 1155a1–10). It is remarkable, in fact, how many ancient philosophers wrote treatises and books on friendship. Plato, Aristotle, Epicurus, Seneca, Cicero—all of them devoted considerable attention to the practice of friendship precisely because they knew that a good life, a life of meaning and purpose, was impossible apart from friends. And yet loneliness and isolation mark our society as never before. In fact, numerous studies have demonstrated that the greatest source of unhappiness in the United States is loneliness—the feeling of isolation and lack of significant social engagement. Increased technological capacities and lack of stable roots have had a significantly negative impact on meaningful and long-lasting friendships. A culture oriented toward maximum pleasure means that friends are expendable; they can be dispensed with when they don't contribute to our pleasure and happiness. A love of achievement means that friends often are selected according to their ability to help us advance in our careers or education. A culture of narcissism that is obsessed with the image that we present to others inhibits our ability to actually care about anyone other than ourselves. An inability to know how to forgive and reconcile when one has harmed or been harmed by a friend results in decreased friendships.

John's Gospel can provide us with guidance and encouragement to pursue a friendship grounded in God's goodness and love. The good news of the gospel is that God's love for us in Christ makes us friends with God. And as if being friends with God in Christ isn't remarkable enough, our friendship with God can transform our horizontal relationships so that we become spiritual friends with one another. Friendship with God (the vertical) creates true friendship with one another (the horizontal). After Jesus has washed his disciples' feet, he declares that his act of love is the basis for a new kind of friendship between himself and his disciples. The greatest act of love imaginable is the love of a friend who gives their life for the sake of their friends, and since Jesus is about to enact this love for his disciples, he says, "You are my friends if you do what I command you" (15:14). Jesus's command or stipulation is that they prove themselves to be his friends by continuing to "love one another as I have loved you" (15:12). In the preceding chapter, we saw a frequent refrain: "As the Father has loved me, so I have loved you" (15:9). This indicates that our friendship is rooted in the divine love shared by Jesus and the Father. One Johannine scholar states it this way: "Jesus has been the ultimate friend—he gave his life for us. Now it is our turn to be Jesus's friend, which means that we love one another as he has loved us."[3] Our friendship with the triune God is what enables us to pursue, sustain, and enjoy *real* loving friendship with one another. And if we have experienced the love of God in our lives, then this love will mark the quality and character of our friendships. Jesus has called us his friends. And he has said that the world will know us by the love that is seen in the community of his disciples.

There is a missionary movement to this kind of Jesus-like friendship. Jesus's friends extend this friendship and love to others in their relationships with one another. Our ability to love others, to refrain from hatred and dislike of those who are not like us, and to extend friendship to one another will only be as strong as our ability to remember how Jesus has extended his love to us. You cannot extend love to others unless you are consistently remembering that you are loved by God. God's extension of friendship with us *necessarily creates a new kind of relationship and friendship with others*. If we as God's people have been made to be God's friends, then one of our tasks is to be a befriending community that embodies God's friendship and can welcome others into a place where friendship, intimacy, and familial love can be experienced.

Summary of Main Points on the Gospel of John

1. Despite there being remarkable differences from the Synoptic Gospels in terms of language, themes, and omissions, John's Gospel also has enough obvious similarities to justify the conclusion that it tells of the same Jesus of Nazareth.
2. The Gospel of John was highly regarded by a variety of Christian groups. Greek manuscripts indicate that it was read together with the Synoptic Gospels from a very early stage. The Gospel was highly valued by Gnostic-like Christians as well as orthodox Christians who found it valuable not least for its guidance in understanding dogmatic topics related to Christology and the Trinity.
3. Since its earliest reception, many have read John's Gospel as offering a uniquely spiritual and theological take on the story of Jesus. While the Gospel clearly stands on its own as a coherent and independent narrative, it may also be the case that the author intends for his writing to work as a supplement or complement for those already familiar with one of the Synoptic Gospels (or at least Synoptic traditions). This dynamic is especially evident in John's taking Synoptic-like themes and transposing them into his uniquely theological key.
4. The differences between John and the Synoptics can be explained, at least in part, in that John's stories and traditions derive from the unique source of the Beloved Disciple—despite the lack of clarity regarding his historical identification. Likewise, the Gospel seems to have been written in order both to invite other Jews to faith in Jesus as the Messiah and to encourage Jewish believers in Jesus who were involved in conflict with the Jewish synagogue.
5. As is often the case, determining the date, authorship, and location of the text is incredibly difficult. Church tradition holds that the author is John the son of Zebedee (or, perhaps, John the Elder), writing sometime toward the end of the first century, and that it was penned from his location in Ephesus.
6. John's Gospel employs symbolism to a great extent. In fact, almost everything—feasts and festivals, water and wine, bread, temple—has symbolic import and finds its meaning in relationship to Jesus.
7. Symbolism often results in the theme of misunderstanding whereby human characters misapprehend Jesus and his teaching by failing to see how the "literal" or "earthly" points to the "symbolic" or "heavenly." The result of misunderstanding is often ironic such that the characters may state something "better than they actually know."

8. There are many key words and phrases in John's Gospel, but some of the most crucial are "Logos," "world," "life, eternal life," "I am," and "Son of Man."
9. The Gospel of John has a number of major narrative threads:
   a. The prologue functions as a hermeneutical point of entry for the reader as it alerts one to major themes of the Gospel such as Christology and revelation, testimony to the truth, Moses and Israel's Scriptures, Jesus and the Jews.
   b. Jesus performs signs that are intended to reveal his glory and thereby lead people to faith. The signs, however, often reveal humanity's preference for the earthly rather than the heavenly, and so they frequently are misunderstood or wrongly pursued.
   c. Jesus is the giver of abundant life who extends God's life and welcome through sharing water, wine, and bread. He washes his disciples' feet to purify them so that they can enter into God's home.
   d. Jesus sends his disciples out, calling them to share in the triune God's mission of love, holiness, and unity.
10. Disciples of Jesus confess Christ's kingship of truth and love, receive life and share it with others, and are called to be friends of God and of one another.

Notes

The endnotes for each chapter appear first, followed by the notes to the sidebars for that chapter.

Chapter 1 What Are the Gospels?

1. See N. T. Wright, *How God Became King: The Forgotten Story of the Gospels* (New York: HarperOne, 2012).

2. Andrew T. Abernethy, *The Book of Isaiah and God's Kingdom: A Thematic-Theological Approach*, New Studies in Biblical Theology 40 (Downers Grove, IL: InterVarsity, 2016), 62.

3. See Douglas A. Campbell, "The Story of Jesus in Romans and Galatians," in *Narrative Dynamics in Paul: A Critical Assessment*, ed. Bruce W. Longenecker (Louisville: Westminster John Knox, 2002), 97–124.

4. See Richard B. Hays, *Echoes of Scripture in the Gospels* (Waco: Baylor University Press, 2016).

5. Klyne Snodgrass, "The Gospel of Jesus," in *The Written Gospel*, ed. Markus Bockmuehl and Donald A. Hagner (Cambridge: Cambridge University Press, 2005), 41.

6. Scot McKnight, *The King Jesus Gospel: The Original Good News Revisited* (Grand Rapids: Zondervan, 2011), 132. See also Matthew W. Bates, *Salvation by Allegiance Alone: Rethinking Faith, Works, and the Gospel of Jesus the King* (Grand Rapids: Baker Academic, 2017), chaps. 2–3.

7. See Martin Hengel, *The Four Gospels and the One Gospel of Jesus Christ: An Investigation of the Collection and Origin of the Canonical Gospels*, trans. John Bowden (London: SCM, 2000), 48–53.

8. Jonathan Pennington, *Reading the Gospels Wisely: A Narrative and Theological Introduction* (Grand Rapids: Baker Academic, 2012), 10.

9. Simon Gathercole, "The Alleged Anonymity of the Gospels," *Journal of Theological Studies* 69 (2018): 447–76.

10. This includes the witnesses of Irenaeus, Tertullian, and Clement of Alexandria as well as important Coptic and Old Latin versions.

11. See the excellent discussion by Michael F. Bird, *The Gospel of the Lord: How the Early Church Wrote the Story of Jesus* (Grand Rapids: Eerdmans, 2014), 245–69.

12. See Graham Stanton, *The Gospels and Jesus*, 2nd ed., Oxford Bible Series (Oxford: Oxford University Press, 2002), 27–29.

13. David E. Aune, *The New Testament in Its Literary Environment* (Philadelphia: Westminster, 1987), 27.

14. Craig S. Keener, *Christobiography: Memory, History, and the Reliability of the Gospels* (Grand Rapids: Eerdmans, 2019), 35–37.

15. Helen K. Bond, *The First Biography of Jesus: Genre and Meaning in Mark's Gospel* (Grand Rapids: Eerdmans, 2020), 45.

16. See Keener, *Christobiography*, 138–60.

17. Richard A. Burridge, *What Are the Gospels? A Comparison with Graeco-Roman Biography*, 2nd ed. (Grand Rapids: Eerdmans, 2004), 185–232.

18. See Bond, *First Biography of Jesus*, 92.

19. Burridge, *What Are the Gospels?*, 289.

20. This is stated with respect to Matthew's Gospel by Dale C. Allison Jr., "Structure, Biographical Impulse, and the *Imitatio Christi*," in *Studies in Matthew: Interpretation Past and Present* (Grand Rapids: Baker Academic, 2005), 144.

21. See Keener, *Christobiography*, 346–64; Burridge, *What Are the Gospels?*, 213–32.

22. Pennington, *Reading the Gospels Wisely*, 33.

23. See David B. Capes, "*Imitatio Christi* and the Gospel Genre," *Bulletin for Biblical Research* 13 (2003): 1–19.

24. On the aspects of the Gospels that are distinctive from Greco-Roman biography, see Pennington, *Reading the Gospels Wisely*, 27–31; Bird, *Gospel of the Lord*, 238–39.

Chapter 1 Sidebar Notes

a. Jonathan Pennington, *Reading the Gospels Wisely: A Narrative and Theological Introduction* (Grand Rapids: Baker Academic, 2012), 5.

b. Scot McKnight, *The King Jesus Gospel: The Original Good News Revisited* (Grand Rapids: Zondervan, 2011), 132.

c. The two most influential form critics were Rudolf Bultmann, *The History of the Synoptic Tradition*, trans. John Marsh (Oxford: Blackwell, 1963) (German original, 1921); Martin Dibelius, *From Tradition to Gospel*, trans. Bertram Lee Woolf (New York: Charles Scribner's Sons, 1935) (German original, 1919).

d. See the foundational work of Richard A. Burridge, *What Are the Gospels? A Comparison with Graeco-Roman Biography*, 2nd ed. (Grand Rapids: Eerdmans, 2004), 105–84.

e. Plutarch, *Alexander*, in *Lives: Demosthenes and Cicero, Alexander and Caesar*, Loeb Classical Library 99, trans. Bernadotte Perrin (Cambridge, MA: Harvard University Press, 1919), 225.

Chapter 2 Where Did the Gospels Come From?

1. See Chris Keith, *Jesus against the Scribal Elite: The Origins of the Conflict* (Grand Rapids: Baker Academic, 2014), 41–43.

2. See Tom Thatcher, *Jesus the Riddler: The Power of Ambiguity in the Gospels* (Louisville: Westminster John Knox, 2006).

3. See Samuel Byrskog, *Jesus the Only Teacher: Didactic Authority and Transmission in Ancient Israel, Ancient Judaism, and the Matthean Community*, Coniectanea Biblica: New Testament 24 (Stockholm: Almqvist & Wiksell, 1994).

4. See Eric Eve, *Writing the Gospels: Composition and Memory* (London: SPCK, 2016), 42.

5. See Michael F. Bird, *The Gospel of the Lord: How the Early Church Wrote the Story of Jesus* (Grand Rapids: Eerdmans, 2014), 23–36.

6. Bird, *Gospel of the Lord*, 24–25.

7. This is brilliantly argued by Dale C. Allison Jr., *Constructing Jesus: Memory, Imagination, and History* (Grand Rapids: Baker Academic, 2010), 392–423.

8. See Seyoon Kim, "Jesus, Sayings of," in *Dictionary of Paul and His Letters*, ed. Gerald F. Hawthorne, Ralph P. Martin, and Daniel G. Reid (Downers Grove, IL: InterVarsity, 1993), 475–80.

9. This argument presumes an early dating for 1 Peter and James.

10. Bird, *Gospel of the Lord*, 30.

11. See Luke Timothy Johnson, *The Writings of the New Testament: An Interpretation* (Minneapolis: Fortress, 1999), 141–42.

12. See the helpful remarks of Loveday Alexander, "What Is a Gospel?," in *The Cambridge Companion to the Gospels*, ed. Stephen C. Barton (Cambridge: Cambridge University Press, 2006), 17–21.

13. Alexander, "What Is a Gospel?," 19.

14. For this example, see James D. G. Dunn, *Jesus Remembered*, vol. 1 of *Christianity in the Making* (Grand Rapids: Eerdmans, 2003), 586–88.

15. For more detail, very helpful is the discussion in Bird, *Gospel of the Lord*, 102–11.

16. Bird, *Gospel of the Lord*, 103.

17. Richard Bauckham, *Jesus and the Eyewitnesses: The Gospels as Eyewitness Testimony* (Grand Rapids: Eerdmans, 2006).

18. See Bird, *Gospel of the Lord*, 48–49.

19. See Eve, *Writing the Gospels*, 45.

20. Bauckham, *Jesus and the Eyewitnesses*, 116–24.

21. Samuel Byrskog, *Story as History—History as Story: The Gospel Tradition in the Context of Ancient Oral History*, Wissenschaftliche Untersuchungen zum Neuen Testament 123 (Tübingen: Mohr Siebeck, 2000), 48.

22. These two steps to the writing of history are based on the work of Lucian of Samosata (second century CE), *How to Write History* 47–56.

23. Bauckham, *Jesus and the Eyewitnesses*, 124.

24. Bauckham, *Jesus and the Eyewitnesses*, chaps. 14 and 15.

25. Bird, *Gospel of the Lord*, 56.

26. See Richard Bauckham, "Historiographical Characteristics of the Gospel of John," in *The Testimony of the Beloved Disciple: Narrative, History, and Theology in the Gospel of John* (Grand Rapids: Baker Academic, 2007), 93–112.

27. Very helpful here is Bauckham, *Jesus and the Eyewitnesses*, 12–30.

28. J. B. Lightfoot and J. R. Harmer, eds. and trans., *The Apostolic Fathers: Greek Texts and English Translations of Their Writings*, ed. and rev. Michael W. Holmes, 2nd ed. (Grand Rapids: Baker, 1992), 565.

29. Bird, *Gospel of the Lord*, 59.

30. Quotation from Eusebius, *The History of the Church*, trans. G. A. Williamson, Penguin Classics (London: Penguin Books, 1989), 169.

31. Bauckham, *Jesus and the Eyewitnesses*, 295–96.

32. See also Birger Gerhardsson, *Memory and Manuscript: Oral Transmission and Written Transmission in Rabbinic Judaism and Early Christianity*, trans. Eric J. Sharpe, Acta Seminarii Neotestamentici Upsaliensis 22 (Lund: Gleerup, 1961).

33. Francis Watson, *Gospel Writing: A Canonical Perspective* (Grand Rapids: Eerdmans, 2013), 349.

34. Dunn, *Jesus Remembered*, 176.

35. Bauckham, *Jesus and the Eyewitnesses*, 264–357.

36. Dunn, *Jesus Remembered*, 177–80.

37. Bird, *Gospel of the Lord*, 97–98.

38. Eve, *Writing the Gospels*, 107.

39. See Chris Keith, *Jesus against the Scribal Elite: The Origins of the Conflict* (Grand Rapids: Baker Academic, 2014), 81.

40. Bird, *Gospel of the Lord*, 61–62.

41. See Watson, *Gospel Writing*, 349–50.

42. Eve, *Writing the Gospels*, 106. See also Allison, *Constructing Jesus*, 1–10.

43. My articulation of this is dependent on Eve, *Writing the Gospels*, 109.

44. Anthony Le Donne refers to this as "typological narrativization." See Anthony Le Donne, *The Historiographical Jesus: Memory, Typology, and the Son of David* (Waco: Baylor University Press, 2019).

45. See Mark Goodacre, "Scripturalization in Mark's Crucifixion Narrative," in *The Trial and Death of Jesus: Essays on the Passion Narrative in Mark*, ed. Geert van Oyen and Tom Shepherd, Contributions to Biblical Exegesis and Theology 45 (Leuven: Peeters, 2006), 33–47.

46. For this example, see Eve, *Writing the Gospels*, 111–14.

47. See Chris Keith, "Memory and Authenticity: Jesus Tradition and What Really Happened," *Zeitschrift für die neutestamentliche Wissenschaft* 102 (2011): 155–77.

48. I am thinking especially of Allison, *Constructing Jesus*.

49. See Craig S. Keener, *Christobiography: Memory, History, and the Reliability of the Gospels* (Grand Rapids: Eerdmans, 2019), 455–58.

50. Eve, *Writing the Gospels*, 81–86.

51. Eve, *Writing the Gospels*, 150.

52. See the discussion in Pennington, *Reading the Gospels Wisely*, 98–103.

Chapter 2 Sidebar Notes

a. Christopher W. Skinner, "Who Was the Beloved Disciple?," Bible Odyssey, https://www.bibleodyssey.org/people/related-articles/who-was-the-beloved-disciple/.

Chapter 3 What Are the Relationships between the Four Canonical Gospels?

1. Jonathan T. Pennington, *Reading the Gospels Wisely: A Narrative and Theological Introduction* (Grand Rapids: Baker Academic, 2012), chap. 4.

2. See Eric Eve, *Writing the Gospels: Composition and Memory* (London: SPCK, 2016), 24–28.

3. See also Mark L. Strauss, *Four Portraits, One Jesus: A Survey of Jesus and the Gospels*, 2nd ed. (Grand Rapids: Zondervan, 2020), 63–65.

4. I recommend that students who want to explore this in more detail begin with the following two works: Mark Goodacre, *The Synoptic Problem: A Way through the Maze*, Biblical Seminar 80 (London: Sheffield Academic, 2001); Stanley E. Porter and Bryan R. Dyer, eds., *The Synoptic Problem: Four Views* (Grand Rapids: Baker Academic, 2016).

5. See Kurt Aland, ed., *Synopsis of the Four Gospels*, rev. ed. (New York: American Bible Society, 2010); for the text in Greek, see Kurt Aland, ed., *Synopsis Quattuor Evangeliorum*, 15th ed. (Stuttgart: Deutsche Bibelgesellschaft, 2005).

6. James D. G. Dunn, *Jesus Remembered*, vol. 1 of *Christianity in the Making* (Grand Rapids: Eerdmans, 2003), 241.

7. See also Eve, *Writing the Gospels*, 42–44.

8. For a brief but helpful summary for the evidence for Markan priority, see Strauss, *Four Portraits, One Jesus*, 65–66.

9. Michael F. Bird, *The Gospel of the Lord: How the Early Church Wrote the Story of Jesus* (Grand Rapids: Eerdmans, 2014), 160.

10. Bird, *Gospel of the Lord*, 162.

11. See Bird, *Gospel of the Lord*, 142–43.

12. Strauss, *Four Portraits, One Jesus*, 73.

13. Thus, sometimes this theory also goes under the name "four-source hypothesis" (i.e., Mark, Q, M, and L).

14. This is classically expressed by B. H. Streeter, *The Four Gospels: A Study of Origins, Treating of the Manuscript Tradition, Sources, Authorship, and Dates* (New York: Macmillan, 1924).

15. See Strauss, *Four Portraits, One Jesus*, 72.

16. Francis Watson, *Gospel Writing: A Canonical Perspective* (Grand Rapids: Eerdmans, 2013), 249–71.

17. See Mark S. Goodacre, *The Case against Q: Studies in Markan Priority and the Synoptic Problem* (Harrisburg, PA: Trinity Press International, 2002).

18. E. P. Sanders and Margaret Davies, *Studying the Synoptic Gospels* (London: SCM, 1989), 67.

19. Watson, *Gospel Writing*, 158–61.

20. G. N. Stanton and N. Perrin, "Q," in *Dictionary of Jesus and the Gospels*, ed. Joel B. Green, Jeannine K. Brown, and Nicholas Perrin, 2nd ed. (Downers Grove, IL: IVP Academic, 2013), 714.

21. Eve, *Writing the Gospels*, 99.

22. See James D. G. Dunn, "Q1 as Oral Tradition," in *The Written Gospel*, ed. Markus Bockmuehl and Donald A. Hagner (Cambridge: Cambridge University Press, 2005), 45–69.

23. Nijay K. Gupta, *A Beginner's Guide to New Testament Studies: Understanding Key Debates* (Grand Rapids: Baker Academic, 2020), 10.

24. On the Gospel of John as stemming from "John the Elder" (a figure referred to by Papias), see Richard Bauckham, *Jesus and the Eyewitnesses: The Gospels as Eyewitness Testimony* (Grand Rapids: Eerdmans, 2006), 358–471.

25. Craig S. Keener, "Gospel of John," in Green, Brown, and Perrin, *Dictionary of Jesus and the Gospels*, 427.

26. Keener, "Gospel of John," 427.

27. See J. Ramsey Michaels, *The Gospel of John*, New International Commentary on the New Testament (Grand Rapids: Eerdmans, 2010), 6–12.

28. Edwyn Clement Hoskyns, *The Fourth Gospel*, ed. Francis Noel Davey (London: Faber & Faber, 1947), 18–19.

29. The view that John is independent from the Synoptics has been most famously argued for by C. H. Dodd, *Historical Tradition in the Fourth Gospel* (Cambridge: Cambridge University Press, 1965).

30. See, however, James W. Barker, *John's Use of Matthew* (Minneapolis: Fortress, 2015).

31. Richard Bauckham, "John for Readers of Mark," in *The Gospel for All Christians: Rethinking the Gospel Audiences*, ed. Richard Bauckham (Grand Rapids: Eerdmans, 1998), 159.

Chapter 3 Sidebar Notes

a. Graham Stanton, *The Gospels and Jesus*, 2nd ed., Oxford Bible Series (Oxford: Oxford University Press, 2002), 22–23.

Chapter 4 Why Only These Four Gospels?

1. On Marcion and Irenaeus's description of his use of a mutilated/corrupted version of Luke, see Judith M. Lieu, *Marcion and the Making of a Heretic: God and Scripture in the Second Century* (Cambridge: Cambridge University Press, 2015), 31–46.

2. Markus Bockmuehl, *Ancient Apocryphal Gospels*, Interpretation (Louisville: Westminster John Knox, 2017), 128.

3. On Porphyry and Augustine, see Robert Louis Wilken, *The Christians as the Romans Saw Them*, 2nd ed. (New Haven: Yale University Press, 2003), 144–47.

4. Francis Watson, *Gospel Writing: A Canonical Perspective* (Grand Rapids: Eerdmans, 2013), 35–36.

5. Jonathan T. Pennington, *Reading the Gospels Wisely: A Narrative and Theological Introduction* (Grand Rapids: Baker Academic, 2012), 52–53.

6. I have been helped here in my understanding of what follows by Pennington, *Reading the Gospels Wisely*, 60–63.

7. Pennington, *Reading the Gospels Wisely*, 64.

8. Pennington, *Reading the Gospels Wisely*, 64.

9. See Craig S. Keener, *Christobiography: Memory, History, and the Reliability of the Gospels* (Grand Rapids: Eerdmans, 2019), 158–60, 303–6.

10. Watson, *Gospel Writing*, 13.

11. Points of convergences between the Gospel writings are developed well by Francis Watson, *The Fourfold Gospel: A Theological Reading of the New Testament Portraits of Jesus* (Grand Rapids: Baker Academic, 2016).

12. Bart D. Ehrman, *Lost Christianities: The Battles for Scripture and the Faiths We Never Knew* (Oxford: Oxford University Press, 2003), 182.

13. I am invoking the title of Ehrman's *Lost Christianities.*

14. C. E. Hill, *Who Chose the Gospels? Probing the Great Gospel Conspiracy* (Oxford: Oxford University Press, 2010), 8–9.

15. See the convincing argument of Dale C. Allison Jr., *The Jesus Tradition in Q* (Harrisburg, PA: Trinity International Press, 1997), 103–19.

16. For a list of prominent scholars, see Hill, *Who Chose the Gospels?*, 213.

17. C. E. Hill, "Canon," in *Dictionary of Jesus and the Gospels*, ed. Joel B. Green, Jeannine K. Brown, and Nicholas Perrin, 2nd ed. (Downers Grove, IL: IVP Academic, 2013), 103.

18. Watson, *Fourfold Gospel*, 17.

19. See the discussion in Michael J. Kruger, *Christianity at the Crossroads: How the Second Century Shaped the Future of the Church* (London: SPCK, 2017), 208–9.

20. On the Muratorian Fragment, see Lee Martin McDonald, *The Biblical Canon: Its Origin, Transmission, and Authority* (Peabody, MA: Hendrickson, 2007), 209–20.

21. Kruger, *Christianity at the Crossroads*, 212.

22. See Hill, *Who Chose the Gospels?*, 69–102.

23. Hill, *Who Chose the Gospels?*, 101.

24. Michael F. Bird, *The Gospel of the Lord: How the Early Church Wrote the Story of Jesus* (Grand Rapids: Eerdmans, 2014), 319.

25. Bockmuehl, *Ancient Apocryphal Gospels*, 61.

26. Bockmuehl, *Ancient Apocryphal Gospels*, 68–71.

27. Hill, *Who Chose the Gospels?*, 86.

28. However, see Bockmuehl, *Ancient Apocryphal Gospels*, 163–83.

Chapter 4 Sidebar Notes

a. Francis Watson, *Gospel Writing: A Canonical Perspective* (Grand Rapids: Eerdmans, 2013), 13.

b. The first line here is disputed. But it seems likely that the Muratorian Fragment is passing on tradition, known to us as early as Papias, that held that the Gospel of Mark is dependent on the remembrances and testimony of Peter.

c. This translation, after the disputed first line, is that of Edmon L. Gallagher and John D. Meade, *The Biblical Canon Lists from Early Christianity: Texts and Analysis* (Oxford: Oxford University Press, 2017), 179.

d. Translation by Alexander Roberts and William Rambaut, in *Ante-Nicene Fathers*, vol. 1, ed. Alexander Roberts, James Donaldson, and A. Cleveland Coxe (Buffalo, NY: Christian Literature Publishing, 1885); revised and edited for New Advent by Kevin Knight, https://www.newadvent.org/fathers/0103311.htm.

e. Michael F. Bird, *The Gospel of the Lord: How the Early Church Wrote the Story of Jesus* (Grand Rapids: Eerdmans, 2014), 326.

f. Oscar Cullmann, ed. and trans., "The Infancy Story of Thomas," in *New Testament Apocrypha*, ed. Wilhelm Schneemelcher and R. McL. Wilson, rev. ed. (Louisville: Westminster John Knox, 1991), 1:444.

g. Christian Maurer and Wilhelm Schneemelcher, ed. and trans., "The Gospel of Peter," in Schneemelcher and Wilson, *New Testament Apocrypha*, 1:225.

h. Quotations from Beate Blatz, ed. and trans., "The Gospel of Thomas," in Schneemelcher and Wilson, *New Testament Apocrypha*, 1:110–33.

i. Quotations from Blatz, "Gospel of Thomas."

Chapter 5 Reading the Gospels in Their First-Century Historical Context

1. Fortunately, this claim is no longer controversial. While many have contributed to the so-called recovery of Jesus's Jewishness, I have been greatly helped by N. T. Wright, *The New*

Testament and the People of God (Minneapolis: Fortress, 1992); *Jesus and the Victory of God* (Minneapolis: Fortress, 1996).

2. Helpful here is Michael L. Satlow, *Creating Judaism: History, Tradition, Practice* (New York: Columbia University Press, 2006), 1–14.

3. See Ekkehard W. Stegemann and Wolfgang Stegemann, *The Jesus Movement: A Social History of Its First Century*, trans. O. C. Dean Jr. (Minneapolis: Fortress, 1999), 7–14.

4. Peter Garnsey and Richard Saller, *The Roman Empire: Economy, Society and Culture*, 2nd ed. (Berkeley: University of California Press, 2015), 71.

5. See Martin Hengel, *Property and Riches in the Early Church: Aspects of a Social History of Early Christianity*, trans. John Bowden (Philadelphia: Fortress, 1974), 12–14.

6. Helen Rhee, *Loving the Poor, Saving the Rich: Wealth, Poverty, and Early Christian Formation* (Grand Rapids: Baker Academic, 2012), 28–29.

7. See especially Roland Boer, *The Sacred Economy of Ancient Israel*, Library of Ancient Israel (Louisville: Westminster John Knox, 2015).

8. On wealthy landowners and large estates in and near Jerusalem, see David A. Fiensy, *Christian Origins and the Ancient Economy* (Eugene, OR: Cascade Books, 2014), 161–63.

9. This theme is highlighted throughout Luke Timothy Johnson, *The Literary Function of Possessions in Luke-Acts*, Society of Biblical Literature Dissertation Series 39 (Missoula, MT: Scholars Press, 1977).

10. E. P. Sanders, *Judaism: Practice and Belief, 63 BCE–66 CE* (Philadelphia: Trinity Press International, 1992), 3.

11. For an accessible view of the diverse groups within first-century Judaism, see Mark L. Strauss, *Four Portraits, One Jesus: A Survey of Jesus and the Gospels*, 2nd ed. (Grand Rapids: Zondervan, 2020), 166–75.

12. Sanders, *Judaism*, 20–22.

13. Shaye J. D. Cohen, *From the Maccabees to the Mishnah*, 3rd ed. (Philadelphia: Westminster John Knox, 2014), 152.

Chapter 5 Sidebar Notes

a. The following studies have influenced my articulation of the material in this sidebar: E. P. Sanders, *Judaism: Practice and Belief, 63 BCE–66 CE* (Philadelphia: Trinity Press International, 1992), 45–303; N. T. Wright, *The New Testament and the People of God* (Minneapolis: Fortress, 1992), 215–338. For an accessible summary, see Mark L. Strauss, *Four Portraits, One Jesus: A Survey of Jesus and the Gospels*, 2nd ed. (Grand Rapids: Zondervan, 2020), 158–66.

b. Translation by R. B. Wright, "Psalms of Solomon," in *The Old Testament Pseudepigrapha*, ed. James H. Charlesworth (Garden City, NY: Doubleday, 1983–85), 2:667–68.

c. For an excellent essay on how Christian teachers and preachers can responsibly engage the Gospels' depiction of the Pharisees, see Amy-Jill Levine, "Preaching and Teaching the Pharisees," in *The Pharisees*, ed. Joseph Sievers and Amy-Jill Levine (Grand Rapids: Eerdmans, 2021), 403–27.

Chapter 6 Reading the Gospels as Narratives

1. Jonathan T. Pennington, *Reading the Gospels Wisely: A Narrative and Theological Introduction* (Grand Rapids: Baker Academic, 2012), 173.

2. Jeannine K. Brown, *The Gospels as Stories: A Narrative Approach to Matthew, Mark, Luke, and John* (Grand Rapids: Baker Academic, 2020), 11.

3. Pennington, *Reading the Gospels Wisely*, 149–50.

4. David Rhoads, Joanna Dewey, and Donald Michie, *Mark as Story: An Introduction to the Narrative of a Gospel*, 3rd ed. (Minneapolis: Fortress, 2012), 73.

5. Rhoads, Dewey, and Michie, *Mark as Story*, 65.

6. Jonathan T. Pennington, *Heaven and Earth in the Gospel of Matthew* (Grand Rapids: Baker Academic, 2009), 7.

7. Brown, *Gospels as Stories*, 65–66.

8. Rhoads, Michie, and Dewey, *Mark as Story*, 130–36.

9. See especially Willard M. Swartley, *Israel's Scripture Traditions and the Synoptic Gospels: Story Shaping Story* (Peabody, MA: Hendrickson, 1994).

10. Many books on the Gospels as stories have helpful sections on the narrator and point of view. I have been most influenced by Rhoads, Dewey, and Michie, *Mark as Story*, 39–61.

11. In what follows I draw on Joshua W. Jipp, "The Beginnings of a Theology of Luke-Acts: Divine Activity and Human Response," *Journal of Theological Interpretation* 8 (2014): 28–32.

12. See Paul Ricoeur, *Time and Narrative*, trans. Kathleen McLaughlin and David Pellauer (Chicago: Chicago University Press, 1984–88), 1:33–37.

13. Brown, *Gospels as Stories*, 149.

14. Ricoeur, *Time and Narrative*, 1:91–94.

15. See Roger Lundin, Clarence Walhout, and Anthony C. Thiselton, *The Promise of Hermeneutics* (Grand Rapids: Eerdmans, 1999), 82.

16. Ricoeur, *Time and Narrative*, 1:53–54.

17. William C. Placher, "How the Gospels Mean," in *Seeking the Identity of Jesus: A Pilgrimage*, ed. Beverly Roberts Gaventa and Richard B. Hays (Grand Rapids: Eerdmans, 2008), 30.

18. Hans W. Frei, *The Eclipse of Biblical Narrative: A Study in Eighteenth and Nineteenth Century Hermeneutics* (New Haven: Yale University Press, 1974), 3.

19. Brown, *Gospels as Stories*, 158.

Chapter 6 Sidebar Notes

a. Seymour Chatman, *Story and Discourse: Narrative Structure in Fiction and Film* (Ithaca, NY: Cornell University Press, 1978).

b. Jack D. Kingsbury, *Matthew as Story* (Philadelphia: Fortress, 1988); David Rhoads, Joanna Dewey, and Donald Michie, *Mark as Story* (Philadelphia: Fortress, 1982); Robert C. Tannehill, *The Narrative Unity of Luke-Acts*, 2 vols. (Philadelphia: Fortress, 1986–90); R. Alan Culpepper, *The Anatomy of the Fourth Gospel: A Study in Literary Design* (Philadelphia: Fortress, 1983).

c. Luke Timothy Johnson, "Imagining the World Scripture Imagines," *Modern Theology* 14 (1998): 166.

Chapter 7 Reading the Gospels for Transformative Discipleship

1. William C. Placher, "How the Gospels Mean," in *Seeking the Identity of Jesus: A Pilgrimage*, ed. Beverly Roberts Gaventa and Richard B. Hays (Grand Rapids: Eerdmans, 2008), 29.

2. See Jonathan T. Pennington, *Reading the Gospels Wisely: A Narrative and Theological Introduction* (Grand Rapids: Baker Academic, 2012), 137–38.

3. For an excellent study of these themes, see Catherine J. Wright, *Spiritual Practices of Jesus: Learning Simplicity, Humility, and Prayer with Luke's Earliest Readers* (Downers Grove, IL: IVP Academic, 2020).

4. Pennington, *Reading the Gospels Wisely*, 159.

5. Pennington, *Reading the Gospels Wisely*, 160.

6. See Dale C. Allison Jr., "Structure, Biographical Impulse, and the *Imitatio Christi*," in *Studies in Matthew: Interpretation Past and Present* (Grand Rapids: Baker Academic, 2005), 142–55.

7. Dale C. Allison Jr., "The Embodiment of God's Will: Jesus in Matthew," in Gaventa and Hays, *Seeking the Identity of Jesus*, 125.

8. Luke Timothy Johnson, *Living Jesus: Learning the Heart of the Gospel* (San Francisco: HarperSanFrancisco, 1999), 4–5.

9. Ulrich Luz, *Matthew 1–7: A Commentary*, trans. Wilhelm C. Linss (Minneapolis: Augsburg, 1989), 99.

Chapter 7 Sidebar Notes

a. Thomas à Kempis, *The Imitation of Christ* (North Brunswick, NJ: Bridge Logos, 1999), 19.

b. On the broader point, see Frances M. Young, *Biblical Exegesis and the Formation of Christian Culture* (Cambridge: Cambridge University Press, 1997), 217–84.

c. Peter W. Martens, "Ideal Interpreters," in *The Oxford Handbook of Early Christian Biblical Interpretation*, ed. Paul M. Blowers and Peter W. Martens (Oxford: Oxford University Press, 2019), 159.

d. Dietrich Bonhoeffer, *Life Together*, trans. John W. Doberstein (San Francisco: Harper & Brothers, 1954), 84–85.

e. See Jessica Hooten Wilson and Jacob Stratman, eds., *Learning the Good Life: Wisdom from the Great Hearts and Minds That Came Before* (Grand Rapids: Zondervan Academic, 2022), 182.

f. Gerard Manley Hopkins, *Selected Poetry*, ed. Catherine Phillips (New York: Oxford University Press, 1996), 115.

Chapter 8 Matthew and History

1. For the evidence from the canon lists, see Edmon L. Gallagher and John D. Meade, *The Biblical Canon Lists from Early Christianity: Texts and Analysis* (Oxford: Oxford University Press, 2017).

2. R. T. France, *Matthew: Evangelist and Teacher* (Downers Grove, IL: InterVarsity, 1989), 17. This volume, though somewhat dated, is excellent.

3. France, *Matthew*, 19–20.

4. See Paul S. Minear, *Matthew: The Teacher's Gospel* (New York: Pilgrim, 1982).

5. Luke Timothy Johnson, *The Writings of the New Testament: An Interpretation* (Minneapolis: Fortress, 1999), 190.

6. See further Patrick Schreiner, *Matthew, Disciple and Scribe: The First Gospel and Its Portrait of Jesus* (Grand Rapids: Baker Academic, 2019), esp. 7–36.

7. See R. Kendall Soulen, *The God of Israel and Christian Theology* (Minneapolis: Fortress, 1996), esp. 25–56.

8. See Elizabeth Schüssler Fiorenza, "The Ethics of Biblical Interpretation: Decentering Biblical Scholarship," *Journal of Biblical Literature* 107 (1988): 3–17.

9. See Susannah Heschel, *The Aryan Jesus: Christian Theologians and the Bible in Nazi Germany* (Princeton: Princeton University Press, 2008).

10. See further Matthias Konradt, *Israel, Church, and the Gentiles in the Gospel of Matthew*, trans. Kathleen Ess, Baylor–Mohr Siebeck Studies in Early Christianity (Waco: Baylor University Press, 2014), 172–93.

11. Sadly, there are too many to name here. On this, see John G. Gager, *The Origins of Anti-Semitism: Attitudes toward Judaism in Pagan and Christian Antiquity* (Oxford: Oxford University Press, 1985).

12. So Boris Repschinski, "'For He Will Save His People from Their Sins' (Matthew 1:21): A Christology for Christian Jews," *Catholic Biblical Quarterly* 68 (2006): 263.

13. See further John Kampen, "The Problem of Christian Anti-Semitism and a Sectarian Reading of the Gospel of Matthew: The Trial of Jesus," in *Matthew within Judaism: Israel and the Nations in the First Gospel*, ed. Anders Runesson and Daniel M. Gurtner, Early Christianity and Its Literature 27 (Atlanta: SBL Press, 2020), 371–97.

14. See Mark Allan Powell, *Fortress Introduction to the Gospels*, 2nd ed. (Minneapolis: Fortress, 2019), 103–7.

15. This option is discussed but rejected by France, *Matthew*, 62–66.

16. Ulrich Luz, *Matthew 1–7: A Commentary*, trans. Wilhelm C. Linss (Minneapolis: Augsburg, 1989), 90.

17. See Richard Bauckham, ed., *The Gospels for All Christians: Rethinking the Gospel Audiences* (Grand Rapids: Eerdmans, 1998).

Chapter 8 Sidebar Notes

a. My list is adapted from that of Mark Allan Powell, *Fortress Introduction to the Gospels*, 2nd ed. (Minneapolis: Fortress, 2019), 96–97.

Chapter 9 Matthew and Narrative (1)

1. So Graham N. Stanton, *A Gospel for a New People: Studies in Matthew* (Louisville: Westminster John Knox, 1992), 71–75.

2. My articulation of this is dependent on Eric Eve, *Writing the Gospels: Composition and Memory* (London: SPCK, 2016), 109.

3. On this theme, see Patrick Schreiner, *Matthew, Disciple and Scribe: The First Gospel and Its Portrait of Jesus* (Grand Rapids: Baker Academic, 2019).

4. See Jack Dean Kingsbury, *Matthew as Story*, 2nd ed. (Minneapolis: Fortress, 1988), 40–42.

5. This structure was argued for and popularized by Benjamin W. Bacon, *Studies in Matthew* (New York: Henry Holt, 1930). I am following the updated arguments by Dale C. Allison Jr., *Studies in Matthew: Interpretation Past and Present* (Grand Rapids: Baker Academic, 2005), 137–42.

6. I am indebted here to the work of Jonathan T. Pennington, *The Sermon on the Mount and Human Flourishing: A Theological Commentary* (Grand Rapids: Baker Academic, 2017), 87–103.

7. R. T. France, *The Gospel of Matthew*, New International Commentary on the New Testament (Grand Rapids: Eerdmans, 2007), 167.

8. Richard B. Hays, *Echoes of Scripture in the Gospels* (Waco: Baylor University Press, 2016), 126; on Jesus's "hermeneutic of mercy," see pp. 123–28.

Chapter 9 Sidebar Notes

a. Ellen T. Charry, *By the Renewing of Your Minds: The Pastoral Function of Christian Doctrine* (Oxford: Oxford University Press, 1997), 80.

b. Jonathan T. Pennington, *Heaven and Earth in the Gospel of Matthew* (Grand Rapids: Baker Academic, 2009), 342–43.

Chapter 10 Matthew and Narrative (2)

1. Portions of the first three narrative threads have been adapted from Joshua W. Jipp, *The Messianic Theology of the New Testament* (Grand Rapids: Eerdmans, 2020), 21–56. Reprinted by permission of the publisher.

2. See Nicholas G. Piotrowski, "'After the Deportation': Observations in Matthew's Apocalyptic Genealogy," *Bulletin for Biblical Research* 25 (2015): 189–203.

3. Richard B. Hays, *Echoes of Scripture in the Gospels* (Waco: Baylor University Press, 2016), 111.

4. Nathan Eubank, *Wages of Cross-Bearing and the Debt of Sin: The Economy of Heaven in Matthew's Gospel*, Beihefte zur Zeitschrift für die neutestamentliche Wissenschaft 196 (Berlin: de Gruyter, 2013), 130.

5. See, e.g., Exod. 21:30; 30:12; Lev. 19:20; 25:51–52; 27:31; Num. 3:46–49.

6. Eubank, *Wages of Cross-Bearing*, 149–54.

7. See also Hays, *Echoes of Scripture*, 134.

8. Nicholas G. Piotrowski, *Matthew's New David at the End of Exile: A Socio-Rhetorical Study of Scriptural Quotations*, Supplements to Novum Testamentum 170 (Leiden: Brill), 146–49.

9. See Boris Repschinski, "'For He Will Save His People from Their Sins' (Matthew 1:21): A Christology for Christian Jews," *Catholic Biblical Quarterly* 68 (2006): 264.

10. Matthias Konradt, *Israel, Church, and the Gentiles in the Gospel of Matthew*, trans. Kathleen Ess, Baylor–Mohr Siebeck Studies in Early Christianity (Waco: Baylor University Press, 2014), 301.

11. See W. D. Davies, *Torah in the Messianic Age and/or the Age to Come*, Journal of Biblical Literature Monograph Series 7 (Philadelphia: Society of Biblical Literature, 1952).

12. On Jesus as a Moses-like figure, see Dale C. Allison Jr., *The New Moses: A Matthean Typology* (1993; repr., Eugene, OR: Wipf & Stock, 2013).

13. George Eldon Ladd, *A Theology of the New Testament*, 2nd ed. (Grand Rapids: Eerdmans, 1998), 94.

14. See Dale C. Allison Jr., *The Sermon on the Mount: Inspiring the Moral Imagination*, Companions to the New Testament (New York: Crossroad, 1999), 58–61.

15. See Jonathan T. Pennington, *The Sermon on the Mount and Human Flourishing: A Theological Commentary* (Grand Rapids: Baker Academic, 2017), 170–79.

16. Note Pennington, *Sermon on the Mount*, 181.

17. Anders Runesson, *Divine Wrath and Salvation in Matthew: The Narrative World of the First Gospel* (Minneapolis: Fortress, 2016), 72–73.

18. Thomas R. Blanton IV, "Saved by Obedience: Matthew 1:21 in Light of Jesus' Teaching on the Torah," *Journal of Biblical Literature* 132 (2013): 407–8.

19. See also Pennington, *Sermon on the Mount*, 91.

20. See especially Deirdre J. Good, *Jesus the Meek King* (Harrisburg, PA: Trinity Press International, 1999).

21. Good, *Jesus the Meek King*, 82–88.

22. I am dependent on Dale C. Allison Jr., "The Embodiment of God's Will: Jesus in Matthew," in *Seeking the Identity of Jesus: A Pilgrimage*, ed. Beverly Roberts Gaventa and Richard B. Hays (Grand Rapids: Eerdmans, 2008), 117–32.

23. See throughout Jonathan T. Pennington, *Heaven and Earth in the Gospel of Matthew* (Grand Rapids: Baker Academic, 2009), esp. 321–23.

24. Konradt, *Israel, Church, and the Gentiles*, 36.

25. See further Dorothy Jean Weaver, "'What Is That to Us? See to It Yourself': Making Atonement and the Matthean Portrait of the Jewish Chief Priests," in *The Irony of Power: The Politics of God within Matthew's Narrative* (Eugene, OR: Pickwick, 2017), 66–84.

26. J. R. Daniel Kirk, *A Man Attested by God: The Human Jesus of the Synoptic Gospels* (Grand Rapids: Eerdmans, 2016), 466–67.

27. See further Wayne Baxter, *Israel's Only Shepherd: Matthew's Shepherd Motif and His Social Setting*, Library of New Testament Studies 457 (London: T&T Clark, 2012), 154–55.

28. Nathan C. Johnson, "The Passion according to David: Matthew's Arrest Narrative, the Absalom Revolt, and Militant Messianism," *Catholic Biblical Quarterly* 80 (2018): 247–72.

29. See the conclusion in Johnson, "Passion According to David," 271–72.

30. See further David C. Sim, *Apocalyptic Eschatology in the Gospel of Matthew*, Society for New Testament Studies Monograph Series 88 (Cambridge: Cambridge University Press, 1996).

31. David E. Garland, *Reading Matthew: A Literary and Theological Commentary on the First Gospel*, Reading the New Testament (New York: Crossroad, 1993), 226.

32. Garland, *Reading Matthew*, 220.

33. Very helpful here is Eubank, *Wages of Cross-Bearing*, 99–102.

Chapter 10 Sidebar Notes

a. Quotations from Fyodor Dostoevsky, *The Brothers Karamazov*, trans. David McDuff (London: Penguin Books, 2003), 325, 335–36, 342.

b. See Pierre Hadot, *Philosophy as a Way of Life: Spiritual Exercises from Socrates to Foucault*, ed. Arnold I. Davidson, trans. Michael Chase (Malden, MA: Blackwell, 1995).

c. See Chris Keith, *Jesus against the Scribal Elite: The Origins of the Conflict* (Grand Rapids: Baker Academic, 2014), 56–68.

d. I am dependent here on the excellent essay by Margaret M. Mitchell, "John Chrysostom," in *The Sermon on the Mount through the Centuries: From the Early Church to John*

Paul II, ed. Jeffrey P. Greenman, Timothy Larsen, and Stephen R. Spencer (Grand Rapids: Brazos, 2007), 22–23.

e. Dallas Willard, *The Divine Conspiracy: Rediscovering Our Hidden Life in God* (San Francisco: HarperOne, 1997). In addition to Willard, see Jonathan T. Pennington, *Jesus the Great Philosopher: Rediscovering the Wisdom Needed for the Good Life* (Grand Rapids: Brazos, 2020).

f. Pennington, *Jesus the Great Philosopher*, 65–66.

g. See Richard B. Hays, *Echoes of Scripture in the Gospels* (Waco: Baylor University Press, 2016), 128.

Chapter 11 Matthew and Discipleship

1. The best book I've seen on this is Dorothy Jean Weaver, *The Irony of Power: The Politics of God within Matthew's Narrative* (Eugene, OR: Pickwick, 2017).
2. R. T. France, *The Gospel of Matthew*, New International Commentary on the New Testament (Grand Rapids: Eerdmans, 2007), 169.
3. Esau McCaulley, *Reading While Black: African American Biblical Interpretation as an Exercise in Hope* (Downers Grove, IL: InterVarsity, 2020), 87.
4. Weaver, *Irony of Power*, 181.
5. Weaver, *Irony of Power*, 182.
6. I have adapted parts of the following from Joshua W. Jipp, *The Messianic Theology of the New Testament* (Grand Rapids: Eerdmans, 2020), 53–55. Reprinted by permission of the publisher.
7. See France, *Gospel of Matthew*, 957–58.
8. Mark Allan Powell, *God with Us: A Pastoral Theology of Matthew's Gospel* (Minneapolis: Fortress, 1989), 3–4.
9. The following section has been revised and expanded from Jipp, *Messianic Theology of the New Testament*, 55–56. Reprinted by permission of the publisher.
10. Richard B. Hays, *Echoes of Scripture in the Gospels* (Waco: Baylor University Press, 2016), 175–85; Matthias Konradt, *Israel, Church, and the Gentiles in the Gospel of Matthew*, trans. Kathleen Ess, Baylor–Mohr Siebeck Studies in Early Christianity (Waco: Baylor University Press, 2014), 265–81.
11. See Michael Patrick Barber, "Jesus as the Davidic Temple Builder and Peter's Priestly Role in Matthew 16:16–19," *Journal of Biblical Literature* 132 (2013): 947–51.

Chapter 11 Sidebar Notes

a. Mary Oliver, "Upstream," in *Upstream: Selected Essays* (New York: Penguin Books, 2016), 8.

b. Mary Oliver, *Devotions: The Selected Poems of Mary Oliver* (New York: Penguin Books, 2017), 131.

c. See especially Taylor Branch, *Parting the Waters: America in the King Years, 1954–63* (New York: Simon & Schuster, 1988).

d. Albert J. Raboteau, *American Prophets: Seven Religious Radicals and Their Struggle for Social and Political Justice* (Princeton: Princeton University Press, 2016), 146.

e. Martin Luther King Jr., "A Christian Sermon on Peace," in *A Testament of Hope: The Essential Writings of Martin Luther King Jr.*, ed. James Melvin Washington (San Francisco: Harper & Row, 1986), 254.

f. Esau McCaulley, *Reading While Black: African American Biblical Interpretation as an Exercise in Hope* (Downers Grove, IL: InterVarsity, 2020), 69.

g. King, "Christian Sermon on Peace," 297.

h. On the distinction, see Mark R. McMinn, *The Science of Virtue: Why Positive Psychology Matters to the Church* (Grand Rapids: Brazos, 2017), 49–51.

i. Matthew Ichihashi Potts, *Forgiveness: An Alternative Account* (New Haven: Yale University Press, 2022), 8.

j. Quoted in Manlio Simonetti, ed., *Matthew 14–28*, vol. 1b of *Ancient Christian Commentary on Scripture: New Testament* (Downers Grove, IL: InterVarsity, 2002), 234.

k. Quoted in Simonetti, *Matthew 14–28*, 234.

l. The following paragraphs are dependent in large part on Coleman Fannin, "Dorothy Day's Radical Hospitality," in *Christian Reflection*, Center for Christian Ethics at Baylor University (Waco: Baylor University Press, 2007), 37–45, https://www.baylor.edu/content/services/document.php/53381.pdf; Dorothy Day, *The Long Loneliness: The Autobiography of Dorothy Day* (San Francisco: Harper & Brothers, 1952).

m. Day and Maurin also started a newspaper and small-scale farms as part of their advocacy for the urban poor.

n. Day, *Long Loneliness*, 285.

o. Dorothy Day, "Love Is the Measure," *The Catholic Worker* 13, no. 5 (June 1946): 2.

Chapter 12 Mark and History

1. For more precise statistics, see Michael J. Kok, *The Gospel on the Margins: The Reception of Mark in the Second Century* (Minneapolis: Fortress, 2015), 3–4.

2. Luke Timothy Johnson, *The Writings of the New Testament: An Interpretation* (Minneapolis: Fortress, 1999), 159.

3. See further C. E. Hill, *Who Chose the Gospels? Probing the Great Gospel Conspiracy* (Oxford: Oxford University Press, 2010), 20–21.

4. Martin Hengel, *The Four Gospels and the One Gospel of Jesus Christ: An Investigation of the Collection and Origin of the Canonical Gospels*, trans. John Bowden (London: SCM, 2000), 39.

5. J. B. Lightfoot and J. R. Harmer, eds. and trans., *The Apostolic Fathers: Greek Texts and English Translations of Their Writings*, ed. and rev. Michael W. Holmes, 2nd ed. (Grand Rapids: Baker, 1992), 569.

6. Nicholas Perrin, "Mark, Gospel of," in *Dictionary of Jesus and the Gospels*, ed. Joel B. Green, Jeannine K. Brown, and Nicholas Perrin, 2nd ed. (Downers Grove, IL: IVP Academic, 2013), 553.

7. Further, see Perrin, "Mark, Gospel of," 559.

8. Hill, *Who Chose the Gospels?*, 213.

9. Richard Bauckham, *Jesus and the Eyewitnesses: The Gospels as Eyewitness Testimony* (Grand Rapids: Eerdmans, 2006), 125.

10. Hengel, *Four Gospels*, 82.

11. See Mark 1:16, 29, 36; 3:16; 5:37; 8:29, 32–33; 9:2, 5; 10:28; 11:21; 13:3; 14:29, 33, 37, 54, 66–67, 70, 72; 16:7.

12. Note, however, the recent suggestion by Joel Marcus, "Mark—Interpreter of Paul," *New Testament Studies* 46 (2000): 473–87.

13. Perhaps the most ambitious attempt to demonstrate Mark's Gospel as a narrative commentary on Paul's Epistles is that of J. C. Fenton, "Paul and Mark," in *Studies in the Gospels: Essays in Memory of R. H. Lightfoot*, ed. Dennis E. Nineham (Oxford: Basil Blackwell, 1957), 89–112.

14. Marcus, "Mark—Interpreter of Paul," 477.

15. See Michael Bird, "Mark: Interpreter of Peter and Disciple of Paul," in *Paul and the Gospels: Christologies, Conflicts and Convergences*, ed. Michael F. Bird and Joel Willitts, Library of New Testament Studies 411 (London: T&T Clark, 2011), 30–61. He argues that Mark is a synthesis of "Petrine testimony" and "Pauline proclamation" (p. 32).

16. This view is often associated with Willi Marxsen, *Mark the Evangelist: Studies on the Redaction History of the Gospel*, trans. James Boyce (Nashville: Abingdon, 1969).

17. See Mark Allan Powell, *Fortress Introduction to the Gospels*, 2nd ed. (Minneapolis: Fortress, 2019), 70–71.

18. For what follows, see Hengel, *Four Gospels*, 78–89.

19. Latinisms: Mark 4:21; 5:9, 15; 6:37; 7:4; 12:14, 42; 15:15, 16, 39, 44–45; Aramaic words: 3:17; 5:41; 7:11, 34; 10:46; 14:36; 15:22, 34.

20. See Udo Schnelle, *The History and Theology of the New Testament Writings*, trans. M. Eugene Boring (Minneapolis: Fortress, 1998), 200–201.

21. For a good discussion of the options, see Perrin, "Mark, Gospel of," 560–61.

22. So Hengel, *Four Gospels*, 78.

23. See Richard Bauckham, ed., *The Gospels for All Christians: Rethinking the Gospel Audiences* (Grand Rapids: Eerdmans, 1998).

24. Helpful here is Powell, *Fortress Introduction to the Gospels*, 71–72.

Chapter 12 Sidebar Notes

a. J. B. Lightfoot and J. R. Harmer, eds. and trans., *The Apostolic Fathers: Greek Texts and English Translations of Their Writings*, ed. and rev. Michael W. Holmes, 2nd ed. (Grand Rapids: Baker, 1992), 569. Papias's statement is also found in Eusebius, *Ecclesiastical History* 3.39.15.

b. The apocalyptic battle between Jesus and the demonic, including the military imagery implied in the "strong man" statements, is noted by Rikki E. Watts, *Isaiah's New Exodus in Mark*, Wissenschaftliche Untersuchungen zum Neuen Testament 2/88 (Tübingen: Mohr Siebeck, 1997), 144–69.

Chapter 13 Mark and Narrative (1)

1. Many rightly make this point. See Mark Allan Powell, *Fortress Introduction to the Gospels*, 2nd ed. (Minneapolis: Fortress, 2019), 59.

2. There is an abundance of examples, but most of them are indebted to David Rhoads, Joanna Dewey, and Donald Michie, *Mark as Story: An Introduction to the Narrative of a Gospel*, 3rd ed. (Minneapolis: Fortress, 2012).

3. See Joanna Dewey, "Mark as Interwoven Tapestry: Forecasts and Echoes for a Listening Audience," *Catholic Biblical Quarterly* 53 (1991): 221–36.

4. See Joanna Dewey, "Oral Methods of Structuring in Mark," *Interpretation* 43 (1989): 32–44; Christopher Bryan, *A Preface to Mark: Notes on the Gospel in Its Literary and Cultural Settings* (Oxford: Oxford University Press), 72–81.

5. Helen K. Bond, *The First Biography of Jesus: Genre and Meaning in Mark's Gospel* (Grand Rapids: Eerdmans, 2020), 88.

6. Bryan, *Preface to Mark*, 83.

7. Many excellent studies have contributed to my knowledge of these devices. I recommend, however, Rhoads, Dewey, and Michie, *Mark as Story*, 47–61; Nicholas Perrin, "Mark, Gospel of," in *Dictionary of Jesus and the Gospels*, ed. Joel B. Green, Jeannine K. Brown, and Nicholas Perrin, 2nd ed. (Downers Grove, IL: IVP Academic, 2013), 556–58.

8. See especially Elizabeth Struthers Malbon, *Mark's Jesus: Characterization as Narrative Christology* (Waco: Baylor University Press, 2009), 195–210.

9. See especially James R. Edwards, "Markan Sandwiches: The Significance of Interpolations in Markan Narratives," *Novum Testamentum* 21 (1989): 193–216.

10. Again, see Dewey, "Mark as Interwoven Tapestry."

11. My proposal is similar to that of Joel Marcus, *Mark 1–8: A New Translation with Introduction and Commentary*, Anchor Bible 27 (New York: Doubleday, 2000), 62–64.

12. Rhoads, Dewey, and Michie, *Mark as Story*, 63.

13. See Francis Watson, *The Fourfold Gospel: A Theological Reading of the New Testament Portraits of Jesus* (Grand Rapids: Baker Academic, 2016), 50–51.

14. Marcus, *Mark 1–8*, 149.

15. See, for example, Matthew W. Bates, *Salvation by Allegiance Alone: Rethinking Faith, Works, and the Gospel of Jesus the King* (Grand Rapids: Baker Academic, 2017); Teresa Morgan, *Roman Faith and Christian Faith:* Pistis *and* Fides *in the Early Roman Empire and Early Churches* (Oxford: Oxford University Press, 2015).

16. Many early manuscripts do not have "Son of God," but I find the arguments for its inclusion to be persuasive. See Tommy Wasserman, "The 'Son of God' Was in the Beginning (Mark 1:1)," *Journal of Theological Studies* 62 (2011): 20–50.

Chapter 13 Sidebar Notes

a. Michael Peppard, *The Son of God in the Roman World: Divine Sonship in Its Social and Political Context* (Oxford: Oxford University Press, 2012), 28. See also Adela Yarbro Collins, "Mark and His Readers: The Son of God among Greeks and Romans," *Harvard Theological Review* 93 (2000): 85–100.

b. Peppard, *Son of God in the Roman World*, 123.

Chapter 14 Mark and Narrative (2)

1. There are many good resources on this, but in my view the most helpful is Joel Marcus, *Mark 1–8: A New Translation with Introduction and Commentary*, Anchor Bible 27 (New York: Doubleday, 2000). In particular, see his introduction to this theme (pp. 71–73).

2. In more detail, see Joshua W. Jipp, *The Messianic Theology of the New Testament* (Grand Rapids: Eerdmans, 2020), 60–61.

3. Mark Allan Powell, *Fortress Introduction to the Gospels*, 2nd ed. (Minneapolis: Fortress, 2019), 74–77.

4. On this as Jesus's first Markan parable, see Elizabeth E. Shively, *Apocalyptic Imagination in the Gospel of Mark: The Literary and Theological Role of Mark 3:22—30*, Beihefte zur Zeitschrift für die neutestamentliche Wissenschaft 189 (Berlin: de Gruyter, 2012).

5. This dynamic is stated well by Marcus, *Mark 1–8*, 301–2.

6. See especially the important work, which has strongly influenced my reading of the Gospel, by Elizabeth Struthers Malbon, *Mark's Jesus: Characterization as Narrative Christology* (Waco: Baylor University Press, 2009).

7. David Rhoads, Joanna Dewey, Donald Michie, *Mark as Story: An Introduction to the Narrative of a Gospel*, 3rd ed. (Minneapolis: Fortress, 2012), 104–6.

8. See Joshua W. Jipp, *Christ Is King: Paul's Royal Ideology* (Minneapolis: Fortress, 2015), 18–29.

9. J. R. Daniel Kirk, *A Man Attested by God: The Human Jesus of the Synoptic Gospels* (Grand Rapids: Eerdmans, 2016), 451.

10. On Markan intercalation and the way in which the technique highlights the most important themes of the Gospel, see James R. Edwards, "Markan Sandwiches: The Significance of Interpolations in Markan Narratives," *Novum Testamentum* 31 (1989): 193–216.

11. Marcus, *Mark 1–8*, 398.

12. So Kirk, *Man Attested by God*, 451.

13. I have learned much on this point from Malbon, *Mark's Jesus*, 129–94.

14. Many have recognized Mark's emphasis on "three" in the literary structure of the "way" section. See, for example, Powell, *Fortress Introduction to the Gospels*, 87.

15. This is the major argument of Jeremy R. Treat, *The Crucified King: Atonement and Kingdom in Biblical and Systematic Theology* (Grand Rapids: Zondervan, 2014).

16. Bartimaeus belongs to the Markan pattern of those minor characters who respond to Jesus with faith (so also 1:40–44; 5:24–34; 7:24–30; 9:14–29). See further Richard B. Hays, *Echoes of Scripture in the Gospels* (Waco: Baylor University Press, 2016), 50–51.

17. Very helpful here is Matthew Thiessen, "The Many for One or the One for Many: Reading Mark 10:45 in the Roman Empire," *Harvard Theological Review* 109 (2016): 447–66.

18. See Timothy C. Gray, *The Temple in the Gospel of Mark: A Study in Its Narrative Role* (Grand Rapids: Baker Academic, 2010), 20–22.

19. Gray, *Temple in the Gospel of Mark*, 25–29.

20. See Joel Marcus, *Mark 8–16: A New Translation with Introduction and Commentary*, Anchor Yale Bible 27A (New Haven: Yale University Press, 2009), 783.

21. Marcus, *Mark 8–16*, 791.

22. See, in more detail, W. R. Telford, *The Barren Temple and the Withered Fig Tree: A Redaction-Critical Analysis of the Cursing of the Fig-Tree Pericope in Mark's Gospel and Its Relation to the Cleansing of the Temple Tradition*, Journal for the Study of the New Testament Supplement Series 1 (Sheffield: JSOT Press, 1980).

23. See Gray, *Temple in the Gospel of Mark*, 38–43.

24. See Gray, *Temple in the Gospel of Mark*, 41.

25. Kirk, *Man Attested by God*, 214.

26. Timothy G. Gombis, *Mark*, The Story of God Bible Commentary (Grand Rapids: Zondervan, 2021), 449.

27. Gray, *Temple in the Gospel of Mark*, 124.

28. See Brant Pitre, *Jesus and the Last Supper* (Grand Rapids: Eerdmans, 2015), 93–95.

29. Pitre, *Jesus and the Last Supper*, 100–104.

30. Many have made this point, but see especially Treat, *Crucified King*.

31. See Peter G. Bolt, *The Cross from a Distance: Atonement in Mark's Gospel*, New Studies in Biblical Theology 18 (Downers Grove, IL: InterVarsity, 2004), 117–21.

32. Dorothy A. Lee, *The Ministry of Women in the New Testament: Reclaiming the Biblical Vision for Church Leadership* (Grand Rapids: Baker Academic, 2021), 35.

33. Very helpful here is Stephen Ahearne-Kroll, *The Psalms of Lament in Mark's Passion: Jesus's Davidic Suffering*, Society for New Testament Studies Monograph Series 142 (Cambridge: Cambridge University Press, 2007).

34. See Frank J. Matera, *The Kingship of Jesus: Composition and Theology in Mark 15*, Society of Biblical Literature Dissertation Series 66 (Chico, CA: Scholars Press, 1982), 121.

35. On the soldiers' activity as mimicking a Roman triumph for a victorious general or ruler, see T. E. Schmidt, "Mark 15.16–32: The Crucifixion Narrative and the Roman Triumphal Procession," *New Testament Studies* 41 (1995): 1–18.

36. See Marcus, *Mark 8–16*, 1050.

37. Bolt, *Cross from a Distance*, 52–54.

38. So Treat, *Crucified King*, 101.

39. Bolt, *Cross from a Distance*, 130–31.

40. Morna D. Hooker, *The Gospel according to Saint Mark*, Black's New Testament Commentaries (Grand Rapids: Baker Academic, 2011), 394.

Chapter 14 Sidebar Notes

a. See especially David Rhoads, Joanna Dewey, and Donald Michie, *Mark as Story: An Introduction to the Narrative of a Gospel*, 3rd ed. (Minneapolis: Fortress, 2012), 130–35.

b. Translations of the *Res Gestae* are from Alison E. Cooley, *Res Gestae Divi Augusti: Text, Translation, and Commentary* (Cambridge: Cambridge University Press, 2009).

c. If one adds the Freer Logion, this would constitute a fourth, but its external evidence is weak (see only Codex Washingtonianus). On the endings in Mark, see Mark L. Strauss, *Mark*, Zondervan Exegetical Commentary on the New Testament (Grand Rapids: Zondervan, 2014), 723.

d. Strauss, *Mark*, 723.

Chapter 15 Mark and Discipleship

1. On this theme, see the excellent study by Suzanne Watts Henderson, *Christology and Discipleship in the Gospel of Mark*, Society for New Testament Studies Monograph Series 135 (Cambridge: Cambridge University Press, 2005).

2. Timothy G. Gombis, *Mark*, The Story of God Bible Commentary (Grand Rapids: Zondervan, 2021), 114.

3. This point was brought home to me by David Rhoads, Joanna Dewey, and Donald Michie, *Mark as Story: An Introduction to the Narrative of a Gospel*, 3rd ed. (Minneapolis: Fortress, 2012), 90–96.

4. For an excellent demonstration of how Paul's understanding of power is indebted to Jesus's example of service and sacrifice, see Timothy G. Gombis, *Power in Weakness: Paul's Transformed Vision for Ministry* (Grand Rapids: Eerdmans, 2021).

5. Gombis, *Mark*, 373.

6. Scot McKnight and Laura Barringer, *A Church Called Tov: Forming a Goodness Culture That Resists Abuses of Power and Promotes Healing* (Carol Stream, IL: Tyndale, 2020), 181.

7. See Alan Noble, *Disruptive Witness: Speaking Truth in a Distracted Age* (Downers Grove, IL: InterVarsity, 2018), 71.

8. See Charles Taylor, *The Ethics of Authenticity* (Cambridge, MA: Harvard University Press, 1991), 43–45.

9. See also 1 Cor. 3:16; 6:19; 2 Cor. 6:14–7:1.

10. Gombis, *Mark*, 395.

Chapter 15 Sidebar Notes

a. Wendell Berry, *A Timbered Choir: The Sabbath Poems, 1979–1997* (Washington, DC: Counterpoint, 1998), 74. Wendell Berry, excerpt from ["A gracious Sabbath stood here while they stood"] from *This Day: Collected and New Sabbath Poems 1979–2012*. Copyright © 1985, 2013 by Wendell Berry. Reprinted with the permission of The Permissions Company, LLC on behalf of Counterpoint Press, counterpointpress.com.

b. On what follows, see Scot McKnight and Laura Barringer, *A Church Called Tov: Forming a Goodness Culture That Resists Abuses of Power and Promotes Healing* (Carol Stream, IL: Tyndale, 2020), 183–90.

c. McKnight and Barringer, *Church Called Tov*, 189.

d. McKnight and Barringer, *Church Called Tov*, 193.

Chapter 16 Luke and History

1. Joel Green, "Luke, Gospel of," in *Dictionary of Jesus and the Gospels*, ed. Joel B. Green, Jeannine K. Brown, and Nicholas Perrin, 2nd ed. (Downers Grove, IL: IVP Academic, 2013), 541.

2. In more detail, see Judith M. Lieu, *Marcion and the Making of a Heretic: God and Scripture in the Second Century* (Cambridge: Cambridge University Press, 2015), 196–209.

3. Translation from Edmon L. Gallagher and John D. Meade, *The Biblical Canon Lists from Early Christianity: Texts and Analysis* (Oxford: Oxford University Press, 2017), 178.

4. Martin Hengel, *The Four Gospels and the One Gospel of Jesus Christ: An Investigation of the Collection and Origin of the Canonical Gospels* (London: SCM, 2000), 38–47.

5. Mark Allan Powell, *Fortress Introduction to the Gospels*, 2nd ed. (Minneapolis: Fortress, 2019), 153.

6. During the time of Luke's writing, overlap between literary genres often resulted in mixed genres. There is plenty of evidence for overlap between ancient history and biography.

7. In more detail, see Francis Watson, *What Is a Gospel?* (Grand Rapids: Eerdmans, 2022), 103–5.

8. See Richard Bauckham, *Jesus and the Eyewitnesses: The Gospels as Eyewitness Testimony* (Grand Rapids: Eerdmans, 2006), 116–20.

9. In more detail, see David P. Moessner, *Luke the Historian of Israel's Legacy, Theologian of Israel's "Christ": A New Reading of the "Gospel Acts" of Luke*, Beihefte zur Zeitschrift für die neutestamentliche Wissenschaft 182 (Berlin: de Gruyter, 2016), 68–107.

10. Bauckham, *Jesus and the Eyewitnesses*, 124.

11. See the helpful discussion in Powell, *Fortress Introduction to the Gospels*, 129–31.

12. In more detail, see Jonathan Bernier, *Rethinking the Dates of the New Testament: The Evidence for Early Composition* (Grand Rapids: Baker Academic, 2022), 52–66.

13. François Bovon, *Luke 1: A Commentary on the Gospel of Luke 1:1–9:50*, trans. Christine M. Thomas, ed. Helmut Koester, Hermeneia (Minneapolis: Fortress, 2002), 8.

Chapter 16 Sidebar Notes

a. Luke Timothy Johnson, *The Writings of the New Testament: An Interpretation* (Minneapolis: Fortress, 1999), 219.

Chapter 17 Luke and Narrative (1)

1. Robert C. Tannehill, *The Narrative Unity of Luke-Acts: A Literary Interpretation*, vol. 1, *The Gospel According to Luke* (Philadelphia: Fortress, 1986), 19. See also Joel B. Green, "Luke, Gospel of," in *Dictionary of Jesus and the Gospels*, ed. Joel B. Green, Jeannine K. Brown, and Nicholas Perrin, 2nd ed. (Downers Grove, IL: IVP Academic, 2013), 543–44; Jeannine K. Brown, *The Gospels as Stories: A Narrative Approach to Matthew, Mark, Luke, and John* (Grand Rapids: Baker Academic, 2020), 43–49.

2. Justo L. González, *The Story Luke Tells: Luke's Unique Witness to the Gospel* (Grand Rapids: Eerdmans, 2015), 51. See also Dorothy A. Lee, *The Ministry of Women in the New Testament: Reclaiming the Biblical Vision for Church Leadership* (Grand Rapids: Baker Academic, 2021), 59–73.

3. Amy Peeler, *Women and the Gender of God* (Grand Rapids: Eerdmans, 2022), 74–75.

4. I have learned much here from the work of C. Kavin Rowe, *Early Narrative Christology: The Lord in the Gospel of Luke* (Grand Rapids: Baker Academic, 2009).

Chapter 18 Luke and Narrative (2)

1. I have learned much here from Luke Timothy Johnson, *Prophetic Jesus, Prophetic Church: The Challenge of Luke-Acts to Contemporary Christians* (Grand Rapids: Eerdmans, 2011); Jocelyn McWhirter, *Rejected Prophets: Jesus and His Witnesses in Luke-Acts* (Minneapolis: Fortress, 2013).

2. Johnson, *Prophetic Jesus, Prophetic Church*, 85.

3. I have written on this in more detail in Joshua W. Jipp, *Saved by Faith and Hospitality* (Grand Rapids: Eerdmans, 2017), 19–24. Reprinted by permission of the publisher.

4. Similarly, see Brendan Byrne, *The Hospitality of God: A Reading of Luke's Gospel* (Collegeville, MN: Liturgical Press, 2000), 48–50.

5. I have written on this in more detail in Jipp, *Saved by Faith and Hospitality*, 161–62.

6. See Joshua W. Jipp, *The Messianic Theology of the New Testament* (Grand Rapids: Eerdmans, 2020), 97–101.

Chapter 18 Sidebar Notes

a. See also Patrick Schreiner, *Matthew, Disciple and Scribe: The First Gospel and Its Portrait of Jesus* (Grand Rapids: Baker Academic, 2019), 155.

b. Quoted in Jessica Hooten Wilson and Jacob Stratman, eds., *Learning the Good Life: Wisdom from the Great Hearts and Minds That Came Before* (Grand Rapids: Zondervan Academic, 2022), 116–17.

c. Jan-Olav Henriksen and Karl Olav Sandnes, *Jesus as Healer: A Gospel for the Body* (Grand Rapids: Eerdmans, 2016), 246.

d. Amanda Porterfield, *Healing in the History of Christianity* (Oxford: Oxford University Press, 2005), 47.

e. Gary B. Ferngren, *Medicine & Health Care in Early Christianity* (Baltimore: Johns Hopkins University Press, 2009), 124.

f. Dominique DuBois Gilliard, *Subversive Witness: Scripture's Call to Leverage Privilege* (Grand Rapids: Zondervan, 2021), 128–29.

Chapter 19 Luke and Discipleship

1. See M. Daniel Carroll R., *The Lord Roars: Recovering the Prophetic Voice for Today* (Grand Rapids: Baker Academic, 2022).

2. Esau McCaulley, *Reading While Black: African American Biblical Interpretation as an Exercise in Hope* (Downers Grove, IL: InterVarsity, 2020), 58.

3. Catherine J. Wright, *Spiritual Practices of Jesus: Learning Simplicity, Humility, and Prayer with Luke's Earliest Readers* (Downers Grove, IL: IVP Academic, 2020), 129.

4. Eric D. Barreto, "A Gospel on the Move: Practice, Proclamation, and Place in Luke-Acts," *Interpretation* 72 (2018): 185.

5. I have written on this extensively in Joshua W. Jipp, *Saved by Faith and Hospitality* (Grand Rapids: Eerdmans, 2017).

6. Henri J. M. Nouwen, *Reaching Out: The Three Movements of the Spiritual Life* (Garden City, NY: Doubleday, 1975), 46.

7. Heather H. Vacek, *Madness: American Protestant Responses to Mental Illness* (Waco: Baylor University Press, 2015), 168–69.

8. Wright, *Spiritual Practices of Jesus*, 67.

9. See William T. Cavanaugh, *Being Consumed: Economics and Christian Desire* (Grand Rapids: Eerdmans, 2008); Daniel M. Bell Jr., *The Economy of Desire: Christianity and Capitalism in a Postmodern World* (Grand Rapids: Baker Academic, 2012).

Chapter 19 Sidebar Notes

a. Robert Chao Romero, *Brown Church: Five Centuries of Latina/o Social Justice, Theology, and Identity* (Downers Grove, IL: InterVarsity, 2020), 215–16.

b. Ruth Irene Padilla DeBorst, "Integral Mission Formation in Abya Yala (Latin America): A Study of the *Centro de Studios Teológicos Interdisciplinarios* (1982–2002) and Radical *Evangélicos*" (PhD diss., Boston University, 2016), 5.

c. C. René Padilla, *Mission between the Times: Essays on the Kingdom* (Grand Rapids: Eerdmans, 1985), 189–90.

d. Esau McCaulley, *Reading While Black: African American Biblical Interpretation as an Exercise in Hope* (Downers Grove, IL: InterVarsity, 2020), 87–89.

e. Marjorie Maddox, "Her Stations of the Cross," in *Poems of Devotion: An Anthology of Recent Poets*, ed. Luke Hankins (Eugene, OR: Wipf & Stock, 2012), 114–16. Used by permission of Wipf and Stock Publishers, www.wipfandstock.com.

f. Denise Levertov, "The Avowal," in *The Collected Poems of Denise Levertov*, ed. Paul A. Lacey and Anne Dewey (New York: New Directions, 2013), 728.

Chapter 20 John and History

1. Luke Timothy Johnson, *The Writings of the New Testament: An Interpretation* (Minneapolis: Fortress, 1999), 525.

2. C. E. Hill, "The Gospel of John," in *The Oxford Handbook of Early Christian Biblical Interpretation*, ed. Paul M. Blowers and Peter W. Martens (Oxford: Oxford University Press, 2019), 606. This paragraph draws on and is indebted to Hill's helpful study.

3. Quoted from Hill, "Gospel of John," 602.

4. On the reception history of John's Gospel, see Mark Edwards, *John*, Blackwell Bible Commentaries (Malden, MA: Blackwell, 2004).

5. Cyril of Alexandria, *Commentary on John*, trans. David R. Maxwell, ed. Joel C. Elowsky, 2 vols., Ancient Christian Texts (Downers Grove, IL: IVP Academic, 2013–15).

6. See Robert Kysar, *John: The Maverick Gospel*, 3rd ed. (Louisville: Westminster John Knox, 2007).

7. On this and for what follows, see Andreas Köstenberger, "John's Transposition Theology: Retelling the Story of Jesus in a Different Key," in *Earliest Christian History: History, Literature, and Theology; Essays from the Tyndale Fellowship in Honor of Martin Hengel*, ed. Michael F. Bird and Jason Maston, Wissenschaftliche Untersuchungen zum Neuen Testament 2/320 (Tübingen: Mohr Siebeck, 2012), 191–226.

8. Johnson, *Writings of the New Testament*, 528–32.

9. On which, see Ruth B. Edwards, *Discovering John: Content, Interpretation, Reception* (Grand Rapids: Eerdmans, 2014), 36–38.

10. For a convincing argument that John situates his Gospel among alternative narratives about Jesus but does not intend to displace prior writings, see Andrew J. Byers, *John and the Others: Jewish Relations, Christian Origins, and the Sectarian Hermeneutic* (Waco: Baylor University Press, 2021).

11. For what follows I am reliant on the arguments of Richard Bauckham, "John for Readers of Mark," in *The Gospels for All Christians: Rethinking the Gospel Audiences*, ed. Richard Bauckham (Grand Rapids: Eerdmans, 1998), 147–71. See also Edwards, *Discovering John*, 35–38; Michael F. Bird, *The Gospel of the Lord: How the Early Church Wrote the Story of Jesus* (Grand Rapids: Eerdmans, 2014), 188–212.

12. Bauckham, "John for Readers of Mark," 153.

13. See Bauckham, "John for Readers of Mark," 150–56.

14. For a useful discussion on John's sources and potential stages of editing, see Mark Allan Powell, *Fortress Introduction to the Gospels*, 2nd ed. (Minneapolis: Fortress, 2019), 184–85.

15. See the classic work of Raymond E. Brown, *The Community of the Beloved Disciple: The Life, Loves, and Hates of an Individual Church in New Testament Times* (New York: Paulist Press, 1979).

16. On the role of the Beloved Disciple within John's Gospel, see Richard Bauckham, *The Testimony of the Beloved Disciple: Narrative, History, and Theology in the Gospel of John* (Grand Rapids: Baker Academic, 2007).

17. See especially Richard Bauckham, *Jesus and the Eyewitnesses: The Gospels as Eyewitness Testimony* (Grand Rapids: Eerdmans), 412–71.

18. David F. Ford, *The Gospel of John: A Theological Commentary* (Grand Rapids: Baker Academic, 2021), 32.

19. In more detail, see Bird, *Gospel of the Lord*, 189–90.

20. See D. A. Carson, "The Purpose of the Fourth Gospel: John 20:30–31 Reconsidered," *Journal of Biblical Literature* 108 (1987): 639–51.

21. See Edwards, *Discovering John*, 45.

Chapter 21 John and Narrative (1)

1. See especially Craig R. Koester, *Symbolism in the Fourth Gospel: Meaning, Mystery, Community*, 2nd ed. (Minneapolis: Fortress, 2003).

2. See Koester, *Symbolism in the Fourth Gospel*, 157–59, 197–98.

3. In more detail, see Jeannine K. Brown, *The Gospels as Stories: A Narrative Approach to Matthew, Mark, Luke, and John* (Grand Rapids: Baker Academic, 2020), 129–35.

4. On representative characters in John's Gospel, see Koester, *Symbolism in the Fourth Gospel*, 34–77.

5. Michael J. Gorman, *Abide and Go: Missional Theosis in the Gospel of John* (Eugene, OR: Cascade Books, 2018), 52–55.

6. See Robert Kysar, *John: The Maverick Gospel*, 3rd ed. (Louisville: Westminster John Knox, 2007), 45–49.

Chapter 21 Sidebar Notes

a. Marianne Meye Thompson, "The Human Jesus in the Gospel of John: The Word Made Flesh," in *Portraits of Jesus in the Gospel of John*, ed. Craig R. Koester, Library of New Testament Studies 589 (London: T&T Clark, 2019), 30.

b. Denise Levertov, "On the Mystery of the Incarnation," in *The Stream and the Sapphire: Selected Poems on Religious Themes* (New York: New Directions Books, 1997), 19.

c. Craig R. Koester, *The Word of Life: A Theology of John's Gospel* (Grand Rapids: Eerdmans, 2008), 56.

Chapter 22 John and Narrative (2)

1. Christopher W. Skinner, *Reading John*, Cascade Companions (Eugene, OR: Cascade Books, 2015), 29.
2. I have been most helped here by John Ashton, *Understanding the Fourth Gospel*, 2nd ed. (Oxford: Oxford University Press, 2007).
3. Luke Timothy Johnson, *The Writings of the New Testament: An Interpretation* (Minneapolis: Fortress, 1999), 535.
4. One of the best treatments of this theme, from which I have learned much, is Andrew T. Lincoln, *Truth on Trial: The Lawsuit Motif in the Fourth Gospel* (Peabody, MA: Hendrickson, 2000).
5. See Jane Heath, "'You Say That I Am a King' (John 18.37)," *Journal for the Study of the New Testament* 34 (2012): 232–53.
6. On this theme, see especially Mary L. Coloe, *God Dwells with Us: Temple Symbolism in the Fourth Gospel* (Collegeville, MN: Liturgical Press, 2001).
7. Skinner, *Reading John*, 47.
8. See Skinner, *Reading John*, 51–56.
9. Helpful here is Ruth B. Edwards, *Discovering John: Content, Interpretation, Reception* (Grand Rapids: Eerdmans, 2014), 142–55.
10. See Andrew J. Byers, *John and the Others: Jewish Relations, Christian Origins, and the Sectarian Hermeneutic* (Waco: Baylor University Press, 2021), 53.
11. Byers, *John and the Others*, 57.
12. I draw here on the argument of Byers, *John and the Others*, 59–94.
13. On these stories as "quest stories," see John Painter, *The Quest for the Messiah: The History, Literature and Theology of the Johannine Community*, 2nd ed. (Nashville: Abingdon, 1993). I have written on this in Joshua W. Jipp, *The Messianic Theology of the New Testament* (Grand Rapids: Eerdmans, 2020), 119–22.
14. An enormous amount has been written on signs in the Gospel of John, but I have found the following most helpful: Craig R. Koester, *Symbolism in the Fourth Gospel: Meaning, Mystery, Community*, 2nd ed. (Minneapolis: Fortress, 2003); Robert Kysar, *John: The Maverick Gospel* (Louisville: Westminster, 1993), 80–86.
15. Koester, *Symbolism in the Fourth Gospel*, 86.
16. On the multifaceted use of faith/belief in the Gospel of John, see Chris Seglenieks, *Johannine Belief and Graeco-Roman Devotion: Reshaping Devotion for John's Graeco-Roman Audience*, Wissenschaftliche Untersuchungen zum Neuen Testament 2/528 (Tübingen: Mohr Siebeck, 2020).
17. On this theme, see especially Craig R. Koester, *The Word of Life: A Theology of John's Gospel* (Grand Rapids: Eerdmans, 2008), 163–70; Dorothy Lee, "The Gospel of John and the Five Senses," *Journal of Biblical Literature* 129 (2010): 115–27.
18. I have written on this theme in Joshua W. Jipp, *Saved by Faith and Hospitality* (Grand Rapids: Eerdmans, 2017), 82–92.
19. See Koester, *Symbolism in the Fourth Gospel*, 198–99.
20. See Koester, *Symbolism in the Fourth Gospel*, 132.

21. Arland J. Hultgren, "The Johannine Footwashing (13.1–11) as Symbol of Eschatological Hospitality," *New Testament Studies* 28 (1982): 539–46.

22. On this theme, see Andreas Köstenberger, *The Missions of Jesus and the Disciples According to the Fourth Gospel: With Implications for the Fourth Gospel's Purpose and the Mission of the Contemporary Church* (Grand Rapids: Eerdmans, 1998); Michael J. Gorman, *Abide and Go: Missional Theosis in the Gospel of John* (Eugene, OR: Cascade Books, 2018), 71–132.

23. Gorman, *Abide and Go*, 140–43.

Chapter 22 Sidebar Notes

a. Richard Bauckham, "Monotheism and Christology in the Gospel of John," in *The Testimony of the Beloved Disciple: Narrative, History, and Theology in the Gospel of John* (Grand Rapids: Baker Academic, 2007), 242.

b. Quoted in Jessica Hooten Wilson and Jacob Stratman, eds., *Learning the Good Life: Wisdom from the Great Hearts and Minds That Came Before* (Grand Rapids: Zondervan, 2022), 43.

c. See S. A. Hunt, "And the Word Became Flesh—Again? Jesus and Abraham in John 8:31–59," in *Perspectives on Our Father Abraham: Essays in Honor of Marvin R. Wilson*, ed. S. A. Hunt (Grand Rapids: Eerdmans, 2012), 81–109.

d. Andrew J. Byers, *John and the Others: Jewish Relations, Christian Origins, and the Sectarian Hermeneutic* (Waco: Baylor University Press, 2021), 86.

e. Caryn A. Reeder, *The Samaritan Woman's Story: Reconsidering John 4 after #ChurchToo* (Downers Grove, IL: IVP Academic, 2022), 180.

f. Mary L. Coloe, *Dwelling in the Household of God: Johannine Ecclesiology and Spirituality* (Collegeville, MN: Liturgical Press, 2007), 102.

g. See Anthony Giambrone, *The Bible and the Priesthood: Priestly Participation in the One Sacrifice for Sins* (Grand Rapids: Baker Academic, 2022), 175–91.

Chapter 23 John and Discipleship

1. Craig R. Koester, *The Word of Life: A Theology of John's Gospel* (Grand Rapids: Eerdmans, 2008), 59.

2. Augustine, *Confessions*, trans. Sarah Ruden (New York: Modern Library, 2017), 1.6.7, p. 8.

3. Gail R. O'Day, "I Have Called You Friends," *Christian Reflection* (2008): 24.

Chapter 23 Sidebar Notes

a. In Frances Smith Foster, ed., *A Brighter Day Coming: A Frances Ellen Watkins Harper Reader* (New York: Feminist Press at the City University of New York, 1990), 208–9.

Index